VOLUME NINETY

Advances in
COMPUTERS

Connected Computing Environment

VOLUME NINETY

ADVANCES IN
COMPUTERS

Connected Computing Environment

Edited by

ALI HURSON
Department of Computer Science
Missouri University of Science and Technology
325 Computer Science Building
Rolla, MO 65409-0350
USA
Email: hurson@mst.edu

ELSEVIER

Amsterdam • Boston • Heidelberg • London
New York • Oxford • Paris • San Diego
San Francisco • Singapore • Sydney • Tokyo
Academic Press is an imprint of Elsevier

Academic Press is an imprint of Elsevier
225 Wyman Street, Waltham, MA 02451, USA
525 B Street, Suite 1800, San Diego, CA 92101-4495, USA
The Boulevard, Langford Lane, Kidlington, Oxford, OX5 1GB, UK
32, Jamestown Road, London NW1 7BY, UK
Radarweg 29, PO Box 211, 1000 AE Amsterdam, The Netherlands

First edition 2013

Library of Congress Cataloging-in-Publication Data
A catalog record for this book is available from the Library of Congress

British Library Cataloguing-in-Publication Data
A catalogue record for this book is available from the British Library

ISBN: 978-0-12-408091-1
ISSN: 0065-2458

For information on all Academic Press publications
visit our web site at *store.elsevier.com*

Printed and bound in USA

13 14 15   10 9 8 7 6 5 4 3 2 1

CONTENTS

PREFACE

Traditionally, Advances in Computers, the oldest Series to chronicle of the rapid evolution of computing, annually publishes several volumes, each typically comprised of five to eight chapters, describing new developments in the theory and applications of computing. The theme of this 90th volume: "*Connected Computing Environment*" is inspired by the advances in technology and interconnected computing devices. Interconnected world is requiring more attention on resource management and resource sharing. Within the spectrum of interconnected computing infrastructures this volume is concentrating on two computing platforms: Sensor networks and Cloud computing. The volume is a collection of six chapters that covers a diverse aspect of related issues. The articles included in this volume were solicited from authorities in the field, each of whom brings to bear a unique perspective on the topic.

In Chapter 1, "Advances in Real-World Sensor Network System," Debraj De et al., survey the existing state-of-the-art of real-world sensor network system designs and their application. The chapter studies sensor networks at different layers. In addition, it details operating system and software development, and middleware of wireless sensor network. Finally, it addresses experience and lessons learned from real-world sensor network deployment and maintenance.

In Chapter 2, "Novel System Architectures for Semantic Based Integration of Sensor Networks," Bobivic and Milutinovic articulate the on-going projects and research initiatives that propose semantic-oriented services for obtaining, delivery, and processing sensor data gathered from integrated sensor networks, and establishing interoperability among various deployed sensor networks. Moreover, as expected by the Sensor Web vision and the Future Internet initiatives, certain architecture is faced with performance requirements while providing complex services. The chapter identifies challenges and design issues of sensor networks integration platforms, and gives a survey of existing approaches specifically emphasizing semantic oriented approaches.

The concept of Mobility in Wireless Sensor Networks is the main theme of Chapter 3. In this chapter Chellappan and Dutta add mobility to the scope of sensor networks and discuss algorithms for exploiting sensor mobility with the goal of extending its coverage. Three standard models namely: Blanket, Barrier, and Event Coverage are surveyed and analyzed based on various metrics such as: quality of coverage, movement distance minimization, communication overhead, and energy constraints. The chapter also highlights open issues in mobility in wireless sensor networks, including some discussions on uncontrolled sensor mobility.

In Chapter 4, "A Classification of Data Mining Algorithms for Wireless Sensor Networks and Classification Extension to Concept Modeling in System of Wireless Sensor Networks Based on Natural Language Processing," Stankovic et al., attempt to create synergy between Data Mining and Natural Language Processing within the scope of wireless sensor networks. The chapter introduces a classification of data mining algorithms for wireless sensor networks for both a single network platform and a System of networks platform. It surveys the selected approaches from the open literature, to help application designers/developers get a better understanding of their options in different areas. The goal is to provide a good starting point for a more effective analysis leading to possible new solutions, possible improvements of existing solutions, and/or possible combination of two or more of the existing solutions into new ones.

Chapter 5, "Multihoming: A Comprehensive Review," Sousa, Pentikousis and Curado detail developments in multihoming due to the explosion of devices with build-in communication capabilities. As noted by the authors, "IP multihoming is a networking concept with a deceptively simple definition in theory. In practice, however, multihoming has proved difficult to implement and optimize for." The chapter introduces the fundamentals, the architectural goals, and system design principles for multihoming. Multihoming support at the application, session, transport, and network layers are also studied and analyzed. Finally, recent developments with respect to multihoming and mobility management are discussed.

Finally Chapter 6, "Efficient Data Analytics Over Cloud," Gupta (Rajeev), Gupta (Himanshu), and Mohania articulate fast handling large amount of data in applications such as telecom, health-care, retail, pharmaceutical, financial services. The chapter argues that the traditional solutions are unable to provide reasonable response times in handling large data volumes and emphasizes that one can either perform analytics on big volume once in days or perform transactions on small amounts of data in seconds to ensure the real-time or near real-time responses. The chapter covers various important aspects of analyzing big data and challenges that need to overcome over the cloud. For *big data* two kinds of systems, namely: NoSQL and MapReduce paradigm such as Hadoop, are discussed. The authors also illustrate various middleware and applications which can use these technologies to quickly process massive amount of data.

I hope that you find these articles of interest, and useful in your teaching, research, and other professional activities. I welcome feedback on the volume, and suggestions for topics for future volumes.

Ali R. Hurson
Missouri University of Science and Technology,
Rolla, MO, USA

CHAPTER ONE

Advances in Real-World Sensor Network System

Debraj De, Wen-Zhan Song, Mingsen Xu, Lei Shi, and Song Tan
Sensorweb Research Laboratory, Department of Computer Science, Georgia State University, Atlanta, Georgia 30303, USA

Contents

Advances in Computers, Volume 90
ISSN 0065-2458, http://dx.doi.org/10.1016/B978-0-12-408091-1.00001-4

1

Abstract

Significant advancements in wireless communication, microelectronic technologies, and distributed systems have revealed the great potential of Wireless Sensor Networks (WSN) for pervasive applications. Sensor networks are being increasingly used for sensing, monitoring, and controlling in various application fields. In the past decade, sensor network technology has stimulated much research interest from the academia to the industry. The technology development is now matured to a point, where real-world and business applications are emerging, and the engineers and investors are increasingly getting involved into its development. This chapter surveys the existing state-of-the-art of real-world sensor network system designs and their application. The authors of this chapter have also described their own hands-on experience and lessons when applying the sensor network technologies in real-world application. The chapter mainly consists of survey of the practical system contributions in: (a) different layers of sensor networks (such as transport layer, network layer and link layer), (b) operating system and software development, middleware of WSN (such as network management, neighbor discovery, topology control, energy management, data storage, localization, time synchronization, and security), and (c) experience and lessons from real-world sensor network deployment and maintenance. Finally this chapter concludes with brief comments on current state of the Sensor Network technologies, its challenges and future opportunities.

1. INTRODUCTION

Sensor networks consist of spatially distributed devices communicating through wireless radio and cooperatively sensing physical or environmental conditions. They provide a high degree of visibility into the environmental physical processes. Wireless Sensor Networks (largely termed as WSN) have been used in pervasive domain of applications such as scientific exploration, infrastructure protection, military, social, assisted living, and many more. Sensor networks are also notably useful in catastrophic or emergency scenarios, such as floods, fires, volcanos, battlefields, where human participation is too dangerous and infrastructure networks are either impossible or too expensive.

However, there are significant challenges to the design for sustainability and reliability for real–world applications. Those challenges come in all forms:

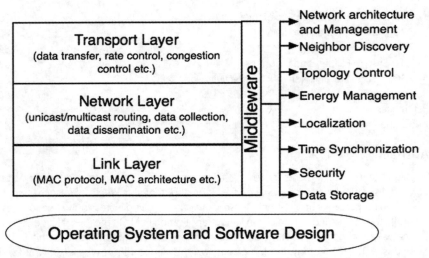

Fig. 1. Different layers and components of Wireless Sensor Networks, where real system level advancements are done and are covered in this chapter.

software, hardware, and application–specific designs. In this chapter we have identified those challenges individually, and have surveyed the important works in the literature for solving those challenges. The important components of Wireless Sensor Networks (WSN) system, covered in this chapter are shown in Fig. 1. This chapter explores the practical advancements in: different layers of WSN (such as transport layer, network layer, and link layer), operating system and development issues, middleware design and real-world sensor network deployment experiences.

Following is the organization of this chapter. First we focus on works in different layers of WSN. In Section 2 we have presented practical advancements in transport layer, involving data transport and data management. In Section 3 we have presented practical advancements in network layer, involving opportunistic routing, data collection, and data dissemination. In Section 4 we have presented practical advancements in link layer, involving radio management. Next we focus on various middleware designs in Section 5. This includes network management, neighbor discovery, topology control, energy management, localization, time synchronization, security, data storage, etc. Then we focus on advancements in operating system and software in Section 6. There we have presented practical developments in operating systems design, network reprogramming, and simulation. In the following Section 7 we have presented practical experiences of real-world sensor network design, deployment, and maintenance. This is focused on scenario of real-time volcano monitoring sensor network deployment. Finally we conclude this chapter in Section 8 with discussion on research challenges and future potentials.

2. TRANSPORT LAYER

Message communication between sensor nodes over unreliable wireless medium is an energy expensive and lossy operation. The transport layer is responsible for handling the congestion among the generated data traffic and for assuring the end-to-end reliability of individual data packets. The traditional transport layer protocols for the Internet are UDP (User Datagram Protocol) and TCP (Transmission Control Protocol). But they cannot be directly applied to sensor networks. This is because, typical characteristics of sensor networks bring unique design challenges at the transport layer. Careful design of transport layer protocol needs to assure important properties like: bulk data transfer, reliability, congestion control, and fair data rate control, while still satisfying factors like minimal overhead, minimal retransmission, minimal energy expense, etc. In this section we have focused on real system solutions in: reliable bulk data collection and rate-controlled fair data collection.

2.1 Reliable Bulk Data Transfer

In many WSN applications (e.g., structural health monitoring, volcanic activity monitoring, etc.) the capability of bulk data transfer over multi-hop network is needed. Those emerging high data rate applications need to transport large volumes of data concurrently from several sensor nodes. Some of these applications are also loss-intolerant. Delivery of such bulk data reliably in the network is hard, because the nature of wireless communication brings several challenges: lossy links, inter-path interference, intra-path interference, and transient data rate mismatches. A key for handling such challenges is a protocol that can reliably transport large sensor data from many sources to one or more sink nodes, without incurring congestion collapse. Now we present some existing works in the literature that have tried to solve this challenge.

2.1.1 Receiver-Initiated Bulk Data Transfer

The *Flush* protocol [18] is a receiver-initiated transport protocol for transferring bulk data across a multi-hop wireless sensor network. *Flush* is a reliable, high goodput bulk data transport protocol for Wireless Sensor Networks. It provides end-to-end data reliability, reduces transfer time, and adapts to

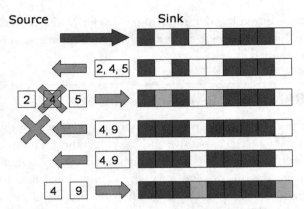

Fig. 2. NACK transmission. *Flush* has at most one NACK packet in flight at once.

time-varying network conditions. To initiate a data transfer, the sink sends a request for a data object to a specific source in the network using the underlying delivery protocol. After a request is made, *Flush* moves through *four phases*: (i) *topology query*, (ii) *data transfer*, (iii) *acknowledgment*, and (iv) *integrity check*.

The *topology query* phase probes the depth of a target node to tune the RTT (Round–Trip Time) and computes a timeout at the receiver. During the *data transfer* phase, the source sends packets to the sink using the maximum rate that does not cause intra–path interference. *Flush* finds the maximum transmitting rate along a path using a combination of local measurements and an interference estimation. The sink keeps track of which packets it receives. When the *data transfer* phase is completed, the *acknowledgment* phase begins. This process repeats until the sink has received the requested data in total. At last, the sink verifies the integrity of the data in *integrity check* phase.

Flush uses an *end-to-end reliability protocol* that is robust to node failures. Figure 2 shows a conceptual session example of the protocol, where the data size is 9 packets, and a NACK (negative acknowledgment) packet can accommodate at most 3 sequence numbers. In the *data transfer* stage, the source sends all of the data packets, of which some are lost (sequence numbers 2, 4, 5, and 9 in the example), either due to retransmission failures or queue overflows. The sink keeps track of all received packets. When it believes that the source has finished sending data, the sink sends a single NACK packet, which can hold up to 3 sequence numbers, back to the source. This NACK contains the first 3 sequence numbers of lost packets 2, 4, and 5. The source then retransmits the requested packets. This process continues until

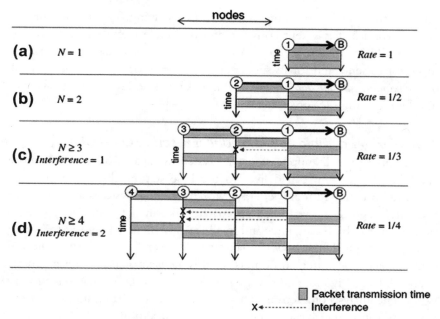

Fig. 3. Maximum sending rate without collision in the simplified pipelining model.

the sink has received every packet. The sink uses an estimate of the RTT (Round–Trip Time) to decide when to send NACK packets in the event that all of the retransmissions are lost.

The *end-to-end selective negative acknowledgments* achieve the reliable data delivery goal of *Flush*. For the minimum transfer time, *Flush* proposes a novel *rate control algorithm* that is based on interference estimation. First, in the simplified conceptual model, there are N nodes arranged linearly plus a base station B. Node N sends packets to the base station through nodes $N - 1,...,1$. Nodes forward a packet as soon as possible after receiving it. There is a variable range of interference I, where a node's transmission interferes with the reception of all nodes that are I hops away.

Figure 3 shows the maximum rate in the simplified pipeline model for key values of N and I. If there is only one node, as in Fig. 3, in section (a), the node can send to the base station at the maximum rate of 1 pkt/s. There is no contention, as no other nodes transmit. For two nodes in (b), the maximum rate falls to 1/2, because node 1 cannot send and receive at the same time. The interference range starts to play a role if $N \geq 3$. In (c), node 3 has to wait for node 2's transmission to finish and for node 1's, because node 1's transmission prevents node 2 from receiving. This is true for any node beyond 3 if I is kept constant, and the stable maximum rate then is $1/3$. Finally, in (d) I is set to 2. Any node past node 3 has to wait for its successor to send, and for its successor's two successors to send. In general, the *maximum transmission rate* in this model for a node N hops away with interference range I is given by: $r(N,I) = \frac{1}{\min(N,2+I)}$.

2.1.2 Maximizing Data Collection Under Resource Constraints

In a number of WSN applications, the system is capable of acquiring more data, than the system can deliver to the base station, due to severe limits on radio bandwidth and energy. Moreover, these systems are unable to take advantage of conventional approaches like in-network data aggregation, given the high data rates and need for raw signals. These systems face an important challenge: how to maximize the overall value of the collected data, subject to resource constraints. In this scenario *Lance* [44] is a general approach to bandwidth and energy management for bulk data collection in WSN. The analysis of a sensor network deployment at Tungurahua volcano has showed how *Lance* can be effective in a field setting.

Lance couples the use of optimized, data-driven reliable data collection with a model of energy cost for extracting data from the network. *Lance*'s design decouples resource allocation mechanisms from application-specific policies, enabling flexible customization of the system's optimization metrics. There are *three design principles* of *Lance*: (i) decouple mechanism from policy, (ii) simplicity through centralized control, and (iii) low cost for maintenance traffic. Figure 4 provides an overview of the *Lance* architecture.

The main components of *Lance* architecture are now described. *Application Data Unit:* Sensor nodes sample sensor data, storing the data to local flash storage. Each *Application Data Unit* (ADU) consists of some amount of raw sensor data, a unique ADU identifier, and a timestamp indicating the time that the first sample in the ADU was sampled.

Summarization function: Each node i applies an application-supplied summarization function, computing a concise summary s_i of the contents of the ADU as it is sampled. Nodes periodically send ADU summary messages to the base station, providing information on the ADUs they have sampled, their summaries, timestamps, and other metadata.

Controller: The *Lance* controller receives ADU summaries from the network. The controller also estimates the download energy cost vector $\overline{c_i}$ for each ADU, based on information on network topology as well as a model of energy consumption for download operations.

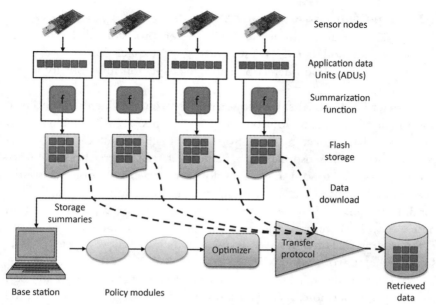

Fig. 4. The *Lance* system architecture. The summarization portions are provided by the application. All other components are generic.

Optimizer: The *Lance* optimizer is responsible for scheduling ADUs for download, based on knowledge of the set of ADUs currently stored by the network, their associated values and costs. *Lance's* optimization process attempts to maximize the value of the ADUs retrieved while adhering to the lifetime target L.

Policy Modules: Policy modules provide an interface through which applications can tune the operation of the *Lance* optimizer. A chain of policy modules executed at the base station which, by modifying the value for each ADU, can implement a range of application-specific policies.

2.2 Rate Controlled Fair Data Transfer

In WSN the finite capacity of wireless medium is shared among the contending sensor nodes. This affects the effective bandwidth from each node to the sink. One way to regulate individual node's effective data rate is to maximize the global utility of the data collection. This requires each node to find a trade off point between degree of interference and amount of successful data sent. Some practical works in the literature have tried to solve this challenge for rate controlled reliable data transport [32, 36].

2.2.1 Rate-Controlled Reliable Data Transfer

RCRT [32] is a rate-controlled reliable transport protocol, suitable for constrained sensor nodes. *RCRT* uses end-to-end explicit loss recovery, but places all the congestion detection and rate adaptation functionality in the sink nodes.

To describe *RCRT*, first we define a sink as an entity which runs on a base station and collects data from one or more sensors. *RCRT* is oblivious to the kind of data sourced by the sensors. More than one sink can be running concurrently in the sensor network. Let the notation f_{ij} describes the flow of data from source i toward sink j. This flow can be delivered from the source over multiple hops to the base station. A sensor i may source several flows f_{ij} for different sink j. Finally, each sink j is associated with a capacity allocation policy P_j which determines how network capacity is divided up across flows f_{ij} for arbitrary i. The simplest P_j is one in which each flow f_{ij} gets an equal share of the network capacity.

RCRT provides reliable, sequenced delivery of flows f_{ij} from source i to sink j. Furthermore, *RCRT* ensures that, for a given application j, the available network capacity is allocated to each flow according to policy P_j. Specifically, each flow f_{ij} is allocated a rate $r_{ij}(t)$ at each instant t that is in accordance with policy P_j. Thus, for a fair allocation policy, all sensors would receive equal $r_{ij}(t)$.

Table 1 describes the various components of *RCRT*. End-to-end reliability is achieved using end-to-end negative acknowledgments. A particular aspect of *RCRT* is that its traffic management functionality resides at the sink. Specifically, each sink determines congestion levels and makes rate allocation decisions. Once sink j decides the rate r_{ij}, it either piggybacks this rate on a negative acknowledgment packet, or sends a separate feedback packet to source i.

Table 1 RCRT components.

Function	Where	How
End-to-end retransmissions	Source and Sink	End-to-end NACKs
Congestion Detection	Sink	Based on time to recover loss
Rate Adaptation	Sink	Based on total traffic, with additive increase and decrease based on loss rate
Rate Allocation	Sink	Based on application-specified capacity allocation policy

At the sink node, *RCRT* has *three distinct logical components*: (i) The *congestion detection component* observes the packet loss and recovery dynamics (which packets have been lost, how long it takes to recover a loss) across every flow f_{ij}, and decides if the network is congested. (ii) Once it determines that the network is congested, the *rate adaptation component* estimates the total sustainable traffic $R(t)$ in the network. (iii) Then, the *rate allocation component* decreases the flow rates $r_{ij}(t)$ to achieve $R(t)$, while conforming to policy P_j. Conversely, when the network is not congested, the rate adaptation component additively increases the overall rate $R(t)$, and the rate allocation component determines $r_{ij}(t)$.

2.2.2 Fair Data Rate Adjustment with Congestion Control
Congestion control has been an active area of networking research for several decades. But relatively less attention has been paid to congestion control for data collection in WSN. One important challenge here is to determine what distributed mechanisms must the sensor network implement in order to dynamically allocate fair and efficient data transmission rates to each node.

In order to dynamically allocate *fair* and *efficient* transmission rates to each node, the work in [36] have proposed *Interference-aware Fair Rate Control* (IFRC) to detect incipient congestion at a node by monitoring the average queue length. IFRC communicates congestion state to exactly the set of potential interferers using a novel low-overhead *congestion sharing mechanism*, and converges to a fair and efficient rate using an AIMD (Additive Increase/Multiplicative Decrease) control law. The fair and efficient rate is assigned to each flow, to at least the most congested fair share rate. A node n_1 is a potential interferer of node n_2 if a flow originating from node n_1 uses a link that interferes with the link between n_2 and its parent. In tree-based communication, the potential interferers of a node include nodes not just in the node's subtree or its neighbor's (parent included) subtrees, but also includes nodes in its parent's neighbor's subtrees.

In IFRC, each node i adaptively converges to a fair and efficient rate r_i for flow f_i using a *distributed rate adaptation technique*. Congestion information with potential interferers are accurately shared. *IFRC consists of three interrelated components*: (i) one that measures the level of congestion at a node, (ii) another that shares congestion information with potential interferers, and (iii) a third that adapts the rate using an AIMD control law.

Measuring congestion levels: IFRC maintains a single queue of packets from all flows passing through a node. This includes flows from all descendants of the node in the routing tree and that sourced by itself. IFRC uses an exponentially weighted moving average of the instantaneous queue length as a measure of congestion: $avg_q = (1 - w_q) \times avg_q + w_q \times inst_q$. IFRC employs multiple thresholds about the queue length, $U(k)$, defined by $U(k) = U(k-1) + I/2^{(k-1)}$, where k is a small integer and I is a constant increment of the queue length. When avg_q is increasing the node halves its r_i whenever avg_q crosses $U(k)$ for any k. Since the difference between $U(k)$ and $U(k-1)$ decreases geometrically with increasing k, the rate halving becomes more frequent as the queue size increases. In this manner, a node continues to aggressively cut its r_i.

Congesting sharing: In IFRC, node i includes the following in the header of its outgoing packet: its current r_i, its current average queue length, a bit indicating whether any child of i is congested, the smallest rate r_l (of node l) among all its congested children, and l's average queue length. For the potential interferers of i that cannot receive this packet, IFRC introduces *two rules. Rule 1:* r_i can never exceed r_j, the rate of i's parent j. *Rule 2:* Whenever a congested neighbor j of i crosses a congestion threshold $U(k)$ (for any k), i sets its rate to the lower of r_i and r_j. The same rule is applied for the most congested child l of any neighbor of i.

Rate adaptation: In IFRC, nodes increases their r_i additively. Every $1/r_i$ seconds, a node i increases its rate by δ/r_i. If i is congested, then when threshold $U(k)$ is crossed, the node halves its current r_i. When i discovers its r_i to be higher than that of its parent j, it sets its rate to r_j. When i overhears a neighbor l's transmission that indicates that l, or one of its children p has crossed a threshold $U(k)$, it sets r_i to either r_l or r_p as necessary. All nodes start from a fixed initial rate r_{init}.

The base station maintains a "rate" r_b and enforces congestion sharing by adapting r_b to congestion indicators from its children. It decreases its rate only when any of its children j crosses $U(k)$ for any k. Initially, IFRC sets r_b equal to the nominal data rate of the wireless channel. It always additively increases r_b, every $1/r_b$ seconds it increments r_b by δ/r_b. For *multiple base station* case, the control packet sent by the base station is modified to include the base station's own rate instead of the current state of the most congested child. For *weighted fairness* case node i in a sensor network is assigned a weight w_i, the allocation scheme is fair if the normalized rate for each flow, $\frac{f_i}{w_i}$ is fair. When only a subset of nodes transmit, IFRC can work without modification in this case.

In conclusion, in this section we have presented practical system solutions to the challenges in transport layer of Wireless Sensor Networks.

This includes the works in: bulk data transfer with reliability and fair data transfer with rate control.

3. NETWORK LAYER

The protocols required in WSN network layer include unicast/multi-cast routing, data collection, and data dissemination. In this section we have presented practical advancements in these components of network layer. Routing protocols for WSN are responsible for maintaining the routes in the network and have to ensure reliable multi-hop communication. Routing in WSN is very challenging due to the inherent characteristics (such as many-to-one and one-to-many routing requirements than just one-to-one routing) that distinguish WSN from other networks. The unique characteristics of WSN require effective methods for data forwarding and processing.

3.1 Opportunistic Routing

In real-world WSN, the quality of a wireless channel fluctuates signifi-cantly with time, and the nodes can aggressively duty cycle to reduce their energy consumption. These factors tend to degrade the performance of traditional routing protocols in WSN, that seek only one optimized route for each source node. To alleviate many of these drawbacks, the concept of *opportunistic routing* is introduced. *Opportunistic routing* for multi-hop net-works can overcome some deficiencies of traditional routing, by using a set of nodes that is available for routing, during the time a packet is needed to be transmitted. Traditional routing protocols choose the best sequence of nodes between the source and destination, and forward each packet through that sequence. In contrast, *opportunistic routing* uses *cooperative diversity*, that takes advantage of broadcast transmission to send information through multiple relay nodes concurrently. Here we have presented some practical works in designing efficient opportunistic routing protocol for multi-hop networks.

3.1.1 Data Transfer Using Opportunistic Routing

ExOR [4] is an integrated routing and MAC protocol, that realizes some of the gains of cooperative diversity on standard radio hardware. *ExOR* increases the throughput of large unicast transfers in multi-hop wireless net-works. This is because it chooses each hop of a packet's route after the transmission for that hop, so that the choice can reflect which intermediate nodes actually received the transmission. This deferred choice gives each transmission multiple opportunities to make progress. As a result *ExOR* can use long radio links (although with higher loss rates), which would be avoided by traditional routing. *ExOR* increases a connection's throughput while using no more network capacity than traditional routing.

A simplified version of *ExOR* works as follows. A source node has a packet that it wishes to deliver to a distant destination. Between the source and destination are other wireless nodes willing to participate in *ExOR*. The source broadcasts the packet. Some subset of the nodes receive the packet. These receiving nodes run a protocol to discover and agree on which nodes are in that subset. The node in the subset that is closest to the destination broadcasts the packet. Again, the nodes that receive this second transmission agree on the closest receiver, which broadcasts the packet. This process continues until the destination has received the packet. One reason of *ExOR*'s improvement over tradition routing is that each transmission may have more independent chances of being received and forwarded. Another reason is that *ExOR* takes advantage of transmissions that reach unexpectedly far, or fall unexpectedly short.

ExOR faces *four key design challenges*. *First*, the nodes need to agree on which subset of them received each packet. This agreement protocol should be light-weight and robust as well. *Second*, *ExOR* must have a metric reflecting the likely cost of moving a packet from any node to the destination. *Third*, *ExOR* must choose only the most useful nodes as participants instead of nodes of entire network. *Finally*, *ExOR* must avoid simultaneous transmissions to minimize collisions. The key design components to address these challenges will be *Forwarder List* and *Scheduling Transmissions*, as described next.

Forwarder list: The source specifies the forwarder list in priority order based on the expected cost of delivering a packet from each node in the list to the destination. The cost metric is the number of transmissions required to move a packet along the best traditional route from the node to the destination, counting both hops and retransmissions. Each node's ETX (expected transmission count) value is the sum of the link ETX values along the lowest-ETX path to destination. If the number of nodes in a network is too large, *ExOR* source include only a subset of the nodes in the forwarder list. The source chooses the forwarder list using network-wide knowledge of inter-node loss rates. The source can acquire this knowledge via periodic link-state flooding of per-node measurements. *ExOR* is relatively insensitive to inaccurate or out-of-date measurements, since a packet's actual path is determined by conditions at the time of transmission.

Scheduling transmissions: ExOR attempts to schedule the times at which nodes send their fragments so that only one node sends at a time. This scheduling allows higher priority nodes to send first, which speeds completion and updates lower priority nodes' batch maps. Each node waits for its turn to transmit. After the source has sent the whole batch, the destination sends packets containing just batch maps, then the participating nodes send the packets in the order in which they appear in the forwarder list, highest priority first. However, a node cannot rely on receiving the last transmission of the node just before it in the transmission order. Instead, a node starts sending at the time it predicts the previous fragment will finish, as indicated by the node's forwarding timer. Whenever a node receives a packet, it updates its transmission tracker. The node then sets the forwarding timer to be equal to the current time plus the estimated send rate times the number of packets remaining to be sent. When a node's forwarding timer elapses, it sends its batch fragment: the packets that it has received, but that its batch map indicates have not been received by any higher priority node. When the lowest priority node has finished forwarding, the schedule starts again.

3.2 Data Collection

Network data collection (also known as *Convergecast* operation) is a common communication pattern across many sensor network applications featuring data-flows from many different source nodes to a single sink node. *Convergecast* in WSN requires proper coordination among the nodes.

3.2.1 Reliable Data Collection Protocol

Data Collection or *Convergecast* in a sensor network is a challenging problem, particularly due to the wireless medium dynamics. Multi-hop routing in a dynamic wireless environment requires that a protocol adapts quickly to the changes in the network (i.e., agility), while the energy-constrains of sensor networks requires that such mechanisms do not require too much communication in the network (i.e., efficiency). *CTP* (Collection Tree Protocol) [12] is a collection routing protocol, that achieves both *agility* and *efficiency*, while offering highly reliable data delivery in sensor networks. CTP protocol can benefit almost every sensor network application, as well as the many transport, routing, overlay, and application protocols that sit on top of collection trees.

Before this work, some of the practical deployments of data collection applications usually observed the delivery ratios ranging in 2%–68%. But the implementation of CTP offers 90%–99.9% packet delivery in highly dynamic environments while sending up to 73% fewer control packets than existing approaches. The major reasons for such performance improvements are the ways CTP deals with: *link dynamics* and *transient loops*. The CTP protocol builds and maintains minimum cost trees to nodes that advertise themselves as tree roots. *Two main mechanisms* of *CTP* makes it robust and agile to link dynamics and transient loops, while also having a low overhead when the topology is stable. Those two mechanisms are *data path validation* and *adaptive beaconing*.

First mechanism is the *data path validation*. Each data packet contains the transmitter's local cost estimate. When a node receives a packet to forward, it compares the transmitter's cost to its own. Since cost must always decrease, if a transmitter's advertised cost is not greater than the receiver's, then the transmitter's topology information is stale and there may be a routing loop. Using the data path to validate the topology in this way allows a protocol to detect possible loops on the first data packet after they occur.

Second mechanism is *adaptive beaconing*. Adaptive beaconing breaks the trade off between timeliness of routing information and energy consumption, achieving both fast recovery and low cost. In a network with very stable links, when a timer interval expires, the beaconing interval is doubled, up to a maximum value t_h. The routing layer resets the interval to t_l on three events as follows:

1. It is asked to forward a data packet from a node whose ETX is not higher than its own. The protocol interprets this as neighbors having a significantly out-of-date estimate and possibly a routing loop. It beacons to update its neighbors.
2. Its routing cost decreases significantly. The protocol advertises this event because it might provide lower cost routes to nearby nodes.
3. It receives a packet with the a "Pull" bit set. The "Pull" bit advertises that a node wishes to hear beacons from its neighbors, e.g., because it has just joined the network and needs to seed its routing table. The "Pull" bit provides a mechanism for nodes to actively request topology information from neighbors.

The architecture of CTP consists of *Data Plane* and *Control Plane*, as illustrated in Fig. 5. The *Control Plane* in CTP plays the role of detecting inconsistencies in the topology and resetting the beacon interval to fix them. *Control Plane* design consists of following *three mechanisms*: (i) routing computation and selection, (ii) control traffic timing, and (iii) resetting the beacon interval. The job of Routing or *Data Plane* is to maintain the route consistency. The Data Plane design consists of *four mechanisms*: (i) per-client

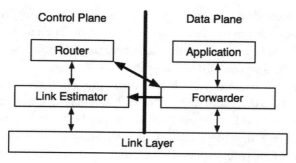

Fig. 5. *CTP* architecture.

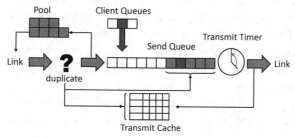

Fig. 6. Data plane design.

queuing, (ii) a hybrid send queue, (iii) a transmit timer, and (iv) a packet summary cache. Figure 6 shows the *CTP* data plane and how these four mechanisms interact.

3.3 Data Dissemination

The Data Dissemination is a network protocol for propagating data objects from one or more source nodes to many other nodes over a multi-hop network. Usually in WSN, data dissemination protocol is used to transmit some information from the sink node to all other nodes in the network. Now we present the practical solutions for data dissemination protocol in WSN.

3.3.1 Reliable Broadcast Across Network

Varying interference levels make broadcasting in wireless medium an unreliable operation in low–power Wireless Sensor Networks. Many routing and resource discovery protocols depend on flooding (repeated per–node broadcasts) over the network. Unreliability at the broadcast–level can result in either incomplete flooding coverage or excessive re-flooding, making path maintenance either unreliable or expensive. Robust Broadcast Propagation (RBP) [41] is a simple protocol that improves the reliability of broadcasting in WSN, for the purpose of data dissemination.

RBP protocol requires only local information, and resides as a service between the MAC (Medium Access Control) and network layer, taking information from both. RBP is based on *two principles*: (i) It exploits network density to achieve near-perfect flooding reliability by requiring moderate broadcast reliability when nodes have many neighbors. (ii) It identifies areas of sparse connectivity where important links bridge dense clusters of nodes, and strive for guaranteed reliability over those links. We next describe the *four steps* needed to meet this goal: (i) *tracking neighbors and floods*, (ii) *basic retransmission to reach a target reliability*, (iii) *adapting that target to network density*, and (iv) *identifying important links that require successful transmission*.

Tracking neighbors and floods: RBP requires that a node know the identity of its one-hop neighbors. Let define the one-hop neighborhood as nodes with which a node has inbound and outbound connectivity above a configurable threshold, over a moving window of broadcasts. This definition eliminates distant and weak neighbors, as well as neighbors with strongly asymmetric links.

Basic retransmission to reach a target reliability: RBP uses a simple algorithm for retransmission. The first time a node hears a broadcast it retransmits the packet unconditionally, as in a normal flood. As additional neighbors transmit the same packet, the node listens (snoops) and keeps track of which neighbors have propagated the broadcast.

Adapting target to network density: A key optimization in RBP is that both retransmission thresholds and the number of retries are adjusted for neighborhood density. Higher density neighborhoods require lower thresholds with fewer retries, since other neighbors are likely to broadcast as part of the same flood.

Identifying important links that require successful transmission: An additional important improvement is directional sensitivity by detection of important links. With the directional sensitivity optimization, nodes keep a histogram of which neighbor was the first to transmit a previously unheard broadcast.

The RBP module tracks the status of each new broadcast packet, indexed by the unique flood identifier, to handle multiple overlapping broadcasts. RBP starts a timer and records the implicit and explicit ACKs for the broadcast. The length of this timer is not dictated by RBP. A relatively long timer is selected to detect relevant neighbors broadcast, since diffusion has a 1 s forwarding delay with 800 ms of jitter. If the forwarding constants of the routing protocol were shorter or longer, a different constant would have been chosen. When the timer expires, the handler decides whether or not to retransmit the message. RBP keeps a duplicate of the original broadcast packet for retransmission. A cleanup timer periodically removes obsolete records. Explicit ACKs and directional sensitivity messages are implemented as unique control messages in diffusion.

3.3.2 Fast and Reliable Data Dissemination

The reliability and the speed of data dissemination are important particularly for real-time feedback–driven sensing applications (e.g., precise agriculture and volcano monitoring WSN). Due to the important role that each individual sensor node plays in the overall network operations, it is vital that all intended sensor nodes receive the command and control information. *Cascades* protocol [33] is designed for a fast and reliable data dissemination, where data from the sink (base station) is propagated to all or a subset of nodes in a data collection sensor network.

Cascades assume a data collection routing protocol is running in the system and there are continuous data flow from sensor nodes to the sink. Thus the nodes form a tree, each node has the knowledge of its parent, and each node can learn its direct children by tracking recent forwarded packets. *Cascades* makes use of the *parent-monitor-children* analogy to ensure reliable dissemination. Each node monitors whether or not its children have received the broadcast messages through snooping children's rebroadcasts or waiting for explicit ACKs. If a node detects a gap in its message sequences, it can fetch the missing messages from its neighbors reactively. Cascades also considers many practical issues for field deployment, such as dynamic topology, link/node failure etc. It therefore guarantees that a disseminated message from the sink will reach all intended receivers and the dissemination is terminated in a short time period.

In essence the algorithm works as follows:

1. For a non-leaf node u, it will send an ACK back to its parent node, once u detects all intended children have rebroadcasted the message (implicit ACK) or confirmed with an explicit ACK; otherwise it retries broadcast periodically. If u is a leaf node, it sends back ACK once a new message is received or snooped.

2. If a node detects a gap in its received data sequence, it will broadcast a request (e.g., NACK) message to notify its parent.

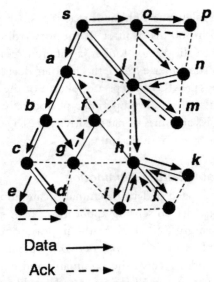

Data ⟶

Ack - - -▶

Fig. 7. Illustration of opportunistic broadcast flow in a tree with *Cascades* protocol. The solid lines sketch the tree structure, and the dashed lines shows the other network links.

Each node rebroadcasts periodically until successful reception is confirmed by all intended children either through rebroadcast or explicit ACK. Questions may be raised for asymmetric links: parent can not reach children or children can not reach parent. To notice that, if this happens permanently, a correct data gathering routing protocol will have updated the data gathering tree due to failed link layer acknowledgment. This is another reason why parent-children relationship is extracted from data gathering tree.

Cascades protocol is as fast as flooding. The broadcast flow does not completely depend on the data gathering tree structure. A snooped new message from neighbor nodes will be accepted and rebroadcasted if necessary. Therefore, it is possible that a parent first hears new data from its child, before it hears it from its parent. It speeds up the dissemination process. For example, in Fig. 7, node a is the parent of node b and f. However, node a's data reaches node b only, then b rebroadcasts the data to its neighbors (as an implicit ACK to node a). At the same time, node h receives data from node l (though l is not node h's parent), and rebroadcasts the data to its neighbors which includes parent f. Additionally, due to the opportunistic dissemination protocol, a non-leaf node may suppress its own rebroadcasting as long as all of its children have ACKed explicitly or implicitly to reduce communication cost. For example, in Fig. 7, assume node a's data does not reach f, but node

h's ACK and node g's data have reached f, then f sends an ACK to a without further rebroadcast. The opportunistic design makes the protocol not just faster, but also more robust as a node does not rely only on its parent node to get disseminated data. If the link reliability between a parent and child is temporarily not good, it still has a good chance of getting the data from some other neighbor nodes.

In conclusion, in this section we have presented practical system solutions to the challenges in network layer of Wireless Sensor Networks. This includes the works in: opportunistic routing, data collection, data dissemination.

4. LINK LAYER

The link layer in sensor network deals with the data transfer among neighboring nodes sharing same wireless link. Due to the lossy wireless communication medium in WSN, reliable and fast data exchange necessitates Medium Access Control (MAC). The MAC protocol design in sensor network is required to satisfy some key properties: energy efficiency, scalability to node density, communication synchronization, bandwidth utilization, etc. The wireless communication states of sensor nodes, especially the wireless radio idle state is the most energy-consuming operation. This makes efficient design of radio MAC protocol crucially important. There is significant amount of research works done on MAC protocol design for Wireless Sensor Networks.

Existing MAC protocols can be categorized basically into two types: (i) *synchronous* and (ii) *asynchronous* protocols. Synchronous MAC protocols specify the time period of wake-up and sleep for radio communication, in order to reduce the unnecessary time and energy wasted in the idle listening state. Nodes periodically exchange SYNC packets for synchronization among themselves in neighborhood so that the data transfer between nodes can be done in the common active schedule. S-MAC [47], T-MAC [43], etc. are practical examples of *synchronous* MAC protocols. On the other hand the asynchronous MAC protocols, unlike synchronous schemes, have no control overhead for synchronization. Examples of asynchronous schemes are B-MAC [34], X-MAC [5], etc. These protocols are based on low power listening (LPL) operation. The sender node communicates to the receiver to wake it up first from duty cycling. Then the data transfer is performed between the sender and the receiver.

4.1 Unified Link Layer Architecture

Efficient design of different MAC protocols need unified software architectures for flexible power management. But the existing practices mostly had one monolithic software implementation, without any separation between power management and core radio functionality. This had made it hard to develop new MAC protocols. It was hard to maintain multiple MAC stacks as operating system evolves. Also the protocols were not reusable across radio or processor platforms.

To solve this issue MAC Layer Architecture (MLA) [19] has proposed a component-based architecture for power-efficient MAC protocol development. Various features common to the existing popular protocols are distilled into a set of reusable components, and the specific functions they provide are optimized. Two types of components are defined in MLA as shown in Fig. 8, the High-level *hardware-independent* components and Low-level *hardware-dependent* components. The MLA architecture is here explained with some help of TinyOS [22] (a popularly used operation system for WSN) terminologies: component, interface, modules. All MAC-level interfaces to the application are exposed through two components, the MacC configuration,

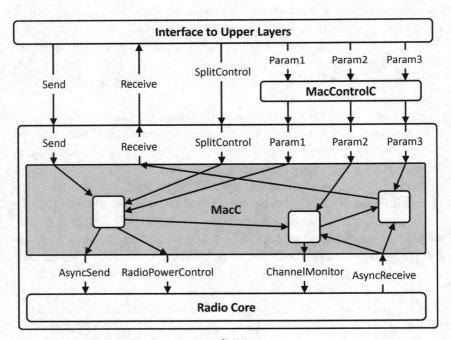

Fig. 8. The application developer's view of MLA.

which composes any reusable MLA components and any protocol-specific components together and the MacControlC, which collects a small number of MAC-specific interfaces. MLA identifies features that many MAC protocols share, and encapsulates them into the two types of components.

4.1.1 Hardware-Independent Components

- *ChannelPollerC* component performs low-power listening by invoking the radio stack's CCA (Clear Channel Assessment) routines at a specified interval.
- *LPL Listener* are provided by *FixedSleepLplListenerC* and *PeriodicLplListenerC* components. When radio activity is detected, *FixedSleepLplListenerC* activates the radio and disables the *ChannelPollerC*. *PeriodicLplListenerC* component instead keeps the *ChannelPollerC* component active at all times, and immediately moves the radio into its sleep state when the channel is free.
- *Preamble Sender* ensures the sender nodes that the recipient nodes are awaken when messages are sent through *PreambleSenderC* component.
- *Time Synchronization* among TDMA and scheduled contention protocols are supported commonly by *BeaconedTimeSyncC* component, which exchanges synchronization packets at regular intervals and adjusts the interval timers of both sender and receiver nodes.
- *Slot Handlers* are supported by *TDMASlothandlerC* and *CSMASlotHandlerC* components. The former provides contention-free packet sending and the latter provides contention-based packet sending.

4.1.2 Hardware-Dependent Components

- *Radio Power Control* interface provides the ability to control the power state of the radio.
- *Low-Cost Packet Resending* are supported by Resend interface.
- *ChannelMonitor* interface provides a simple, platform-independent wrapper around complex radio-specific CCA procedures.
- *CcaControl* interface allows a MAC protocol to control the radio layer's CCA checks and subsequent back-off behavior.
- *Low-Latency I/O* MLA exposes the radio's send and receive operation through *AsyncReceive* and *AsyncSend* interfaces as shown in Fig. 9. All I/O events that the MAC layer does not consume are passed through an *AsyncIOAdapter*, which converts asynchronous I/O into their synchronous counterparts by posting tasks or scheduling a thread.

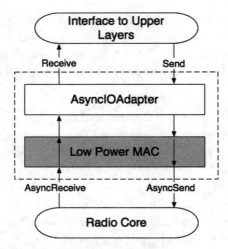

Fig. 9. Asynchronous to synchronous I/O adaptation.

– *Alarms:* The *Alarm* interface in TinyOS 2.0 are used in MLA. Besides this, MLA requires that each platform implement generic *AlarmMilliC*, *Alarm32khzC*, and *AlarmMicroC* components.
– *Local Time* MLA introduce *LocalTime32khz32C*, *LocalTimeMilli16C*, etc. to wrap hardware counters of the corresponding width and frequency, using some interface.

4.2 Preamble Based MAC Protocol

Asynchronous MAC protocol B-MAC utilizes a long preamble message to achieve low power communication. But the kind of LPL approaches with long preamble have some drawbacks: (a) excess latency at each hop, (b) suboptimal energy consumption, and (c) suffering from excess energy consumption at non-target receivers. X-MAC [5] proposes solutions to each of these drawbacks by employing a shortened preamble approach that also keeps the basic advantages of LPL, such as low power communication, simplicity, decoupling of transmitter and receiver sleep schedules. A visual timeline representation of asynchronous LPL with long preamble and X-MAC with short preamble are shown in Fig. 10. The X-MAC protocol has been implemented in various operating systems for sensor networks such as TinyOS, Mantis Operating System (MOS), etc.

X-MAC reduces the overhearing problem due to long preamble by dividing that one long preamble into a number of short preamble packets, each containing the ID of the destination node. The stream of short preamble packets effectively constitutes a single long preamble. When a node wakes

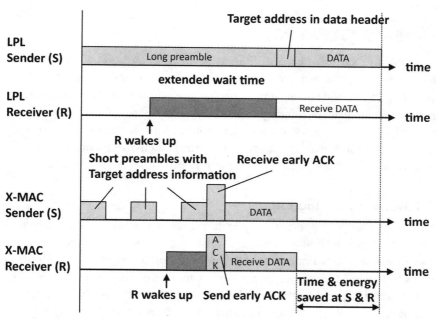

Fig. 10. Comparison of the timelines between extended preamble in LPL and short preamble in X-MAC.

up and receives a short preamble packet, it compares the destination node ID (included in the packet) with it's own ID. If the node is not the destination, it returns to sleep mode immediately. But if the node itself is the intended destination, it remains awake for the subsequent data packet.

In addition to shortening the preamble, X-MAC also addresses the problem of multiple transmitters sending the entire preamble even though the receiver is already awake. In such situation for X-MAC, when a transmitter is attempting to send but detects a preamble and is waiting for a clear channel, the node listens to the channel and if it hears an acknowledgment frame from the node that it wishes to send to, the transmitter will backoff a random amount and then send its data without a preamble. The randomized backoff is necessary because there may be more than one transmitter waiting to send, and the random backoff will mitigate collisions between multiple transmitters.

In conclusion, in this section we have presented practical system solutions to the challenges in link layer of Wireless Sensor Networks. This includes the works in: link layer architecture design and MAC protocols.

5. MIDDLEWARE

Middleware can bridge the gap between applications and the lower level components in order to resolve many challenges in Wireless Sensor Networks and to provide more application features. Sensor network middleware is basically a software infrastructure that combines together, the hardware, operating systems, protocol stacks, and applications. A state-of-the-art middleware solution is expected to contain a runtime environment that supports and manages multiple application requirements and system services.

5.1 Network Management

In order to support pervasive applications, WSN is envisioned to have features like autonomy, self-awareness, scalability, etc. Thus, network management becomes very important to keep the whole network and application work properly. The task of Network management mainly consists of managing, monitoring, and controlling the behavior of a network. Network management in traditional networks primarily focuses on minimizing response time, improving bandwidth, data persistence, etc. But network management in WSNs needs to focus on many other directions also, such as: network fault detection, network visualization tools, management of resources, debugging tools to localize fault in network, etc.

5.1.1 Tiered Architecture for Sensor Network

The future large-scale sensor network deployments will need to be tiered, for the purpose of robustness and manageability. For such tiered network design, *Tenet architecture* [13] presents a tired sensor network system design, consisting of sensor motes in the lower tier and *masters* (relatively unconstrained 32-bit platform nodes) in the upper tier. Tenet provides master node with increased network capacity and constrains multi-mode fusion only to the master tier. In this way, Tenet architecture simplifies application development and results in a generic mote tier networking subsystem that can be reused for a variety of applications.

The Tenet architecture is guided by Tenet Principle as follows. *Multi-node data fusion functionality and multi-node application logic should be implemented only in the master tier. The cost and complexity of implementing this functionality in a fully distributed fashion on motes outweighs the performance benefits of doing so.* This principle does allow motes to process locally generated data. Applications run on one or more master nodes and *task* motes to sense and locally process data. The result are sent back to the application program in the master node. Then the application can fuse the data and re-trigger the next sensing. More than one application can run concurrently on Tenet. The *main design principles* in Tenet architecture are: asymmetric task communication, address-ability, task library, robustness, and manageability. A Tenet task is composed of arbitrarily many tasklets linked together in a linear chain. Each tasklet may be thought of as a service to be carried out as part of the task. Tasklets expose parameters to control this service. Tenet's networking subsystem has two functions: to disseminate tasks to motes and to transport task responses back to masters. There are four guided design requirements: (i) the subsystem should support different applications on tiered networks, (ii) routing must be robust and scalable, (iii) tasks should be disseminated reliably from any master to all motes, and (iv) task responses should be transported with end-to-end reliability.

5.1.2 Network Management

In interactive sensor network management, the system collects information about network states in order to identify whether faults have occurred. The system can also interact with network nodes and adaptively reconfigure the network. The Sensor Network Management System (*SNMS*) [42] is an interactive system for monitoring the health of sensor networks. *SNMS* provides two main management functionalities: (a) query-based network health data collection and (b) event logging. With the query system users can collect and monitor physical parameter values of the nodes (e.g., remaining battery power, surrounding temperature, etc.). With the event-driven logging system users can set some event parameters and then nodes in the network will send report if they meet the specified event parameter thresholds. *SNMS* mainly supports two data traffic patterns: data collection and data dissemination. The main advantage of *SNMS* is that it introduces overhead only for human queries and so has minimal impact on memory and network traffic. SNMS also minimizes energy consumption by bundling the results of multiple queries into a single reply message instead of returning replies individually.

5.1.3 Lightweight Network Management

Based on earlier discussed network management system *SNMS* [42], a lightweight and transparent management framework for TinyOS sensor networks, called *L-SNMS* is designed in [48]. *L-SNMS* minimizes the overhead of management functions including memory usage overhead, network

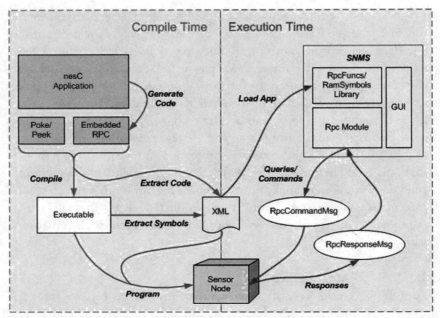

Fig. 11. The RPC solution to reduce the overhead of sensor node management in *L-SNMS*.

traffic overhead, and integration overhead. Remote Procedure Call (RPC) in network management allows the PC to access the functions and variables of a statically-compiled program on a wireless embedded device at runtime. Figure 11 shows the generation process of an RPC during compile time, and the Remote Procedure Calls during runtime. The compile time actions are supported by TinyOS, which adds the RPC function stub to the SNMS server. The Lightweight network management tools have been designed and used in an air-dropped wireless sensor network for volcano hazard monitoring [38].

5.1.4 Network Diagnosis

Network diagnosis is essential in network management for wireless sensor network. Due to the ad hoc nature, once deployed, the inner structures and interactions within a WSN are difficult to observe from the outside. This necessitates an online diagnosis approach which can passively observe the network symptoms from the sink node. *PAD* [26] provides a lightweight network diagnosis mechanism for sensor networks. PAD system is a probabilistic

Fig. 12. Oceansense project.

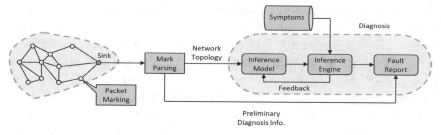

Fig. 13. PAD system overview.

diagnosis approach for inferring the causes of abnormal phenomena, by the root or sink node.

PAD employs a packet marking scheme for efficiently constructing and dynamically maintaining the inference model. PAD does not incur additional traffic overhead for collecting desired information. Instead, it introduces a probabilistic inference model that encodes internal dependencies among different network elements for online diagnosis of an operational sensor network system. Such a model is capable of additively reasoning root causes based on passively observed symptoms. PAD prototype is implemented in sea monitoring sensor network testbed called *Oceansense* (Fig. 12).

The work is claimed to be the first to investigate a passive method of diagnosing the Wireless Sensor Networks. The working of PAD is shown in Fig. 13. PAD is mainly composed of *four components*: a packet marking module, a mark parsing module, a probabilistic inference model, and an inference engine. The packet marking module resides in each sensor node and sporadically marks routine application packets passing by. At the sink side, the mark parsing module extracts and analyzes the marks carried by the received data packets. The network topology can thus be reconstructed and dynamically updated according to the analysis results. The mark parsing module also generates preliminary diagnosis information such as packets loss on certain links, route dynamics, and so on. The inference model builds a graph of dependencies among network elements based on the outputs from the parsing module. Using the inference model and observed negative and positive symptoms as inputs, the inference engine is able to yield a fault report, which reveals the root causes of exceptions by setting the posterior probabilities of each network component being problematic. The inference results are also taken as feedback to help improve and update the inference model.

5.1.5 Wireless Link Quality Estimation Using Cross-Layer Information

Wireless link quality estimation in ad hoc wireless network is an important challenge. Accurate link quality estimates are a prerequisite for efficient network operations in wireless networks, because poor link estimates can cause a 200% or greater slowdown in network throughput [7]. Despite its importance, link estimation remains an open problem, in part because many factors conspire to make it challenging. The work in [11] argues that estimating links accurately requires combining of information from different layers: network later, link layer and physical layer. This work proposes narrow, protocol-independent interfaces for the different layers, which in total provide *four bits of information*: one from the physical layer, one from the link layer, and two from the network layer. Using these interfaces, the work designs a wireless link estimator that is tested to reduce packet delivery costs by up to 44% over current approaches and maintains a 99% delivery ratio over large, multi-hop networks in different standard testbeds.

Figure 14(a)–(e) shows the interfaces each layer provides to a link estimator, for different routing protocols. For the *Four Bit link estimator*, together the three layers provide four bits of information: two bits for incoming packets, and one bit each for transmitted unicast packets and link table entries.

- The *physical layer* provides a single bit of information. If set, this *white bit* denotes that each symbol in received packet has a very low probability of decoding error. A set white bit implies that during the reception, the medium quality is high. The converse is not necessarily true: if the white bit is clear, then the medium quality may or may not have been high during the packet's reception.

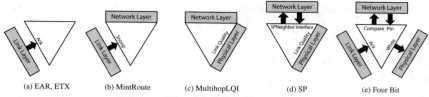

Fig. 14. Link estimators information usage by several different wireless link estimators: EAR, ETX[8], MintRoute[45], Multi-hopLQI [2], SP[35] and Four Bit scheme. A link estimator, represented by the triangle, interacts with up to three layers. Attached boxes represent unified implementation. Outgoing arrows represent information the estimator requests on packets it receives. Incoming arrows represent information the layers actively provide.

— The *link layer* provides one bit of information per transmitted packet: the *ack bit*. A link layer sets the ack bit on a transmit buffer when it receives a layer 2 acknowledgment for that buffer. If the ack bit is clear, the packet may or may not have arrived successfully.
— The *network layer* provides 2 bits of information, the *pin bit* and the *compare bit*. The pin bit applies to link table entries. When the network layer sets the pin bit on an entry, the link estimator cannot remove it from the table until the bit is cleared. A link estimator can ask a network layer for a compare bit on a packet. The compare bit indicates whether the route provided by the sender of the packet is better than the route provided by one or more of the entries in the link table.

The proposed hybrid estimator combines the information provided by the three layers with periodic beacons in order to provide accurate, responsive, and useful link estimates. The estimator maintains a small table of candidate links for which it maintains ETX values. It periodically broadcasts beacons that contain a subset of these links. Network layer protocols can also broadcast packets through the estimator, causing it to act as a layer 2.5 protocol that adds a header and footer between layers 2 and 3. The estimator follows the basic table management algorithm. But it does not assume a minimum transmission rate, since it can leverage outgoing data traffic to detect broken links. Link estimate broadcasts contain sequence numbers, which receivers use to calculate the beacon reception rate. The estimator uses the white and compare bits to supplement the standard table replacement policy. When it receives a network layer routing packet which has the white bit set from a node that is not in the link estimation table, the estimator asks the network layer whether the compare bit is set. If so, the estimator flushes a random unpinned entry from the table and replaces it with the sender of the current packet.

5.2 Neighbor Discovery

Neighbor discovery is a challenging problem to solve and design in real systems, especially in mobile sensor networks. Here we have presented a practical solution to this problem in the literature.

5.2.1 Neighbor Discovery among Unsynchronized Nodes

A practical solution to the neighbor discovery problem has been proposed and designed in [10]. *Disco* is an asynchronous neighbor discovery and rendezvous protocol that allows two or more nodes to operate their radios at low-duty cycles (e.g., 1%) and yet still discover and communicate with one another during infrequent, opportunistic encounters without requiring any prior synchronization information.

Disco works as following, two nodes, i and j, pick two numbers, m_i and m_j, such that m_i and m_j are relatively prime (co-primes) and $1/m_i$ and $1/m_j$ are approximately equal to i's and j's desired duty cycles, respectively. Time is divided into fixed-width reference periods and consecutive periods are labeled with consecutive integers. Nodes i and j start counting the passage of these periods at times a_i and a_j, with their respective counters, c_i and c_j, initialized to zero, and with i and j counts synchronized to the reference period. If $c_i | m_i$ (c_i is divisible by m_i), then i turns on its radio for one period and beacons (or listens, or does both, depending on application requirements). Similarly, if $c_j | m_j$, then j turns on its radio for one period and beacons. When both i and j turn on their radios during the same period, they can exchange beacons and discover each other.

Let us consider a concrete example. Let node i select $m_i = 3$ (so i's duty cycle is: $DC \approx 33\%$), start counting at reference period $x = 1$ (so that $a_i = 1$), with counter values c_i. Similarly, let node j select $m_j = 5$ (so j's duty cycle is: $DC \approx 20\%$), start counting at reference period $x = 2$ (so that $a_j = 2$), with counter values c_j. Figure 15 illustrates this time line and counter values.

The *Chinese Remainder Theorem* requires the moduli m_i and m_j be co-primes to guarantee a solution to the simultaneous congruences. So the moduli cannot be chosen independently by the nodes since such choices could lead to values of m_i and m_j that are not co-primes. It would, of course, be preferable to let nodes choose the moduli that best satisfy their individual duty cycle requirements rather than require a static or central assignment.

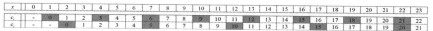

x	0	1	2	3	4	5	6	7	8	9	10	11	12	13	14	15	16	17	18	19	20	21	22	23
c_i	-	0	1	2	3	4	5	6	7	8	9	10	11	12	13	14	15	16	17	18	19	20	21	22
c_j	-	-	0	1	2	3	4	5	6	7	8	9	10	11	12	13	14	15	16	17	18	19	20	21

Fig. 15. An example discovery time line. Two nodes, i and j, start their counters, c_i and c_j, at time $x = 1$ and $x = 2$, with periods $m_i = 3$ and $m_j = 5$, and duty cycles of approximately 33% and 20%, respectively. The dark cells indicate times when the nodes i and j turn on their radio. Both nodes are awake at times $x = 7$ and $x = 22$. This pattern repeats when $x = 7 + 15k$, for all $k \in \mathbb{Z}^+$.

Besides, restricting the moduli to co-primes is not scalable since there are only a handful of numbers that can satisfy both the target duty cycle (typically 1–5%) and co-prime requirement. Furthermore, if $m_i = m_j$, then nodes i and j may never discover each if they wake up with the same period but different phase. One way to allow each node to select the best duty cycle for itself while still ensuring discovery occurs is to require each node i to pick two primes, p_{i1} and p_{i2}, such that $p_{i1} \neq p_{i2}$ and the sum of their reciprocals (approximately) equals the desired duty cycle as follows:

$$DC \approx \frac{1}{p_{i1}} + \frac{1}{p_{i2}}.$$

Each node increments a local counter and if a node's local counter is divisible by either of its primes, the node turns on its radio for a single interval, whose length is the only global parameter. This approach ensures that no matter what duty cycles are independently selected at different nodes, for every pair of nodes i and j, there will be at least one pair in the set $\{(p_{i1},p_{j1}),(p_{i1},p_{j2}),(p_{i2},p_{j1}),(p_{i2},p_{j2})\}$ that are relatively prime, satisfying the Chinese Remainder Theorem. Note, however, that simply requiring p_{i1} and p_{i2} to be co-primes does not satisfy the requirements of the theorem, and therefore cannot ensure discovery. Therefore, to ensure correctness, *Disco* uses prime pairs rather than co-primes.

The choice of primes can have a large impact on discovery latency. The ratio of the worst-case discovery latency between an auspicious and an unfortunate set of prime pairs is bounded by the duty cycle. For example, a 10% duty cycle results in no worse than a 1:10 ratio, a 2% duty cycle is bounded by a 1:50 ratio, and a 1% duty cycle results in at worse a 1:100 ratio. If we let $c = 1/DC$, we have:

$$\frac{1}{c} \approx \frac{1}{p_{i1}} + \frac{1}{p_{i2}},$$

$$p_{i2} \approx \frac{p_{i1} \cdot c}{p_{i1} - c}.$$

The limit of the ratio between the auspicious and unfortunate worst-case latencies is:

$$\lim_{p_{i1} \to c+1} \frac{p_{i1}^2}{p_{i1}p_{i2}} = \frac{(c+1)^2(c+1-c)}{(c+1)(c+1)c} = \frac{1}{c} = DC.$$

These observations suggest that picking the prime pairs requires care: a good choice can result in low-discovery latency but a poor choice can result in much longer worst-case discovery latency. Low-discovery times are possible if one of the primes is very close to the reciprocal of the duty cycle while the other prime is a much larger number. If this approach is taken, then it becomes important to randomize the choice of prime pairs to reduce the chance that two nodes will have picked the same pair if they both select the same duty cycle.

5.3 Topology Control

Topology control determines network-wide physical connectivity by configuring RF (Radio Frequency) power, radio frequencies, and physical data rate, and thus has significant impact on network reliability, capacity, and lifetime. It can reduce the energy consumption of packet transmissions and channel contention. Moreover, it can enhance disruption-resilience and reliability in disruptive networks. Topology control for Wireless Sensor Networks faces significant challenges since wireless characteristics are usually dynamic and complex.

5.3.1 Topology Control Adaptive to Link Dynamics

A practical topology control algorithm must be robust against environmental and workload dynamics while introducing minimal communication, processing, and memory overhead. To design such topology control algorithm, Adaptive and Robust Topology control (ART) [14] proposes a novel and practical topology control algorithm.

ART is designed based on the key observations in an empirical study done in the work, and has the following salient features: (i) ART is designed to be a robust topology control algorithm: indirect measurements of link quality is not used because they are not sufficiently robust in different indoor environments; (ii) ART is an adaptive algorithm in the sense that it changes the transmission power of a link based on its observed PRR (Packet Reception Ratio). Moreover, ART employs a lightweight adaptation mechanism and does not employ prolonged bootstrapping phase for link profiling; (iii) ART can dynamically adapt the transmission power in response to high channel

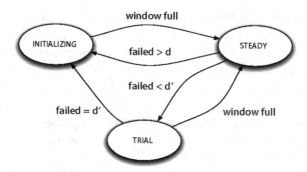

Fig. 16. ART state transition diagram.

contention; (iv) ART is specifically designed to be efficient, so that it can be realistically deployed on memory-constrained wireless sensor platforms with low-runtime overhead.

Figure 16 summarizes the ART algorithm as a state diagram. ART individually tunes the transmission power over each of a node's outgoing links. A link is initially set to transmit at its maximum power. ART monitors all outgoing packet transmissions and keeps a record of whether each transmission failed or succeeded in a sliding window of size w. While the window is filling, it is said that the link is "initializing." When the sliding window is full, ART compares the number of recorded transmission failures to two thresholds d and d', where $d > d'$. The link remains in this "steady" state as long as the number of failures is between these two thresholds.

If the recorded number of failures is above d, then ART adjusts the link power to improve its quality. ART may raise the link's transmission power to improve its quality under low contention, but may lower its transmission power under high contention. ART uses a simple gradient-based mechanism to detect high contention based on recent history. After selecting a new power setting, ART flushes the transmission window and re-enters the initializing state.

If the number of failures is below d', then ART enters a "trial" state where it temporarily lowers the power by one level. If the link experiences d' more transmission failures at any time while in the trial state, then it returns to the previous power level, flushes its transmission window, and goes back to the initializing state. If the link's window fills with fewer than d' recorded transmission failures, then the new power setting is made permanent and the link goes back to the steady state.

5.3.2 Topology Control with Transmission Power Control

The phenomenon that quality of radio communication between low power sensor devices varies significantly with time and environment, indicates that the topology control algorithms using static transmission power, transmission range, and link quality, are not effective in the real-world applications. To address this issue, *online transmission power control* is necessary, that can adapt to external changes. ATPC [25] is a lightweight algorithm of adaptive transmission power control for Wireless Sensor Networks.

In ATPC, each node builds a model for each of its neighbors, describing the correlation between transmission power and link quality. With this model, a feedback-based transmission power control algorithm is employed to dynamically maintain individual link quality over time. The *main objectives* of ATPC are: (i) to make every node in a sensor network find the minimum transmission power levels that can provide good link qualities for its neighboring nodes in order to address the spatial impact and (ii) to dynamically change the pairwise transmission power level over time in order to address the temporal impact. Through ATPC, it is possible to maintain good link qualities between pairs of nodes with the in situ transmission power control.

Figure 17 shows the main idea of ATPC. A neighbor table is maintained at each node and a feedback closed loop for transmission power control runs between each pair of nodes. The neighbor table contains the proper transmission power levels that this node should use for its neighboring nodes and the parameters for *linear predictive models* of transmission power control. The proper transmission power level is defined here as the minimum transmission

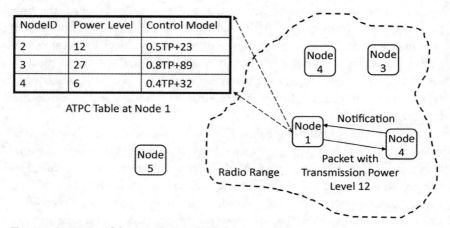

NodeID	Power Level	Control Model
2	12	0.5TP+23
3	27	0.8TP+89
4	6	0.4TP+32

ATPC Table at Node 1

Fig. 17. Overview of the pairwise ATPC design.

power level that supports a good link quality between a pair of nodes. The *linear transmission power predictive model* is used to describe the in situ relation between the transmission powers and link qualities. The empirical data collected in this work indicate that this in situ relation is not strictly linear. Therefore, this predictive model is an approximation of the reality. To obtain the minimum transmission power level, feedback control theory is applied to form a closed loop to gradually adjust the transmission power. It is known that feedback control allows a linear model to converge within the region when a non-linear system can be approximated by a linear model, so it is possible to safely design a small-signal linear control for the system, even if the linear model is just a rough approximation of reality.

ATPC has *two phases*: (i) initialization phase and (ii) runtime tuning phase. In the *initialization phase*, a mote computes a predictive model and chooses a proper transmission power level based on that model for each neighbor. In the *runtime tuning phase*, a lightweight feedback mechanism is adopted to monitor the link quality change and tune the transmission power online. Figure 18 shows an overview of the feedback mechanism in ATPC. To simplify the description, a pair of nodes are shown. Each node has an ATPC module for transmission power control. This module adopts a predictive model for each neighbor. It also maintains a list of proper transmission power levels for neighbors of this mote. When node A has a packet to send to its neighbor B, it first adjusts the transmission power to the level indicated by its neighbor table in the ATPC module, and then transmits the packet.

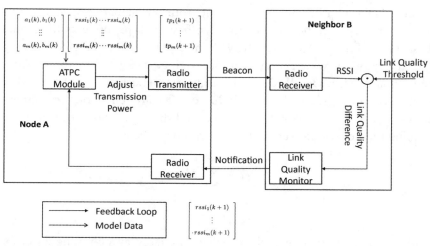

Fig. 18. Feedback closed loop overview for ATPC.

When receiving this packet, the link quality monitor module at its neighbor B takes a measurement of the link quality. Based on the difference between the desired link quality and actual measurements, the link quality monitor module decides whether a notification packet is necessary.

A notification packet is necessary when: (a) the link quality falls below the desired level, or (b) the link quality is good but the current signal energy is so high that it wastes the transmission energy. The notification packet contains the measured link quality difference. When node A receives a notification from its neighbor B, the ATPC module in node A uses the link quality difference as the input to the predictive model and calculates a new transmission power level for its neighbor B.

5.4 Energy Management

Energy consumption in sensor network is still one of the main obstacles in applying the technology to various services requiring high Quality-of-Service (QoS) and long network lifetime. Hence efficient energy management policy on and among sensor nodes is a key in designing robust and long lasting sensor network operations. In this section we present practical works on designing energy management architecture for WSN.

5.4.1 Architecture for Energy Management

Matching workload to the resource availability across the sensor network requires integration with application components (that produce energy load), distributing load, and availability information to facilitate node decision making. This requires awareness of the connection between load, availability, and application-level fidelity. Geoffrey et al. [6] presents Integrated Distributed Energy Awareness (*IDEA*), a sensor network service enabling effective network-wide energy decision making. *IDEA* distributes information about each node's load rate, charging rate, and battery level to other nodes whose decisions affect it. *IDEA* enables awareness of the connection between the behavior of each node and the application's energy goals, guiding the network toward states that improve performance.

$$L_i(S) = \sum_{j=1}^{k} L_i^j(s_j), \tag{1}$$

$$S^* = \arg\max O(\bar{L}(S), \bar{B}, \bar{C}) \cdot \alpha + u(S) \cdot (1 - \alpha). \tag{2}$$

IDEA is intended to address the problem of energy-aware tuning in sensor network applications. In *IDEA*, the term *client* is used to refer to either an application or an individual software component that wishes to perform energy tuning. Clients interact with the *IDEA* runtime residing on each sensor node to make decisions that impact energy consumption and data fidelity. Then, the problem can be formally defined as follows. At a given time, let's denote the global state of all nodes in the network as $S = \{s_1, s_2, ..., s_k\}$. The combined energy load at node i induced by this selection of states is as in equation (1). Based on the current battery levels B_i and charging rates C_i, an energy objective function is defined as $O(L(S), B, C)$ that represents the global energy impact of the global state assignment S. Likewise, this state assignment has an associated application–defined utility $u(S)$ that represents the intrinsic desirability of the state. The choice of $u(S)$ can be provided by the application as a static function. The system's goal is to determine the optimal state as in equation (2). The term α represents the trade off factor between energy impact and intrinsic utility. Setting $\alpha = 1$ optimizes only for energy; $\alpha = 0$ only for application–defined utility.

IDEA seeks to perform optimization in a *decentralized* fashion, with the goal of closely approximating the globally optimal solution. The overview of the *IDEA* architecture is shown in Fig. 19. Each node monitors its own

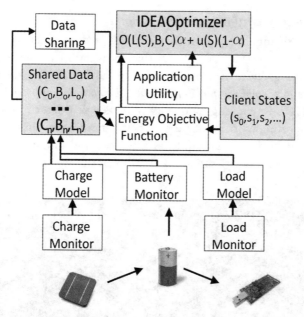

Fig. 19. Overview of *IDEA* architecture. *IDEA* combines load and charge monitoring and modeling, energy data distribution, and an application-provided energy objective function into a single service.

load rate, charging rate, and battery level. Monitoring output is passed onto a modeling component that produces models of load and charging behavior. Model parameters are distributed to other nodes via a data sharing component, which maintains a distributed table allowing energy information to be queried by energy objective functions. *IDEA* monitors the accuracy of each node's local model parameters, re-propagating them as necessary to maintain the distributed energy information.

5.5 Localization

One of the important challenges for sensor networks is the need for localization. In order to understand sensor data in a proper spatial context, or for computation of navigation throughout a sensing region, information of sensor node position is necessary. Localization algorithms can be classified into *range-free* and *range-based* methods. *Range-free* methods use node proximity and connectivity. *Range-based* methods use location metrics such as ToA (Time of Arrival), TDoA (Time Difference of Arrival), RSS (Received Signal Strength) and AoA (Angle of Arrival) to estimate the distance between two nodes.

5.5.1 Ranging Quality-Based Localization

The real-world implementation of *GreenOrbs*, a sensor network system in the forest (shown in Fig. 20), shows that localization in the wild remains very challenging due to various interfering factors. In this scenario *CDL* [46] proposes a *Combined and Differentiated Localization* approach. The central idea of *CDL* is that ranging quality is the key that determines the overall localization accuracy. In its pursuit of better ranging quality, *CDL* incorporates virtual-hop localization, local filtration, and ranging-quality aware calibration. *CDL* inherits the advantages of both *range-free* and *range-based*

Fig. 20. *GreenOrbs* deployment in the campus woodland.

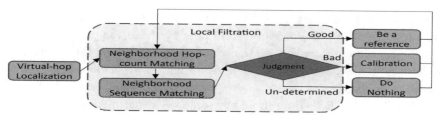

Fig. 21. The work flow of *CDL*.

methods, and keeps pursuing better ranging quality throughout the localization process.

CDL considers locating a network of wireless nodes on a two dimensional plane by using the connectivity information and RSSI readings. A few nodes, which know their own coordinates once they are deployed, are used as landmarks. The design of *CDL* mainly consists of (a) virtual-hop localization, (b) local filtration, and (c) ranging-quality aware calibration. Figure 21 illustrates the *CDL* workflow. Virtual-hop localization initially estimates node locations using a range-free method. In order to approximate the distances from the nodes to the landmarks, it counts virtual hops, compensating particularly for the errors caused by the non-uniform deployment problem. Subsequently, *CDL* executes an iterative process of filtration and calibration. In each filtration step, *CDL* uses two filtering methods to identify good nodes whose location accuracy is already satisfactory. Neighborhood hop-count matching filters the bad nodes by verifying a node's hop-counts to its neighbors. Furthermore, neighborhood sequence matching distinguishes good nodes from bad ones by contrasting two sequences on each node. Each sequence sorts a node's neighbors using a particular metric, such as RSSI and estimated distance. Those identified good nodes are regarded as references and used to calibrate the location of bad ones. Links with different ranging quality are given different weights. Outliers in range measurements are tolerated using robust estimation.

5.5.2 Range-Free Localization

In many WSN applications, the requirement of low system cost prohibits many range-based methods for sensor node localization. On the other hand, range-free localization, depending only on connectivity, may under-utilize the proximity information embedded in neighborhood sensing. In response to the above mentioned limitations, *RSD* [49] represents a range-free approach to capturing a relative distance between 1-hop neighboring nodes from their

neighborhood orderings, that serve as unique high-dimensional location signatures for nodes in the network. With little overhead, the proposed design
can be conveniently applied as a transparent supporting layer for many state-
of-the-art connectivity-based localization solutions to achieve better positioning accuracy.

The design of RSD is motivated by some key experimental observations
in the outdoor environments: (a) network-wide monotonic relationship
between radio signal strength and physical distance does not hold, but (b)
per-node monotonic RSS-Distance relationship holds well, i.e., any single
node's RSS sensing results for its neighboring nodes can be used as an indicator for the relative "near-far" relationship among neighbors.

Based on these, RSD is designed with the concept of *range-free relative
distance among 1-hop neighboring nodes*. Given the RSS sensing results for
neighboring nodes, a node can obtain a neighborhood ordering with two
steps: (i) sorting its 1-hop neighbors according to their signal strength by
decreasing order and (ii) adding itself as the first element in the sorted node
list. The example is shown in Fig. 22. For any node u_i, its neighborhood
ordering S_i is considered as a high-dimensional signature of the node in the
network. S_i has a vector format and contains all 1-hop neighbors of node u_i
with some important features.

$$SD(S_i, S_j) = F_e(S_i, S_j) + F_i(S_i, S_j) + F_p(S_i, S_j) \times 0.5, \tag{3}$$

$$RSD(u_i, u_j) = SD(S_i, S_j). \frac{\sqrt{K}}{K(K-1)/2}. \tag{4}$$

The term *Signature Distance* (SD) quantifies the difference between two
high-dimensional signatures. SD is the first step toward a relative distance
that effectively reflects the physical distance relationships among neighboring nodes in the network. There are three types of potential node-pair

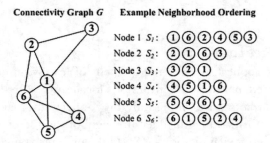

Fig. 22. Neighborhood ordering.

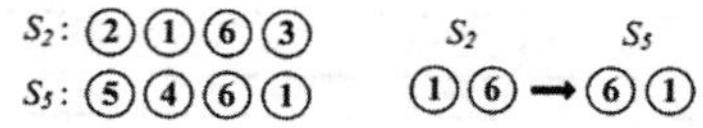

S_2: ② ① ⑥ ③ S_2 S_s
S_s: ⑤ ④ ⑥ ①   ① ⑥ → ⑥ ①

Fig. 23. Explicit node-pair flip.

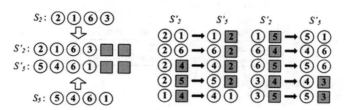

Fig. 24. Implicit node-pair flip.

Fig. 25. Possible node-pair flip.

flips between two signatures S_i and S_j: (a) *explicit flip*, (b) *implicit flip*, and (c) *possible flip*. The corresponding examples are shown in Figs. 23–25. Based on these, the signature distance between S_i and S_j is defined as follows. The signature distance $SD(S_i, S_j)$ is equal to the summation of the number of explicit flips $F_e(S_i, S_j)$, implicit flips $F_i(S_i, S_j)$, and possible flips $F_p(S_i, S_j)$ times 0.5 (50% probability of flip for possible node pairs), as shown in equation (3). However, in some cases, SD can be biased due to spatially non-uniform bisector line density throughout the network area, violating some conditions. Based on this the work has proposed a more robust relative distance, i.e., *Regulated SD* (RSD), to address this problem. RSD is a robust metric of the proximity among 1-hop neighboring nodes. The computation of RSD is defined as in equation (4).

Equation (4) refines $SD(S_i, S_j)$ with a factor $\frac{\sqrt{K}}{K(K-1)/2}$, where $K = |S_i \cup S_j|$ is the total number of nodes in the neighborhood of node u_i and u_j combined. In this equation, $K(K-1)/2$ calculates the number of local bisector lines, used to normalize $SD(S_i, S_j)$ with the local bisector density; $\sqrt{K}$ estimates the diameter of this neighborhood, which puts the factor of neighborhood size into consideration.

The design of *RSD* can be implemented as a supporting layer that is transparent to the localization algorithms. As shown in Fig. 26, the smallest

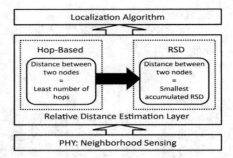

Fig. 26. *RSD* algorithm design.

accumulated *RSD* is used along a path between two nodes instead of the shortest path hop count as the estimated relative distance. Specially, the accumulated *RSD* between two nodes is defined as: (i) For 1-hop neighboring nodes u_i and u_j, accumulated *RSD* equals $RSD(u_i, u_j)$ computed with equation (4); (ii) For non-neighboring nodes u_i and u_j, accumulated *RSD* is calculated as the summation of the *RSD* values of neighboring nodes along a path between u_i and u_j.

5.6 Time Synchronization

The problem of Time Synchronization in Sensor Networks is to synchronize the local clocks of individual sensor nodes in the network. There have been extensive study in the literature, still practical Time Synchronization protocol with higher order of accuracy, scalability and independence of topology is an open problem.

5.6.1 Network Flooding Based Time Synchronization

One of the early practical time synchronization protocol is Flooded Time Synchronization protocol (*FTSP*) [28]. It is especially tailored for applications requiring stringent precision on resource limited wireless platforms. *FTSP* uses low communication bandwidth and is robust against node and link failures. *FTSP* achieves the robustness by utilizing periodic flooding of synchronization messages, and implicit dynamic topology update. It achieves high precision synchronization by utilizing MAC-layer timestamping and comprehensive error compensation including clock skew estimation.

The work has identified the non-deterministic delays in the radio message delivery in WSN. These delays can be in magnitudes larger than the required precision of time synchronization. Therefore in *FTSP* these delays are carefully analyzed and compensated for. The delays factors involved are:

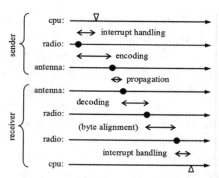

Fig. 27. The timing of the transmission of an idealized point in the software (cpu), hardware (radio chip), and physical (antenna) layers of the sender and the receiver.

send time, access time, transmission time, propagation time, reception time, receive time, interrupt handling time, encoding time, decoding time, and byte alignment time. Figure 27 summarizes the decomposition of delivery delay of the idealized point of the message as it traverses over a wireless channel.

The *FTSP* synchronizes the time of a sender to possibly multiple receivers utilizing a single radio message timestamped at both the sender and the receiver sides. It has a structure with a root node and other nodes are synchronized to the root. The root node transmits the time synchronization information with radio message to all the receivers. The message contains the sender's timestamp of the global time at the time of transmission. The receiver node records its local time when the message is received. Then from the sender's transmission time and the reception time, the receiver can estimate the clock offset. The message is MAC layer timestamped on both the sending and receiving side. To compensate due to clock drift for high precision, *FTSP* uses linear regression. *FTSP* was designed for large multi-hop networks. The root is elected dynamically and is periodically re-elected. Root node is responsible for keeping the global time of the network. The receiving nodes synchronize themselves to the root node and organize in an ad hoc fashion to communicate the timing information amongst all other nodes. *FTSP* provides multi-hop time synchronization. *FTSP* is relatively robust against node and link failures, and dynamic topology changes.

5.6.2 Time Synchronization Using AC Power Line Signal

A low-power hardware module, for achieving global clock synchronization by tuning to the magnetic field radiating from existing AC power lines, has been developed by [37]. The signal can be used as a global clock source for battery operated sensor nodes to eliminate drift between nodes over time even when they are not passing messages. Since these phase offsets tend to be constant, a higher level compensation protocol can be used to globally synchronize a sensor network.

Hardware Design: The design consists of hardware and software components. In hardware, the work presents the design of an LC tank receiver circuit tuned to the AC 60 Hz signal which is called a *Syntonistor*. The *Syntonistor* incorporates a low-power microcontroller that filters the signal induced from AC power lines generating a pulse-per second output for easy interfacing with sensor nodes. In firmware, a clock–recovery technique running on the local microcontroller that minimizes timing jitter and provides robustness to noise. In software, the work provides a protocol that sets a global time by accounting for phase offsets.

First, the work describes the hardware and firmware components that accurately detect the energy radiating from AC power lines. The EM (ElectroMagnetic) receiver is shown in Fig. 28. The circuit diagram in Fig. 29 shows the major components of the *Syntonistor*. The power–line magnetic field is detected by an antenna composed of an inductor (L) and capacitor (C) tank circuit. The LC component of the circuit is tuned to a resonant frequency of 60 Hz.

Firmware Design: The main task of firmware running on PIC12F683 processors is to filter the incoming pulses and generate a stable pulse per second (PPS) output which the sensor node can use for synchronization purposes. The signal tends to suffer from jitter as well as occasional periods of lost reception. Filtering such a signal in the time domain to recover a

Fig. 28. AC power-line EM receiver (*Syntonistor*) next to a coin.

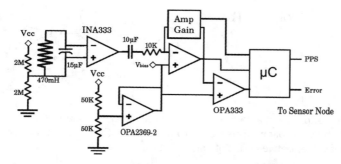

Fig. 29. Schematic for wireless power line clock synchronization module.

clock is commonly solved using a Phase–Locked Loop (PLL). In the design, a proportional–integral (PI) PLL controller is implemented in software.

Synchronization Protocol: After each node gains a globally rate adjusted clock, there are following challenges in the protocol layer: (1) determining a common starting time point; (2) determining phase offsets between neighbors; (3) recovering from errors when synchronization fails.

The protocol begins when a master node broadcasts a message at its rising PPS edge that contains its wall-clock time. The message is flooded across the network. After the flood has propagated across the network, each node should maintain a synchronization time point as well as the phase offset between its local PPS signal and that from the master. Also, periodic broadcasts with neighbors can be used to build a 1–hop neighbor list containing relative phase offsets between neighbors which is a useful tool for detecting errors. Each node in the network will have a synchronization accuracy limited by the local jitter in the *Syntonistor* which is about 2 ms as well as the accumulated jitter from the radio communications, but not the *Syntonistor* error from previous hops.

The Fig. 30a illustrates the protocol, where node M is the master and nodes $a,b,c,...,g$ are other nodes constituting a multi-hop network. The nodes are able to estimate phase offset of their local PPS signal to that of the master. The phase offset between the master and node i is given by Θ_i. This synchronization flooding is only required at network initialization time. If new nodes join the network, they can communicate with existing infrastructure nodes to obtain a phase offset. Once the phase offsets with respect to the master are calculated, the relative phase between any two nodes can be calculated by treating their phase offsets from the master as directed vectors, and the phase difference between them is just a vector

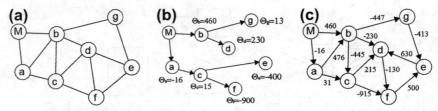

Fig. 30. Operation of initialization phase of phase offset calculation. (a) Shows a set of nodes. (b) Shows a spanning tree used to determine offsets from a master clock. (c) Phase offset values between sets of nodes that can be used for error checking.

sum of the two vectors. This is explained in Fig. 30c, where each node has a list of phase offsets from its neighbors. It is interesting to note that this sum of phases along a closed loop in the directed vectors graph is always zero. This property provides robustness against a node failure and improves reliability by allowing the nodes to crosscheck their phase offset. Besides, the *Syntonistor* has the ability to detect when the timing of the incoming signal unexpectedly increases beyond the normal jitter threshold.

5.7 Security

With the significant growth of Wireless Sensor Networks into pervasive applications, the need of effective security mechanisms is also growing. Sensor networks, a lot of time contain sensitive data, and operate in hostile unattended environments. Therefore it is imperative that the security mechanisms are integral part of whole system design. The challenges in developing security mechanisms for sensor networks is apparently different from that of traditional computer network security. This is due to different factors like limited resource, limited computing capability, disruptive application environments etc.

5.7.1 Link Layer Security Architecture

TinySec [17] is claimed to be the first fully-implemented link layer security architecture for Wireless Sensor Networks. Sensor Networks' constraints like small memory, slower processing unit, limited energy, and small packet overload, etc. put limitations to implementing efficient security mechanisms. *TinySec* has attempted to address these system constraints.

    TinySec is a lightweight, generic security package that can be integrated into sensor network implementations. *TinySec* provides the following *basic security properties*: (i) message authentication and integrity through MAC (Message Authentication Codes), (ii) message confidentiality through

Table 2 Summary of different keying mechanisms for link layer security.

Keying Mechanism	Benefits	Costs
Single network-wide key	Simple and easy to deploy. Supports passive participation and local broadcast.	Not robust to node compromise.
Per-link keys between neighboring nodes	Graceful degradation in the presence of compromised nodes.	Needs a key distribution protocol. Prohibits passive participation and local broadcast.
Group keys	Graceful degradation in the presence of compromised nodes. Supports passive participation and local broadcast.	Requires key distribution. Trades off robustness to node compromise for added functionality.

encryption, (iii) semantic security through an Initialization Vector, and (iv) replay protection. *TinySec* supports *two different security options*: (i) authenticated encryption (called TinySec-AE) and (ii) authentication only (called TinySec-Auth). For authenticated encryption (TinySec-AE), *TinySec* uses Cipher Block Chaining (CBC) mode, and encrypts the data payload and authenticates the packet with a MAC. The MAC is computed over the encrypted data and the packet header. In authentication only mode (TinySec-Auth), *TinySec* authenticates the entire packet with a MAC, but the data payload is not encrypted.

Keying Mechanism: Keying mechanism determines how cryptographic keys are distributed and shared throughout the network. The *TinySec* protocol is not limited to any particular keying mechanism. Any of the mechanisms can be used in conjunction with *TinySec*. Table 2 shows a summary of trade offs among different possible keying mechanisms in sensor networks.

Implementation of Security Architecture: The work has implemented *TinySec* on the Berkeley sensor nodes Mica, Mica2, and Mica2Dot platforms (each uses Atmel processors). Additionally, *TinySec* is integrated into the TOSSIM simulator, which runs on an Intel x86 platform. Others have ported *TinySec* into Texas Instruments microprocessor. *TinySec* is actually portable to both new processors, as well as new radio architectures. *TinySec* is implemented in 3000 lines of nesC code, the programming language used for sensor network operating system TinyOS. The implementation of *TinySec* requires 728 bytes of RAM and 7146 bytes of program space. The default TinyOS 1.1.2 radio stack is modified to incorporate *TinySec*.

5.7.2 Physical Attack on Sensor Node

Most security protocols for Wireless Sensor Networks assume that the adversary can gain full control over a sensor node through direct physical access (node capture attack). But the topic of assessing the amount of effort an attacker has to undertake in a node capture attack, was unexplored for some years. The work in [3] has evaluated different physical attacks against sensor node hardware. The *physical attacks can be categorized* in decreasing severity as follows: (i) gaining complete read/write access to the microcontroller, (ii) reading out RAM or flash memory, in whole or in part, (iii) influencing sensor readings, and (iv) manipulating radio communications.

Security Attack Methods on Hardware: There are three different examples of attacks on RAM and flash memory, such as (i) *JTAG attack*, (ii) *bootstrap loader attack*, and (iii) *external flash attack*.

JTAG attack: All nodes examined in the work has a JTAG connector on board allowing easy access to the memory data. However, the nodes with TI MSP430 has a fuse which can be blown to disable all JTAG functionality. The ATmega128 has software-controlled lock bits to disable memory access via JTAG.

Bootstrap loader attack: The BSL password has a size of 16×16 bit and is equivalent to the flash memory content at addresses 0xFFE0 to 0xFFFF where the interrupt vector table is located. An attacker might be able to guess the password by brute force, when an object of the program is in possession. One consequence of the fact that the password is equal to the interrupt vector table, is that anyone possessing the password can know the interrupt vector table information. Therefore, the work has proposed and tested a technique called *interrupt vector randomization*. The work has written a program that preprocesses a program image before installation on a node. The tool replaces the original interrupt vector table with a series of 16 randomly chosen, previously unused code addresses. Unconditional branch instruction to the original interrupt handler routine are placed at each of these addresses.

External flash attack: Some applications store valuable data on the external EEPROM. The simplest form of attack is eavesdropping on the conductor wires connecting the external memory chip to the microcontroller, possibly using a suitable logic analyzer. A more sophisticated attack would connect a second microcontroller to the I/O pins of the flash chip. If the node's microcontroller will not access the data bus while the attack is in progress, it can be completely unnoticed. Instead of using own chip, the attacker could simply overwrite the program in the nodes' microcontroller and put own program on it to read the external memory contents.

5.7.3 Security Key Deployment in Sensor Network

The existing protocols for secure key establishment all rely on an unspecified mechanism for initially deploying secrets to sensor nodes. However, no commercially viable and secure mechanism exists for initial setup. Without a guarantee of secure key deployment, the traffic over a sensor network cannot be presumed secure. To address this problem, the work in [20] presents a user-friendly protocol for the secure deployment of cryptographic keys in sensor networks. A *collection of five techniques* are proposed to prevent an attacker from eavesdropping on key deployment. Message-In-a-Bottle (*MIB*) [20] is a user-friendly protocol for initial key deployment in sensor networks. *MIB* is claimed to be the first secure key setup protocol designed for low cost, commodity sensor nodes. It enables fast, secure wireless key deployment for multiple nodes.

The solution to secret key set up between a trusted base station node and each new uninitialized node needs the following properties: (i) key secrecy, (ii) key authenticity, (iii) forward secrecy, (iv) demonstrative identification, (v) robustness to user error, (vi) cost effectiveness, and (vii) no public key cryptography. *MIB* satisfies these requirements. Following are the participants in *MIB* and description about how they interact with one another.

Base Station: The base station, a PC-class machine that controls the entire network, delegates key deployment to two devices: the *keying device* and the *keying beacon*.

New Node: The new node can be in one of *three states*: uninitialized, initialized, or rejected. When node M is first powered on or reset, it has no prior keying information and is uninitialized. Once the node receives a key, it is initialized. The key is the shared secretly between the base station and the new node.

Keying Device: During key deployment, the keying device and the uninitialized node are placed inside a *Faraday cage*. The keying device sends keying information to the node when the Faraday cage is closed.

Keying Beacon: During key deployment, the keying beacon remains outside of the Faraday cage. The keying beacon has three purposes: (i) detect when the Faraday cage is closed; (ii) jam the communication channel to prevent an eavesdropper from overhearing keying information leaked from the Faraday cage; and (iii) inform the user of the status and outcome of the deployment.

5.7.4 Wireless Snooping Attack in Sensor Network

Wireless sensors are becoming ubiquitous in homes and residential environments. However, Activities of Daily Living (ADLs) of home residents are typically very personal and private, and must be kept secret from third parties. A new privacy leak in residential wireless ubiquitous computing systems is presented in [40]. The work has proposed guidelines for designing future systems to prevent this problem.

The work has showed that private activities in the home such as cooking, showering, toileting, and sleeping, all can be observed by eavesdropping on the wireless transmissions of sensors in a home, even when all of the transmissions are encrypted. This is called *Fingerprint and Timing-based Snooping* (*FATS*) attack. The work has demonstrated and evaluated the *FATS* attack on eight different homes containing wireless sensors. They also have proposed and evaluated a set of privacy preserving design guidelines for future wireless ubiquitous systems, and have showed how these guidelines can be used in a hybrid fashion to prevent against the *FATS* attack with low implementation costs.

FATS Attack: The work has developed the multi-tier *FATS* inference algorithm to infer information about a home and its residents from just the timing and fingerprints of radio transmissions. The inference algorithm is provably robust to the diversity of homes, people, and sensed objects in deployments and can infer detailed resident activity information with high accuracy. The inference algorithm is explained in terms of its logical view, as in Fig. 31. The algorithms is divided into *four tiers*. In Tier 0 the adversary only has access to timestamps, but not fingerprints. In Tier I the adversary uses fingerprints to associate each message with a unique transmitter. In Tier II specific features are first extracted from the combined transmissions of all

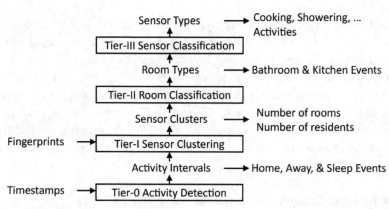

Fig. 31. The *FATS* inference algorithm.

devices in a spatial cluster. In Tier III another classifier is used to determine the likelihood of a sensor being the motion sensor, stove sensor etc.

5.8 Data Storage

Data storage has become an important issue in sensor networks as a large amount of collected data needs to be archived for future information retrieval and analysis. Storage is essential ingredient of any data–centric sensor network application. Common uses of storage in WSN applications include archival storage, temporary data storage, storage of sensor calibration tables, in–network indexing, in–network querying, and code storage for network reprogramming.

Data storage issue in sensor networks is a very different problem than storage in other computing systems. The demand for data storage comes from the requirements of sensor network nodes to store information collected in real–time, in order to later relay or serve to queries. Due to it's unique features and constraints, the main goals for efficient data storage management in sensor networks are: (a) minimizing storage size for data block to maximize the amount of data retention, (b) minimizing energy expenditure for data storage and retrieval, (c) supporting efficient response to complex query on the stored data, and (d) delivering efficient data management under constrained storage capacity etc. There are several methods proposed in the literature for data storage management, with most of them achieving a trade off among these different goals.

5.8.1 Flash Memory Based Storage for Sensor Network

Recent gains in energy efficiency of new–generation NAND flash storage have strengthened the case for in–network storage by data–centric sensor network applications. *Capsule* [29] presents an energy-optimized log-structured object storage system for flash memories in sensor platforms that enables sensor network applications to exploit storage resources in a multitude of ways. *Capsule* employs a *hardware abstraction layer* to hide the vagaries of flash memories, supports energy-optimized implementations of commonly used storage objects, and provides checkpointing and rollback of objects states. *Capsule* uses a *three layer architecture* (shown in Fig. 32), composed of: (i) a flash abstraction layer (FAL), (ii) an object layer, and (iii) an application layer.

Flash Abstraction Layer: For the flash abstraction layer, *four issues* have been explored. *First*, a log-structure design has been employed, which means it treats the storage device as a *log*. The log-structured file system sequentially traverses the device from start to the end, writing data to pages. *Second*, a

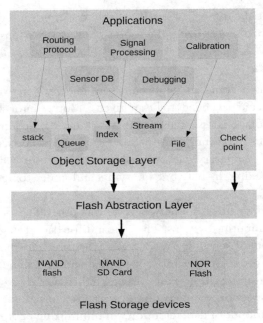

Fig. 32. Object storage architecture.

cleaner task is used for reclaiming memory. The cleaner exposes a compaction interface to which objects holding high priority data are wired at compile time. The flash abstraction layer keeps tracking the usage of the flash that has been used and when the percentage of usage reaches a predetermined threshold, the cleaner sends an event to the *Capsule* object, which has to implement the compaction interface. Once all the wired objects have performed compaction, the FAL marks the older blocks for deletion. *Third*, with respect to error handling, the FAL provides a simple checksum for each chunk and it uses a single-error-correction double-error-detection algorithm (SECDED) to generate codes at the page level. The error correction function can be chosen as on or off. *Fourth*, the FAL offers a read and write interface for accessing the flash directly.

Object Storage Layer: For the object storage layer, the work demonstrates *four key concepts*. *First*, the work identifies a core set of basic objects (Stack, Queue, Stream, and Index) that are the first-order objects in *Capsule*, and a set of composite objects (Stream-Index, File) which are composed from multiple basic objects. *Second*, a list of design of basic objects are provided. The Stack object provides push and pop operation. *Third*, for the Composite Storage Objects, two of them are presented. One is stream-index object.

The other is file system, which is composed of two objects: the file object and a singleton file-system object. *Fourth*, The work implements checkpointing support using a *checkpoint* component, which exposes two operations: *checkpoint* and *rollback*.

Application Layer: Applications can use one or more of the objects in *Capsule* with simple and intuitive interfaces. The work has evaluated three applications of the *Capsule* system: archival storage, indexing, and querying of stored sensor data, and batching packets in flash to improve communication efficiency.

5.8.2 Database for Flash Based Storage in Sensor Network

There are many WSN applications where it is desirable to store data within the sensor network, rather than transmit it all to a central database. In these applications, rather than uploading the entire raw data stream, one may save energy and bandwidth by processing queries locally at a cluster-head or a more capable node, and then uploading only the query response or the compressed or summarized data. Motivated by this requirement, *FlashDB* [31] designs a database for sensor networks using flash based storage.

FlashDB is a self-tuning database optimized for sensor networks using NAND flash storage. It uses a novel self-tuning index that dynamically adapts its storage structure to workload and underlying storage device. The work formalizes the self-tuning nature of an index as a two-state task system and proposes a 3-competitive online algorithm that achieves the theoretical optimum. In addition, a framework to determine the optimal size of an index node that minimizes energy and latency for a given device, is provided. The evaluation shows that the indexing scheme outperforms existing schemes under all workloads and flash devices considered. *FlashDB* consists of *two main components* (shown in Fig. 33): (i) a *Database Management System* that implements the database functions including index management and query compilation and (ii) a *Storage Manager* that implements efficient storage functionalities such as data buffering and garbage collection. The primary focus of this work is the self-tuning Index Manager (that uses a B^+-tree data structure) of FlashDB's database management system and related functionalities of the Storage Manager. B^+-tree is a popular indexing data structure used in various database systems.

Logical Storage (LS) belongs to the *Storage Manager*. *Logical Storage* provides a logical sector address abstraction over physical flash pages. The upper level components access sectors through two APIs: *ReadSector* and *WriteSector*. The B^+-tree (ST) design enables the *FlashDB* to store an index in one of two

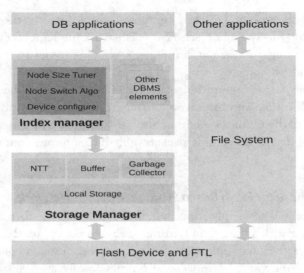

Fig. 33. *FlashDB* architecture.

modes: *Log* or *Disk*. When a node is in *Log* mode, each node update operation is written as a separate log entry so that reading a node in *Log* mode needs to read and parse all its log entries. When a node is in *Disk* mode, the whole node is written together on consecutive pages. *Storage Manager* component's B$^+$-tree (ST) brings two components: a *Log Buffer* and a *Node Translation Table (NTT)*. The Log buffer can hold up to one sector of data and be only used by the nodes currently in *Log* mode. The NTT maps logical B$^+$-tree (ST) nodes to their current modes and physical representations. *FlashDB* supports checkpointing and rollback of indices. Checkpointing requires making both in-memory states and in-flash data persistent. *FlashDB* replaces the sector addresses in a checkpointed NTT with their physical addresses and store the NTT. Rollback requires loading the NTT into memory, creating new logical addresses in Logical Storage that map to the physical addresses in in-flash NTT, and placing the logical addresses in the restored NTT in memory.

5.8.3 Tiered Architecture for Data Management in Sensor Network
A number of emerging large-scale hierarchical WSN applications need a predictive storage for sensor networks, that attempts to provide the interactivity of the data streaming approach with the energy efficiency of the direct sensor querying. *PRESTO* [24] is such a predictive storage architecture.

PRESTO is a two-tier sensor data management architecture comprising of proxies and sensors, that cooperate with one another for acquiring data and processing queries. The design of *PRESTO* has three key features: (i) *model-driven push*, (ii) *support for archival queries*, and (iii) *adaptation to data and query dynamics*. (i) *Model-driven push*: PRESTO employs seasonal ARIMA-based time series models to predict sample data based on the historical observed data at each sensor. This model is possessed by both *PRESTO* proxy and remote sensors. The remote sensor check sensed data against this model, and push data only when the observed data deviates from the values predicted. (ii) *Support for archival queries*: PRESTO exploits proxy cache and flash storage in sensor nodes to handle archival queries. By associating confidence intervals with the model predictions and caching values predicted by the model in the past, a *PRESTO* proxy can directly respond to archival queries using cached data so long as it meets error tolerance. (iii) *Adaptation to data and query dynamics*: Long-term changes in data trends are handled by periodically refining the parameters of the model at the proxy. Changes in query precision requirements are handled by varying the threshold used at a sensor to trigger a push.

System Architecture for Data Management: PRESTO exploited a *two-tier data management architecture* (shown in Fig. 34), with *PRESTO Proxy* at the upper tier and *PRESTO Sensor* in the lower tier. For system operation, PRESTRO proxy constructs a model of the temporal correlation of data observed from each sensor in the initial stage. The model and parameters are transmitted to each sensor. Sensors use this model for predicting next sample data, and sensed data is only transmitted when the difference between predicted sample and sensed data exceed a certain threshold. Since the model is also known to proxy, proxy can compute the predicted value and use it as an approximation of actual observation. Upon receiving a query, proxy generates a *confidence interval* for each predicted value. If *confidence interval* is larger than query error tolerance, the proxy pulls the actual sensed values from sensors;

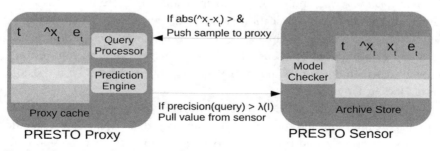

Fig. 34. The *PRESTO* data management architecture.

otherwise, use the predicted value as an approximation to answer the query. Additionally, the model parameters are adaptively refined and conveyed back to the corresponding sensor, who uses them to push subsequent values.

In conclusion, in this section we have presented practical system solutions to the challenges in middleware of Wireless Sensor Networks. This includes the works in: network management, neighbor discovery, topology control, energy management, localization, time synchronization, security, and data storage.

 # 6. OPERATING SYSTEMS AND SOFTWARE

6.1 Operating System

The design of operating system for WSN deviates from traditional operating system design due to significant and specific characteristics like constrained resources (energy, computation, storage etc.), high dynamics, and inaccessible deployment.

6.1.1 Event-Driven Operating System

TinyOS [22] is one the most early and largely used operating system designed for sensor networks. It's design is motivated by *four broad requirements* in WSN: limited resources, reactive concurrency, flexibility, and low power requirements. TinyOS is a flexible, application-specific operating system for sensor network. TinyOS combines flexible, fine-grained components with an execution model that supports complex safe concurrent operation and nicely meets the challenges in sensor network, such as limited resources, event-centric concurrent applications, and low-power operation. A TinyOS program consists of *components*, each of which is an independent entity that exposes one or more *interfaces*. Components have *three computational abstraction*: *commands*, *events*, and *tasks*. Commands and events are mechanisms for inter-component communication, while tasks are used to express intra-component concurrency. TinyOS provides a large number of components, including abstractions for: sensors, single-hop networking, ad hoc routing, power management, timers, and non-volatile storage. Figure 35 lists the core interfaces in TinyOS.

Component Model: TinyOS's programming model, provided by the nesC language, centers around the notion of *components* that encapsulate a specific set of services, specified by *interfaces*. An application connects components using a *wiring specification*, which defines the complete set of components

Interface	Description
ADC	Sensor hardware interface
Clock	Hardware clock
EEPROM Read/Write	EEPROM read and write
HardwareId	Hardware ID access
I2C	Interface to I2C bus
Leds	Red/yellow/green LEDs
MAC	Radio MAC layer
Mic	Microphone interface
Pot	Hardware potentiometer for transmit power
Random	Random number generator
ReceiveMsg	Receive Active Message
SendMsg	Send Active Message
StdControl	Init, start, and stop components
Time	Get current time
TinySec	Lightweight encryption/decryption
WatchDog	Watchdog timer control

Fig. 35. Core interfaces provided by TinyOS.

that the application uses. A component has *two classes of interfaces*: those it *provides* and those it *uses*. These interfaces define how the component directly interacts with other components. Interfaces are bidirectional and contain both *commands* and *events*. A *command* is a function that is implemented by the providers of an interface, an *event* is a function that is implemented by its users. The nesC language has two types of components: *modules* and *configurations*. Modules provide code for calling and implementing commands and events. A module declares private state variables and data buffers. Configurations are used to wire other components together, connecting interfaces used by components to interfaces provided by others.

Execution Model and Concurrency: In TinyOS, the core of the execution model consists of run–to–completion *tasks* that represent the ongoing computation, and *interrupt handlers* that are signaled asynchronously by hardware. The scheduler can execute tasks in any order, but must obey the run–to–completion rule. The task are atomic with respect to each other. However, tasks are not atomic with respect to interrupt handlers or to commands and events they invoke. To facilitate the detection of race conditions, TinyOS defines the following. (i) *Synchronous Code (SC)*: code that is only reachable from tasks; (ii) *Asynchronous Code (AC)*: code that is reachable from at least one interrupt handler. The basic invariant nesC must enforce is, *Race-Free Invariant:* any update to shared state is either SC–only or occurs in an atomic section. The core TinyOS communication abstraction is based on *Active*

Messages(AM). Upon reception of an Active Message, a node dispatches the message (using an event) to one or more handlers that are registered to receive messages of that type. AM provides an unreliable, single-hop datagram protocol, and provides a unified communication interface to both the radio and the built-in serial port.

6.1.2 Dynamic Loading Based Operating System

For the designer of an operating system for sensor network, the challenge lies in finding lightweight mechanisms and abstractions that provide a rich enough execution environment while staying within the limitations of the constrained devices. *Contiki* [9] is such a lightweight and flexible operating system for Wireless Sensor Networks. *Contiki* provides dynamic loading and unloading of individual programs and services. It also supports preemptive multi-threading, which is implemented as a library on top of an event-driven kernel.

System Components: A running *Contiki* system consists of: the *kernel*, *libraries*, the *program loader*, and a set of *processes*. All process, including both the application programs and services can be dynamically replaced at runtime. Communication between processes always goes through the kernel. A process is defined by an event handler function and an optional poll handler function. The process state is held in the process' private memory and the kernel keeps a pointer to the process state. A *Contiki* system is partitioned into two parts: the *core* and the *loaded programs* as shown in Fig. 36. The partitioning is made at compile time and is specific to the deployment.

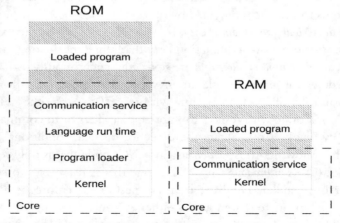

Fig. 36. Partitioning into core and loaded programs.

The core typically consists of the Contiki kernel, the program loader, the most commonly used parts of the language runtime and support libraries, and a communication stack with device drivers for the communication hardware. The core is compiled into a single binary image and usually not modified after deployment, although it is possible. Programs are loaded by the program loader. It may obtain the program binaries either from the communication stack or the attached storage such as EEPROM.

Kernel architecture: The *Contiki* kernel is composed of a lightweight event scheduler that dispatches events to running processes and periodically calls processes' polling handlers. All program execution is trigged either by events dispatched by the kernel or through the polling mechanism. The kernel supports both *asynchronous* and *synchronous* events. Asynchronous events are enqueued by the kernel and are dispatched to the target process some time later. Synchronous events are similar except that it immediately causes the target process to be scheduled. Besides events, the kernel supports a *polling mechanism* which is used by processes that operates hardware status checking. The *Contiki* kernel uses a single shared stack for all process execution.

Services: A *service* is a process that implements functionality that can be used by other processes. It can be dynamically replaced at runtime and must therefore be dynamically linked. Services are managed by a *service layer* conceptually next to the kernel. A service consists of a *service interface* and a process that implements the interface. Application programs use a stub library to communicate with the service. When a service is to be replaced, the kernel informs the running version of the service by posting a special event to the service process. In response to this event, the service must remove itself. The kernel passes a pointer that points to the internal state description of the service process to the new service process. The memory for holding the state must be allocated from a shared source.

Libraries: The programs can be linked with libraries in three ways. First, statically linked with libraries as part of core. Second, statically linked with libraries as part of the loadable program. Third, calling services that implements a specific library, which can be dynamically replaced at rum-time.

Communication support: Communication is implemented as a service in *Contiki* in order to enable rum-time replacement. It also provides for multiple communication stacks to be loaded simultaneously. The communication stack may be split into different service as shown in Fig. 37.

Multi-Threading: Preemptive multi-threading is implemented as a library on top of the event-driven kernel. The library consists of two parts: a platform independent part that interfaces to the event kernel, and a platform-specific

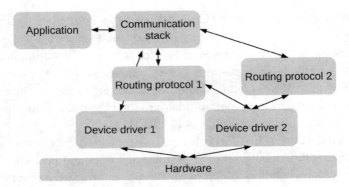

Fig. 37. Loosely coupled communication stack.

part implementing the stack switching and preemption primitives. Each thread requires a separate stack. The API of the library is shown as the following two Figures.

6.1.3 Resource-Aware Programming Based Operating System

A growing class of sensor network applications require high data rates and computationally intensive node-level processing. When deployed into environments where resources are limited and variable, achieving good performance requires applications to adjust their behavior as resource availability changes. *Pixie* [27] is such an operating system to enable *resource-aware programming*.

PIXIE Architecture: Pixie is a new sensor node operating system designed to support the needs of data-intensive applications. In *Pixie*, a sensor node has direct knowledge of available resources, such as energy, radio bandwidth, and storage space, and *Pixie* can control resource consumption at a fine granularity. The technical contribution of *Pixie* OS has *three aspects*. (i) First, *Pixie* enables resource awareness by making resources a first-class entity in the programming model. (ii) Second, *Pixie* incorporates efficient runtime estimation of available resources, such as energy and radio bandwidth. Their approach to energy usage estimation is based on a simple software model and performs accurate energy estimation on standard mote platforms with no additional hardware support. (iii) Third, *Pixie*'s resource broker abstraction enables a broad range of reusable adaptation strategies, including adaptive duty cycling, varying computational fidelity, and tuning radio bandwidth, while shielding application code from the details of low-level resource management.

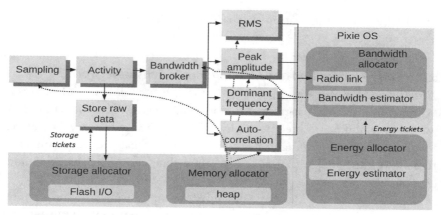

Fig. 38. PIXIE architecture overview.

There are four key components of the *Pixie* system, as illustrated in Fig. 38. (i) The first is a dataflow programming model that structures applications as a graph of interconnected stages, where each stage represents some unit of computation or I/O. The use of a dataflow model gives the operating system both visibility and control over the application's resource usage. (ii) Second, *Pixie* uses the concept of resource tickets, an abstraction representing a bounded-duration right to consume a given quantity of a given resource. Ticket design is central to the resource awareness and control in *Pixie*. (iii) The third component is a set of resource brokers, reusable software modules that encode policies for resource management. Brokers are specialized stages responsible for providing feedback on and arbitrating access to resources, such as energy, radio bandwidth, or flash storage. (iv) Finally, each physical resource managed by *Pixie* has a corresponding *resource allocator* that performs three functions: (a) estimating the amount of available resource at runtime; (b) allocating tickets for that resource on demand; and (c) enforcing ticket redemptions. *Pixie* employs resource allocators for radio, flash storage, energy, and memory, although the model can be readily extended to other physical resources.

6.2 Network Reprogramming

Network reprogramming allows for over-the-air application updates in sensor networks. Network reprogramming consists of two main components: (i) the installation mechanism for loading the code onboard a sensor node

and (ii) the code propagation mechanism for disseminating software to a
sensor node.

6.2.1 Code Propagation and Maintenance in Sensor Network

While code is propagating, a network can be in a useless state due to the
existence of multiple programs running concurrently. Transition time is a
wasted time, and that wasted time is translated into wasted energy. Therefore,
an effective reprogramming protocol must also propagate new code quickly.
To achieve this, Trickle [23] is an algorithm designed for propagating and
maintaining code updates in WSN.

Basic Primitives: Trickle's basic primitive is simple: every so often, a mote
transmits code metadata if it has not heard a few other motes transmit the
same thing. This allows Trickle to scale to thousand-fold variations in network density, quickly propagate updates, distribute transmission load evenly,
be robust to transient disconnections, handle network repopulations, and
impose a maintenance overhead on the order of a few packets per hour per
mote. Trickle sends all messages to the local broadcast address. There are two
possible results to a Trickle broadcast: either every mote that hears the message is up to date, or a recipient detects the need for an update. Detection
can be the result of either an out-of-date mote hearing someone has new
code, or an updated mote hearing someone has old code.

Gossip based Message Exchange: Trickle uses "polite gossip" to exchange
code metadata with nearby network neighbors. It breaks time into intervals,
and at a random point in each interval, it considers broadcasting its code
metadata. If Trickle has already heard several other motes gossip the same
metadata in this interval, it politely stays quiet: repeating what someone else
has said is rude. When a mote hears that a neighbor is behind the times (it
hears older metadata), it brings everyone nearby up to date by broadcasting
the needed pieces of code. When a mote hears that it is behind the times,
it repeats the latest news it knows of (its own metadata); following the first
rule, this triggers motes with newer code to broadcast it.

More formally, each mote maintains a counter c, a threshold k, and a timer
t in the range $[0,\tau]$. k is a small, fixed integer (e.g., 1 or 2) and τ is a time
constant. When a mote hears metadata identical to its own, it increments c.
At time t, the mote broadcasts its metadata if $c < k$. When the interval of size
τ completes, c is reset to zero and t is reset to a new random value in the
range $[0,\tau]$. If a mote with code ϕ_x hears a summary for ϕ_{x-y}, it broadcasts
the code necessary to bring ϕ_{x-y} up to ϕ_x. If it hears a summary for ϕ_{x+y}, it
broadcasts its own summary, triggering the mote with ϕ_{x+y} to send updates.

Code Propagation Algorithm: Using the Trickle algorithm, each mote broad-casts a summary of its data at most once per period τ. If a mote hears k motes with the same program before it transmits, it suppresses its own transmis-sion. In perfect network conditions—a lossless, single-hop topology C there will be k transmissions every τ. If there are n motes and m non-interfering single-hop networks, there will be km transmissions, which is independent of n. The km transmission count depends on three assumptions: no packet loss, perfect interval synchronization, and a single-hop network. Instead of fixing the per-mote send rate, Trickle dynamically regulates its send rate to the network density to meet a communication rate, requiring no apriori assumptions on the topology.

The random selection of t uniformly distributes the choice of who broad-casts in a given interval. This evenly spreads the transmission energy load across the network. If a mote with n neighbors needs an update, the expected latency to discover this from the beginning of the interval is $\frac{\tau}{n+1}$. Detection happens either because the mote transmits its summary, which will cause others to send updates, or because another mote transmits a newer summary. A larger τ has a lower energy overhead (in terms of packet send rate), but also has a higher discovery latency. Conversely, a small τ sends more messages but discovers updates more quickly.

6.2.2 Reliable Code Propagation

Because of the resource constrained nature of sensor nodes, an effective code dissemination algorithm should attempt to minimize: (i) the amount of energy required and (ii) minimize the length of time required to distribute the data. It is also needed to provide sufficient support for incremental code upgrades, since program data evolves with time. As a algorithm with such design, Deluge [16] is reliable data dissemination protocol for propagating large amounts of data (i.e., more than can fit in RAM) from one or more source nodes to all other nodes over a multi-hop wireless sensor network.

Deluge is an epidemic protocol and operates as a state machine where each node follows a set of strictly local rules to achieve a desired global behavior: the quick, reliable dissemination of large data objects to many nodes. In its most basic form, each node occasionally advertises the most recent version of the data object it has available to whatever nodes that can hear its local broadcast. If S receives an advertisement from an older node R, S responds with its object profile. From the object profile, R deter-mines which portions of the data need updating and requests them from any neighbor that advertises the availability of the needed data, including S.

Nodes receiving requests then broadcast any requested data. Nodes then advertise newly received data in order to propagate it further. A node operates in one of three states at any time: MAINTAIN, RX, or TX. The set of local rules an individual node follows is a function of its current state and specify what actions and state transitions to take in response to events.

6.3 Sensor Network Simulator

In the literature it was needed to investigate how to exploit the characteristics of the sensor network domain to obtain a scale, fidelity, and completeness that would be intractable in a general purpose context.

6.3.1 Sensor Network Simulator for TinyOS Based System

TOSSIM [21] is an early practical sensor network simulator that is designed for TinyOS [22] based sensor network applications. TOSSIM captures the behavior and interactions of networks of thousands of TinyOS motes at network bit granularity. Figure 39 shows a graphical overview of TOSSIM. The TOSSIM consists of *five parts*: (i) support for compiling TinyOS component graphs into the simulation infrastructure, (ii) a discrete event queue, (iii) a small number of re-implemented TinyOS hardware abstraction components, (iv) mechanisms for extensible radio and ADC models, and (v) communication services for external programs to interact with a simulation. Figure 39 shows the overview of TOSSIM.

TOSSIM utilizes the structure and whole system compilation system of TinyOS to generate discrete-event simulations, directly from TinyOS component graphs. TOSSIM runs the same TinyOS code that runs on real sensor mote hardware. TOSSIM requires replacement in just a few low-level components (e.g., the regions shaded in Figure 39). In this way TOSSIM translates hardware interrupts into discrete simulation events. The simulator event queue delivers those interrupts that drive the execution of a TinyOS application. The remainder of TinyOS code remains unchanged. The TOSSIM simulator engine also provides a set of communication services in order to interact with external applications. These services allow applications to connect to TOSSIM over a TCP socket to monitor or actuate a running simulation.

In conclusion, in this section we have presented practical system solutions to the challenges in operating system and software design of Wireless Sensor Networks. This includes the works in: operating system, network reprogramming, and sensor network simulator.

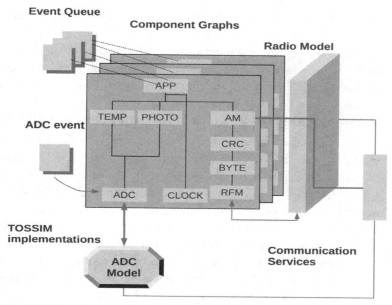

Fig. 39. *TOSSIM* architecture: frames, events, models, components, and services.

7. EXPERIENCE OF REAL-WORLD SENSOR NETWORK DEPLOYMENT

In recent times a number of Wireless Sensor Networks have been deployed in varied environments for real-world application purpose. These application experiences serve to explore the requirements, constraints, and guidelines for general sensor network system design. In this section we present our own experience of deployed sensor network applications and research challenges associated. The scenario presented is designing stable remote volcano monitoring system, using wireless sensor network in hazardous environment.

7.1 Volcano Monitoring

In the last 15 years, volcanic eruptions have killed more than 29,000 people and have caused billions of dollars in damage [1]. In conventional monitoring stations the amount of data transmitted is limited by the bandwidth of the hardware and hardships of siting used telemetry links. As a result, many active volcanoes maintain networks of fewer than 10 stations. This lacks sufficient real-time and high-fidelity data for volcano analysis and eruption prediction [30]. Wireless Sensor Networks have the potential to greatly enhance the understanding of volcano activities by allowing large distributed deployments of sensor nodes in difficult-to-reach or hazardous areas. In this section we have provided detailed description of volcano monitoring sensor network deployment experience in Mount St. Helens, Washington, USA.

7.2 First Deployment of Volcano Monitoring Sensor Network

This presents the design and initial deployment experience of an air-dropped wireless sensor network for volcano hazard monitoring [39]. The project is called *Optimized Autonomous Space—In-situ Sensor-web* or *OASIS*. The next section describes the second deployment of this effort and the long-term monitoring experience. Self-contained stations were deployed into the rugged crater of Mount St. Helens (shown in Fig. 40) in only one hour with a helicopter. The stations communicate with each other through an amplified 802.15.4 radio and establish a self-forming and self-healing multi-hop network. The transmit distance between stations were up to 8 km with favorable topography. Each sensor station collects and delivers real-time continuous seismic, infrasonic, lightning, and GPS raw data to a gateway. The presented system design and deployment experience proves that the low-cost sensor network system can work in extremely harsh environments.

7.3 Main Contribution

The main contribution of this work is the design of a robust sensor network optimized for rapid deployment during periods of volcanic unrest

Fig. 40. The panorama of the rugged volcano crater with a diameter of 2 km.

and provide real-time long-term volcano monitoring. The deployed system has attempted to meet the requirements of the USGS scientists: synchronized sampling, real-time continuous raw data, one-year robust operation, remote configurability, and fast deployment. The system supports UTC-time-synchronized data acquisition with 1 ms accuracy, and is remotely configurable. It has been tested in the lab environment, in the outdoor campus, and in the volcano crater. Despite the heavy rain, snow, and ice as well as wind gusts exceeding 160 km/h, the sensor network has achieved a remarkable packet delivery ratio above 99% with an overall system uptime of about 93.8% over the 1.5 months evaluation period after deployment.

7.4 Hardware Design

Each node, a three-legged *Spider* sensor station (shown in Figs. 41 and 42) is about 4 feet tall (including the lifted antenna), and weighs about 80 kg. The sensor station contains the following hardware components and specifications: 6 dBi omnidirectional antenna on a steel pipe, AIR–ALKALINE batteries, a 900-MHz Freewave radio modem connected the sink station to the gateway over a 10 km radio link, 30×20 cm^2 small weatherproof box,

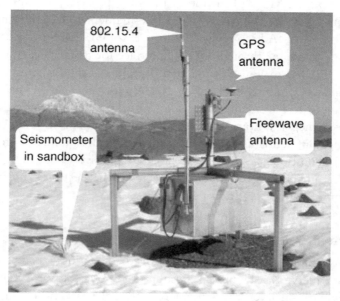

Fig. 41. Spider station (the sink node is shown) inside volcano crater.

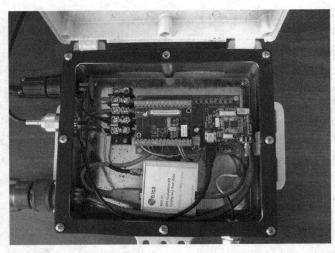

Fig. 42. The electronics box contains iMote2, MDA320CA, U-Blox LEA-4T GPS receiver.

iMote2 wireless sensor mote, acquisition board (MDA320CA), GPS receiver (LEA-4T), and expansion connectors.

The wireless sensor mote iMote2 has PXA271 processor that can be configured to work from 13 to 416 MHz. It has 256 KB SRAM, 32 MB SDRAM, and 32 MB flash. iMote2s PXA271 processor is configured to operate in a low-voltage (0.85 V) and low-frequency (13 MHz) mode in normal operations. A low-power U-Blox LEA-4T L1 GPS receiver is connected to the iMote2 through UART interface for raw data capturing, and through GPIO 93 for Pulse Per Second (PPS) signal capturing. The seismic sensor Silicon Designs Model 1221 J-002, is a low-cost MEMS accelerometer for use in zero to medium frequency instrumentation applications that require extremely low noise. The infrasonic sensor, model 1 INCH-D-MV is a low-range differential pressure sensor to record infrasound, low-frequency (<20 Hz) acoustic waves generated during explosive events. The seismic, infrasonic, and lightning sensors are connected to the electronics box through weatherproof connectors and cables.

7.5 Software Design

Each sensor node runs TinyOS, the de facto operating system for Wireless Sensor Networks. Figure 43 illustrates the node software architecture. In the application layer, the sensing module collects various sensing and utility data with synchronized timestamping. The network management

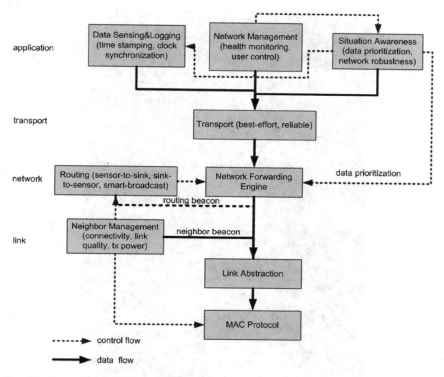

Fig. 43. The OASIS node software architecture.

module reports network health status and processes command and control from remote users. The situation awareness module detects events, prioritizes data, and implements priority-aware data delivery protocols. The transport layer provides reliable delivery for critical data such as seismic event data, and best-effort delivery for other data. The network layer supports sensor-to-sink and sink-to-sensor routing. With the sensor-to-sink routing, sensor nodes form a spanning tree rooted at the sink node and deliver data toward the sink via multi-hop relays. The link layer estimates the link quality, which serves as link metric for the network layer to determine routing paths.

7.6 Deployment Experience

On 15th October 2008, five stations were air-dropped and successfully deployed into the crater of Mount St. Helens and streamed data to the Internet. The deployment map is illustrated in Fig. 44. Figure 45 illustrates the system configurations. The rugged crater has a diameter of around 1 mile.

Fig. 44. Air-drop deployment and the panorama of the network.

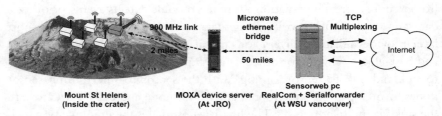

Fig. 45. The system configuration of the air-dropped volcano monitoring sensor network.

During the deployment, the air-dropped nodes immediately formed a data collection tree, and delivered real-time sensor data to the sink node through the multi-hop network. The sink node then relayed the data to gateway (e.g., MOXA device server) at JRO through a Freewave radio modem. Then, the gateway relayed the data stream to the Sensorweb Research Lab through

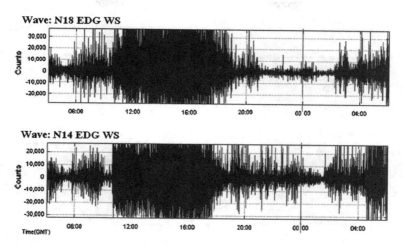

Fig. 46. Heavy gusts observed by the infrasonic sensor of nodes 18 and 14.

a microwave link of 90 km. In the lab, a Serial–Forwarder Java tool forwards data between the sensor network and the Internet.

During the operation, nodes experienced high temperature variations, heavy gusts, rains, and even snows during the second half month of the deployment. Very strong gusts were recorded by the infrasonic sensors. The infrasonic sensors are essentially pressure sensors, and hence are able to capture those heavy gusts (Fig. 46). Figure 47 is the illustration of detected event data by OASIS station and existing USGS stations. The dynamic range, resolution, and signal-to-noise ratio of the OASIS seismic signal compared favorably with short-period and broadband seismic station in the crater. For the purpose of earthquake event detection and warning, it can be seen the system was able to accurately detect earthquake events with a precise timestamp. The biggest advantage of the sensor is its ability to be set on the ground without regard to orientation.

The cost of money and deployment effort of the OASIS system are significantly lower than that of all the old stations, which use telemetry for data acquisition and require higher energy consumption. The gold–standard broadband seismic station costs more than $10K$ USD, while the OASIS station costs about $2K$ USD (which includes GPS, infrasonic, and lightning sensors, besides a seismometer). Figure 48 summarizes the major differences among the different stations been used so far. The money cost counts the hardware and deployment labor cost.

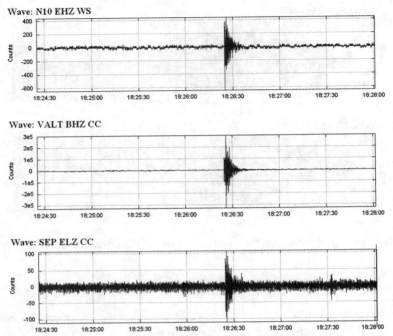

Fig. 47. Waveform of detected earthquake on three types of stations: (N10) OASIS station node 10, (VALT) USGS broadband seismic station, and (SEP) USGS typical short-period seismic station.

Station / Carac	Digital	GPS	Seismic	Ultrasonic	Lightning
Dual-freq GPS(1)	yes	yes	no	no	no
Short period(2,4)	no	no	yes	(no,yes)	no
Broadband(3)	yes	no	yes	no	no
Oasis station	yes	yes	yes	yes	yes

Station / Carac	Real-time	Self-healing	Power Cons	Money Cost
Dual-freq GPS(1)	no	no	++	++
Short period(2,4)	yes	no	+	++
Broadband(3)	yes	no	+++	+++
Oasis station	yes	yes	+	+

Fig. 48. Comparison between monitoring stations.

In conclusion, specifically designed for rapid deployment during volcanic unrest, this volcano monitoring system was mainly focused on achieving real-time high-fidelity, remote reconfigurability, and a high-degree of robustness. The high data yield of the deployed system validates its robustness.

The presented system design and deployment experience proves that the low-cost sensor network system can work in extremely harsh environments.

7.7 Second Deployment of Volcano Monitoring Sensor Network

Continuing the previous work, this section presents more experience about the design, the second deployment and the evaluation of a real-world sensor network system [15] in an active volcano, the Mount St. Helens. Most system research to date have focused more on performance improvement and less on system robustness. In the deployed system design, to address this challenge, automatic fault detection and recovery mechanisms were designed to autonomously roll the system back to the initial state if exceptions occur. Also, a light-weight adaptive linear predictive compression algorithm and localized TDMA MAC protocol were designed to improve network throughput.

With these techniques and other improvements on intelligence and robustness based on a previous trial deployment, 13 stations were air-dropped into the crater and around the flanks of Mount St. Helens in July 2009. The deployed in situ sensor network had *two branches*. Each branch operated with a separate data collection sink and radio channel. The first branch (*branch 1*) network (node 1–node 6) was mostly placed inside the crater. The second branch (*branch 2*) network (node 8–node 14) was deployed around the flank forming a semicircle. During the deployment, the nodes autonomously discovered each other even in-the-sky, and formed a smart mesh network for data delivery immediately. This work has conducted rigorous system evaluations and discovered many interesting findings on data quality, radio connectivity, network performance, as well as the influence of environmental factors.

7.8 System Overview

The deployment map of 13 nodes are shown in Fig. 49. Figure 50 illustrates the end-to-end configuration of the full OASIS system. The ground sensor network delivered real-time volcanic signals to the sink nodes at JRO (Johnston Ridge Observatory) through multi-hop relays. The sink nodes are connected to the gateway through serial connection. The gateway (MOXA device server DE-304) relayed the data stream to a WSUV (Washington State University at Vancouver) server through a microwave link of 50 miles. In the lab, a customized TinyOS tool SerialForwarder in WSUV server forwards the data between the sensor network and the Internet. Multiple control clients may connect to it, access the sensor data stream, and control the network in real-time.

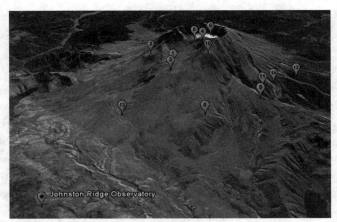

Fig. 49. The deployment map of 13 nodes on Mount St. Helens Volcano. The sink nodes 0 and 7 are placed at JRO.

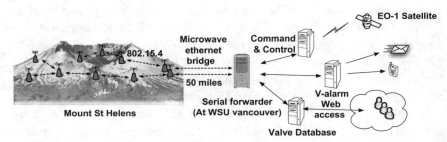

Fig. 50. The system configuration of OASIS.

7.9 Automatic Fault Detection and Recovery

Nasty bugs may occur in hard to reachable deployed nodes after deployments. It is, therefore, crucial to have an exception-handling mechanism to recover nodes automatically from software and hardware failures. To achieve this, the system has exploited the benefits of watchdog. The iMote2s hardware watchdog can restart the node under exceptions such as dead loop, memory errors, and stack overflow. In addition, software failures can also be caused by unexpected logic errors. To reduce the reboot cost to the minimum, important parameters and states, such as sampling rate and RF channel/power, are written to Flash when configured by remote users, and are restored once a node reboots. With those fault tolerant mechanisms, the system is able to continuously operate normally after the deployment.

7.10 Remote Command and Control

The remote command and control is based on a flexible Remote Procedure Call (RPC) mechanism. It allows a PC to access the exported functions and any global variables of a statically-compiled program on sensor nodes at runtime. To ensure the reliable dissemination of RPC messages over multi-hop paths, a reliable data dissemination protocol called Cascades [33] is designed. The RPC mechanism gives users great flexibility to read/write system variables and run any exported functions. Operations such as set/get sampling rate, beacon interval, power level, radio channel and event report level threshold are provided to remote clients. The RPC mechanism also provides visibility into network failures and helps to correct bugs.

7.11 Configurable Sensing

The sensor driver performs synchronized sampling operation and maintains sensing parameters, such as sampling rate, ADC channel, and data priority. All these parameters could be tuned according to environmental and resource situations to conserve energy or increase fidelity. When energy conservation becomes a priority, users can remotely close a non-critical data channel by simply setting the sampling rate to 0. At the deployment all raw data were collected for scientific analysis, but users also can change the base data priority to 0, then the OASIS station will send out event data only. If a sensor is broken or the hardware interface is disconnected, its channel can be closed to save energy and bandwidth.

7.12 Over-the-Air Network Reprogramming

After a field deployment, the network functionality may need improvement or fix new software failures. Thus, it is important to support remote software upgrades. Deluge [16] is the de facto network reprogramming protocol that provides an efficient method for disseminating code update over the wireless network and having each node program itself with the new image. Deluge originally does not support the iMote2 platform, and it is not trivial to port it to support the iMote2 platform. Deluge was also improved to ensure that it could handle some adverse situations. Following are such important features. (1) *Image integrity verification:* If a node reboots during the download phase, it has to be ensured that it correctly resumes the download. To address this issue, a mechanism is implemented where the image integrity during startup is verified. If the image has been completely downloaded, then the system continue with the normal operations; otherwise it erases the entire downloaded image and reset the meta data to enable a fresh re-download. (2) *Image version consistency:* The original Deluge is based on sequence number. However, if the gateway lost track of the sequence number and did not use a higher sequence number, then Deluge will not respond to new request of code update. This problem was fixed by using the compilation timestamp to differentiate new image from old image.

7.13 Data Quality Evaluation

One important aspect of evaluating a real-world sensor network system is the data quality. To assess the quality of collected data, it was compared with that from broadband station VALT, which is the state-of-the-art instrument in seismology. Figure 51 shows 50-min seismic raw reading from OASIS node

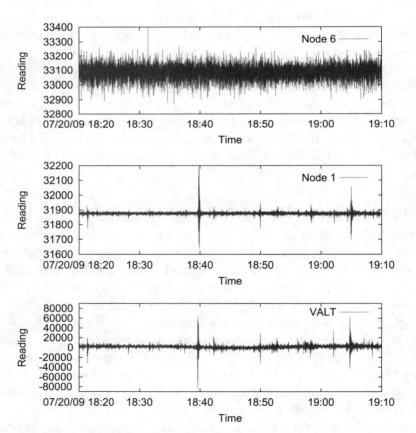

Fig. 51. Comparison of the seismic waveform data (node 6, node 1, and VALT).

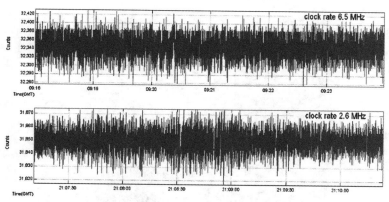

Fig. 52. (Top) The 6 least significant bits of some seismic data samples are cut due to the ADC overclocking problem. (Bottom) The seismic data samples without distortion.

6, node 1, and VALT station during the time period from UTC 07/20/2009 18:20 to UTC 07/20/2009 19:10. After scaling, the noise level of VALT and OASIS station is almost the same. It can be clearly observed that the OASIS station with geophone seismic sensor can achieve similar data quality.

7.14 System Debugging Experience

During a trial deployment in 2008, it was found that some seismic data samples lost their 6 LSBs (Least Significant Bit) and have distortions, as shown in Fig. 52 (Top). Eventually, it was figured out that the 6.5 MHz clock rate of iMote2 driving the ADC driver was the cause of the data distortion.

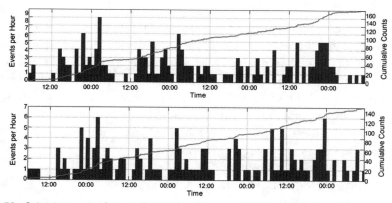

Fig. 53. Seismic events detected during a 6-day period: (Top) Broadband station VALT; (Bottom) OASIS node 1.

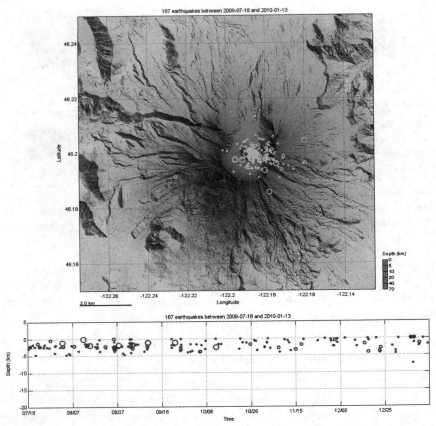

Fig. 54. (Top) The spatial distribution of earthquake events. (Bottom) The temporal distribution of earthquake events.

The ADC chip ADS8344 can only work normally at 2.4 MHz clock mode. In other words, the external clock cycle should be no less than 400 ns (2.4 MHz) to correctly accomplish the conversion. Originally the SPI clock rate was configured to be 6.5 MHz (typical iMote2 clock rate), which is too high for ADS8344. Thus the SPI Serial clock rate was changed to 2.6 MHz by configuring a higher clock divisor. This SPI clock rate was still slightly higher than the specification, but ADS8344 worked normally and the data distortion was eliminated (Fig. 52 Bottom).

7.15 Event Detection Accuracy

In Fig. 51, it can be observed that OASIS node 1 and VALT detect seismic events at the same time. Figure 53 compares the number of events detected

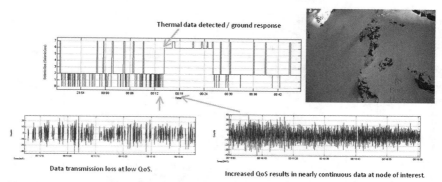

Fig. 55. Space-to-ground triggering raised the data priority to the highest level, resulting in reliable delivery of the data stream from node 4.

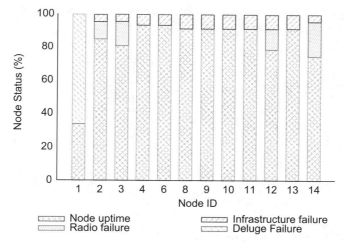

Fig. 56. The node status during the first 47 days.

during an active period from 07/21/2009–07/26/2009. OASIS node 1 triggers 140 seismic events while VALT detects 160. The VALT station is more sensitive, because it has a very low frequency response up to 0.01 Hz, while the corner frequency of the OASIS station is 2 Hz. Therefore, VALT can detect more subtle events than the OASIS station, but it is also more expensive as said earlier.

Figure 54 (Top) shows the location and magnitude of the 187 earthquakes that happened in the first 6 month deployment period from 07/18/2009 to 01/13/2010. The size of the circles denotes the earthquake magnitude. From

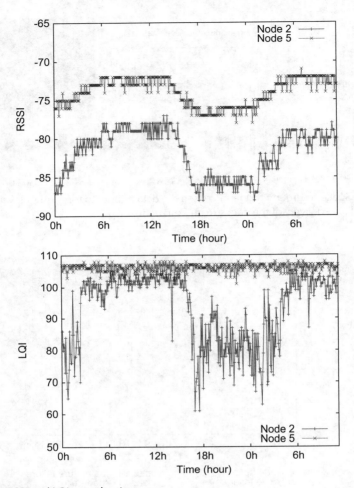

Fig. 57. RSSI and LQI over the time.

Fig. 54 (Top) it can be seen that while the crater is most active area, some strong earthquakes also took place on the flanks. Figure 54 (Bottom) shows the earthquake time. It was observed that earthquakes were more frequent during the first 3 month.

7.16 Data Prioritization

Figure 55 shows the space-to-ground triggering and the prioritized data delivery mechanism in the ground network. For example, as snow accumulates in the Mount St. Helens, OASIS node 4 was gradually buried under

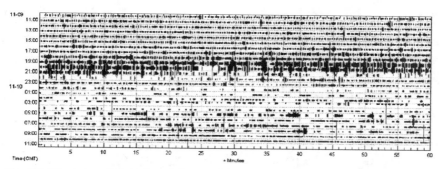

Fig. 58. The intermittent data delivery of OASIS node 12 between 11/09/2009 and 11/10/2009.

snow. During that process, the data stream of node 4 experienced more and more packet loss. However, once the data priority was raised to highest level due to space triggering, the data during that period were reliably delivered.

7.17 System Failures and Diagnosis

The uptime evaluation is fully end-to-end, i.e., a node is considered to be up only if its data is successfully logged in the database, no matter where the failure is in between. Figure 56 shows the status of each node during the period from 07/15/2009 to 09/01/2009. The uptime of the nodes varied from 34% to 93.6% with different types of failures. From 08/16/2009, the UPS for the Internet router at the control center was down for two days, and caused failure of data importing. On 08/23/2009, due to an exception in the data importer tool, the network *branch 2* was offline for 1 day.

7.18 Link Quality and Network Connectivity

Evaluation on link quality (RSSI/LQI) and packet loss were also conducted. The end-to-end packet loss is measured as the ratio of the number of lost data bits over the total number of bits expected in each time unit. Each node in the network reported the RSSI (Received Signal Strength Indicator) and LQI (Link Quality Indicator) of beacon packets from its neighbors every 5 min. Figure 57 plots the change of the RSSI and LQI of links 2→0 (node 2 is the sender and node 0 is the receiver) and 5→0 over a time period of 36 h. The network connectivity can become intermittent in extreme conditions. For example, node 12 occasionally lost its communication connection to the network when the link quality dropped (Fig. 58).

In conclusion, the successful design and deployment of volcano monitoring wireless sensor network in Mount St. Helens demonstrated that a low-cost sensor network system can provide real-time continuous monitoring in harsh environments. This has greatly promoted the confident use of sensor networks for real-world applications.

8. CONCLUSION

A Wireless Sensor Network (WSN) is a wireless network consisting of spatially distributed autonomous tiny devices, each containing a set of sensors and actuators. The purpose of WSN is to seamlessly monitor physical or environmental conditions, and trigger actuation based on application needs. Wireless Sensor Networks have emerged as a key technology to enable a huge amount of ubiquitous applications. These bring more challenges in systematically designing and improving various layers and components of WSN. Due to it's typical characteristics and applications needs, WSN system design is different from general networking in a lot of aspects. Practical system design in WSN brings critical challenges at different layers and components. In this chapter we have explored the practical system solutions to these challenges in: (a) different layers of WSN (transport, network, and link layer), (b) operating system design and middleware (network management, network reprogramming energy management, data storage, localization, time synchronization, and security), and (c) real-world sensor network deployment and maintenance.

It has been nearly a decade from advent of Wireless Sensor Networks. There has been significant improvements in WSN system design. The advancements have been focused on different layers, middleware, and operating system design. The problems in WSN that have been explored heavily and can be considered solved (with acceptable performance) are: MAC protocol, data dissemination, data collection, routing, localization, time synchronization. However there has been comparatively lesser development in a number of design challenges. The problems that are relatively unsolved are: energy management, security, fault tolerance, scalability, network management, hardware design, ubiquitous sensor development, actuation, application-specific system designs. These hold great new unexplored opportunities for the next decade of Wireless Sensor Networks (WSN).

Acronyms

WSN	Wireless Sensor Networks
UDP	User Datagram Protocol

TCP	Transmission Control Protocol
RTT	Round Trip Time
ACK	Acknowledgment
NACK	Negative acknowledgment
ADU	Application Data Unit
RCRT	Rate Controlled Reliable Transport
IFRC	Interference-aware Fair Rate Control
ETX	Expected Transmission Count
CTP	Collection Tree Protocol
RBP	Robust Broadcast Propagation
LPL	Low Power Listening
MAC	Media Access Control
MLA	MAC Layer Architecture
TDMA	Time Division Multiple Access
EWMA	Exponentially Weighted Moving Average
RSSI	Received Signal Strength Indicator
SNMS	Sensor Network Management System
RF	Radio Frequency
CMRR	Common Mode Rejection Ratio
PRR	Packet Reception Ratio
QoS	Quality-of-Service
ToA	Time of Arrival
TDoA	Time Difference of Arrival
AoA	Angle of Arrival
RSS	Received Signal Strength
SD	Signature Distance
FTSP	Flooded Time Synchronization Protocol
EM	Electro-Magnetic
ADL	Activities of Daily Living
FATS	Fingerprint and Timing-based Snooping
FAL	Flash Abstraction Layer
SECDED	Single-Error-Correction Double-Error-Detection
GPIO	General Purpose Input/Output
LS	Logical Storage
API	Application Programming Interface
NTT	Node Translation Table
AM	Active Message
EEPROM	Electrically Erasable Programmable Read-Only Memory

RAM	Random Access Memory
TOSSIM	TinyOS simulator
PPS	Pulse Per Second
PLL	Phase-Locked Loop
OASIS	Optimized Autonomous Space In-situ Sensor-web
USGS	United States Geological Survey
JRO	Johnston Ridge Observatory
RPC	Remote Procedure Call
UPS	Uninterruptible Power Supply
ROM	Read-Only Memory
MEMS	MicroElectroMechanical Systems
UTC	Coordinated Universal Time
ADC	Analog-to-Digital Converter
SPI	Serial Peripheral Interface
LQI	Link Quality Indicator

REFERENCES

[1] <http://www.pbs.org/wnet/nature/forces/lava.html>.
[2] <http://www.tinyos.net/tinyos-1.x/tos/lib/MultiHopLQI>, 2004.
[3] A. Becher, Z. Benenson, M. Dornseif, Tampering with motes: real-world physical attacks on wireless sensor networks, in: Proceedings of the 3rd International Conference on Security, Pervasive Computing (SPC'06), 2006, pp. 104–118.
[4] Sanjit Biswas, Robert Morris, ExOR: opportunistic multi-hop routing for wireless networks, in: Proceedings of the Special Interest Group on Data Communication (SIGCOMM'05), of SIGCOMM '05, Philadelphia, Pennsylvania, USA, vol. 35, ACM, October 2005, pp. 133–144.
[5] Michael Buettner, Gary Yee, Eric Anderson, Richard Han, X-MAC: A short preamble MAC protocol for duty-cycled wireless sensor networks, in: Proceedings of the ACM Conference on Embedded Networked Sensor Systems (SenSys'06), Boulder, Colorado, USA, November 2006.
[6] W. Geoffrey, Challen, Jason Waterman, Matt Welsh, IDEA: integrated distributed energy awareness for wireless sensor networks, in: The 8th Annual International Conference on Mobile Systems, Applications and Services (MobiSys'10), June 2010.
[7] B.N. Chun, P. Buonadonna, A. AuYoung, C. Ng, D.C. Parkes, J. Shneidman, A.C. Snoeren, A. Vahdat, Mirage: a microeconomic resource allocation system for sensornet testbeds, in: The 2nd IEEE Workshop on Embedded Networked Sensors (EmNets'05), 2005.
[8] D.D. Couto, D. Aguayo, J. Bicket, R. Morris, A high-throughput path metric for multi-hop wireless routing, in: Proceedings of the ACM International Conference on Mobile Computing and Networking (MobiCom'03), San Diego, California, USA, September 2003.
[9] Adam Dunkels, Bjorn Gronvall, Thiemo Voigt, Contiki—a lightweight and flexible operating system for tiny networked sensors, in: Proceedings of the 29th Annual IEEE International Conference on Local Computer Networks (LCN '04), IEEE Computer Society, Tampa, FL, USA, 2004, pp. 455–462.

[10] Prabal Dutta, David Culler, Practical asynchronous neighbor discovery and rendezvous for mobile sensing applications, in: Proceedings of the 6th ACM conference on Embedded Network Sensor Systems (SenSys '08), Raleigh, NC, USA, 2008, pp. 71–84.

[11] Rodrigo Fonseca, Omprakash Gnawali, Kyle Jamieson, Philip Levis, Four-bit wireless link estimation, in: HotNets'07, 2007.

[12] Omprakash Gnawali, Rodrigo Fonseca, Kyle Jamieson, David Moss, Philip Levis, Collection tree protocol, in: Proceedings of the 7th ACM Conference on Embedded Networked Sensor Systems (SenSys), 2009.

[13] Omprakash Gnawali, Ki-Young Jang, Jeongyeup Paek, Marcos Vieira, Ramesh Govindan, Ben Greenstein, August Joki, Deborah Estrin, Eddie Kohler, The tenet architecture for tiered sensor networks, in: The 4th International Conference on Embedded Networked Sensor Systems (SenSys'06), 2006.

[14] Gregory Hackmann, Octav Chipara, Chenyang Lu, Robust topology control for indoor wireless sensor networks, in: Proceedings of the 6th ACM Conference on Embedded Network Sensor Systems (SenSys '08), Raleigh, NC, USA, November 2008.

[15] Renjie Huang, Wen-Zhan Song, Xu Mingsen, Nina Peterson, Behrooz Shirazi, Richard LaHusen, real-world sensor network for long-term volcano monitoring: design and findings, in: IEEE Transactions on Parallel and Distributed Systems, 2011.

[16] Jonathan Hui, David Culler, The dynamic behavior of a data dissemination protocol for network programming at scale, in: Proceedings of the 2nd ACM Conference on Embedded Networked Sensor Systems (SenSys'04), Baltimore, MD, USA, November 2004.

[17] Chris Karlof, Naveen Sastry, David Wagner, TinySec: a link layer security architecture for wireless sensor networks, in: Proceedings of the ACM Conference on Embedded Networked Sensor Systems (SenSys'04), Baltimore, Maryland, USA, November 2004.

[18] Sukun Kim, Rodrigo Fonseca, Prabal Dutta, Arsalan Tavakoli, David Culler, Philip Levis, Scott Shenker, Ion Stoica, Flush: a reliable bulk transport protocol for multihop wireless networks, in: Proceedings of the ACM Conference on Embedded Networked Sensor Systems (SenSys'07), November 2007.

[19] Kevin Klues, Gregory Hackmann, Octav Chipara, Chenyang Lu, A component-based architecture for power-efficient media access control in wireless sensor networks, in: Proceedings of the ACM Conference on Embedded Networked Sensor Systems (SenSys'07), Sydney, Australia, November 2007.

[20] Cynthia Kuo, Mark Luk, Rohit Negi, Adrian Perrig, Message-in-a-bottle: user-friendly and secure key deployment for sensor nodes, in: The ACM Conference on Embedded Networked Sensor System (SenSys'07), 2007.

[21] Philip Levis, Nelson Lee, Matt Welsh, David Culler, TOSSIM: accurate and scalable simulation of entire tinyos applications, in: Proceedings of the First ACM Conference on Embedded Networked Sensor Systems (SenSys'03), 2003.

[22] Philip Levis, Sam Madden, Joseph Polastre, Robert Szewczyk, Alec Woo, David Gay, Jason Hill, Matt Welsh, Eric Brewer, David Culler, TinyOS: an operating system for sensor networks, in: W. Weber, J. Rabaey, E. Aarts (Eds.), Ambient Intelligence, Springer-Verlag, 2004.

[23] Philip Levis, Neil Patel, David Culler, Scott Shenker, Trickle: a self-regulating algorithm for code propagation and maintenance in wireless sensor networks, in: Proceedings of the 1st USENIX/ACM Symposium on Networked Systems Design and Implementation (NSDI'04), San Francisco, CA, USA, November 2004.

[24] Ming Li, Deepak Ganesan, Prashant Shenoy, PRESTO: feedback-driven data management in sensor networks, in: 3rd Symposium on Networked Systems Design and Implementation (NSDI'06), San Jose, CA, USA, May 2006.

[25] Shan Lin, Jingbin Zhang, Gang Zhou, Lin Gu, John A. Stankovic, Tian He, ATPC: adaptive transmission power control for wireless sensor networks, in: Proceedings of the Fourth International Conference on Embedded Networked Sensor Systems (SenSys '06), ACM Press, New York, NY, USA, 2006, pp. 223–236.

[26] Yunhao Liu, Kebin Liu, Mo Li. Passive diagnosis for wireless sensor networks, IEEE/ACM Trans. Netw. 18 (4) 2010.

[27] Konrad Lorincz, Bor-rong Chen, Jason Waterman, Geoff Werner-Allen, Matt Welsh, Resource aware programming in the pixie OS, in: Proceedings of the Sixth ACM Conference on Embedded Networked Sensor Systems (SenSys), November 2008.

[28] Miklós Maróti, Branislav Kusy, Gyula Simon, Ákos Lédeczi, The flooding time synchronization protocol, in: Proceedings of the Second ACM Conference on Embedded Networked Sensor Systems (SenSys), Baltimore, MD, USA, November 2004.

[29] Gaurav Mathur, Peter Desnoyers, Deepak Ganesan, Prashant Shenoy, Capsule: an energy-optimized object storage system for memory-constrained sensor devices, in: Proceedings of the Fourth International Conference on Embedded Networked Sensor Systems (SenSys'06), ACM Press, New York, NY, USA, 2006, pp. 195–208.

[30] S. Mcnutt, Seismic monitoring and eruption forecasting of volcanoes: a review of the state of the art and case histories, in: Monitoring and Mitigation of Volcano Hazards, 1996, pp. 99–146.

[31] S. Nath, A. Kansal. FlashDB: dynamic self-tuning database for NAND flash, in: Proceedings of the ACM/IEEE International Conference on Information Processing in Sensor Networks (IPSN'07), Cambridge, MA, 2007.

[32] Jeongyeup Paek, Ramesh Govindan, RCRT: rate-controlled reliable transport for wireless sensor networks, in: Proceedings of the ACM Conference on Embedded Network Sensor Systems (SenSys '07), November 2007.

[33] Yang Peng, WenZhan Song, Renjie Huang, Xu Mingsen, Behrooz Shirazi, Cascades: a reliable dissemination protocol for data collection sensor network, in: IEEE Aerospace Conference, Big Sky, MT, USA, March 2009.

[34] Joseph Polastre, Jason Hill, David Culler, Versatile low power media access for wireless sensor networks, in: The Second ACM Conference on Embedded Networked Sensor Systems (SenSys), 2004.

[35] Joseph Polastre, Jonathan Hui, Philip Levis, Jerry Zhao, David Culler, Scott Shenker, Ion Stoica, A unifying link abstraction for wireless sensor networks, in: Proceedings of the ACM Conference on Embedded Networked Sensor Systems (SenSys'05), San Diego, California, USA, 2005.

[36] Sumit Rangwala, Ramakrishna Gummadi, Ramesh Govindan, Konstantinos Psounis. Interference aware fair rate control in wireless sensor networks, in: Proceedings of the Special Interest Group on Data, Communication (SIGCOMM'06), September 2006.

[37] Anthony Rowe, Vikram Gupta, Raj Rajkumar, Low-power clock synchronization using electromagnetic energy radiating from AC power lines, in: Proceedings of the ACM Conference on Embedded Network Sensor Systems (SenSys '09), November 2009.

[38] Wen-Zhan Song, Renjie Huang, Mingsen Xu, Andy Ma, Behrooz Shirazi, Richard Lahusen, Air-dropped sensor network for real-time high-fidelity volcano monitoring, in: The Seventh Annual International Conference on Mobile Systems, Applications and Services (MobiSys), June 2009.

[39] Wen-Zhan Song, Renjie Huang, Xu Mingsen, Behrooz A. Shirazi, Richard LaHusen, Design and deployment of sensor network for real-time high-fidelity volcano monitoring, IEEE Trans. Parallel Distr. Syst. 21 (11) (2010) 1658–1674.

[40] Vijay Srinivasan, John Stankovic, Kamin Whitehouse, Protecting your daily in-home activity information from a wireless snooping attack, in: the 10th International Conference on Ubiquitous, Computing (UbiComp'08), 2008.

[41] Fred Stann, John Heidemann, Rajesh Shroff, Muhammad Z. Murtaza, RBP: robust broadcast propagation in wireless networks, in: Proceedings of the Fourth International Conference on Embedded Networked Sensor Systems (SenSys'06), ACM Press, New York, NY, USA, 2006, pp. 85–98.

[42] Gilman Tolle, David Culler, Design of an application-cooperative management system for wireless sensor networks, in: Second European Conference on wireless sensor networks (EWSN), January 2005.

[43] Tijs van Dam, Koen Langendoen, An adaptive energy-efficient MAC protocol for wireless sensor networks, in: The First ACM Conference on Embedded Networked Sensor Systems (SenSys), 2003.

[44] Geoffrey Werner-Allen, Stephen Dawson-Haggerty, Matt Welsh, Lance: optimizing high-resolution signal collection in wireless sensor networks, in: Proceedings of the Sixth ACM Conference on Embedded Network Sensor Systems (SenSys '08), Raleigh, NC, USA, November 2008.

[45] A. Woo, T. Tong, D. Culler, Taming the underlying challenges of reliable multihop routing in sensor networks, in: Proceedings of the ACM Conference on Embedded Networked Sensor Systems (SenSys'03), Los Angeles, California, USA, November 2003.

[46] Wei Xi, Yuan He, Yunhao Liu, Jizhong Zhao, Lufeng Mo, Zheng Yang, Jiliang Wang, Xiangyang Li, Locating sensors in the wild: pursuit of ranging quality, in: Proceedings of the Eigth ACM Conference on Embedded Networked Sensor Systems (SenSys'10), Zurich, Switzerland.

[47] W. Ye, J. Heidemann, D. Estrin, An energy-efficient MAC protocol for wireless sensor networks, in: 21st Conference of the IEEE Computer and Communications Societies (INFOCOM), June 2002.

[48] Fenghua Yuan, Wen-Zhan Song, Nina Peterson, Yang Peng, Lei Wang, Behrooz Shirazi, Lightweight sensor network management system design, in: The Fourth IEEE International Workshop on Sensor Networks and Systems for, Pervasive Computing, March 2008.

[49] Ziguo Zhong Tian He, Achieving range-free localization beyond connectivity, in: Proceedings of the Seventh ACM Conference on Embedded Networked Sensor Systems (SenSys'09), ACM, Berkeley, California, 2009, pp. 281–294.

ABOUT THE AUTHORS

Debraj De (dde1@student.gsu.edu) is a Ph.D. candidate in Sensorweb Research Laboratory, Department of Computer Science, Georgia State University. His current research interests include Smart Environments, Internet of Things, Wireless Sensor Networks, Smart Healthcare, Artificial Intelligence, Pervasive Computing, and Distributed Systems.

Wen-Zhan Song (wsong@gsu.edu) is an associate professor in Department of Computer Science, Georgia State University, and the Director of Sensorweb Research Laboratory there. He received his Ph.D. in Computer Science from Illinois Institute of Technology, USA, in 2005. His current research interests include the sensing, computing, communication, control and security issues in Cyber-Physical Systems; applications and systems for Environment Monitoring, Smart Grid, Mobile Health.

Mingsen Xu (mxu4@student.gsu.edu) has received Ph.D. in Computer Science from Sensorweb Research Laboratory, Department of Computer Science, Georgia State University in 2013. His current research interests include Wireless Sensor Networks, Network Coding, real-time and embedded systems, and Distributed Systems.

Lei Shi (lshi1@student.gsu.edu) is a Ph.D. student in Sensorweb Research Laboratory, Department of Computer Science, Georgia State University. His current research interests include Wireless Sensor Networks, in-network processing, and Distributed Systems.

Song Tan (stan6@student.gsu.edu) is a Ph.D. student in Sensorweb Research Laboratory, Department of Computer Science, Georgia State University. His current research interests include Smart Grid, Wireless Sensor Networks.

CHAPTER TWO

Novel System Architectures for Semantic-Based Integration of Sensor Networks

Zoran Babovic[*] and Veljko Milutinovic[†]

[*]Innovation Center of the School of Electrical Engineering, University of Belgrade, Serbia
[†]School of Electrical Engineering, University of Belgrade, Serbia

Contents

Advances in Computers, Volume 90
ISSN 0065-2458, http://dx.doi.org/10.1016/B978-0-12-408091-1.00002-6

91

Abstract

There are many on-going projects and research initiatives that are proposing new semantic-oriented services for obtaining, delivery, and processing sensor data gathered from integrated sensor networks. Rich information models based on the ontologies for heterogeneous sensor data description are necessary for achieving interoperability among various deployed sensor networks while providing context-related information with raw sensor data. As expected by the Sensor Web vision and the Future Internet initiatives, certain architecture is faced with performance requirements while providing complex services. This study identifies main challenges and design issues of sensor networks integration platforms, and gives a survey of existing approaches specifically emphasizing semantic-oriented approaches. The survey includes non-semantic approaches that are improved by employing semantics on certain levels, as well as approaches fully based on semantic technologies. As their original contribution, the authors propose a new architecture designed as an infrastructural platform for enabling semantic-based sensor networks integration. The key idea behind the proposed innovation is to utilize a flexible distributed repository called column store for keeping semantically modeled sensor data providing a scalable platform capable of supporting huge amounts of sensor data and large numbers of users. Moreover, column store is employed for push-based data propagation and support for including more complex processing elements.

1. INTRODUCTION

The term Semantic Interoperability refers to the ability of two or more systems, not only to exchange data, but also to understand the semantic meaning of the exchanged data, which is of crucial importance for applications that require heterogeneous systems interoperability. In this context, the term Heterogeneous Systems refers to the systems defined in isolation from each other that use different data formats as well as different data exchange protocols while communicating with each other. Consequently, a basic characteristic of Semantic-Based Integration is the existence of a large data variety and data exchange formats, the diversity of which could result in fatal consequences in the sense that existing data cannot be used by remote systems, while at the same time it is crucial for remote systems problem solving.

Scenarios requiring semantic interoperability of heterogeneous systems are typical of applications in which: (a) Wireless Sensor Networks (WSNs) produce data to be utilized by other systems, or (b) Two or more wireless sensor networks exchange data. According to the first scenario, the WSN is a data producer, while in the second scenario, the WSN is both the producer and the consumer of large data quantities.

The progress in the sensing technology and electronic devices miniaturization with decreased energy requirements and increased processing power implies both various sensor type development and deployment in the real world. Sensor networks are used for environment observation and collecting information concerning different physical phenomena, which can be utilized to derive more knowledge about natural events and situations. However, although many autonomously deployed sensor networks exist, the deeper knowledge remains hidden, because of the lack of deployed networks integration and interoperability. The essential idea is that certain sensors, installed for a particular service, may represent a useful data source for other services possibly published by different parties.

This observation has inspired researchers to intensify efforts on investigation of new platforms and paradigms, in order to provide infrastructure for integration of sensor networks on the Web, with appropriate user services. This technology set is known as the Sensor Web [1, 2], or the Sensor Internet, and has recently been included in many initiatives. Most work in this area is done in creating platforms capable of integrating heterogeneous sensor data, different sensing device types, operating systems and low-level programming paradigms, and routing protocols, while providing a common view to outside users who are interested in getting information about the observed real world parameters. An additional improvement of the developed platforms lies in the involvement of semantics into sensor observations. This approach assumes that raw data are supplied with context-related information including spatial, temporal, and thematic metadata. This helps to better utilize, manage, understand, and search sensor data sources, with possibilities of providing more complex services. This enhanced platform is usually labeled as the Semantic Sensor Web [7, 40].

In brief, the viewpoint of the work here presented implies fusion of heterogeneous sensor data sources, the collected sensor data management relying on semantic data representation and semantic processing, and the relevant services provision to Sensor Web applications. This chapter shows a survey of available architectures for providing semantic-based integration of heterogeneous sensor networks. In Section 2 we discuss the main challenges and design issues that certain architecture deals with. An existing similar surveys overview is given in Section 3, while the surveyed approaches classification methodology is elaborated in Section 4. The surveyed architectures presentation and their comparison are provided in Section 5 and Section 6, respectively. An original contribution of authors is described in Section 7. Finally, Section 8 provides a global conclusion.

2. PROBLEM STATEMENT

It is clear that many challenges are placed before the sensor networks integration architectures. Despite the fact that researchers approach this problem from different points of view such as: targeting different objectives, end-users, and application domains, we can identify several challenges and topics that certain architecture should address [9].

2.1 The Basic Organization

The first issue we discuss is the basic organization within the architecture. The typical approach is a multi-layered organization that logically divides the system components. Data layer encapsulates low-level communication with underlying sensor networks, which may include communication over a middleware oriented interface or through native query language of certain sensor data source. The processing layer encompasses the functions responsible for filtering, aggregation, and transformation of the sensed data, maintenance of the semantic data model, as well as more intelligent functions that leverage the semantic-based reasoning. The application layer is responsible for interaction with end-users by providing a set of services and supplying data in appropriate formats. Variations in this organization allow different interfaces among these layers, a further separation into more layers, or grouping some of these layers into a single layer. Depending on the distribution and interaction between layers there are also client-server, hierarchical, and peer-to-peer organizations.

2.2 Scalability

Scalability may refer to the case when the sensor data volume is increased, or when the number of supported users and applications that interact with the integrated sensor system grows. A good architecture should appropriately scale up and preserve the necessary performance requirements. A typical problem with scalability in the available approaches is the case when one of the critical functions of the entire system is centralized, regardless what that functionality is. This might be the centralized storage system for archiving sensor data, the data annotation unit, the query processing engine, the query resolver, the service provider, etc. It is a challenge to make these critical functions distributed and scalable.

2.3 Sensor Data Modality

Currently deployed sensor networks vary in sensed data characteristics. Therefore, architecture should support as much as possible different data modalities, in order to support efficient data fusion. Users may have the ability to obtain event-driven sensor data, acquisitional and streaming sensor data, archived/stored data, and aggregated or filtered data. Another categorization of the sensor data provision patterns includes push-based sensor data propagation (driven either by detection of some events, or programmed time intervals) and poll-based access (when sensor tasking is initiated by users). A properly configured sensor data collection should ensure that the system cannot be overloaded if gathered sensor data rate is not adjusted carefully.

2.4 Flexibility of Supported Sensor Networks

There is a large number of sensor devices that run different operating systems such as TinyOS, Contiki, and FreeRTOS [70] using different communication protocols as IEEE 802.15.4, ZigBee, 6LoWPan, Bluetooth, etc. [69, 70] currently on the market. Generally, it might be left to the sensor data providers to adapt to the specified interface of an architecture, in order to be integrated usually through the gateway components, or the architecture provides its own implementation for interaction with certain class of sensor networks or middleware layer. A middleware layer is a software infrastructure that connects sensor network platforms, operating systems, protocol stack, and applications [67]. Several middleware solutions such as database style access [24], macro-programming paradigm, publish–subscribe message passing mechanism, virtual machine-based interaction, mobile agents-based access, and service-oriented access [67, 69], can be used to access sensor networks.

2.5 Sensor Networks Capability Awareness

The most common principle in the Sensor Web platforms design is the following: complexities of the underlying sensors and networks are hidden from the users and not considered while obtaining sensor data.

However, in order to improve energy efficiency and to extract more precise information from the observed environment by optimizing network management and sensor data access, some architectures may maintain relevant information of technical capabilities of sensors, their accuracy, power constraints, as well as the network topology and routing protocols. Such optimization may introduce additional overhead while keeping capability information in parallel with performing other operations. Users can be provided with this type of information, while security concerns are being taken into account. The ontological infrastructure is a powerful mechanism for describing sensor capabilities.

2.6 Sensor Networks Management and Actuation Functions

Some implementations may allow end-users to have a full or a limited control over sensor networks resources, which may include setting of sensors' working mode parameters, or perhaps access to actuation function. Since access to this set of functions cannot be simply shared among interested users, the appropriate arbitration mechanism must be provided together with authorization policies.

2.7 Ontologies

A more flexible way for interpreting and managing sensor network data is possible by defining the application domain core concepts and their relationships with sensors through ontology development. By utilizing the defined concepts, users, and applications are able to interact with the integrated sensor networks on a higher level, which enables interoperability. Guarino [32] has suggested development of "different kinds of ontology according to their level of generality" and classified them as: top-level or upper ontology for describing general concepts independent of any domain, domain and task ontology addressing particular domain or tasks by specializing upper ontology concepts, and the application ontology covering domain entities roles while performing the defined activities. This ontology network approach is often utilized in semantic sensor networks, by means of developing separate sensor network domain and the application domain ontologies, and reusing some of the most common upper layer ontologies for achieving interoperability.

The most comprehensive work on sensor ontology has been done by the World Wide Web Consortium (W3C) Semantic Sensor Network Incubator Group, which developed the Semantic Sensor Network (SSN) Ontology [36] that covers sensor devices and sensor networks, their capabilities, as well as Sensor Web applications. This ontology tends to become widely accepted, while enabling extensions with domain-specific ontologies. It extends the DOLCE + DnS UltraLite upper ontology [39]. Compton et al. [33] gave a survey of available sensor ontologies. Among others, they emphasize the OntoSensor ontology [34] that is built on the Open Geospatial Consortium Sensor Web Enablement's (OGC SWE) SensorML specification and reuses the IEEE Suggested Upper Merged Ontology [38], however, it does not cover observation and measurement data. Another significant ontology is the CSIRO Semantic Sensor Ontology [35] that is used as a starting point for the development of the W3C's SSN Ontology. Some projects reuse the NASA Semantic Web for Earth and Environmental Terminology (SWEET) Ontology [37] as an upper ontology. For representing ontologies, in general the Semantic Web technologies such as the W3C Web Ontology Language (OWL) [5] are used, although the Resource Description Framework (RDF) Schema [4] can be used, as well.

2.8 Applied Semantics

The introduction of ontology into the system enables possibility of employing data semantics within various architecture levels. With regard to the accepted information model, semantics could be also utilized for available services description, representation of observation and measurements data, sensor data sources properties, semantic queries, as well as internal processing elements characteristics.

2.9 The Data Representation Model

The next important design issue is the sensor data model for representing the collected data. Generally, using a simple sensor data model, for instance a model based on binary or relational formats, enables better performance, lower storage and communication requirements, but since this is a low–level data model, it could result in poor interoperability of the heterogeneous sensor data. The eXtensible Markup Language (XML) can be used as an intermediate format for sensor data encoding. While keeping data storage size requirements reasonably low, it enables the interoperability of sensor networks, but lacks the ability to enrich data with semantics. Higher abstraction of sensor data representation employs Semantic Web technologies for encoding data as Resource Description Framework (RDF) data representation model [3], suitable for expressing concepts and relationships defined in the accepted ontology. A discussion on potentials and requirements of certain sensor models is given in [8, 31].

2.10 Query Language

The most convenient way for users to access and search for desirable sensor data is through query languages, whose selection is influenced but does not have to be limited to the chosen internal data model. If sensor data model is relational based, SQL, or its derivations, are the natural choice. This choice leaves users to deal with raw data, and additional processing has to be included in order to extract more knowledge from the data. Selection of XML documents for data representation leaves an opportunity of various formats for expressing queries, a standard one being the XPATH. Higher abstraction of data representation, encoded as RDF triples relying on ontologies, expects that users express their queries using SPARQL, or a similar semantic query language. In the available systems, some extensions of these query languages could be found. In the case of existence of a few data formats in the system, the query translation or transformation should be performed at some level. However, the simplest query approach is to use a custom query format by allowing users to specify query parameters within the request. Unfortunately, this approach is neither extensible nor flexible.

2.11 Knowledge Inference

As one of the main benefits of introducing the semantic technologies in the sensor networks is the ability to infer high-level knowledge from the gathered observations, by reasoning over ontology descriptions and a set of logic rules. The reasoning process includes improved search with generalized concepts, high-level events detection within raw sensor data, logical and domain reasoning by implementing certain algorithms that utilize the logic programming and description logic. There are many available reasoning engines on the market that might be utilized by certain architectures for this purpose [19, 23].

2.12 The Application Interface and Data Format

Relying on standard interfaces and data format facilities, developers can create a wide set of applications running on different platforms and device types, ranging from thin mobile application, to web application, and standard desktop application. Better interoperability is achieved through using standard-based interfaces, the most common of which are: the web service described with Web Service Definition Language (WSDL) and the Representational State Transfer (REST) [25, 26] style of interaction based on the HTTP protocol. The requested data should be delivered according to some defined format that can be the same as the internal data representation format used in the system over the selected interface. Or, the data can be converted to an application-specific format. Standard representations include XML data encodings and ontology-based data representation as RDF triples. However, there are some proposals to embed semantic annotation in the XML formatted data using RDFa [42], or XLINK [43] technologies. These semantic annotations may include context-relevant data as temporal, spatial, and thematic metadata [7]. Additionally, data can be also delivered using JavaScript Object Notation (JSON) format, or HTML-based documents, etc.

2.13 Discovery of Services

The function that enables users to get information related to the available services which are provided by the integration system is called the discovery of services. In contrast, the providers of sensor data sources are able to register their services with appropriate description mechanisms. Certain architecture can allow dynamic registration and hence discovery of such services, while others have only a static set of available services. Users might have a possibility to discover relevant services through queries that are usually semantically enabled. Such approach relies on the semantic descriptions of registered services.

2.14 Service Composition

One of the most sophisticated functions that certain architecture can offer to users is the ability to declaratively specify the desirable service by defining either complete data flow starting from basic sensor data sources, or just specifying properties of the resulting data stream. Although it is not mandatory, relying on the semantic technologies is the most convenient way for implementing this feature. Typically, there is a special component called a planner responsible for creating requested type of service.

2.15 Quality of Service and Information

We assume quality of service and information from the application perspective, which includes the following issues: (1) confidence refers to confidence in both data values and associated metadata information, as well as to confidence in processing elements characteristics [17], (2) accuracy, depending on the provided model of sensor technical capabilities, (3) availability, driven by sensor networks characteristics and constraints as working mode, network topology, and underlying protocol, and (4) delivery, referring to data delay and latency in the environment with unreliable connections, etc.

2.16 Security

In the scenario when many providers publish their sensor resources to a large community of end-users, security of such services has to be addressed. On the one hand, access control concerns the policy enforcement and credentials for particular users, or group of users, to access certain sensor networks, or sensor data, or even sensor data type (archived or real-time). On the other hand, users must be guaranteed the authentication of such provided data. With implementation of appropriate accounting functions, sensors providers are able to offer services to users by charging their usage. Privacy issues include situations when real-world entities do not allow that their activities or states can be monitored or tracked. Various aspects of security can be enforced either at communication level or at data storage level.

Some architectures aim to provide a ubiquitous platform for Sensor Web applications covering many application-domains and user groups, addressing the majority of the aforementioned issues. In contrast, simpler architectures target one application-domain and some specific issues. Having introduced the classification criteria and the surveyed architectures, we will give a comparative analysis of presented architectures with regard to the implementation of the issues discussed above.

3. EXISTING SURVEYS AND THEIR CRITICISM

There are several surveys that tackle techniques and approaches overlapping with those used in semantic sensor networks. Those surveys cover topics such as middleware architectures for wireless sensor networks [66, 67], sensor network integration without concerning semantic approaches [68], analysis of the existing state-of-the-art frameworks and integration sensor services [69, 70], and semantic specifications of sensor networks [33]. Authors of this article are not aware of the existence of any similar survey that addresses the architectural requirements for semantics-based integration of sensor networks.

Henricksen and Robinson [66] published a survey of middleware approaches for sensor networks, considering context-aware systems. Authors have identified four categories of middleware: database-inspired approaches, tuple space approaches, event-based approaches, and service discovery-based approaches. None of these approaches involve any data semantics.

The context-aware systems are described from the perspective of benefits, if they are used for sensor networks applications, with a touch on semantic technologies used for their implementations. Authors have envisioned convergence of middleware approaches and context-aware systems in the future architectures of heterogeneous sensor networks.

Fedor et al. [68] provided an overview of sensor networks' integration frameworks and architectures. Authors gave a simple classification on client-server and peer-to-peer architectures. Non-functional and functional properties comparison of the surveyed approaches is provided. However, there is no discussion regarding semantic techniques and semantics-enabled sensor networks that are more sophisticated approaches to sensor networks integration.

The survey provided by Compton et al. [33] covers various approaches to proposing ontologies that capture concepts and their relationships from the sensor networks point of view. More specifically, the survey discusses concepts related to physical environment observed by sensor networks, technical characteristics of sensor device capabilities, and the application-domain concepts. However, no analysis is provided as to efficient employment of these ontologies by appropriate architectures. Finally, the survey addresses a generic architecture for semantic sensor networks.

The overview of state-of-the-art solutions regarding sensor integration frameworks, sensor networks protocols, security, as well as semantic technologies was provided as deliverables in the EU FP7 projects SENSEI [69] and the Internet of Things [70]. Despite the fact that these are very comprehensive overviews of recent technologies, they do not cover concrete architectures available for semantic sensor networks.

4. CLASSIFICATION CRITERIA AND THE CLASSIFICATION TREE

The major two problems in creating a new taxonomy are: the classification criteria and the classification tree. Here, the classification criteria have been chosen to reflect the essence of the research basic viewpoint. The classification tree has been obtained by successive application of the chosen criteria. The leaves of the classification tree are the examples (research efforts), which are elaborated briefly later on, in the Presentation of Existing Solutions section of this paper.

In this study, we have also included architectures not dealing with the data semantics, but the architectures of which have influenced research in certain direction. In addition to this, we have shown how semantic data enrichment improves efficiency of used approach.

Since the role of the sensor networks integration platform is to act as an interface between sensor networks and users application, researchers are able to tackle the problem either at the sensor networks level, i.e., bottom–up, or at the applications level, i.e., top–down approach. Therefore, as the main classification criteria of the surveyed architectures, we classify architectures according to the selected approach, which may include: *sensor networks-oriented approach* and *application-oriented approach*. In the first approach, researchers try to solve the sensor networks heterogeneity, sensor networks technical characteristics, constraints, protocols, and produced observations and measurement, by means of proposing an optimal way for handling, representing, storing, and aggregating the available sensor data sources to upper layers in the system, and thus to applications. In the second approach, researchers tend to enable an as-conform-as-possible interface and an interaction mechanism for users and applications, which enable them to get the information they are interested in, from the integrated sensor networks, by releasing them from the complexities and specifics of those sensors networks.

Within the first class, we can identify three subgroups: *database centered* architectures, approaches based on *query translation*, and *sensor virtualization-* based approaches. All these subgroups can be further divided into the approaches with and without data semantics employment.

The database centered solutions are characterized with a database as a central hub of all the collected sensor data, and consequently all search and manipulation of sensor data are performed over the database. It is a challenge to map heterogeneous sensor data to a unique database scheme. An additional mechanism should be provided for real-time data support, because this type of data is hardly to be cached directly due to its large volume. The main concern with this approach is the scalability, since the database server should handle both insertions of data coming from the sensor nodes, as well as to perform application queries. This approach can benefit from the possibility to enable support for data mining and machine learning techniques over the stored pool of sensor data.

The query translation approach utilizes natural form of sensor data and the associated query languages in order to transform users query to the target query language of a certain source. This approach implies a need to maintain the information of available data sources, primarily the native query language of certain data source, format and the nature of produced data, but it may also include information about sensors capabilities, network topology, power constrains for better query optimization. The results of native queries should be assembled into target data format. Potentially, a performance drawback lies in the fact that two conversions per each user request must be done in the runtime: when a query is translated to a native query, and again when query results should be converted into the target format.

In *the sensor virtualization* approach, sensors and other devices are represented with an abstract data model and applications are provided with the ability to directly interact with such abstraction using an interface. Whether the implementation of the defined interface is achieved on the sensor nodes sinks or gateways components, the produced data streams must comply with the commonly accepted format that should enable interoperability. Generally, any common data format, that leverages the semantic data model, could be used for representing data representation, or even multiple data formats targeting at different levels of data abstractions, might coexist in parallel depending on the user needs. This approach is a promising one and offers good scalability, high performance, and efficient data fusion over heterogeneous sensor networks, as well as flexibility in aggregating data streams, etc.

As stated above, *application-oriented approaches* try to offer the most efficient way to user applications to get needed information from the integrated sensor networks. However, focusing on the provision of the high-level interaction between applications and underlying system, with enabling knowledge inferring features, sometimes suffers from the performance aspects, which prevent these solutions' wider acceptance. We have identified four subgroups that share the same basic principle of top-down approach: the *service-oriented architecture approaches*, *service-composition approaches*, *rule-based data transformation approaches*, and *agent-based systems*.

The service-oriented-architecture approaches provide a standard service interface with defined methods and data encodings for obtaining observation and measurements from desired sensors. Furthermore, it might offer functions such as getting information of sensors characteristics, ability to subscribe on selected sensors data values, submitting queries, optionally the actuation functions, etc. The dominant interaction in these architectures is the request–reply model, and to a lesser extent the event-based delivery of sensors data. A drawback of this approach is that it does not have an ability to fuse stream–based sensor data along with archived or acquisitioned data types. Although there are no explicit constraints on concrete implementation, this approach tends to be vertically oriented and covers only one application domain.

The service-composition-oriented approaches allow users the ability to define arbitrary services or data streams with specific characteristic of interest. The system will try to compose such a data flow by applying specific processing over appropriate data sources, which will result in producing a data stream that conforms to the requested specification. Full user request expressiveness could be achieved by enabling a semantic model-based description of desired data streams and processing capabilities: semantics-based reasoning could be utilized when looking for an optimal composition of available components. This approach seems to offer the most flexible solutions from the applications perspective, although the performance may be degraded due to real-time discovery of service composition.

The *rule-based data transformation* seems as the most common approach for utilizing semantic data models. Inferring new knowledge or detecting high-level events are achieved by the mapping functions relying on the relationships between the concepts captured in the domain model ontological representation and sensor data observations and measurements. There could be multiple transformations through the architecture according to the different layers in the information model. Data are transformed from lower level formats to semantic-based representations enabling semantic search and reasoning algorithms application.

The *agent-based systems* consist of several types of agents. Agents are software components capable of performing specific tasks. They collaboratively achieve desired functionalities. For the internal agent communications some of standard agent platforms or a specific implementation can be used. Typically, agents belong to one of several layers based on the type of functionalities they are responsible for. Also there might be several agent types in one logical layer. Agents from upper layers employ agents from lower layers. Whether the agents employ sensor data semantics, or whether semantic models are used for the agent processing capabilities description depends on the concrete implementation.

The classification tree, derived from the aforementioned classification criteria, is presented in Fig. 1, and is composed of seven leaves. Each leaf of the classification tree is assigned a name, as described above. The list of existing solutions (examples) is given according to the applied classification for each leaf (class). We have provided only the names of approaches and major references in a separate paragraph in order to enable interested readers to study further details.. For the sake of simplicity, we give an arbitrary name to a solution that does not have an explicit name given by authors. We use

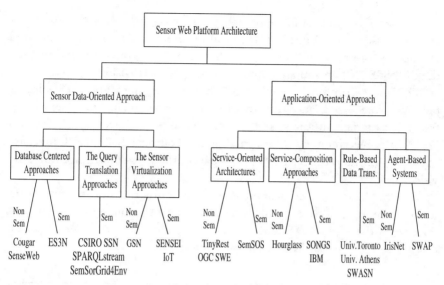

Fig. 1. The classification tree of Sensor Web architectures.

either the name of institution that authors came from, or the name of the main strategic issue characteristic for that solution.

The database centered solutions include non–semantic approaches such as the Cougar database system [10], one of the first research works toward sensor networks integration, and SenseWeb [11], which is an example of maximum utilization of the described approach. The ES3N [13] is an example of semantics-based database centered approach.

All solutions pertaining to query translation approaches employ semantic technologies and include: the CSIRO semantic sensor network [14], the $SPARQL_{STREAM}$–based approach [22], and the SemSorGrid4Env [47, 48], which is the most comprehensive solution in this group.

The most recent research efforts in this field belong to sensor virtualization approaches. The non–semantic approach is used in the GSN [18], while the solutions proposed in large-scale EU funded projects such as the SENSEI [50] and the Internet of Things (IoT) [51, 52] utilize semantics of data.

The service-oriented architectures include simple and yet efficient non–semantic solutions such as TinyREST [53] and the OGC SWE specifications of the reference architecture [2] implemented by various parties [54, 55]. A semantics–enabled approach is used in the SemSOS [56].

The service-composition approaches tend to offer the most flexible interaction to users and Hourglass [16] is an example of a non–semantic-based solution. More powerful solutions utilize semantic approaches and include the SONGS [17] and an architecture developed at IBM [59].

The most common architectures that employ semantic technologies belong to rule-based data transformation approaches and include: a semantics-based sensor data fusion system developed at the University of Toronto [20], pluggable architecture designed at the National Technical University of Athens [23], and the SWASN [61], a part of the Ericsson's CommonSense vision [62].

Finally, the agent-based approaches have both the non–semantic and semantic representatives: the first one is an Internet–scale sensor infrastructure called the IrisNet [15, 63], while the second one is the SWAP [64], a multi–agent system for Sensor Web architectures.

5. PRESENTATION OF EXISTING SOLUTIONS

After the criteria and the classes are defined and explained, this survey is continued with an overview and analysis of selected research efforts in each category along with the following six dimensions: (a) The 7 Ws of the research (again: who, where, when, whom, why, what, how), (b) Essence of the approach (the main strategic issue which differs from the research presented before), (c) Details of the approach (the main tactical issues of interest for the research presented here), (d) Further development trends of the approach (e) A criticism of the approach (looking from the viewpoint of our research), and finally (f) Possible improvements that could overcome the noticed drawbacks (which is what the future research of others can benefit from).

5.1 Sensor Data-Oriented Architectures
5.1.1 Database Centered Architectures
5.1.1.1 Cougar

A first step toward wide area sensors networks was done by Bonnet et al. [10] at Cornel University in 2001, and it is called the Cougar sensor database system. The work focuses on query processing over sensor database because a typical interaction model includes aggregate and correlation queries. The query pattern has been identified within the factory warehouse application scenario.

The sensor database model in the Cougar consists of a list of sensors and their related attributes organized as relations, as well as sensor data that are represented as time series based on a sequence model. This sequence model is defined as a 3-tuple containing a set of records that are outputs of signal-processing functions, ordering domain that corresponds to a discrete time scale, and elements (usually natural numbers) of the ordering domain which are referred to as positions. Each sensor inserts a set of records in the base sequence at the position corresponding to the time when a new output is generated by processing function. Sequence operators are applied to the input sequences when producing a unique output sequence and they include operations like select, project, compose, and aggregate over a set of positions. The basic architecture of the Cougar is depicted in Fig. 2.

The focus of this research is on the sensor query processing over designed sensor database. The following types of queries have been considered: long running queries, queries resulting in a series of notifications of system activity, queries that combine and aggregate data generated by different sensors over time window with selecting certain sensors based on some conditions (usually geographical location). During sensor queries execution, relational data are manipulated with relational operators, while sequence data are manipulated with sequence operators, although there are exceptions to this rule. The Cougar system uses distributed approach for processing sensor queries which assume that different queries may extract different sensor data and only relevant data are extracted from the sensor network.

In Cougar for a certain sensor type, an appropriate Sensor ADT (Abstract Data Type) object is defined. ADT objects are supported by object–relational

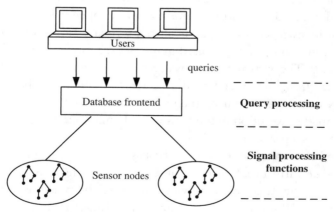

Fig. 2. The basic architecture of the Cougar.

databases and their interfaces correspond to the specific signal-processing functions, which are actually scalar functions. For example, a typical relation in the sensor database schema for temperature sensor may be *T* *(loc location, floor int, sn sensorNode)*, where *sensorNode* is a sensor ADT object, containing methods as *getTemp(), detectAlarmTemp(treshhold)*, etc. SQL language is used for expressing sensor queries, but with little modifications: the "FROM" clause includes a relation containing a sensor ADT attribute, "SELECT" and "WHERE" clause may include expressions over sensor ADTs. Using a previously defined ADT object, an example of a sensor query is:

>   *SELECT T.sn.getTemp()*
>   *FROM T*
>   *WHERE T.floor = 2*
>   *AND $every(60);*

This query will return measurements of all temperature sensors on the second floor every minute. Query processing is executed on the database front-end, while signal-processing functions are performed at the sensor nodes level.

Sensor ADT functions have several limitations due to sensor database characteristics: these functions may induce high latency due to their location or because they are asynchronous (may return a value after arbitrary amount of time), and during long-running queries sensor ADT functions return multiple outputs. In order to overcome limitations of ADT functions, authors implemented their own mechanism called virtual relation that is a tabular form of sensor ADT functions. A record in a virtual relation contains the input arguments of the sensor ADT method, and additionally three attributes: an identifier of a device, the output value of the method, and the time-stamp value corresponding to the point of time when the output value is obtained. Records in a virtual relation are only appended, and each sensor device has its own records fragment in the virtual relation for that sensor type. These virtual relations are used in query execution plan together with base relations. The virtual relation is accessed through a virtual scan using cursor-based *fetch_wait* procedure, during which the cursor is blocked until all records are returned. During the join between a base relation and a virtual relation, the execution of the Sensor ADT functions is done within the virtual scans as a part of nested loops.

This architecture uses the standard database technology that is mature and offers good performance. However, some of the vital functions in Cougar are centralized on the database server which limits scalability of the system. The sensor data model is poor and can hardly support all variations of available sensors which also imply low interoperability. The processing functions are simple, and there is no option of providing multiple processing, or fusion of several sensor data streams.

5.1.1.2 SenseWeb

SenseWeb is sensor data-oriented architecture with a database centered approach designed by Kansal et al. [11] at Microsoft in 2007. Authors designed the SenseWeb with the aim of enabling flexible and uniform sharing of sensor resources among sensor contributors and user applications. There are a number of applications that use the SenseWeb. Pollution monitoring implemented by researchers at Vanderbilt University, the national scale weather study deployed by a research team at Nanyang Technological University, and assisted living facilities developed by researchers at University of Virginia, are three applications of SenseWeb just to name a few.

The architecture consists of several components. The *Coordinator* as a central component, sensors, *Sensor Gateways*, and *Mobile Proxy* is responsible for providing sensor data, while *Data Transformers* and *Applications* interact with end-users. The SenseWeb architecture is depicted in Fig. 3.

The *Coordinator* is the central component and provides system access to all applications and sensor contributors. Functions in the *Coordinator* are separated into two components: the *Tasking Module* and the *SenseDB*, which

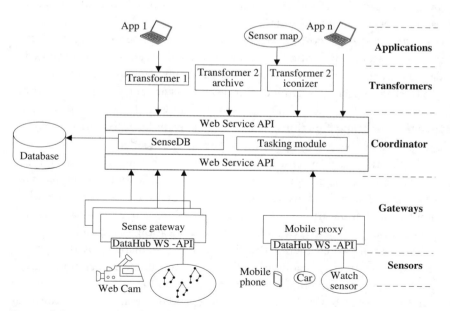

Fig. 3. The SenseWeb's open architecture.

is a streaming sensor database. The *Tasking Module* is responsible for hand-ling applications' requests for sensor data and it tries to gather required data using additional sensor information such as capabilities, sharing willingness, and other attributes. The *SenseDB* is the central sensor database for caching retrieved sensor data and hence reducing access to sensors or *Sensor Gate-ways*. Cached data along with the data from sensors are streamed to certain applications with requested aggregation. A special spatial-temporal structure called COLR-Tree (Collection R-Tree) [12] has been developed to improve spatial-temporal search, and aggregation of cached data. The *SenseDB* is also responsible for indexing sensor characteristics and other shared resources in the system, which can be discovered by user applications.

The SenseWeb enables interaction with various types of sensors that generally have different characteristics. They run on different platforms and communicate with different protocols. Sensor gateway provides a unique interface to various sensors in order to hide their complexities. Other SenseWeb components access the *Sensor Gateways* via web service API in order to get sensor streams, sensor characteristics, or to submit their data demands. Each sensor contributor can maintain its own *Sensor Gateway*, using local database for optimizing sensor streams. There is a default implemen-tation of the *Sensor Gateway* called *DataHub*, whose aim is to communicate with sensors through web service interface by using provided drivers. *Mobile proxy* is a special gateway created for mobile sensors. It provides location-based access to sensor measurements.

Data transformers convert data semantics through processing and serve processed data to applications. The various functions could be achieved with data transformers such as conversions of data units, data fusion, and streaming of visualization services. Application developers are able to implement new transformers using the primitive access methods and combining domain-specific processing functions. Transformers are indexed by the *Coordinator* and can be discovered by applications and used if needed.

Applications utilize sensor data and they can be generally divided into manual and automated applications. In manual applications, users manually issue sensor data requests usually through some graphical user interface, while in automated applications sensor data requests are issued automatically in a specified way and used by other parts of the application for different purposes.

This architecture reaches the limits of non-semantic-based approach because it provides a stable and efficient solution for integrating a large set of sensor data and efficient search capabilities. However, the interaction with the SenseWeb is at the sensor data level and misses high-level features as interface using domain concepts, high-level events detection, and knowledge inference is evident.

5.1.1.3 ES3N

This prototype architecture was developed by Lewis et al. [13] at University of Georgia in 2006, and demonstrates a semantic-based database approach enabling data management of heterogeneous sensor data employing semantic technologies for data representation, storage, and query processing. Although this pioneering project powers only a single sensor network and a single application from the agricultural domain, principles used in this work can be used for the fusion of sensor data collected across many diverse sensor networks.

The multi-layered organization is depicted in Fig. 4. Authors created their own ontology exported in the OWL language respecting the application specification by defining classes, attributes, and constraints. Defined constraints address relationship conditions that imply some of the actuation functions. Jena API [41] is used for keeping the ontology model in the

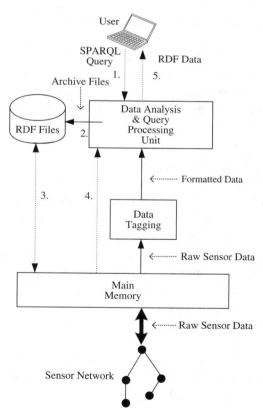

Fig. 4. The ES3N multi-layered approach architecture.

memory, storing data to the database, and query processing. After arrival, sensor data are tagged with timestamps, added as resources to the onto- logy model, and stored to the data repository as daily Resource Descrip- tion Framework (RDF) [3] collections, but temporarily stay in the main memory. The SPARQL is used as query language and it is executed by the Jena API over the data residing in the main memory. If query requests some historical data, ES3N (Exploiting Semantics in Sensor Networks for Silos) will import appropriate RDF files from the database repository into the memory model and perform requested query. Users are able to pose three types of queries: exploratory, monitoring, and range queries. Exploratory queries target a record at a specific date and time, monitoring queries return all RDF records collected at certain date, and range queries allow search- ing for some records made at certain time interval while satisfying specified attribute conditions. An appropriate application interface is developed for an efficient representation of query results.

Authors are aware of the ES3N's limitations due to its simplicity. They are considering potential improvements by using more powerful RDF–based storage.

As one of first works on semantic sensor networks, this architecture suffers from lack of scalability (due to the centralized storage access), support for streaming data, limited flexibility, and extensibility as a consequence of a poor information model that addresses only one application domain.

5.1.2 *The Query Translation Architectures*
5.1.2.1 CSIRO SSN

Li and Taylor [14] from CSIRO ICT Center, Australia, proposed a semantic service-oriented framework in 2008, focusing on the query rewriting tech- nique. The architecture exposes a semantic sensor service through a web service interface with applying declarative semantics. The research is moti- vated by the observation that query processing in sensor networks is very specific due to the constraints of sensor devices, the variable sampling rates of sensor data, and the mobility of sensors.

Proposed architecture shown in Fig. 5 tries to solve several identified challenges and objectives for providing efficient semantic sensor network services such as semantics of capability modeling, wireless sensor networks' (WSN) power management, maintenance of sensor network state, data per- sistence, handling of events and responses, programming issues, and security aspects.

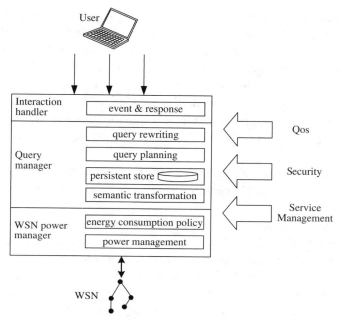

Fig. 5. The semantic sensor network service framework proposed by the CSIRO.

The semantic sensor service system is constituted of the core component, *the service proxy*, which is organized into three layers: *the interaction handler*, the *query manager*, and *the WSN power manager*. The *service proxy* is a mediator between users and WSNs using functionalities of *the interaction handler*. The next stage in the service stack is query processing performed by *query rewriting*, *query planning*, with the support of *persistent store* and *semantic transformation*. The process of efficient query processing is achieved by consideration of the *energy consumption policy* and *power management* strategies managed in the *WSN power manager*. The aspects as *Quality of Service (QoS), security*, and *service management* are applied to all components. The service management includes operations such as management of service life-cycle, service registration, invocation, and closure.

A semantic approach is present in the aspects of describing sensor network state and sensor capability models in order to provide more information about technical issues of sensors and their observations, measured phenomena, and static parameters of sensor networks as well as their dynamical changes. The OWL is used for describing used ontologies.

The main focus in the framework is query optimization regarding energy conservation at the sensor network level. A query rewriting method at compile-time with applying unification-based propagation optimization is proposed. This technique utilizes information about sensor network hardware and software, declaratively expressed in Snlog [44], the WSN programming language. The optimization is achieved through several techniques. Compacting queries code results in less computation on the sensor nodes and thus more energy will be saved. Also messages will be routed only to the relevant nodes. Minimization of storage requirements on the nodes is done by addressing only relevant nodes and by removing redundancy in the code executed on the nodes.

Authors have plans to further investigate query optimization to better handle unpredictable WSN characteristics, as well as energy and bandwidth limitations.

In this work, sensor network issues other than query rewriting are only declaratively described, and hence it is hard to assess at the advantages and drawbacks of this architecture. Applied semantics is focused only on sensor nodes capabilities. Generally, the impression is that the architecture is sensor level centered and end-users are not able to interact with the system using application-domain concepts utilizing semantic-based techniques.

5.1.2.2 *SPARQL*STREAM

This research was done by Calbimonte et al. [22] at Polytechnic University at Madrid and University of Manchester in 2010. They investigated ontology-based access to relational streaming data sources, including sensor networks, through declarative continuous queries. The solution aims to provide ability to users to pose queries over ontology, and to get results in the RDF format. Internally, the ontology queries will be translated to query language of the relational data source, and relational query results will be transformed again from the relational format to the RDF. The motivation application scenario is based on emergency planner application for detection and response to forest fire in Spain.

The solution relies on two existing technologies. The first one is Relational to Ontology (R2O) mapping [45] that defines relationships between relational and ontology schemes. There are several possible cases for mapping operations. In *direct mapping* a single relation maps to an ontology class, relational attributes maps to ontology instance property values, and for each row in the relation, a new ontology instance will be generated; *join/union* handles situations when several relations map to one ontology class; *projection* is used when all relational attributes are not required for the mapping and some of them are ignored; *selection* operation extracts subset of relational

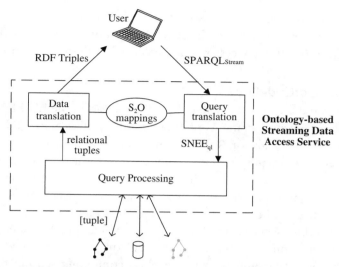

Fig. 6. The ontology-based access to streaming data sources approach.

rows for producing related ontology instances. The continuous query language SNEEql [46], an extension of the SQL, is used for processing data streams. The SNEEql can be used for querying event-streams (tuples are produced when an event occurs), acquisitional-streams (tuples are produced at defined time interval), and stored data.

The architecture of this approach is shown in Fig. 6. The service accepts queries expressed in an extension of the SPARQL for querying RDF streams called SPARQL$_{STREAM}$. Authors developed S2O, an extension of the R2O, which is used for expressing mappings between terms of ontologies to terms of data streams in order to enable *query translation* into continuous query language SNEEql. The evaluator performs distributed *query processing* over sensor networks and relational data sources. This technique supports both push- and poll-based sensor data gathering, in-network query processing, and other data sources specifics. The *Data translation* component converts returned query results into ontology-based streams.

Authors emphasized that this was the first step toward a framework for the integration of distributed heterogeneous streaming and stored data sources through ontological models. Further improvements assume support for more data sources.

This research focuses on the process of translation of SPARQL$_{STREAM}$ into SNEEql with specifying the appropriate syntax and semantics. The improvement of this approach is geared toward data fusion of streaming and archived data, as well as acquisitioned and event-based data. We can also notice that issues like support for sensors mobility and Radio-frequency Identification (RFID) devices are not concerned in this architecture.

5.1.2.3 SemSorGrid4Env

This work was done by Gray et al. [47] in 2011 as part of the EU FP7 (European Union's Seventh Framework Programme) project SemSorGrid4Env (Semantic Sensor Grids for Rapid Application Development for Environmental Management) [48]. This is an effort to solve a real application scenario when the application context requires integration and correlation of data from multiple autonomous sensor networks and other data sources. One of such demanding applications is an environmental monitoring, for example a coastal flooding scenario used in this implementation. This architecture powers the decision support system by translating ontology-based queries to queries over data sources, which enables combining sensing data, the stored database data, the real-time traffic data feed, the weather forecast data, etc. Authors proposed a generic service architecture that employs semantic technologies to enable interaction between various service components and interpretation of such heterogeneous data using application-domain concepts.

The first step in this implementation was the identification of important requirements that should be addressed with the proposed architecture. These requirements include: precise definitions of event conditions, correlation and integration of heterogeneous data sources, discovery of relevant data sources, and efficient presentation and control of information. For data representation of such complex information spaces, the ontology model is composed of several different ontologies covering various domains. Upper ontologies SWEET [37] and DOLCE+DnS Ultralite [39] are used for enabling interoperability with other ontologies. Sensor infrastructure related ontologies involve sensor networks related ontology (the W3C's SSN ontology [36] is used), ontologies specifying the services and the datasets provided by the infrastructure, as well as metadata scheme about relations and relational streams. External data sources related ontologies are responsible for addressing the geographic and the administrative regions needed in the application scenario. Domain relevant ontologies include the flood emergency planning ontology. All ontologies are implemented in OWL.

The proposed architecture is depicted in Fig. 7 and consists of the services distributed in three tiers, although a certain service is able to call any other services from a different tier. Internal architecture services comply

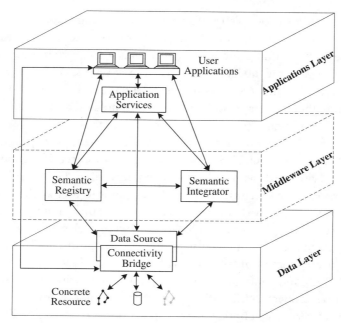

Fig. 7. Conceptual view of the SemSor4Grid service architecture.

with web service standards. However, in order to allow the discovery and the usage of external services that do not follow standard web service specification, the architecture uses semantically annotated property documents which describe non-functional properties of a service, for instance data sets and their features provided from the service. The *Data Tier* contains various data source services, which interact with raw data using their natural query processing languages, for example SQL for relational data, and SNEEql [46] as a continuous query language for sensor data. The *Data source services* publish a property document about the data that they provide, and the supported operations like querying, retrieving, and subscribing to data. A data source service may publish multiple datasets described with spatial–temporal and thematic properties and with its schema if it is appropriate. The *Middleware Tier* comprises two types of services. The *Semantic Registry Service* which supports the registration and the discovery of relevant services based on their service property documents. It keeps a repository of property documents and offers search and access functions through stSPARQL [49] (extension of SPARQL for querying spatial–temporal data) queries by using terms from the domain ontologies. The *Semantic Integrator Service* maintains an integrated view and ontological-based access to the heterogeneous data sources. It accepts queries expressed using concepts from the ontologies, consults the registry service regarding interaction mechanism for certain data sources, translates the received query to a set of data source specific queries, and assembles returned answers into ontological instances. This service is able to perform distributed query processing over the integrated data sources. The *Application Tier* provides the application services that enable to user applications a resource-oriented view of the underlying service-oriented architecture. With using a REST interface, the application services supply web applications with the data formats they can process (GML, GeoJSON, HTML). While providing the semantic integrated viewpoint to user applications, the applications services rely on the property document mechanism provided by the integrator services in order to locate and exploit relevant service.

For the next features authors plan to implement a push-based data transfer through the architecture, integration with existing services as specified in the OGC SWE [2], and configurable mechanism for supporting REST services.

The presented work efficiently solves the problem of various data sources fusion. However, we can notice that the data streams processing is limited to the processing capabilities of corresponding query languages and thus it lacks in the ability to apply complex processing functions and create complex data streams by combining multiple processing.

5.1.3 Sensor Virtualization Architectures
5.1.3.1 GSN

The GSN (Global Sensor Network) was developed by Aberer et al. [18] at EPFL, Switzerland in 2006. It is a middleware layer that enables fast and flexible deployments of sensor networks while abstracts the implementation of underlying heterogeneous technologies.

The key abstraction in the system is a virtual sensor, used for specification of sensor data streams or data streams received from other virtual sensors. Data streams in GSN are sequences of tuples with timestamp values. A virtual sensor may have several input data streams and provides only one output stream. The specification of a virtual sensor is provided with a declarative deployment descriptor. It involves the description of metadata for identification and discovery, the structure of data streams which is consumed or produced by the virtual sensor, processing of data streams in the virtual sensor specified in SQL language, and other functional properties such as data persistence, error handling, and physical deployment. In order to connect to the GSN, developers should implement an appropriate wrapper for their

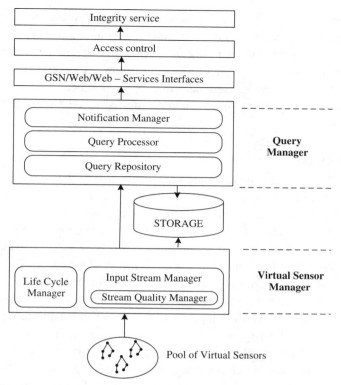

Fig. 8. The GSN container architecture.

data streams. There are several already implemented wrappers, for instance for TinyOS devices. It is possible to combine sensor data streams with stored data. The production of the output stream is event-driven and processing is done when the input data stream arrives. There are several options for reducing input streams data rate during processing in order to prevent over-loading the system. The key component of GSN architecture is the GSN container shown in Fig. 8, where virtual sensors are deployed and managed. GSN containers communicate with each other in a peer-to-peer fashion using standard Internet protocols, thus creating decentralized organization with efficient scalability. Internal architecture of a GSN container is a layered one. The *Virtual Sensor Manager* is a layer responsible for managing virtual sensors, their input streams and production of output streams. In the *Query Management* layer, queries are processed and their results are delivered to consumers. Also, a separate layer manages interaction with the GSN con-tainer by providing appropriate interfaces.

This solution provides a global-scale platform for an easy integration of various sensor networks, while simultaneously achieving high performance. However, the processing capability of supplied query language is low, and end-users have to do additional processing in order to extract more information from data streams. Generally, due to the absence of data semantics, the interoperability is low, and users are required to deal with mostly raw data.

5.1.3.2 SENSEI

The SENSEI [50] was a large-scale project funded by the European Commission within the FP7 (Seventh Framework Programme) and included 19 institutions from industry, universities, research centers, and small-to-medium sized enterprises across Europe. Since this is a large project attempting to offer a comprehensive solution and addresses many issues and challenges as mentioned in Section 2, a detailed description will be given. The project commenced at the beginning of 2008 and lasted to 2011, with the goal of achieving the following outcomes: "a highly scalable and secure architecture framework with corresponding protocol solutions that enable easy plug and play integration of a large number of globally distributed Wireless Sensors & Actuator Networks (WS&AN) into a global system—providing support for network and information management, security, privacy and trust and accounting; an open service interface and corresponding semantic specification to unify the access to context information and actuation services offered by the system for services and applications; efficient WS&AN island solutions consisting of a set of cross-optimized and energy aware protocol stacks." This will facilitate the horizontal re-use of the sensing, actuation and processing resources for a large number of services and applications across a variety of business domains. The SENSEI architecture and the corresponding mechanisms should promote an open market place for providers of real-world information/actuation resources and interested consumers. The application domains that SENSEI addresses include transport, a smart city, buildings and homes, health care, security, asset management, entertainment, etc. It is anticipated that the results of this project will contribute to the shaping of Future Internet standards.

On a high level the SENSEI architecture follows a layered model with three major horizontal layers, as shown in Fig. 9. SENSEI defines a *(Real World) Resource Layer* on top of a *Communication Service Layer*, which is the connectivity ground. The *Communication Services* include the internal *WS&AN communication services* and they are partly addressed in the SENSEI.

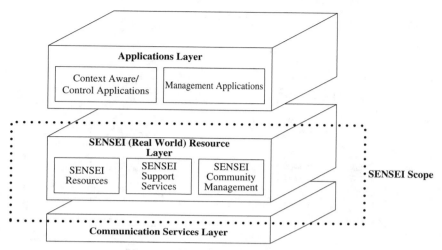

Fig. 9. High-level overview of the SENSEI architecture.

On the *Application Layer* multiple diverse applications and services gain unified access to real-world information (through sensing/context services) and interaction capabilities (through actuation/control service) via interfaces provided by the *SENSEI Resource Layer*. The *SENSEI Resource Layer* also encompasses *SENSEI Support services* that consist of the following components: the *Execution Manager* that enables discovery and supports long-term interactions (sessions), and the *Semantic Query Resolver* provides a function for the composition and dynamic creation of SENSEI Resources. *SENSEI Community Management* set of functions includes user account management, identity management, and security and privacy functions implemented through a novel Authentication, Authorization and Accounting (AAA) architecture. This AAA architecture is based on client credentials and produces an access control decision for the provider.

The central concept in the SENSEI architecture as well as in the *Resource Layer* (see Fig. 10) is a *Resource* and it represents a basic abstraction of devices such as sensors, actuators, processors, or software components. A *Resource* can range from a simple concept (single node parameter), to a complex one (composition of multiple sensors). Resources can be categorized as *physical resources* (sensors, actuators, or combinations of these) which monitor or affect the physical world, and *virtual resources* (typically software components) which affect the virtual world or process the physical world resource information. A *Resource* is described by an associated *Resource Description*. The device hosting a resource is referred to as the *Resource Host* (for example sensor nodes, mobile

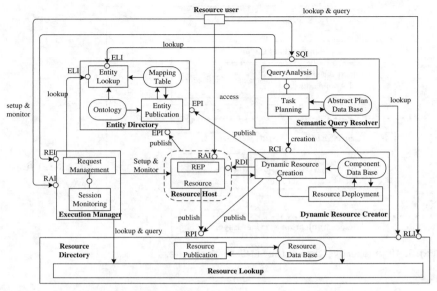

Fig. 10. The SENSEI resource layer architecture.

phones, or some access points). *Resource End Point* (REP) is the software process which represents the physical resource, and can be addressed by a unique Uniform Resource Identifier (URI). It is executed on a device called *REP host*, and has to provide the *Resource Access* function that implements *Resource Access Interfaces* (RAIs) and optionally a *Resource Publication* (RP) function that implements the *Resource Publication Interface* (RPI) by publishing the related *Resource Description*. There may be also multiple REPs to access the same *Resource*, either providing the same RAIs or different ones.

Finally, resources may be associated with one or more real-world entities. Examples of real world entities (also known as *Entities* or *Entities of Interest (EoI)*) are persons, places, or objects that are considered relevant to provide a service to users. A *Resource* provides information or interaction capabilities concerning associated *Entities*.

Resource Users are typically context-aware applications that require real-world information, applications that require real-world actuation, management applications that are used for the management of one or more WS&AN islands, or composite *Resources* that make use of other *Resources*. A *Resource User* interacts with a *Resource* via the *Resource endpoint* (REP) using the *Resource Access Interface* (RAI). For interaction between *Resource Users* and some *Resources* a rendezvous mechanism is implemented in the *Resource Directory*. *Resource Users* are able to look up the *Resource Directory* via *Resource*

Lookup Interface (RLI), to discover registered *Resources*, whose RP functions are stored in the *Resource Database*.

The *Entity Directory* maintains the associations and dependencies between real-world *Entities* and *Resources*. The *Entity Directory* complements the *Resource Directory* in that the focus of the *Resource Directory* is on *Resources* themselves while the *Entity Directory* focuses on *Entities*.

The *Semantic Query Resolver* (SQR) receives queries from users interested in particular *Resources* or *Entities of Interest*. These queries are analyzed by the *Query Analysis* function and recursively decomposed into (a set of) subqueries. For each of these subqueries resources are needed to provide the required functionality, which results in the creation of the *Task Plan* and if all *Resources* are available, the *Task Plan* becomes the *Execution Plan*.

Yet in some cases, *Resources* required for answering a request may not exist. In this case the SQR can check, whether it is possible to dynamically create such a *Resource*. *Resource Template Descriptions* (RTDs), stored in the *Resource Directory*, are used for the dynamic creation of non-instantiated *Resources*. RTDs are published by *Resource Hosts* that offer the dynamic creation of the *Resources*. The Resource Creation functionality of the *Resource Host* internally looks up the required code identified through the *Resource* (Template) ID and instantiates the *Resource* with the provided parameters, creating an REP at the same time. The *Resource Host* can also register the newly created REP/*Resource* with the *Resource Directory* and the associated *Entity of Interest* to the *Entity Directory*.

The functions of the execution management system component are implemented by the *Execution Manager*. Using the *Request Execution Interface* (REI), the *Semantic Query Resolver* can invoke the *Execution Manager* to process requests for real-world information and actuation tasks. A *Request Management* function keeps track of the incoming queries and invokes appropriate *Resources*. Additionally, it can set up sessions between *Resource Users* and *Resources* in cases of long lasting requests (e.g., events).

Information Model: Resources in the SENSEI domain can provide sensor level information as well as the context information about the entities of the real world modeled by the *Information Model*. Allocation resources are also modeled by another model. *Resources* are conceptually modeled by the *Resource Model*, which contains at least one associated *Resource Description* encoded in an XML format, and several *Operations* offered for interactions with the *Resource*. Operation description provides syntactic information about access, and may also have semantic information used for automatic interpretations of the operations' inputs, outputs, pre-conditions and post-conditions. The *Information model* includes a three level data abstraction: *Raw Data*, the *Observation and Measurement* (O&M), and *Context Information*. The *Raw Data layer* refers to data obtained from sensor nodes and may be enriched with specific metadata (units, Quality of Information). The *O&M layer* is similar to the OGC SWE [2] with the improvement that is based on the SENSEI SensorData Ontology and enables addition of any type of metadata, which is an improvement compared to the approach described in [7]. The *Context Information* layer models high-level context-related data about *Entities of Interests* and their properties. The *Context Information* can also include QoI parameters, as well as cost parameters. The Information model is implemented using an ontology representation through RDF. Information can be transformed across layers, and *Resource Users* can specify levels of information that they need.

System interaction: SENSEI supports several use case interactions. In the basic one the developer is able to find the required resources through the rendezvous functionality of the *Resource Directory* and to get the required information for direct runtime interaction with the *Resource* based on RAI description. For mobile resources, by using the *Resource Identifier, Resource Users* can look up the current locator of the *Resource* in the *Resource Directory* at runtime and interact with it as before. Another supported use case is when the set of resources is not known at design time, but has to be determined at runtime. The *Semantic Query Resolver* allows *Resource Users* to issue declarative requests specifying what context or sensor information is required or what actuation task is to be executed. The *SQR* then analyzes the request and finds resources that can be used to satisfy the request including Quality of Information and Quality of Actuation requirements, and it may invoke dynamic resource creation if needed. Alternatively, the *Execution Manager* can execute the request on behalf of the *Resource User*. In a simple one-time request scenario, the *Execution Manager* directly executes the request and returns the information. In the long-term subscription scenario, the *Execution Manager* sets up sessions between the *Resources* and the *Resource User* according to the execution plan. The *Execution Manager* only handles the control aspects, whereas the data flow happens directly between the *Resources* and *Resource Users* and thus enables scalability with such decentralization. During a long-term request the *Execution Manager* can monitor the state of important aspects, and if a relevant change is detected, the execution plan may be changed without intervention of the *Resource User*.

The *SENSEI Plug-and-Play (PnP)* functionality defines how SENSEI and Non-SENSEI resources are attached to the SENSEI system at the run-time.

This proposed approach is based on a loosely coupled Service-Oriented Architecture and can be viewed as a unifying middleware able to integrate different WS&AN technology-dependent solutions. In SENSEI, different SAN islands implementing different technologies are integrated using homogeneous PnP policies running on *REP Hosts*. So WS&AN islands implementing different resource discovery and mobility management mechanisms, optimal for their particular technology and application domain (UPnP, Bluetooth, SLP, Zigbee), can be integrated into SENSEI through gateways that implement the PnP functionality. Integration of any *Resource* is achieved by two operations: registration of the *Resource* to the *Resource Directory* and optionally to the *Entity Directory* if the *Resource* is linked with a certain *Entity of Interest*, and providing access to the *Resource* by implementing the access functions.

Actuation: SENSEI also enables access to actuation functions of *Resources* by direct access to the actuator REPs, or using the *Semantic Query Resolver* (*SQR*) through a unified actuation interface and advanced actuation functionalities. The *SQR* plans the execution of actuation requests that consist of one or more *Actuation Tasks*. These tasks are expressed in terms of the conditions required for execution of the actuation function. Executing an actuation request is fully symmetric with querying for context or sensor information and the same components and mechanisms are used, with the difference that the actuator resource is typically able to perform only one actuation task at a time and it is necessary to provide conflict resolution for simultaneous actuation tasks requiring a common actuator.

TestBed: The project includes deployment of a Pan-European Testbed system for demonstrating the concrete implementation of the SENSEI services. The core components and resources are installed across Europe at project partners' sites. The REST approach is followed since all SENSEI components expose their services as REST resource, accessible by HTTP protocol using URL identifier and standard methods as GET, POST, PUT, and DELETE. The RESTlet framework [27] is mostly used for implementation components from the *Resource Layer*, WS&AN gateways and *REPs* (native SENSEI, ZigBee, mobile phone based, server based), heterogeneous resources (6loWPAN, ZigBee, IEEE802.15.4 based WS&AN islands), etc. A smart city scenario is used as an example of a realized use case.

The authors recognized several issues that should be extended or improved in the current SENSEI architecture: support for RFID devices, mobile phone based sensing platforms, virtual objects, support for higher dynamicity of the real world environment, and a mechanism for automatic identification of entities of interest and their binding to sensing/actuation resources. Other recognized research opportunities include techniques for the management of a large amount of real world data streams as a caching strategy, and distributed stream processing.

In this project much work has been focused on supporting the easy integration of a large set of sensor/actuators devices, and the way web users can find and obtain information from the real world. However, in our opinion, support for complex functions such as inference of the new knowledge, reasoning over a knowledge base, and ability for users to discover such intelligent functions might be significantly improved. We have also recognized the lack of support for management of historical sensor data, acquisition policy for real-time data streams, and fusion of real-time data with archived data. Yet another desirable feature would be the ability to look-up across large amounts of both raw sensor and contextual data using temporal, spatial, and other attributes.

5.1.3.3 Internet of Things (IoT) Architecture

The Internet of Things (IoT) Architecture [51, 52] is the EU FP7 project commenced in 2010 with a vision of making the physical world accessible over the Internet by providing the interoperability of solutions at the communication level, as well as at the service level across various platforms. It is in effect the continuation of the SENSEI project [50], with an extended list of institutions and stakeholders coming mainly from the business area. Consequently, the requirements are similar to those defined in the SENSEI with an additional focus on the business use case scenarios. The aim of the project is to reuse as much of the state-of-the-art existing frameworks and technologies that comply with IoT vision. Use cases include transportation/logistics, a smart city, a smart factory, retail, eHealth, and environmental monitoring.

Based on an evaluation of the different stakeholders requirements in IoT and the generic scenario, the reference model of the IoT domain view was created and included several key concepts. The generic IoT scenario assumes that the IoT should mediate interaction between a generic user and the *entities* from the physical environment. Physical entities are objects or the environment, e.g., humans, cars, store, and they have digital associations called virtual entities, and can be either active elements (software code), or passive elements (database entry). The association between the physical and digital world is achieved by attaching *devices* to physical entities or placing them in the environment. Devices can be *sensors* that enable monitoring of the physical entities, *tags*, which provide entities identification capabilities, or *actuators*, which can modify the physical state of the entity. *Resources* are software components that provide information about physical entities or enable the controlling of devices. *Storage* is a special type of resource that stores information coming from *resources* and thus provides information about the physical entities. A *Service* provides a well-defined and standardized interface, offering all necessary functionalities for interacting with physical entities and related processes. The *services* may range from low-level exposed functionalities of hosted *resources*, to high-level business-process services that may include invocation of low-level services. Only *services*, *devices*, and possibly *resources* are discoverable, while this is not the case for physical entities. Associations between *services* and *entities* are either static, or dynamic, for example when an *entity* is mobile.

The proposed information model [71] represents a described domain view by addressing the *Entity model*, the *Resource model*, and the *Service model*. In the *Entity model* represented with the OWL-DL, the central concept is an *entity* and can have certain domain attributes, temporal features (time zone, date and time range) and location features (geo coordinates, global and local identifiers). The *Resource model* is built around a *resource* concept that contains properties of location, resource description, access interface, and resource type that is a link to an external sensor ontology (e.g., W3C's SSN). The resource interface type instances include REST [25], service-oriented architecture (SOA), as well as remote procedure calls (RPC). The IoT *Service model* provides infrastructure for enabling IoT users to make a search using terms concerning entities from different domains (see Fig. 11). A *service profile* contains a link to a certain *entity*, as well as to the *resources* that provide *services* about the *entity*. A link to an *entity* can be dynamically inferred. The OWL-S profile's object properties are used for representing a *service profile*. The *service profile* describes services and provides a link between the *Service model* and the *Entity model*, as well as a link to the sensor data ontology model. It has been proposed that the semantic data can be represented in the form of Linked Data [28]. For the purpose of the indexing and searching of the semantically described services a probabilistic machine learning mechanism is considered [29], as well as techniques for reasoning over sensor data and resource descriptions [30].

At the time of writing, the IoT project was at the middle of its specified duration and only the reference architecture was available. The functional decomposition of the IoT reference architecture shown in Fig. 12 is also

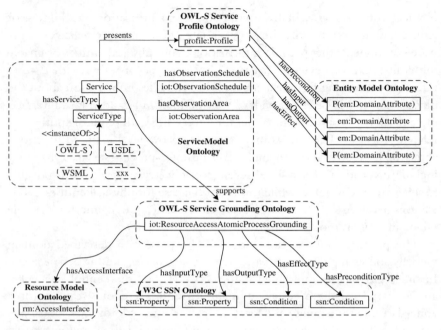

Fig. 11. The IoT semantic service model.

organized based on the key concepts identified in the domain view and consists of the following seven functional groups:

- *Applications:* This group encapsulates the functionalities provided by applications that are built on the top of an implementation of the IoT-A architecture. The business–process modeling component provides functionalities for modeling and execution of IoT-aware business processes.
- *Process execution and service orchestration:* This functionality group organizes and exposes IoT resources and related APIs so that they become available to external entities and services. The service composition and orchestration component provides IoT-service orchestration and flexible process composition with increased quality of information, while the process execution component executes IoT-aware process models modeled in the application layer.
- *Virtual-entity (VE) and information:* This group maintains and organizes information related to physical entities, enables search for services about physical entities and their exposing associated resources. The results of the search for a particular physical entity are addressed by the service related to this physical entity. The Virtual-entity (VE) resolution provides lookup for services exposing resources of virtual entities, discovery of relevant

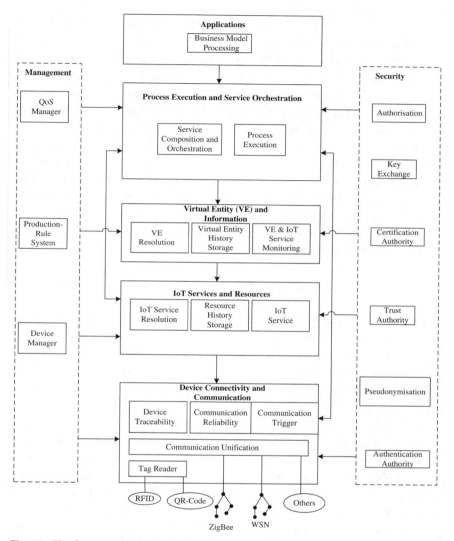

Fig. 12. The functional view of the IoT reference architecture.

services about virtual entities, and updating associations between physical entities and resources. The Virtual-entity history storage keeps historical information about virtual entities. The virtual–entity & IoT–service monitoring maintains associations between virtual entity, resources, and exposed services related to a certain physical entity.

- *IoT service & resource:* This functional block provides access to service descriptions by providing links to the exposed resources and to the func–

tionalities required by services for processing information. Also it notifies application software and services about events related to resources and corresponding physical entities. The IoT-service resolution component maintains information about services based on their descriptions. The resource history storage keeps and processes historical measurements generated by resources. The IoT-service interprets and processes information based on rules or processes defined by a user/application.

- *Device connectivity and communication:* This functional group encompasses a set of methods and primitives for device connectivity and communication. Also, this group contains methods for content-based routing. The device traceability component provides methods for functions of device traceability as checking device authorization, transmission activity, and device roaming. The Communication Reliability provides methods for data flow according to data sensitivity and delay tolerance and includes getting the route for a specific content, transmit delay sensitive information, and setup time-sensitive communication. The Communication Trigger initiates the establishment of communications based on policies, events, or schedules. The Communication Unification component provides a uniform access to IoT devices.

In addition, the *Management* and the *Security* functional blocks provide functionalities to all above functional groups for efficient computational resource management, as well as for access-control, privacy, and identity management.

The final implementation has not yet been provided, while only the reference architecture has. However, it is noticeable where the architectural changes are compared to the SENSEI architecture which is a precursor of IoT architecture. The IoT offers a richer information model that allows an architecture with a more emphasized service related part, as well as separation of SENSEI resources to virtual entities and IoT resources. Also, IoT will provide historical data storage of both virtual entities and resources, which lacks in SENSEI architecture. This implies separated directories for managing resources and virtual entities, which may increase scalability and performance of the system.

5.2 Application-Oriented Architectures
5.2.1 Service-Oriented Architectures
5.2.1.1 TinyREST

This research work describes implementation done by Luckenbach et al. [53] as part of the cooperation between Fraunhofer FOKUS and Samsung

Electronics in 2005. The implementation of a simple prototype TinyREST protocol demonstrates an easy integration of sensor networks into the Internet. The motivated scenario is the smart home/environment system.

The architecture has two main components: the *HTTP-2-TinyREST Gateway* that stands as a middleware and is connected with sensor devices and *Home Server* that stands as a gateway for users as depicted in Fig. 13. The idea is to offer users utilizing standard HTTP messages to interact with sensors and actuators. The GET method is used for getting the state of the sensor. Using the POST method users are able to command an actuator to take some action. With the SUBSCRIBE method users can register their interest for specific sensor/actuators outputs/events and to be notified later. The *Location Manager*, a component hosted on *Home Server* as a part of Home Services Framework, is responsible for mapping sensors/actuators addresses expressed via device or group identifiers to more human readable addresses encoded in URL. The *HTTP-2-TinyREST Gateway* component converts received users HTTP requests to the specific TinyREST messages understandable by sensor/actuator devices. After conversion, the gateway routes those messages to the appropriate device or broadcasts them. One example of the request for taking sensor reading is: <GET>/gatewayIP/roomSensor/temperature. Sensor nodes running on TinyOS platform are devices which can support TinyREST messages. Specifically, in the demonstration prototype, MicaZ sensor nodes are used.

We have included this architecture in this survey because it is one of the first demonstrations of the REST [25] based application interaction, which is later widely accepted as the most suitable interface for Sensor Web applications. The sensors mapping mechanism through URIs is very effective, but discovery services are not provided as well as search over sensor data, data processing and many other functions.

5.2.1.2 OGC SWE

Open Geospatial Consortium (OGC) Sensor Web Enablement (SWE) [2, 21] is an initiative started in 2003 with the goal to enable principles of the Sensor Web. Sensor Web is described as a concept of web-connectable and accessible sensor networks and sensors that are controlled by different owners and have different characteristics. For this goal, several data encodings, models, and service interfaces have been proposed within SWE. This framework has been continually improved, and the new generation SWE 2.0 is described in [84]. The OGC is an international consortium of industry, academic and government organizations who participate in developing open

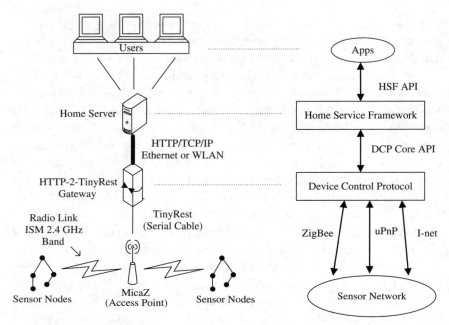

Fig. 13. The TinyREST architecture.

standards for geospatial and location services. The practical implementation of OGC SWE specifications has been done by the EU FP6 project SANY [55], and the 52North Sensor Web Community [54].

The OGC's SWE targets the following functionalities of the Sensor Web: Discovery of sensor systems, observations, and observation processes that match user needs, provision of sensors' capabilities and quality of measurements, users' ability to issue requests for tasking of sensors, subscription to relevant alerts on sensors data that satisfy defined criteria, retrieval of real-time sensor observations, and ability of software to process obtained observations using provided sensor parameters.

In the SWE framework, beside physical sensors, sensors resources may include archived observations, the result of simulations, or processing algorithms. In order to establish aforementioned functionalities, the SWE includes several specifications for data encodings of sensors and their observations, as well as interface definitions of web services:

- **Sensor Model Language** (SensorML) specification contains standard models and XML Schema for describing sensors systems and any processes such as the measurement procedure or the post-measurement processing. This specification also defines common data definitions known as the SWE Common that are used in the entire OGC SWE framework. There are a number of potential usages of SensorML. It can be used for discovery of sensors and sensor systems based on providing rich metadata. On-demand processing of observations can be executed by parties who do not have any knowledge about the sensors, but only a description of the process encoded in SensorML. The entire life span of an observation from the production over the processing to the interpretation can be described in SensorML, and some parts reused later, or simulated. Other SWE services such as SOS, SAS, and SPS can be established based on a SensorML description. Other features include the development of plug-n-play sensors and autonomous sensor networks, and archiving of fundamental sensor parameters. The main concept in the SensorML is a process, which can be either physical or non-physical. The process has inputs, outputs, and parameters, where all of them are expressed using SWE Common data types. Additionally, the process can have various metadata. Individual processes could be further composed into a complex process that is either a *ProcessChain* or a *System,* a physical equivalent of a *ProcessChain*. Currently the work on SensorML 2.0 is still in progress, but some planned features are known. These include a property inheritance hierarchies mechanism for reducing the size of sensor metadata descriptions, and an extension with the precise and well-defined description of a sensor's protocol and interface. Furthermore, the SWE Common 2.0 has been extracted in the separate specification.

- **Observation & Measurement** (O&M) comprises of a standard model and XML Schema for encoding measured sensor data. The central concept in the O&M is an *Observation* that is an act of observing a feature of interest property which results in producing a value. The feature represents some identifiable object that will be observed. The value is the result of a procedure which can be a sensor, observer, analytical procedure, simulation or numerical process. This procedure is described as a process in SensorML. The *Observation* structure contains properties referring to the following resources: the feature of interest, the used procedure for producing the result value, the observed property, the result and the quality of the result value, and temporal and other parameters describing the observation event. The spatial property of the observation is given by a location property of the feature of interest. The type of observation result is "any," which means it can be modeled using any encoding. For achieving better interoperability, the result part of the observation should be encoded using SWE Common data types. In O&M version 2.0 the conceptual model and encoding implementation are divided and the O&M 2.0 conceptual model has become an ISO international standard after harmonization with ISO foundation models. Further on, temporal properties of the observation have been slightly redesigned, and a spatial profile has been added. Additionally, the O&M 2.0 contains a new property for expressing relationships between observations, while the container for a collection of observations has been removed from the data model.

- **Transducer Model Language** (TML) refers to a conceptual approach and XML Schema for supporting real-time data streaming to and from sensor systems, and related metadata. This specification is rarely used, and there will be no further development of it within the SWE 2.0.

- **Sensor Observation Service** (SOS) includes the specification of standard web service interface for requesting, filtering, and retrieving observations and sensor system information. SOS unifies the way of interaction with remote, in-situ, fixed, and mobile sensors. It particularly employs O&M specification for modeling sensor observation responses and SensorML for sensors and sensor systems. SOS provides sensor system observations collections through *Observation Offerings*, characterized with the sensor system which has produced observations, spatial-temporal parameters of observations, phenomena that are sensed, and a region that is the subject of sensor observations. Typical operations include *GetObservation* for obtaining observations, *DescribeSensor* for getting sensor description, and *GetCapabilities* for retrieving the service metadata. The main advancements in SOS 2.0 include increased interoperability. This is achieved by introducing mandatory temporal and spatial operators, as well as by using O&M 2.0 as a mandatory and default response format. Moreover, SOS 2.0 brings new improvements such as capabilities redesign, result handling redesign by adding new operations for result insertions and result retrieval, and facilitating usage of SOS by invoking selected operations using HTTP GET and by passing parameters as key-value pairs in the URL of the service endpoint.

- **Sensor Planning Service** (SPS) provides a standard web interface for requesting user driven acquisitions and tasking of sensors as well as the submission of the collection of requests to sensors and configurable processes. The provided interface enables the complete process of controlling, planning, and tracking the status of sensor tasks. Typical operations are *Submit* for submitting a task, *GetStatus* for getting status of submitted tasks, and *GetFeasibility* for checking if a task is feasible for a sensor. SPS is often used together with SOS and WNS, while for describing the planning parameters users use SWE Common data types. SPS 2.0 has several changes and improvements. First, SPS 2.0 is in accordance with a new SWE Service model which assumes that all operations are derived from the abstract request type defined in SWES and tasking parameters conform to the SWE Common 2.0 data model. Second, the task handling has been redesigned as well as the status model. Third, SPS is not relying anymore on WNS for asynchronous communication with clients, but supports a publish/subscribe model.

- **Sensor Alerting Service** (SAS) includes a standard web service interface for publishing and subscribing to alerts from sensors. SAS runs a pattern-matching algorithm on received sensor data and upon satisfying an alert condition, it distributes an alert notification to subscribed clients. These alerts may refer to the detection of various events, for example when measured values are above the threshold value, detection of motion or specific pattern in sensor observations, or even detection of certain sensor status like low battery, shutdown or similar. SAS enables sensors to dynamically connect to the service and publish their metadata and observation data, while users are able to define their own event conditions. Also, SAS provides available alerts to which clients can subscribe. SAS delivers alerts through WNS, and using Extensible Messaging and Presence Protocol (XMPP). The response of SAS is encoded in a simple format defined within the SAS, and it is not aligned with O&M. The SWE 2.0 introduces several improvements primarily by offering a publish/subscribing mechanism which enables eventing. The development of SAS has been replaced by a new service called the *Sensor Event Service*. The main strategic orientation is to rely on existing protocols and standards for asynchronous notification. Also the O&M is used for response encodings, which improves interoperability with other SWE services. A new advancement includes the introduction of two new filter languages, *Event Pattern Markup Language* (EML) and the *OGC Filter Encoding* (FES). The EML enables detection of relations between events and even the possibility to derive new information.

- **Web Notification Service** (WNS) contains specification for a standard web service interface for asynchronous delivery of messages or alerts from any other web service. The WNS provides two types of asynchronous notifications with and without expecting a response from the user provided with the information. There are several possible communication channels including SMS, email, instant message, http-call (HTTP POST), XMPP, and others.

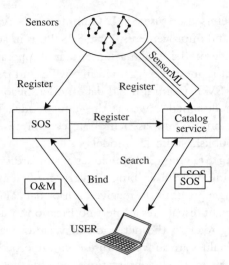

Fig. 14. SWE services and encodings interactions.

There are several usage scenarios for users in order to obtain desirable sensor observation using SWE services. A *catalog service* offers discovery functions of sensors which register themselves to the catalog via SensorML description, or a SOS registers those sensors to the catalog. An interaction starts when the user issues a search request to the catalog requesting certain sensor observation data (see Fig. 14). The catalog returns to the user a list of SOS instances which are able to provide such observations. The user connects to the SOS and gets observation data encoded in O&M. If the catalog does not respond with any SOS instance upon user's request, then the user may search for an appropriate SPS that could task desirable sensors in order to produce the observation data that the user needs. If the catalog returns an SPS, the user submits a task to the SPS, which forwards it to the sensor. The SPS can notify the user about data availability either immediately, or with a certain delay using asynchronous service WNS. The user receives information on how to obtain observation data using the appropriate SOS. The last scenario covers the situation when a user is interested in getting the observation that satisfies some conditions. In that case, the user gets information about an appropriate SAS from a catalog and subscribes to that SAS. The SAS will then continuously receive observations from sensors, perform checking with the subscription condition and alert the user if the match is found. The alert is delivered to the user either directly or via WSN.

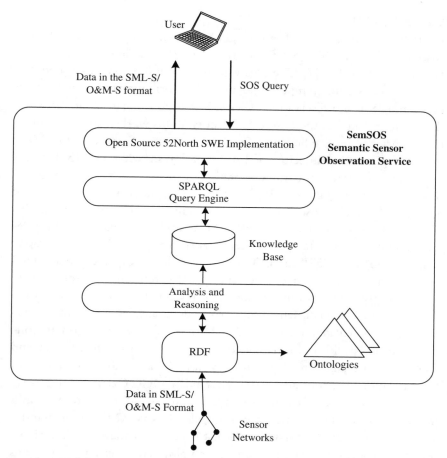

Fig. 15. A High-level view of the SemSOS architecture.

By providing this set of specifications, the OGC's SWE aims to achieve interoperability among sensor networks and sensors mostly by syntactic specification, without providing any semantics of data. Because of this, there are many efforts to extend this framework with either semantic annotations, or with providing an ontology that relies on the OGC' SWE data model. Furthermore, recent architectures use the REST [25] style of interaction with users instead of standard web service, in fact an implementation in this direction has been done in SOS 2.0. We can also notice that there is no specification supporting service composition feature through relevant queries.

5.2.1.3 SemSOS

In 2009 Henson et al. [56] from Wright State University proposed a framework that extends OGC SWE specifications [2] by adding semantic annotations to sensor data [7]. The idea is to provide more context-related data which contains spatial, temporal and thematic information to the applications consuming Sensor Observation Service. Semantic annotations are based on descriptions stored in the ontology. Authors of this work called this semantically enriched service Semantic Sensor Observation Service (SemSOS).

The high-level architecture of this approach is shown in Fig. 15. The first extension is related to the implementation of OGC Observation and Measurements encodings in OWL [5], because the OWL allows for the creation of a concept hierarchy as well as placing constraints on the relationships. This representation is called O&M-OWL. Specifically, this extension includes spatial, temporal, and feature concepts taken from the GML (Geography Markup Language) [57], the OWL-Time ontology [58], and the accepted domain ontology respectively. For the spatial extension, concepts such as point, polygon, and coordinates are used. Temporal concepts include time instant and time interval which supports interval queries containing operators like *within*, *contains*, and *overlaps*. The feature concepts depend on the concrete domain-specific ontology, and for instance concepts such as blizzard and snow storm are taken from an ontology describing weather conditions. In order to embed semantic annotations in standard OGC O&M-XML format, authors use XLINK [43] that enables the creation and description of links among resources. This representation is called O&M-XML and its translation to and from the O&M-OWL format is straightforward. For inferring a new knowledge, a rule-based reasoning is employed over sensor observations data using Jena's internal rule engine [41]. The new derived relationships can then be used to query high-level feature concepts in SemSOS.

The practical implementation of the SemSOS is achieved through the overriding of 52'North SOS [54] implementation of data access functions by replacing those functions with Jena API [41]. The replaced functions are used for storing and accessing the O&M-OWL data. The stored ontology instances are queried via SPARQL [6] which is constructed from the incoming SOS query parameters. The query results are represented as RDF graphs annotated in O&M-OWL. Finally, the last step in the process is the translation of RDF data to the O&M-XML format that respects OGC SWE syntax and contains semantic annotations for clients who are able to interpret it.

Authors have declared their plans to incorporate an abductive reasoning engine in this implementation because it is described as "the inference to the best explanation." Furthermore, they have plans to extend other OGC SWE specifications with semantic annotations as SensorML, Sensor Planning Service, and Sensor Alert Service.

This proof of concept implementation is not a comprehensive solution at this stage. The idea to extend standard OGC SWE encodings with semantic annotation looks like a promising way for the fast and efficient provision of the semantically enriched services to end-users with respecting related standard specifications. It is questionable how this implementation will scale in a situation with increased volume and types of sensor data, since double data transformation per one service request may incur significant processing overhead. Also the query engine and the knowledge base would easily become a bottleneck in the system. Additionally, handling of sensor data streams is not addressed in this approach.

5.2.2 Service Composition Architectures
5.2.2.1 Hourglass

Hourglass is described as an "Internet-based infrastructure for connecting a wide range of sensors, services and application in a robust fashion" and was developed by Shneidman et al. [16] at Harvard University in 2004. The system is designed with a goal to enable a connection over both reliable and unreliable wireless links to sensor nodes, support for access to data and services belonging to isolated sensor networks or an application-specific domain, and an efficient data flow mechanism between data producers and consumers. The demonstrated implementation covers a metropolitan medical scenario.

The key concept in Hourglass is a *circuit* and represents a data path between data consumers and data providers through the system. A *circuit* includes several *services* that perform certain operations on data and implement specified interfaces. These interfaces include functions such as *data consuming, data producing,* while *operators* implement both functionalities. The complexity of underlying sensor networks is hidden by implementing interfaces. For instance, if sensors have limited resources, there is a possibility to interface with the rest of the system through a *data producer proxy* which implements a specific protocol. Also, services can be *generic,* which are used by a wide set of applications, or *application-specific* services, which are intended for use by one application. Typical generic services are the *buffer service* used for buffering data during disconnection and sending buffered data after reconnection, the *filter service* that reduces data flow by applying a filter defined in an appropriate filter expression format (XPATH filters are used in the case of XML data), and *persistent storage services* that enable the saving of data in the storage. Services are organized into *service providers* that encompass one or more nodes and are integrated as units in the system. The *Circuit Manager* is responsible for circuit creation based on the *circuit definition* that is a description of the circuit's internal service interconnections expressed in the *Hourglass Circuit Description Language (HCDL),* an XML form of language. Information about available services and circuits is kept in the *registry* which is a distributed repository. When a service is activated, it registers its properties to the repository. Registered properties include service endpoint information, service *topic* that enables the matching of a desired type of services during search, and *lease time* that is used for the tracking of service liveness. Additionally, service information may contain *predicates* describing conditions that service provided data should comply with.

The process of circuit establishment starts when an application (data consumer in this interaction) creates an unrealized HCDL description of the desired circuit with specifying relevant services. It gets the appropriate set of data producers from a registry, which is used for updating the *circuit definition*, and such a partially realized *circuit definition* is passed to the *Circuit Manager* to realize remaining services. The *Circuit manager* consults the registry based on the set of operators, provided topics, and predicate attributes for appropriate services. If full circuit realization is possible, it contacts all involved services of the circuit and provides them with relevant descriptions necessary for establishing circuit links. Data stream flow is separated from the data control message flow, and data item streams can be associated with multiple circuits in the system. For detecting disconnections, the heart-beat message mechanism is employed. In order to resume normal data flow after reconnection, a *buffering service* can be activated upon disconnection of a certain service provider. An example of a circuit is depicted in Fig. 16.

The authors found that there is a lot of space for improvement of this architecture. Issues include a circuit management, a naming resolution, and efficient content-based routing algorithms during a circuit establishment. Also, the scalability can be increased by involving hierarchical service providers.

This is the first approach that offers the ability to users to declaratively describe a desired service. The provided description mechanism does not seem very expressive and flexible, as might be the case with the semantic-based descriptions. The architecture uses push-based data propagation, and there is no possibility for users to issue an arbitrary search over sensor data that includes poll based data collection. To conclude generally, this architecture

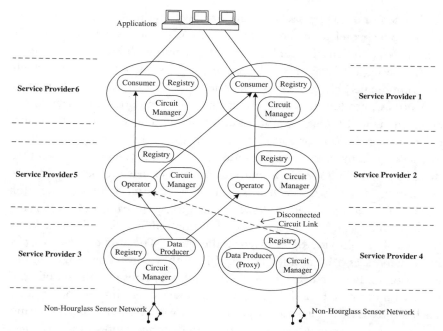

Fig. 16. An example of a circuit in the Hourglass architecture.

offers a good starting point for further extensions and improvements by leveraging semantic technologies.

5.2.2.2 SONGS

In SONGS (Service-Oriented Network proGramming of Sensors) architecture designed by Liu and Zhao [17] at Microsoft in 2005, end-users are able to express requests for certain semantic data streams that are based on a domain-specific ontology. The parking garage scenario is used for demonstrating SONGS implementation.

SONGS is powered by the hierarchical architecture consisting of sensors, *field servers*, and *gateway servers*. Sensors of various types are used to measure the physical environment and to provide data at different rates and with different characteristics. The *field servers* are used to convert raw data received from sensors into the most common and usable formats, such as XML. The *gateway servers* interact with users, process their queries, and contain an intelligent component for solving user requests by converting them into tasks for *field servers*.

The sensor ontology has been developed within this research work. Most of the concepts relate to the application domain, and less about the sensor data. This should enable users to query the system with high-level events.

At the logical level, the architecture provides semantic services which are components able to process semantic input data streams, to add certain semantics, or produce new semantic streams to output ports. The data flow is depicted in Fig. 17. This execution is event-driven. The semantic data streams carry the semantic information relying on the specific domain ontology. Services are composed from semantic services components by connecting their corresponding input and output ports which have to be semantically compatible. There is no need to specify certain services. It is enough for users to issue a query with a desired semantic data stream, and the service planner will try to find a service composition among all available services that is able to provide the answer to the query. The *service planner* that is implemented as a logic inference engine with a constraint programming extension CLP-R, actually converts service descriptions into the set of logic rules with constraints, and decomposes the user's query into set of services. Each service is then assigned to a particular network node while considering certain parameters in order to optimize this service embedding. A *service scheduler* is a component that runs on each node and accepts part of the service composition described with the *micro-server tasking markup language*, or MSTML. It tries to reuse some of the existing service tasks for a new service task and after optimization a new task is scheduled for execution. The execution of service tasks is monitored, and if some resources are changed, the execution can be re-planned by the planner. The inference engine performs backward chaining in order to provide the user query with all constraints satisfied.

The system users are allowed to require the confidence of answer, which is an example of providing the quality of information. This answer confidence depends on the confidence in the detection of basic events, and the subsequent relationship between output and input confidences of particular service components present in the service-composition graph.

The focus of this architecture is on providing high-level information, which completely hides the specifics of the underlying sensor networks and gathered raw sensor data. However, some users are interested in getting information from specific sensors, but the used ontology does not offer ground for interoperability at the sensor data level. Also, this architecture does not scale effectively, since some components such as planner are centralized and should perform demanding computations. Nevertheless, this architecture

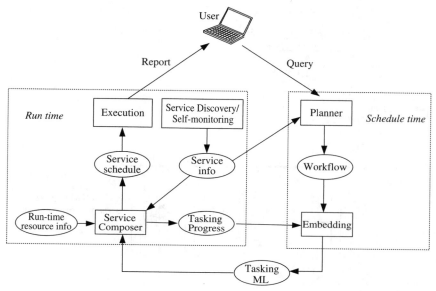

Fig. 17. Data flow in the SONGS architecture.

can be significantly improved by the appropriate separation of the ontology into an upper and sensor related ontology, as well as by increasing scalability capabilities.

5.2.2.3 IBM

Bouilet et al. [59] from IBM proposed an architecture relying on a semantics-based middleware in 2007. The essence of this approach is to enable an automatic application composition by describing the sensor data sources, processing components, and user queries using a semantic model based on terms and relationships taken from an OWL ontology. The motivating scenario is a real traffic service with the goal of providing integrated information from heterogeneous sensor data sources to various users such as drivers, police, and transportation department.

For the implementation of this idea a middleware layer in the System S which is a distributed stream processing system is used. It is shown in Fig. 18.

In this architecture, users pose their inquiries that actually describe the semantics of the desired results. A *planner* is a component responsible for con-structing applications by finding the appropriate combination of data sources and processing elements (PE). The *Data Sources Manager* (DSM) component

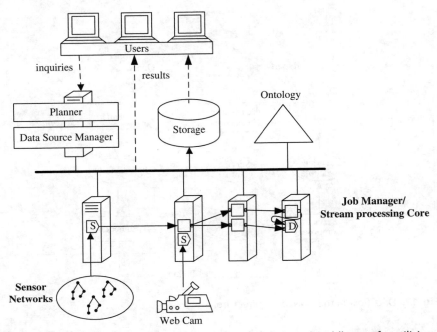

Fig. 18. The architecture of the system S with semantic-based middleware for utilizing.

manages data sources. The *Job Manager* (JMN) deploys applications for execution of a *Stream Processing Core* (SPC).

The semantic model is crucial for the determination of possible interconnection of key components, which are the data sources and the processing elements (PEs). This model is utilized in the semantic application construction. The authors developed their own ontology that covers sensor types and types of produced data, together with temporal and spatial information.

In this work, a data stream is modeled as a continuous stream of Stream Data Objects (SDOs). The semantic description of a data source comprises information of the data elements contained in an SDO, as well as the semantics of those data elements represented as RDF triples which are based on the domain ontology. A *Processing Element* (PE) is semantically described through the semantics of its allowed input streams, as well as the semantics of produced output streams of that PE. For a description of stream requirements a stream pattern is used. This pattern is expressed as a pair of data elements set and their semantics. The authors developed a special language for representing the semantic descriptions of PEs and data sources called Semantic Graph-based Component Description Language (SGCDL).

A process of possible interconnection of data streams and PEs is defined by the matching of stream patterns of PEs' input streams with the description of data streams. This matching is achievable if for every variable in the stream-pattern, a substitution can be found inheritable from the input stream. For finding this matching, description logic program reasoning is used. In effect, the pattern describes how much data and semantics the compatible stream should have, and generally the stream pattern is more specific. An inference process utilizes definitions and relationships from the domain ontology.

The goal of the application's composition process is to produce a processing graph that generates streams that satisfy the semantic stream patterns which represent user or application inquiries for needed information. The stream pattern has a similar syntax as SPARQL. The *planner* is a component responsible for finding streams that satisfy requirements of the stream pattern. The *planner* achieves this process by combining a set of streams with the compatible PEs until it finds a stream produced by some PE which matches the goal stream pattern. The implemented planner works in two phases. In the first phase, it does pre-reasoning on different PEs and their outputs, while trying to generate new facts about the streams. This task of reasoning is OWL-DLP (OWL description logic programs), decidable in polynomial time. The original and the inferred facts about components are translated into a language called SPPL (Stream Processing Planning Language). The SPPL descriptions of different components are persisted and re-used for multiple queries. In the second phase, upon receiving the information request, the *planner* translates the query into an SPPL planning goal that should be produced by the *SPPL solver* component. The *SPPL solver* tries to find the goal stream by connecting appropriate components at the same time respecting their semantic descriptions. At the end, the plan is deployed in the System S stream processing system.

The authors stated that this architecture can be easily extended with new functions if new semantic descriptions used for describing PEs are added to the existing ontology. The results of these experiments are provided and the average response time of the *planner* per one user inquiry is around 2.5 s.

The provided interaction interface is very user friendly, although it is not standard based. However, the experiment results do not indicate satisfactory performance in the case of global-scale deployment. This could be improved if the planner implementation is done in a distributed fashion. Also, there is no support for historical data. In order to provide better interoperability, the used ontology can reuse some of the recommended upper ontologies and available sensor ontologies.

5.2.3 Rule Based Data Transformation Architectures
5.2.3.1 University of Toronto

This architecture proposed by Wun et al. [20] from University of Toronto in 2007 uses the Content-based Publish/Subscribe (CPS) event-driven messaging system, deployed as a middleware for interaction with sensor networks and for semantic-based data processing functions. The prototype deployment is used for environmental monitoring as well as factory equipment monitoring.

The CPS system dispatches received event notifications to clients who are interested in such events. The central component is a *broker*, which accepts publications issued by *publishers*, and tries to forward those publications to appropriate *subscribers* based on their subscriptions. The matching process is based on strict syntax, while publications are expressed in the form of attribute-value tuples and subscriptions are filtering constraints. The semantic extension of CPS used in this system is called S-ToPSS (Semantic-Toronto Publish/Subscribe System) and improves matching by exploitation of concepts and their relationships stored in the domain ontology. Three techniques are used for matching implementation. *Synonym translation* is based on mapping of terms equivalence. *Taxonomy translation* uses hierarchical relationships between terms and enables matching when publications contain more generalized terms than those used in subscriptions. The third technique uses the mapping functions which enable translation of one or more attribute-value tuples of raw data to one or more semantically related attribute-value tuples. This last technique could be used for detection of high-level events. Thus, the work in question gives the example of earthquake detection in the North American region based on measurements from three seismic stations in the US.

The CPS used as a middleware for sensor networks is called Micro-ToPSS, and achieves CPS sensor functions by extending the TinyScript language [60] and its associated Virtual Machine (VM). There is a possibility for using either unscripted or scripted API for applications running on Micro-ToPSS. The unscripted API is related to sensor nodes and efficient data-centric-oriented routing, while the scripting API is a more flexible and dynamic way for developing applications through a set of scripts called handlers. Both APIs provide standard CPS functions for publishing and subscribing to sensor data which can be filtered depending on the application needs.

The architecture of the system is depicted in Fig. 19. The Micro-ToPSS middleware platform is deployed on each sensor node in order to facilitate event-driven data collection within the network respecting application

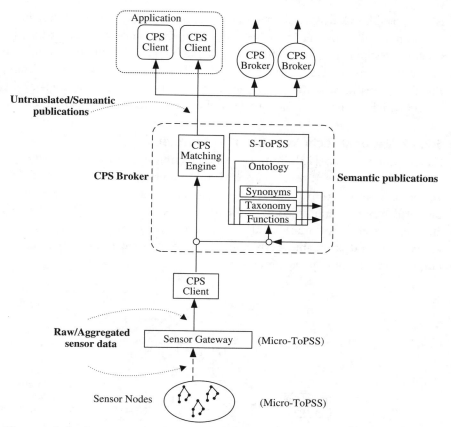

Fig. 19. The architecture and data flow in the system with semantic data fusion based on the content-based publish/subscribe messaging system.

needs. Such data collection is achieved by either issuing subscriptions or by Micro-ToPSS handlers. Collected, aggregated sensor data pass through the *Sensor Gateway* over web service interface, after which they are repackaged by CPS clients into sensor publications and issued to a *broker overlay network*. Brokers run a semantic engine within S-ToPSS, relying on the domain ontology and enable applications to be subscribed to both raw and aggregated data, with added semantics or not. The semantic data fusion is achieved by providing the application with the ability to subscribe for the correlation between data originating from different sensor networks. In this architecture, the application and sensor network interfaces are independent of any ontology definitions and their dynamic changes.

The details regarding data representation format, used ontology, and application interface are not provided. Therefore, a deeper analysis of this research is not possible. Conceptually, the detection of semantic events by utilizing ontology based mapping functions seems effective. Since only event-based streams are supported, it is obvious that this architecture should be extended in order to support fusion of stream-based data and historical sensor data. Thanks to this improvement, functions such as the detection of high-level events which occurred in the past could be offered to users.

5.2.3.2 National Technical University of Athens

Zafeiropoulos et al. [23] from National Technical University of Athens designed this architecture in 2008 with the intention of offering a flexible and extensible solution for heterogeneous sensor data sources integration by performing semantic data transformation based on mapping rules. The architecture employs ontological infrastructure in order to extract a new knowledge, and to enable both high-level events detection by reasoning engine and semantic query processing.

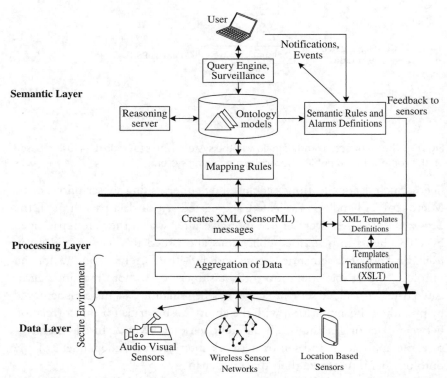

Fig. 20. A modular three-tier architecture based on data transformation by mapping rules.

The overall architecture is divided into three layers as depicted in Fig. 20: the *Data layer*, the *Processing layer*, and the *Semantic layer*. The *Data layer* covers sensor data discovering, collection, data acquisition policy (event-based or polled), and data aggregation. This layer distinguishes three sensor type classes: classical WSN sensors (temperature, humidity, etc.), location-based sensors (GPS, Bluetooth, etc), and multimedia data sources (cameras, microphones). Depending on the sensor class, specific transport protocols for communication with the upper layer are assumed, ranging from TCP/IP based (sockets, HTTP, web services) to secure enabled protocols. The *Processing layer* is responsible for the transformation of the raw sensor data into a more common format such as XML. The XML schema is not fixed, but the OGC SWE specification for data encodings is used as a primary choice. This approach allows the integration of an external solution such as the GSN [18] that also produces XML encoded streams after the processing of raw sensor data.

The *Semantic layer* performs higher-level data processing relying on the pluggable application-specific ontologies. Communication with the *Processing layer* is achieved through a web service interface. Upon arrival, a new message will be processed in the *XML Mapping and Semantic Rules* engine that comprises two set of rules, mapping rules and semantic rules. Both rules are based on the pattern "on *event* if *condition* then *action*." Using the XML mapping rules, XML messages will be converted to the ontology instances, while the semantic rules will be utilized for producing new ontological instances from the existing ones. When all the necessary semantic information is extracted, a *Knowledge Base* is created and manipulated by the *Reasoning Server*, which can also be imported among many available solutions. The manipulation of the ontological model and semantic query processing is implemented by using the Jena engine [41], as well as rule based reasoning.

The described pluggable architecture offers a flexible and extensible platform. The authors have not provided experimental results which are necessary for assessing the performance of this implementation. Passing all sensor data through the central mapping processing unit is the main drawback of this architecture, because applying the rules and conversion of the data format is not a computationally cheap operation. A potential improvement could be achieved with the distribution of mapping components and of the ontology instances repository.

5.2.3.3 SWASN

SWASN (Semantic Web Architecture for Sensor Networks) developed by Huang and Javed [61] at Ericsson and the Royal Institute of Technology,

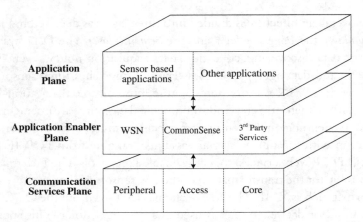

Fig. 21. The technology planes in the CommonSense architecture.

Sweden, in 2008, offers an architecture which utilizes Semantic Web technologies for the purpose of better understanding, interpreting, and sharing of heterogeneous sensor data, their querying, and inferring new information from these data. The SWASN is focused on a specific part of the wider architecture for ubiquitous sensing proposed by Ericsson, CommonSense [62]. A fire emergency example is used for the demonstration purposes.

CommonSense is a multi-tier service-oriented architecture trying to integrate various sensor data sources including standard sensors deployed in WSNs or attached to mobile phones, handheld computers, RFIDs, etc. There are several roles identified in the architecture. *WSN providers* provide data from and control access to sensor networks. *Service providers* are responsible for providing appropriate services to end-users. *CommonSense providers* interconnect other available providers. The architecture is mapped to three technology planes as shown in Fig. 21: *Communication Services, Application Enablers*, and *Applications Plane*. Applications are created using blocks from the *Application Enablers* that include identification services, security services, and information processing services. SWASN addresses the information processing service enablers domain.

The SWASN architecture is separated into four layers (see Fig. 22):

- *Sensor Network Data Sources* consist of heterogeneous sensor networks with gateways used for gathering sensor data.
- The *Ontology Layer* maintains several ontologies for the semantic description of sensor data. There is a possibility for every WSN to have its own ontology. Received sensor data from sensor gateways are mapped into ontology-based data representation. This layer can also contain a context-aware ontology for inferring more knowledge.

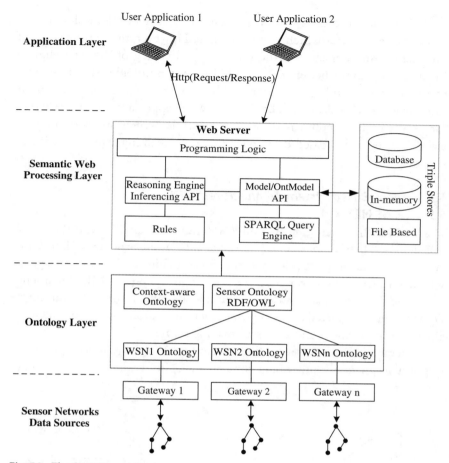

Fig. 22. The SWASN architecture.

- The *Semantic Web Processing Layer* processes semantic data by employing the Jena API [41]. Jena is used for several functions: to produce RDF graphs of the sensor data, to facilitate persistence of sensor data by creating their models either in RDF or OWL, and to enable querying of RDF sensor data via SPARQL. Additionally, for a more high-level information inference mechanism, the reasoning engine contained in Jena is used, as well as a generic-rule engine. In the provided study, a special focus is given to the context data defined in an appropriate context-aware ontology that is utilized in this layer.
- The *Application Layer* contains client applications working with sensor data which are accessed through a standard web server using HTTP protocol.

This architecture allows for the existence of several ontological representations of sensor data which is very flexible. However, the performance of this architecture depends on the processing efficiency of the Jena engine. In order to achieve better interoperability, used ontologies should extend the same upper ontology. Another drawback of this architecture is the poor support for various data modality. The provided application interface allows for only a request-reply based interaction, while asynchronous data delivery driven by event-based data collection and streaming sensor data is not supported.

5.2.4 Agent-Based System Architectures
5.2.4.1 IRIS NET

The IrisNet (Internet-scale Resource-Intensive Sensor Network Services) was designed by Gibbons et al. [15, 63] at Intel and Carnegie Mellon University in 2003 and provides a hierarchical architecture based on agents which enables a common data view through a single XML document. Collected data are partitioned across multiple sites which contain commodity PC machines connected to the Internet. Demonstration applications include a parking space finder and a coastal imaging service.

A hierarchical architecture is depicted in Fig. 23. An *organizing agent* (*OA*) responsible for query processing runs on each site. Potentially, there could

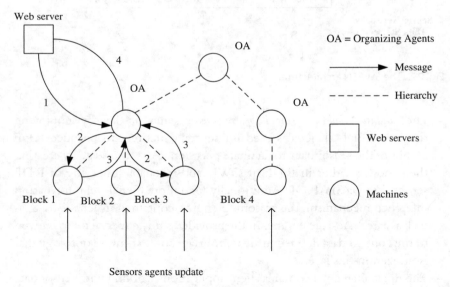

Fig. 23. The hierarchical architecture of the IrisNet.

be several sensing services, but one organizing agent is dedicated to only one sensing service. Each available sensing service corresponds to one specific stored XML document which is distributed in the database and managed by several organizing agents. Other type of agents, called *sensor agents* or *sensor proxies*, collect data from nearby sensors, process them, and send update queries to the site that owns the data, actually to the organizing agents. Additionally, a huge amount of raw sensor data is filtered by *senselets* in the sensing-service fashion. The *senselet* is the execution code, which is run by sensor agents, before an update query is sent to the appropriate host. The scalability of the system is achieved with a large number of sensor proxies. The number of updates that the system is able to handle linearly grows with the number of OAs among which the data are distributed.

In order to enable easy posing queries by users, IrisNet supports XPATH declarative query language for expressing queries over distributed databases which contain fragments of the XML document. The XML data format is chosen because of the heterogeneity and diversity of the sensor data, the ability to change the schema over time and hence to allow dynamic addition and deletion of certain attributes. Since the system should support widely deployed sensor networks, the XML could easily model such hierarchically organized data. The query processing starts when a query is routed to a specific site. An organizing agent queries its local database and cached data, and if it finds that some data are missing, it sends a subquery to the appropriate sites in order to get the necessary data. This process could potentially be recursive, since these sites may further send subqueries to additional sites. The answers to all subqueries are combined into the query result which is returned to the user.

IrisNet has proposed several techniques for optimizing query processing over wide area sensor database:

- Scalable execution of XPATH queries over distributed sensor database by using logical hierarchy of sites.
- Subquery results are cached at a database on the site that receives an answer, thus enabling later reusing either complete or particular data from cached results. A simple cache management policy is used, so the cached data are never removed, but only updated with the fresh copies. There is another possibility to specify the tolerance on query-based consistency for using stale (cached) data in order to quickly answer new queries. The query consistency predicate will consider the timestamp associated with the cached data in order to determine if it is sufficiently fresh.

- Self-starting distributed queries are executed by forwarding queries to the lowest common ancestor (LCA) of the query result, by using DNS-style mappings of site names. The site name is extracted from the query. These DNS lookups are also used to find the IP address of the site that has a missing data.
- A novel query-evaluate-gather (QEG) technique is proposed for detecting which data located on the site is part of the query, and how to obtain missing parts. The XPATH query is actually compiled to the Extensible Stylesheet Language (XSLT) program that is used for querying the database by iterating through the nodes in the document. Depending on the state of the node's status flag, appropriate subqueries should be issued. This compilation of XPATH to the XSLT program can be a significant performance drawback, and certain optimizations should be performed. One of the possible optimizations considered the organizing agent first compiling a dummy XPATH query, and then for real queries, to modify this compiled XSLT program.

Since the mapping of logical nodes to the physical nodes in the hierarchy is not fixed, the processing power of the system could vary depending on the actual architecture. Primarily the architecture depends on the distribution of data updates, as well as on query distribution. For a large number of queries, the most powerful architecture conveys the distribution of updates as well as querying, together with the hierarchical organization, although two-level organization could perform better for certain types of queries [63].

This is an example of a very scalable architecture. On the other hand, there is no real temporal-enabled search and complex processing functions over a large amount of collected data. The architecture is not flexible in the sense of adding new services, since for every new service a new distributed XML document has to be created.

5.2.4.2 SWAP

Moodley and Simonis [64] designed the SWAP (Sensor Web Agent Platform) framework in 2006 by relying on the multi-agent system (MAS) infrastructure together with ontological infrastructure. The architecture aims to extend OGC SWE's functionalities and to offer Sensor Web applications discovery and deployment services, and efficient sensor data fusion. A prototype implementation of the SWAP is used for the Advanced Fire Information System (AFIS), the first near real-time satellite-based fire monitoring system in Africa.

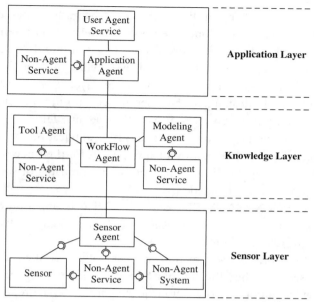

Fig. 24. The Three-tier agent-based architecture designed within the SWAP framework.

The framework is running on the top of a three-layered architecture (see Fig. 24) with separate *Sensor Layer, Knowledge Layer,* and *Application Layer*. In each layer, there are special types of agents that communicate among each other utilizing ontological infrastructure for both conceptual data description and semantic data description.

The *Sensor layer* contains sensor agents that are responsible for interacting with sensors and actuators either directly or via some of OGC's SWE services (SOS, SAS, SPS). Sensor agents exchange messages structured according to the specifications provided in the relevant ontology, for both message format and message content payload description. This message metadata provides information about phenomena that is measured, the unit of measure, as well as for temporal attributes.

All expert knowledge in the system is maintained in the *Knowledge layer*. There are three types of agents there: the *workflow agents*, which are the core components, the *tools agents*, used for performing predefined processes with no other resources demanding, and the *modeling agents*, capable to perform complex processing that may require additional data archived or not. Typical execution scenario starts from the workflow agent which accepts data from sensor agents and invokes appropriate tools and modeling agents in order to run necessary operations on provided data. Processed data could be forwarded further to other workflow agents or to be pushed up to the *Application layer* if all processing is done. All processing in this layer is sensor independent, and the knowledge interpretation is based on multiple ontologies.

The *Application layer* interacts with end-users while offering Sensor Web applications. There are two types of agents in this layer: *application agents* and *user agents*. The application agents are used for composing specific applications based on outputs received from workflow agents. The user agents are responsible for providing custom view of available applications to end-users. Users are able to select combination of applications for their needs, and they are notified by user agents if new applications are available or some of the existing applications are changed.

The SWAP uses NASA SWEET ontology [37] as an upper ontology. For describing processes and tasks in the *Knowledge layer*, it has used OWL-S [65], an extension of OWL for modeling processes.

Despite that some issues are only conceptually described, the SWAP architecture seems to be efficient and flexible enough. There is no information provided about supported user queries, internal data representation, format of sensor data received from sensor agents, etc. Also the architecture lacks the potential for new knowledge inference based on gathered data.

After presentations of surveyed architectures, in the next section the study continues with a comparative analysis of described approaches.

6. COMPARATIVE ANALYSIS

In this section we will give an overall comparison of surveyed architectures and provide data in connection with the issues outlined in Section 2.

Database centered solutions typically use relational database management system (RDBMS) as data storage management solution, that is deployed on a single node. Such solutions limit scalability of such an approach and, therefore, these solutions are not suitable to be used in global-scale application scenarios. There are several techniques for mapping RDF triples to RDBMS [90], so that semantic data representation could be easily applied in this architecture. Data processing based on RDBMS internal processing mechanism, implemented through stored procedures or triggers, offer medium level data processing capabilities. In the next section we describe one possible improvement to this approach by introducing new distributed repository based on column store.

Authors of query translation-based architectures are fully employing semantic technologies focusing on semantic query language and its conversion to sensor data source languages. Additional research attention is dedicated to semantic description of data sources which facilitates sensor data fusing with other semantic data streams. These research efforts have produced various extensions of SPARQL such as SPARQL$_{STREAM}$ and stSPARQL. In the case of intensive sensor data traffic with large number of users, in connection with this approach, the only concern is the real–time performance.

Sensor virtualization approaches follow REST-like design principles by abstracting sensor data with virtual resources. In semantic enabled solutions, the rich information model enables relationships between real–world entities of interest and sensors, thus enabling support for many application scenarios. Resources distribution together with scalable look–up mechanism offers the most scalable solutions among the presented ones. Moreover, the most comprehensive solutions implemented in large EU projects such as SENSEI and Internet of Things share this approach. These solutions fully address many of aforementioned design issues such as security, quality of service, sensor networks heterogeneity, and modality. However, solutions from this group poorly support access to archived data while being open to significant potential improvements by supporting data mining over historical sensor data.

Service-oriented architectures use standards-based solutions. The primary standardization achievements and influence in Sensor Web community have been done by OGC' SWE working group, which proposes architecture based on interaction between sensor data consumers and providers relying on service orchestration and XML data encodings. The alternatives offer REST service interface instead of the standard web service, extension of XML with semantic annotations of sensor data, and support to semantic query language. Due to syntax-based interoperability, many of these components may be reused as elements of other approaches. However, the lack of fully employed semantic modeling limits the use of these architectures to vertical application domain.

The service-composition-oriented approaches are at experimental stage without aiming at providing comprehensive Sensor Web platforms. Nevertheless, composing desired sensor data streams feature are very flexible from user perspective. The strength of these solutions lies in the power of internal processing elements and efficient description of processing capabilities. Therefore, these solutions depend on the richness of accepted semantic model, as well as on the performance of real–time finding of desired processing chain. Our impression is that certain hybrid approach adhering to the service-composition principles with a more scalable approach, could achieve significant architectural advancements.

The rule-based data transformation approaches as straightforward semantics-based architectures provide users with semantic query languages and semantic sensor data representation. Knowledge inference is typically based on descriptive logic reasoning. These solutions leverage multi-layered architecture through which push-based data propagation is applied. Relying on the ontology, rule-based data transformation is applied on the highest layer in order to infer new knowledge or produce real-world events related data. So, information model dictates the capabilities of these solutions. Scalability could be significantly increased through loosely coupled layers connection and more distributed organization within certain layer. Also this approach would benefit from support for more data modality.

Agent-based systems distribute responsibilities for various functionalities among different agents and hence promising approach for scalability. However, to offer a comprehensive and an efficient platform there is a lot of room for potential improvements: employing semantic approaches for querying data produced by processing agents, describing and composing desired agent processing, offering rich semantic data representation, supporting different data modality, etc. which should be powered by appropriate ontology network. We believe that agents-based paradigms could be more often included in other architecture for solving particular issues.

Generally, we can notice an evolution in the available approaches. Earlier solutions offered more low-level-oriented services, with optimized query processing in distributed environments, a simple data model and thus limited interoperability. More recent approaches tend to take the advantage of sensor data semantics and available sensor network ontologies by providing complex services, intelligent functions such as knowledge inference, increased interoperability, support for more application domains, and often aiming to offer a ubiquitous Sensor Web platform.

Finally, in Table 1, we provide summarized data for sensor data-oriented architectures, while Table 2 summarizes data for application-oriented architectures.

7. AN ORIGINAL CONTRIBUTION OF AUTHORS

The aim of our research is to develop an architecture capable of collecting heterogeneous sensor data and to enable Internet users to do both search and subscription functions over the gathered sensors data. Additionally, an important goal is to enable data mining algorithms to be applied over the archived data. One of the motivation scenarios includes monitoring and

Table 1 The overview of sensor data-oriented architectures.

Solution	Basic Organization	Scalability	Data Modality Support	SN Flexibility	SN Capability	SN Management & Actuation	Ontology	Employed Semantics	Data Representation	Query Language	Knowledge Inference	App. Interface and Data Format	Discovery of Service	Service Composition	QoS & QoI	Security
Cougar [10]	Client-server	Low to medium	Medium level, fetch based, time series, archived	–	Particularly –	–	–	–	ADT objects	Extended SQL	–	Native DB service interface	–	–	–	–
SenseWeb [11]	Three logical layers	Medium	High level, Stream data, Archived, mobile	High, Via drivers or DataHub	Particularly No	No	–	–	Relational data format	SQL	No	Web service	Yes, transformers discovery	No	Aggregation of unavailable data	Medium
The ES3N [13]	Multi-layered	Low	Low level. Archived and acquisitional data	?	No	No	Own implementation	Data, queries	RDF	SPARQL	Via queries	?	No	No	No	No
CSIRO SSN [14]	Vertical service-oriented	Low	Medium level, fetch-based access, stored data	Medium, declarative program. Sralog	Yes, with semantic models	Yes,	Own implementation in OWL	SN state, sensors capabilities	XML?	?	No	Web service ?	Yes	No	Declared	Declared
SPARQL-STREAM [22]	Stream-processing oriented	Medium to Low	Medium level, Streaming relational data, push and poll	Medium, SNEEql supported	No	No	Sensors and domain related	Queries, Data Mapping	Relational data	SPARQL-STREAM	Via queries	RDF	No	No	No	No

continued

Table 1 Continued.

Solution	Basic Organization	Scalability	Data Modality Support	SN Flexibility	SN Capability	SN Management & Actuation	Ontology	Employed Semantics	Data Representation	Query Language	Knowledge Inference	App. Interface and Data Format	Discovery of Service	Service Composition	QoS & QoI	Security
SemSorGrid4Env [47, 48]	Three-layers service-oriented	Medium to High	High level, streams, feeds, stored data	Medium-high, over natural query languages	Particularly, by describing service providers	No	Four levels, SWEET & DOLCE, SSN, domain	Queries, data sources description, sensor data	Native data format	Ontology based	Via queries	REST, HTML, GML, GeoJSON	Yes, via stSPARQL	No	?	?
GSN [18]	Peer-to-peer	High	Medium level, Streams, stored data	Medium, through wrappers	No	No	–	–	XML	SQL	No	XML	No	Low, creation of complex streams	?	?
SENSEI [50]	Directory based	High	High level, no support for archived data	High	?	Yes, arbitration is provided	SWEET. SemSorOntology, Context Ontology	Sensor & entity data, resource semantic look-up	O&M XML and RDF in parallel	Semantic queries for resources	?	REST, three data level	Yes, lookup of dynamic entities, resources	Medium, resource creation	High, sessions monitoring	High, AAA Architecture
IoT [51, 52]	?	?	High level, RFID, and mobile also	High	Supported by the information model	?	Multiple layers, SSN	Services, sensor, and entity data	?	?	?	REST, WS, OWL-S, RPC	Yes, lookup of service profiles	Should be provided	High, through all stages	High, through all stages

Table 2 The overview of application-oriented architectures.

Solution	Basic Organization	Scalability	Data Modality Support	SN Flexibility	SN Capability	SN Management & Actuation	Ontology	Employed Semantics	Data Representation	Query Language	Knowledge Inference	App. Interface and Data Format	Discovery of Service	Service Composition	QoS & QoI	Security
TinyREST [53]	Client-Server	Low	Low	Via device support protocol	Network deployment	Yes, actuation	–	–	?	–	–	REST + HTML	Home service framework	No	No	No
OGC SWE [2, 21]	Vertical oriented	Medium	Medium, poll, event, streaming	SensorML compatible	SensorML support	?	No	–	XML	XML structured in SOS interface	–	Web service, XML	Yes	No	Data precision and accuracy	Low, Web-service roles
SemSOS [56]	Vertical oriented	Medium	Low, poll, stored	SensorML	SensorML	?	O&M, GML, OWL-Time	O&M data, OWL queries	OWL instances	SPARQL	JENA engine	Web Svc, XML with XLINK annotation	Yes	No	Data precision and accuracy	Low, Web-service roles
Hourglass [16]	Peer-to-peer	Medium-high	Medium, stream & persisted data	Medium to low	Yes, by service announcements	No	–	–	?	No	No	?	Yes, by service announcements	Yes, by declaring circuit structure	Medium, buffering, heart-beat monitoring	No
SONGS [17]	Hierarchical	Low	Event-based	Low ?	Yes, by run-time resource info	Yes	Application-domain oriented	Services, data streams,	XML ?	Semantic based	CLP-R Constraint Progr. Extension	?	Yes, by user queries	Yes, via queries of semantic streams	Data confidentiality	No
IBM [59]	Distributed stream processing	Medium	Data streams, event-based	?	No	No	Single, spatial and temporal	Data streams, Process. elem.	RDF	SPARQL-like	OWL-Yes, OWL-DLP	?	Yes, Via user queries	Yes, via stream pattern queries	?	?

continued

Table 2 Continued.

Solution	Basic Organization	Scalability	Data Modality Support	SN Flexibility	SN Capability	SN Management & Actuation	Ontology	Employed Semantics	Data Representation	Query Language	Knowledge Inference	App. Interface and Data Format	Discovery of Service	Service Composition	QoS & QoI	Security
University of Toronto [20]	Publish/subscribe message passing	Medium	Event-based sensor data	Through TinyScript VM	No	No	Sensors to high-level events mapping	High-level events detection	?	No	Semantic engine	?	No	No	No	No
NTUA [23]	Pluggable architecture	Medium	Event-based and polled access	High	No	No	?	Mapping rules, sensor data	RDF and XML	XPATH & SPARQL ?	Jena reasoning engine	Web service	No	No	No	Secure data protocols
The SWASN [61]	Four layers service-oriented	Medium	Push and poll based	Through gateways	No	No	Hybrid, sensors, location, domain	Sensor data, transformation	RDF	SPARQL	Jena reasoning engine	HTTP	No	No	No	No
IrisNet [15, 63]	Hierarchical	High	Processing with senselets	?	No	No	–	–	XML	XPATH	No	HTTP	No	No	Tolerance of cached data consistency	No
The SWAP [64]	Three-tier	High	Poll-based, Event-based	?	?	No	SWEET, OWL-S, OWL-Time	Processing agents descriptions	Semantic based ?	?	No	Web service	Yes by application agents	?	?	?

control applications in the public district heating system in one Belgrade municipality.

The identified requirements, especially regarding data mining functionalities, have motivated us to use a database centered approach. Therefore, we have focused on finding optimal mappings of a common sensor data format to a relational database and the corresponding indexing and acquisition policy. Furthermore, we assumed that stored sensor data could be easily mapped to either the XML format or the RDF format, using appropriate metadata and format translators.

In our solution, we propose a model with related meta–objects for representing sensor data and observations. Our work is influenced by the OGC's SWE work, although we do not follow strictly their data model. We have identified several meta–objects for modeling the sensor networks domain. The first one is *MetaProperty,* used as a description of certain physical or virtual data properties. The *MetaProperty* is used for describing a *Property* object. It is assumed that every property value could be expressed in one of the following simple basic data types: *integer, long, double, boolean, date,* and *string.* A property could be simple or complex. Simple property has only one value, while complex property can have several simple or complex properties. For distinctions among inner properties, we introduced the property naming. Typical property types are: *Temperature, Humidity, Light, Latitude, Longitude,* etc., which are all simple properties. One example of complex property is *GeoLocation.* We provide definitions of *Meta Properties* with either XML configuration file, or over web application. The definition of *GeoLocation Meta Property* is as following:

```
<metaProperty>
<name>GeoLocation</name>
<description>Location coordinates</description>
<version>1</version>
<basicType>0</basicType>
<defaultValue></defaultValue>
<isSimpleProperty>false</isSimpleProperty>
<hasPredefinedValues>false</hasPredefinedValues>
<innerProperty>
<order>0</order>
<innerPropertyName>lat</innerPropertyName>
<metaPropertyName>Latitude</metaPropertyName>
<propertyDescription>Latitude Coordinate</propertyDescription>
<isRequired>true</isRequired>
</innerProperty>
<innerProperty>
<order>1</order>
<innerPropertyName>long</innerPropertyName>
<metaPropertyName>Longitude</metaPropertyName>
<propertyDescription>Longitude Coordinate</propertyDescription>
<isRequired>true</isRequired>
</innerProperty>
</metaProperty>
```

For the vector type of properties, we have assumed the use of the basic data type called *set,* which contains several other properties of the same type (complex property includes only a defined number of different/same type of properties).

The next meta-object is the *MetaSensor* that defines all possible data values that could be contained in the related sensor type. Furthermore, every value is defined by an appropriate *MetaProperty*. Sensors are described in this way similarly like sensor capabilities in the OGC's work. In our solution, the *Sensor* is an instance of related *MetaSensor*, which defines what properties (value types) could have that sensor, or what properties (defined by *MetaProperty*) could be changed during time. For instance, we can define *MetaSensor* of type *BasicTemperatureSensor*, which can have the following properties (value types): temperature value, a unit of that temperature value (°C, °F, K...), precision (which could be defined as constant during all measurements, or could vary from one measurements to another), location (geo location of the sensor, which could be constant or variable—implying the sensor is static or mobile). Consequently, the *SensorObservation* is an object for capturing all changeable properties of its *Sensor* during time.

The mandatory values for all sensors are flags if a sensor is active or not (if it works or not), and if sensor is online or not (if a message could be routed to it), and these values are updated depending on the sensor's state. The meta-definitions, which are a set of all *MetaSensor* and *MetaProperty* objects, could be dynamically extended during time.

The topology of sensor networks is modeled in the following way: *SensorNetwork* represents an autonomously deployed sensor network containing several *SensorNodes* and *Sensors*. One *SensorNode* has several *Sensors,* but in our model we allowed existence of *Sensor* that belongs to the *SensorNetwork*, but is not attached to any *SensorNode*. The information about integrated networks is available to users in typical discover service functions, if they are interested to interact on low level.

Since we have modeled domain space by utilizing the object model, all used meta-objects, and data objects are actually class instances implemented in Java. Data objects as *Sensor* and *SensorObservation* keep all their properties in hash data structures, as key (property name) value (*Property* object) pairs. All data objects are persisted to the database, with appropriate mappings. The main challenge here is how to efficiently store different sensor types and their observations in relational database, since different sensor types can have a different number of properties. We mapped objects that have a variable number of properties into two tables: one major table, that keeps basic object values and mandatory properties, and another table that keeps all data properties. The concrete column fields are shown in Table 3 and Table 4 for

Table 3 The sensor_observation relational table schema for mapping the SensorObservation basic values.

id Primary Key [bigint]	network_id [bigint]	sensor_id [bigint]	sensor_name [var char]	is_last_ [boolean]	timestamp [timestamp]

Table 4 The sensor_observation_properties relational table schema for mapping the SensorObservation variable properties.

id Primary Key [bigint]	observation_id Foreign Key [bigint]	property_ name [var char]	property_ type [bigint]	value_ long [bigint]	value_ double [double]	value_ string [var char]

the *SensorObservation* object mapping. The essence of properties mapping is to map one simple property to one row of *sensor_observation_properties* table. Compact format comprises the following mappings of basic types: *integer, long, boolean,* and *date* basic data types are mapped to *value_long* column; *double* basic type is mapped to *value_double* column; *string* basic type is mapped to *value_string* column.

The number of *Sensor* objects increases slowly during time, as new sensors are registered. Hence, we cache all *Sensor* objects in internal memory structures in order to improve performance. The number of *SensorObservation* objects could be huge, depending on the defined observation interval. Therefore, we keep in memory only the latest observation of a *Sensor* while all other values are persisted to the database. The *sensor_observation* and *sensor_observation_properties* are append-only tables, so we use indexing in order to improve performance, more precisely, by creating index on *property_name*, *property_type*, and data values columns. We investigate usage of special index structures based on the Quad Tree [82] for most common type of queries which are spatial-temporal.

The system architecture is depicted in Fig. 25. The sensor networks are connected through the *Sensors Data Connector* component. A common interface is offered, which should be implemented by specific *Connector* in order to enable sensor data flow integration by the system. Certain *Connector* should know the underlying network specifics and could generally be located on sensor network sink components, or desktop machines,

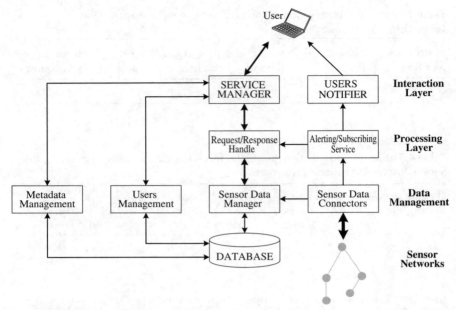

Fig. 25. The system architecture of the database centered approach to enabling efficient mapping of sensor data.

capable of more processing. Many available protocols can be utilized for communication between the *Connector* and the system. We have used standard TCP/IP socket connection protocol in our prototype solution, because it is a lightweight solution. The XML format can be used for data transfer. If the *Connector* is implemented in Java programming language, Java serializable objects may also be used as data format. The *Connector* is allowed to register new sensors to the system, but its main responsibility is to provide new sensor observations of already registered sensors. Registration of new sensor networks must be carried out through another interface, currently offered via web portal.

Upon receiving new sensor observations, two operations will be performed: they will be persisted to the relational database using object-relational mappings in the *Sensor Data Manager*, and passed to *Subscribing/Alerting* component for further processing. Users are able to subscribe to raw sensor observations data, in order to be notified of new data arrival through a defined channel. We have implemented asynchronous web notification using Google Web Toolkit (GWT) Comet technology [83] in our prototype. This service is low-level oriented, and it requires the users to explore sensor capabilities and features.

The powerful functions could be achieved through alerting services. With the arrival of new sensor observations, the specific processing will be performed to check the defined conditions for certain sensors. These conditions could be very simple, for instance to compare observation value with threshold value. Another option is to perform a comparison of different sensor observations produced on the same sensor node by different sensors. For example, a certain condition could check if the temperature is less than a defined value and humidity is higher than certain threshold, which implies the rain detection. The full power of this module is possible when latest observations are mixed with the archived sensor data, using more complex functions, when some data mining algorithms could be applied in order to find hidden rules, association among sensors, trends, detect anomalies, etc. At this level, the semantics of data could also be leveraged with the translation of low-level events using ontology models, when complex events could be detected and users notified.

The described architecture fulfilled the requirements of one application domain and a limited number of users. However, we were aware of its limited scalability in the case of handling huge sensor data volume and great number of sensor data providers, while at the same time supporting many application domains, as well as many Internet users. Therefore, we have investigated a possible improvement of this architecture by looking for a suitable distributed storage structure that is capable of storing and searching over a huge volume of collected sensor data. The similar problem has appeared with the Internet-scale data management, high data availability and support of up to millions of Internet users sharing Internet-scale applications services, such as web search services, social networks sites, global-scale retail, global auction sites, and others. In these applications, the traditional relational database management systems (RDBMS) based on relational data model has failed in offering efficient platform for powering such class of applications. These requirements have motivated researchers to develop new distributed storage systems often called NoSQL ("Not Only SQL") which offer high data availability while being capable of handling petabytes of data distributed over thousands of commodity machines deployed nodes. Contrary to traditional RDBMS features, these systems do not offer relational data model and SQL as query language, referential data integrity, and support a weak rather than a strong data consistency. NoSQL solutions are typically based on key-value stores, with uninterpreted data as values. In most cases, data processing is performed by MapReduce distributed processing jobs [89] consisting of simple functions over key-values pairs, where specific tasks are separated in a few phases in order to enable fault-tolerant processing. Distributed hash tables, developed for fast lookups in large-scale peer-to-peer systems, are used in the core of these systems.

Basically, several classes of these distributed store systems can be identified: key-value stores, column stores, document stores, and graph databases [95]. Standard key-value stores offer high-performance inserts and reads of unstructured data mapped by appropriate keys. Furthermore, they provide simple interface and a basic set of functionalities for inserting, retrieving, and data removal using keys. Column stores organize data in columns referenced by row keys as well as with column keys. However, there is no strict schema for columns which can be dynamically added or removed in contrast to strict database schema present in the RDBMS. These systems are influenced by the Bigtable [72] which is "a sparse, distributed, persistent multidimensional sorted map" designed and used at Google for a number of their applications. In document stores, the basic data units are structured documents. These solutions provide retrieving documents using keys functions, as well as adding and removing elements from documents' structures. Graph databases maintain data as nodes and edges among nodes, suitable for mapping the data that follow graph organization.

Rather than envisioning our Sensor Web architecture as a solution for specific use case scenario, we envision it as an infrastructural platform for supporting many application domains leveraging semantic data representation based on various ontologies. Additionally, this can be used as a platform for publishing Linked Sensor Data [86–88] following principles of Linked Data [85]. We focused on several design issues of semantic sensor networks platform to solve using distributed data stores. First, we want to efficiently store sensors data and observations data represented as time series data, suitable for later search and mining. Even though the data may be also kept in simpler formats, such as XML or binary format, Resource Description Framework (RDF) is the primary data representation format. Secondly, we want to enable publish/subscribe mechanism not only to sensor data, but also to processing elements results, properties of the domain entities, things or similar concepts supported by relevant ontologies. Thirdly, a semantic-based search and knowledge inference should be provided through distributed sensor data. A special focus has been given to the most common semantic searches in the semantic sensor networks, which are spatial-temporal searches. As suggested in Linked Data design issues [85], we use the Uniform Resource Identifier (URI) for referring sensors, sensor observations, as well as processing elements, and other entities. Such an approach facilitates direct interaction with these resources using REST interaction style.

Finally, we have selected column store as our architecture distributed storage due to its scalability, its ability to maintain huge amount of distributed data together with distributed processing, and flexible data model. Column stores support no strict schema for columns which is suitable for mapping heterogeneous sensor data, encoded as RDF triples, thus enabling arbitrarily sensor resources linking. There are several open-source column stores solutions based on the Google's Bigtable data model and distributed architecture [72] such as Apache HBase [92] and Cassandra [73, 94], but the HBase has a data model closer to the Bigtable. The HBase is a distributed data store built on top of the Hadoop [93] which is a platform for scalable, distributed computing offering distributed processing through MapReduce framework [89] and high-throughput access to data via Hadoop Distributed File System (HDFS).

In HBase data are organized in tables. The data model in the HBase provides that a value stored in a table cell is indexed by a row key, a column key, and a timestamp key in the notation: (row:byte[ ], column:byte[ ], time:int64)->value:byte[ ]. The rows are lexicographically ordered according to row keys. The column keys are grouped into column families and column family name is used as a prefix for every column key in the notation *column_family:column_name*. One column family can contain usually a large number of the same type column keys, which can by dynamically added or removed. Timestamps enable the multiple data versions existence in one cell, ordered by decreasing timestamp value. Moreover, there is an option to specify the garbage collection policy per column family with either keeping the certain number of the last versions of a cell, or keeping versions that are fresh enough. The physical unit of data distribution is the column family.

Our research goes in the direction of finding an optimal mapping of the semantic sensor data representation to the column store, i.e., the Bigtable data model, specifically addressing spatial-temporal characteristics of such data and accessing patterns that include intensive inserts of new instances. This entails sensor data keeping, as well as keeping related domain concepts represented as RDF triples appropriately indexed. In the absence of standard query language in column store, index structures enable fast look-up of stored data, as well as specific organization for spatial and temporal data.

There are several approaches for mapping RDF triples to data storage in order to enable efficient query processing and data retrieval. The straightforward technique is a triple store, where all RDF triples are stored in one table with three columns containing subject, property, and object, but this approach suffers from poor performance in the case of a large number of triples. Property tables keep data in a few tables consisting of clustered similar properties. The disadvantage of this approach is the null values presence in some columns and the difficult properties selection to be grouped together. Abadi et al. in [90] have advocated mapping of RDF triples by vertical partitioning using table-per property approach in column stores. They maintain two-column tables containing *subjectID* as a row key and *objectID* as a value, per each property in the data model. Weiss et al. [91] have proposed maintenance of six indices for covering all combinations of *<subject, predicate, object>* triple in the notation *<spo>*, *<sop>*, *<pso>*, *<pos>*, *<osp>*, and *<ops>*. This approach achieves better performance than the previous one, but introduces five times higher storage overhead.

In our approach we focused on finding solution with balanced storage requirements and indices maintenance cost in the case of inserts of new data. Also, we have emphasized the support for the most common queries type in semantic sensor networks, which are spatial-temporal. The two tables are used for keeping *<spo>* and *<pos>* indices. The table responsible for *<spo>* index is organized around subjects' properties, where the subject's URI is a row key, properties are used as columns keys, and corresponding objects' URIs or literals (strings, data values) are stored as cell values. The HBase data model allows the use of arbitrary columns number within one row, which enables using only existing properties of certain subject as columns keys. As a consequence of this, there are no sparse columns like in RDBMS implementations. This organization facilitates retrieving all the RDF triples of one subject, since column families represent the data distribution basic unit. The second table practically implements table-per property-indices [90], in our case *<pos>* index, by using *predicate:object* as a row key, and a *subject* as a column key thus supporting multi-valued properties. This organization is often labeled as *<po_s>* index. The list of all existing properties is kept in the auxiliary table cached in the main memory. Additional improvement can be done by shortening keys through dictionary encodings of resources' and predicates' (property names) URIs.

At this moment we do not have full implementation of SPARQL. However, one SPARQL query can be decomposed to several basic query conditions expressed as triple patterns. There are eight possible triple patterns as the following: *<spo>*, *<?po>*, *<s?o>*, *<sp?>*, *<s??>*, *<?p?>*, *<??o>*, and *<???>*. Our index tables are created for supporting search of possible triple patterns on the following way. The subject-oriented table is used for handling $<s?o>$, $<sp?>$, and $<s??>$ triple patterns, while $<po\_s>$ index table is used for handling $<?po>$ and $<?p?>$ patterns. Both index tables could be consulted for $<spo>$ and $<???>$ patterns. In our organization, the critical triple pattern is $<??o>$. Since we do not maintain $<osp>$ index except for spatial data, the critical pattern can be handled by performing as many lookups as is the number of distinct predicates on $<po\_s>$ index table. This can be additionally improved by employing caching of recent $<??o>$ search results.

Sensor data include sensors information and observations produced by sensors. We assume that information model is based on the ontological network that follows multi-level organization as proposed by Guarino in [32], which enables that sensor data could be in relationships with other domain concepts. In accordance with the described RDF triples mapping, we store semantic representation of sensors, sensor observations, and domain concepts. The mapping is illustrated in Fig. 26.

In the subject-oriented table, a separate column family is reserved for storing related content. Data producers typically provide new sensor observations in non-semantic format, such as XML or even binary format. Upon inserting a new content, a corresponding MapReduce job converts new

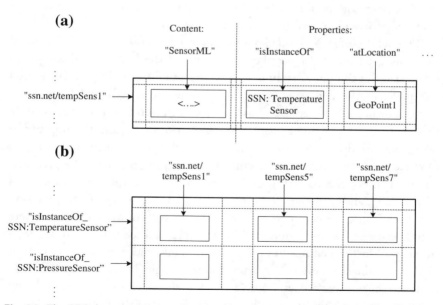

Fig. 26. The RDF data mapping to the Bigtable data model. (a) Subject centered index table and (b) Predicate index table.

observations to RDF triples using available open-source libraries. In the map phase, RDF triples are generated from the new content, while the process of inserting appropriate values in the index tables is performed in the reduce phase. There are two inserts per one RDF triple in this organization. Furthermore, the OGC SWE's Observation and Measurement (O&M) data representation format may be also kept in parallel.

Sensor observations are stored in the separate table suitable for keeping time series data, a row per observation mapping, where the sensor URI and observation timestamp concatenation is used as a key. Since row keys are lexicographically sorted, this organization enables all sensor observations of one sensor being stored in a successive order, suitable for retrieving observations falling in certain time range. Among other properties, columns referring to the most recent and the oldest observation are kept for one sensor. Depending on the data rate the interval of stored observations can be defined.

We use a separate index table designed following principles similar to QuadTree [82] in order to efficiently search spatial data. Our focus is on indexing 2D space, and thus latitude and longitude geographic coordinates are being used for representing a location of a certain geographic point. The implementation is based on the characteristics of the HBase's *Scan* operator and the fact that row keys are sorted. If a key is used as the start row key of the *Scan* operator and it is between two row keys in lexicographic order, the *Scan* operator will return the later row as the result.

The whole area is divided in rectangle cells, and one cell is mapped to a row indexed by *lat_long* key consisting of the latitude and longitude coordinates of the upper right corner of the cell. Depending on the desired resolution of the cell size, we can determine the length of *lat_long* keys. Both coordinates are expressed as positive string-encoded integers, where first three digits are integer part of the real coordinate, and the number of the remaining digits determines precision of the cell location and size. For instance, using five digits after decimal point is enough to have the precision around 1m. For the sake of simplicity, we choose that one coordinate key is 6 bytes long, and thus the whole row key is 12 bytes long. If this precision is not sufficient, we can increase the length of the coordinates' keys. There could be several points contained in one rectangle cell. If the number of points within the cell reaches the maximum allowed number of points, or bucket size, the cell is divided in a new four rectangles trying to equally divide points to the new rectangles. Points are kept in the table row of corresponding rectangle cell via columns, represented by *long_lat* of the point as a column key, and geographical point (*GeoPoint*) URI as value. The length of row keys doesn't prevent us from using column keys comprised of coordinates encoded with more digits. Since *GeoPoint* is typically used as an object in the relationships with other resources, a separate table is used for mapping *GeoPoint* and corresponding resources, where *GeoPoint* URI is used as a row key, and resources' URI (subjects' URI) as column keys, and property names as values (an example of specific <*osp*> index). Additionally, a cell row contains columns referring to the longitude value of the left cell edge and the latitude value of the bottom cell edge, as well as pointer to the next left cell having lower longitude coordinate and pointer to the next bottom cell having lower latitude coordinate.

The process of finding the cell, where a certain point falls inside, is performed in two steps. In the first step the lookup is performed be means of the HBase's *Scan* operator with the target point's latitude coordinate as a start row key, and the result is the cell having latitude coordinate greater or equal to the point's latitude, and the smallest longitude coordinate. In the second step, the lookup is performed using the key comprised of the cell latitude, found in the first step, and the target point longitude. As the result, the *Scan* operator directly returns the row representing the cell where target point belongs. One example of finding target cell is shown in Fig. 27. After finding target cell, the search of certain space range or lookup for k–nearest points can be performed using pointers to the neighborhood cells.

The architecture supports both poll- and push-based data provision. The standard data access is poll based, provided via HTTP protocol and the GET method, with relevant resource URI encoded in the request's URL. Current implementation supports basic triple patterns search, but it is envisioned that the system should support the full SPARQL queries execution for search

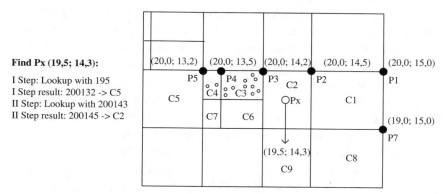

Fig. 27. Search of target cell in the spatial index table.

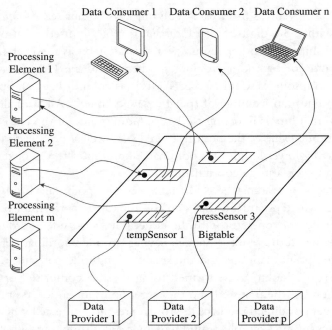

Fig. 28. The conceptual organization of the architecture relying on the column store repository.

over semantic data. Push based data propagation is implemented relying also on column store as depicted in Fig. 28 with the application of similar techniques implemented in large-scale distributed computing architectures such as the Distributed Shared Memory [74–81]. The objective is to enable interested users or processing elements to subscribe to new data, or to be alerted if new data meet certain conditions. The subscriptions of relevant data are stored under separate column family in the subject centered table, with columns referring to subscribed users, or processing elements URIs. Data consumers may be either notified of new data availability, or new data content may be pushed to them by using appropriate channels. The most commonly used technologies for asynchronous server data propagation are the web technologies Comet [97] and WebSocket [96]. There is another table serving processing elements information, typically for storing notifications of new data arrival, while processing functions are implemented by appropriate MapReduce jobs. In the case of complex functions, such processing can be performed on external machines. Produced data can be stored in the repository, and similarly notification can be further propagated to interested parties. The bottleneck caused by large data processing is avoided by distributed processing elements.

Column stores seem to be very suitable distributed storage solutions for building semantic sensor networks platforms since both real-time data and archived data can be efficiently provided to data consumers using these solutions. However, there are lots of research efforts that have to be invested in order to find the appropriate reasoning algorithm over big repository of semantic data, which can enable extraction of more knowledge. Furthermore, distributed processing, available through MapReduce jobs, should be properly employed for implementation of data mining techniques.

8. SUMMARY: GLOBAL CONCLUSION

With the proliferation of deployed sensor networks, as well as mobile phones embedded with various sensors, we may expect increasingly heterogeneous real world information made available to users. This escalating information heterogeneity requires an appropriate integration platform design of such diverse sensor data sources. Despite many proposed solutions, there is neither consensus nor wide acceptance of any specific platform.

As we have presented in this study, recent research efforts in finding efficient Sensor Web architecture have spawned in several directions. The objective of our study is to provide a comprehensive view of current achievements in this field, to identify the most prominent techniques and technologies in use, and to highlight potential directions for further improvements of existing architectures. We may conclude that, regardless of the used approach, more flexible and more powerful architecture can be designed by employing data semantics.

Various research directions can be identified depending upon the used approach. Important observation is made according to which sensor virtualization approach leads toward the most comprehensive and efficient architecture design. Inspired by REST design principles, the primary challenge with this design approach is to create a flexible information model that will satisfy the needs of a large number of use case scenarios, and a scalable look-up mechanism for management and discovery of such pool of virtual resources, as well as real world entities and their relationships. The query translation approaches can also provide a stable architecture that supports data sources variety. Researchers continue to investigate semantic query language extensions that could be leveraged by translating into sensor data source natural query languages. The most user friendly approach is the service-composition oriented approach. Nevertheless, it suffers from the performance point of view. However, performance degradation can be relieved by distribution of processing. Additional attention should be devoted to hybrid approach with combination of service-composition-oriented approaches and more scalable ones.

Several research efforts envision Linked Sensor Data platforms as the most promising ones. Authors of this study proposed an architecture offering infrastructural support for such a platform by opening up a new avenue for further improvements pertaining to database-oriented solutions. This innovation relies on a column store distributed repository which could efficiently satisfy both the performance and flexibility requirements of semantics-enabled Sensor Web architectures.

All approaches leveraging data semantics could benefit from a progress related to advanced reasoning algorithms contributed by the Semantic Web research community. Furthermore, spatial-temporal extensions of SPARQL, as well as efficient structures for enabling spatial-temporal data processing will significantly contribute to existing solutions enhancement.

ACKNOWLEDGMENTS

The work presented here was supported by EU FP7 ProSense (project no. 205494) and by the Serbian Ministry of Education and Science (project III44006).

Table of Abbreviations

6LoWPAN	IPv6 over Low power Wireless Personal Area Network
ADT	Abstract Data Type
CSIRO	Commonwealth Scientific and Industrial Research Organisation
DnS	Descriptions and Situations
DOLCE	Descriptive Ontology for Linguistic and Cognitive Engineering
EU FP7	European Union's Seventh Framework Programme
GML	Geography Markup Language
GPS	Global Positioning System
GSN	Global Sensor Network

GWT	Google Web Toolkit
HTML	HyperText Markup Language
HTTP	Hypertext Transfer Protocol
IoT	Internet of Things
JSON	JavaScript Object Notation
NoSQL	"Not Only SQL"
O&M	Observation and Measurement
OGC SWE	Open Geospatial Consortium Sensor Web Enablement
OWL	Web Ontology Language
RDBMS	Relational Database Management System
RDF	Resource Description Framework
RDFa	Resource Description Framework in Attributes
REST	Representational State Transfer
RFID	Radio-Frequency Identification
SAS	Sensor Alerting Service
SensorML	Sensor Model Language
SNEEql	Sensor Network Engine Query Language
SOS	Sensor Observation Service
SPARQL	Simple Protocol and RDF Query Language
SPS	Sensor Planning Service
SQL	Structured Query Language
SSN	Semantic Sensor Network
stSPARQL	Spatio-Temporal SPARQL
SWEET	Semantic Web for Earth and Environmental Terminology
TCP/IP	Transmission Control Protocol/Internet Protocol
TinyOS	Tiny Operating System
URI	Uniform Resource Identifier
URL	Uniform Resource Locator
W3C	World Wide Web Consortium
WSDL	Web Service Definition Language
WSN	Wireless Sensor Network
XLINK	XML Linking Language
XML	eXtensible Markup Language
XPATH	XML Path Language
XSLT	Extensible Stylesheet Language

REFERENCES

[1] K. Delin, S. Jackson, The Sensor Web: a new instrument concept, in: Proceedings of the SPIE International of Optical Engineering, vol. 4284, pp. 1–9, 2001.

[2] M. Botts, G. Percivall, C. Reed, J. Davidson, Sensor Web Enablement: Overview and High-Level Architecture, The Open Geospatial Consortium whitepaper, 20 August 2008.

[3] Resource Description Framework (RDF), <http://www.w3.org/TR/rdfconcepts/>, accessed 20 January 2012.

[4] The RDF Schema (RDF-S), <http://www.w3.org/TR/rdf-schema/>, accessed 20 January 2012.

[5] The Web Ontology Language (OWL), <http://www.w3.org/TR/owl-ref/>, accessed 20 January 2012.

[6] The SPARQL Query Language for RDF, <http://www.w3.org/TR/rdf-sparqlquery/>,
accessed 20 January 2012.

[7] A. Sheth, C. Henson, S. Sahoo, Semantic Sensor Web, IEEE Internet Computing 12 (2008) 78–83.

[8] P. Barnaghi, S. Meissner, M. Presser, K. Moessner, Sense and Sens'ability: Semantic Data Modelling for Sensor Networks, ICT-MobileSummit 2009 Conference Proceedings, IIMC International Information Management Corporation, 2009.

[9] O. Corcho, R. Garcia-Castro, Five Challenges for the Semantic Sensor Web, in: Semantic Web Journal 1 (1) (2010) 121–125.

[10] P. Bonnet, J. Gehrke, P. Seshadri, Towards sensor database systems, in: Proceedings of Mobile Data Management, Lecture Notes in Computer Science, vol. 1987, Springer, Hong Kong, January 2001.

[11] A. Kansal, S. Nath, J. Liu, F. Zhao, SenseWeb: an infrastructure for shared sensing, IEEE Multimedia 14 (4) (2007) 8–13.

[12] Y. Ahmad, S. Nath, COLR-Tree: communication-efficient spatio-temporal indexing for a sensor data web portal, in: ICDE08, 2008, pp. 784–793.

[13] M. Lewis, D. Cameron, S. Xie, B. Arpinar, ES3N: a semantic approach to data management in sensor networks, in: Semantic Sensor Networks Workshop (SSN06), Georgia, USA, Athens, November 2006.

[14] L. Li, K. Taylor, A framework for semantic sensor network services, in: Sixth International Conference on Service Oriented Computing, 2008.

[15] P.B. Gibbons, B. Karp Ke, S. Nath, S. Seshan, Iris-Net: an architecture for a worldwide Sensor Web, IEEE Pervasive Computing 2 (2003) 22–33.

[16] J. Shneidman, P. Pietzuch, J. Ledlie, M. Roussopoulos, M. Seltzer, M. Welsh, Hourglass: an infrastructure for connecting sensor networks and applications, Harvard Technical Report TR-21-04, 2004.

[17] J. Liu, F. Zhao, Towards semantic services for sensor-rich information systems, in: Second International Conference on Broadband Networks, 2005, pp. 44–51.

[18] K. Aberer, M. Hauswirth, A. Salehi, Infrastructure for data processing in large-scale interconnected sensor networks, in: International Conference on Mobile Data Management, May 2007, pp. 198–205.

[19] B. Motik, U. Sattler, A comparison of reasoning techniques for querying large description logic aboxes, in: Proceedings of the 13th International Conference on Logic for Programming, Artificial Intelligence (LPAR06), LNCS, Springer-Verlag, 2006.

[20] A. Wun, M. Petrovic, H.A. Jacobsen, A system for semantic data fusion in sensor networks, in: Proceedings of the 2007 Inaugural International Conference on Distributed Event-Based Systems (DEBS '07), ACM, New York, USA, 2007, pp. 75–79.

[21] I. Simonis, OGC Best Practices 06–021r4: OGC Sensor Web Enablement Architecture, Open Geospatial Consortium, Wayland, MA, USA, 2008.

[22] J.P. Calbimonte, O. Corcho, A.J.G. Gray, Enabling Ontology-based Access to Streaming Data Sources, in: Nineth International Semantic Web Conference (ISWC2010), Shanghai, China, November, 2010.

[23] A. Zafeiropoulos, N. Konstantinou, S. Arkoulis, D.-E. Spanos, N. Mitrou, A Semantic-Based Architecture for Sensor Data Fusion, in: Proceedings of the Second International Conference on Mobile Ubiquitous Computing, Systems, Services and Technologies (UBICOMM '08) 2008 Washington, DC, USA, 2008, pp. 116–121.

[24] S.R. Madden, M.J. Franklin, J.M. Hellerstein, W. Hong, TinyDB: an acquisitional query processing system for sensor networks, ACM Trans. Database Syst. 30 (1) (2005) 122–173.

[25] R.T. Fielding, Architectural Styles and the Designs of Network-based Software Architectures, University of California, Irvine, 2000.

[26] R.T. Fielding, R.N. Taylor, Principled design of the modern web architecture, ACM Trans. Internet Technol. 2 (2) (2002) 115–150.

[27] The RESTlet framework, <http://www.restlet.org/>, accessed 20 January 2012.

[28] P. Barnaghi, M. Presser, K. Moessner, Publishing linked sensor data, in: Proceedings of the Third International Workshop on Semantic Sensor Networks (SSN), in Conjunction with the Nineth International Semantic Web Conference (ISWC 2010), 2010.

[29] G. Cassar, P. Barnaghi, K. Moessner, Probabilistic Methods for Service Clustering, in: Proceedings of the Fourth International Workshop on Semantic Web Service Matchmaking and Resource Retrieval, 2010.

[30] W. Wang, P. Barnaghi, Semantic annotation and reasoning for sensor data, in: Proceedings of the Fourth European conference on Smart sensing and context (EuroSSC2009), Springer-Verlag, Guildford, UK, 2009.

[31] A.P. Sheth, Changing focus on interoperability in information systems: from system, syntax, structure to semantics, in: M. Goodchild, M. Egenhofer, R. Fegeas, C. Kottman (Eds.), Interoperating Geographic Information Systems, Kluwer Academic Publishers, 1999, pp. 5–30.

[32] N. Guarino, Formal ontology in information systems, in: Proceedings of the International Conference on Formal Ontology in Information Systems—Volume 2001.

[33] M. Compton, H. Neuhaus, K. Taylor, K.-N. Tran, A survey of the semantic specification of sensors, in: Proceedings of the Second International Workshop on Semantic Sensor Networks (SSN09), Washington DC, USA, October 26, 2009.

[34] D. Russomanno, C. Kothari, O. Thomas, Sensor ontologies: from shallow to deep models, in: Proceedings of the 37th Southeastern Symposium on System Theory, 2005, SSST '05, March 2005, pp. 107–112.

[35] H. Neuhaus, M. Compton, The semantic sensor network ontology: a generic language to describe sensor assets, in: Pre-Conference Workshop on Challenges in Geospatial Data Harmonisation (AGILE 2009), Hannover, Germany, 2009.

[36] The W3C Semantic Sensor Network Incubator Group, SSN Ontology, <http://www.w3.org/2005/Incubator/ssn/XGR-ssn-20110628/>, accessed 20 January 2012.

[37] The NASA SWEET Ontology, <http://sweet.jpl.nasa.gov/ontology/, accessed 20 January 2012.

[38] The IEEE Suggested Upper Merged Ontology (SUMO), <http://www.ontology portal.org/>, accessed 20 January 2012.

[39] The DOLCE+DnS Ultralite Ontology, <http://www.loa.istc.cnr.it/ontologies/ DUL.owl>, accessed 20 January 2012.

[40] M.N. Lionel, Y. Zhu, J. Ma, M. Li, Q. Luo, Y. Liu et al., Semantic sensor net: an extensible framework, in: Networking and Mobile Computing , vol. 3619, Springer, Berlin/Heidelberg, 2005, pp. 1144–1153.

[41] The Jena—A Semantic Web Framework for Java, <http://incubator.apache.org/jena/>, accessed January 20 2012.
[42] The RDFa (Resource Description Framework in Attributes), <http://www.w3.org/TR/xhtml-rdfa-primer/>, accessed 20 January 2012.
[43] The XML Linking Language (XLINK), http://www.w3.org/TR/xlink/>, accessed 20 January 2012.
[44] D.C. Chu, L. Popa, A. Tavakoli, J.M. Hellerstein, P. Levis, S. Shenker, I. Stoica, The design and implementation of a declarative sensor network system, in: The Fifth ACM Conference on Embedded Networked Sensor Systems (SenSys 2007), Sydney, Australia, 2007, pp. 175–188.
[45] J. Barrasa, O. Corcho, A. Gomez-Perez, R2O, an extensible and semantically based database-to-ontology mapping language, in: SWDB2004, 2004, pp. 1069–1070.
[46] C.Y. Brenninkmeijer, I. Galpin, A.A. Fernandes, N.W. Paton, A semantics for a query language over sensors, streams and relations, in: BNCOD '08, 2008, pp. 87–99.
[47] A.J.G. Gray, R. Garca-Castro, K. Kyzirakos, M. Karpathiotakis, J.P. Calbimonte, K. Page, J. Sadler, A. Frazer, I. Galpin, A. Fernandes, N. Paton, O. Corcho, M. Koubarakis, D. De Roure, K. Martinez, A. Gmez-Prez, A semantically enabled service architecture for mashups over streaming and stored data, in: Proceedings of the Eighth Extended Semantic Web Conference (ESWC2011), May 2011.
[48] The SemSorGrid4Env FP7-ICT-223913, <http://www.semsorgrid4env.eu/>, accessed 20 January 2012.
[49] M. Koubarakis, K. Kyzirakos, Modeling and querying metadata in the Semantic Sensor Web: the model stRDF and the query language stSPARQL, in: Seventh Extended Semantic Web Conference (ESWC 2010) Part I, 2010, pp. 425–439.
[50] The SENSEI—Integrating the Physical with the Digital World of the Network of the Future, IST-FP7, project no. 215923, <http://www.sensei-project.eu/>, accessed 20 January 2012.
[51] The Internet of Things, <http://www.internet-of-things.eu/>, accessed 20 January 2012.
[52] The Internet of Things Architecture, EU FP7-257521, <http://www.iot-a.eu/public>, accessed 20 January 2012.
[53] T. Luckenbach, P. Gober, S. Arbanowski, A. Kotsopoulos, K. Kim, TinyREST: a protocol for integrating sensor networks into the Internet, in: Proceedings of the REALWSN 2005, 2005, pp. 1–5.
[54] The 52North Sensor Web Community, <http://52north.org>, accessed 20 January 2012.
[55] Sensors Anywhere, FP6 EU Project, <http://sany-ip.eu/>, accessed 20 January 2012.
[56] C. Henson, J.K. Pschorr, A.P. Sheth, K. Thirunarayan, SemSOS: semantic sensor observation service, in: Proceedings of the 2009 International Symposium on Collaborative Technologies and Systems (CTS 2009), Baltimore, MD, 2009.
[57] The Geography Markup Language (GML), <http://www.opengeospatial.org/standards/gml>, accessed 20 January 2012.
[58] The Time Ontology in OWL (OWL-Time), <http://www.w3.org/TR/owl-time/>, accessed 20 January 2012.
[59] E. Bouilet, M. Feblowitz, Z. Liu, A. Ranganathan, A. Riabov, F. Ye, A semantics-based middleware for utilizing heterogeneous sensor networks, in: DCOSS'07, 2007.
[60] P. Levis, D. Gay, D. Culler, Active sensor networks, in: NSDI, 2005.
[61] V. Huang, M. Javed, Semantic sensor information description and processing, in: Proceedings of the Second International Conference on Sensor Technologies and Applications, 2008.

[62] S. Krco, M. Johansson, V. Tsiatsis, A CommonSense approach to real-world global sensing, in: Proceedings of the SenseID: Convergence of RFID and Wireless Sensor Networks and their Applications workshop, ACM SenSys 2007, Australia, Sydney, 2007.

[63] A. Deshpande, S. Nath, P. Gibbons, S. Seshan, Cache-and-query for wide area sensor databases, in: SIGMOD 2003, San Diego, CA, June 2003.

[64] D. Moodley, I. Simonis, New architecture for the sensor web: the SWAP framework, in: Fifth International Semantic Web Conference, ISWC 2006, GA, USA, Athens, 2006.

[65] The OWL-S: Semantic Markup for Web Services, <http://www.w3.org/Submission/OWL-S/>, accessed 20 January 2012.

[66] K. Henricksen, R. Robinson, A survey of middleware for sensor networks: state-of-the-art and future directions, in: Proceedings of the International Workshop on Middleware for Sensor Networks, Melbourne, Australia, 2006, pp. 60–65.

[67] S. Hadim, N. Mohamed, Middleware challenges and approaches for wireless sensor networks, IEEE Distrib. Syst. Online 7 (3) 2006.

[68] S. Fedor, A. Gluhak, S. Krco, Sensor Networks' Integration, in: Lj.j Gavrilovska, S. Krco, V. Milutinovic, I. Stojmenovic, R. Trobec (Eds.), Application and Multidisciplinary Aspects of Wireless Sensor Networks, Springer, 2011, pp. 87–117.

[69] The SENSEI, D3.1. State of the Art—Sensor Frameworks and Future Internet, <http://www.ict-sensei.org/images/Documents/senseiwp3d3.1.pdf>, accessed 20 January 2012.

[70] The Internet of Things, IoT-A Project Deliverable D1.1, SOTA report on existing integration frameworks/architectures for WSN, RFID and other emerging IoT related Technologies, <http://www.iot-a.eu/public/public-documents/documents-1/1/1/d1.1/atdownload/file>, accessed 20 January 2012.

[71] P. Barnaghi, M. Bauer, S. Meissner, Service modeling for the Internet of Things, in: Computer Science and, Information Systems (FedCSIS2011), 2011, pp. 949–955.

[72] F. Chang, J. Dean, S. Ghemawat, W.C. Hsieh, D.A. Wallach, M. Burrows, T. Chandra, A. Fikes, R.E. Gruber, Bigtable: a distributed storage system for structured data, in: Proceedings of the Seventh Conference on USENIX Symposium on Operating Systems Design and Implementation—Volume 7, 2006, pp. 205–218.

[73] A. Lakshman, P. Malik, Cassandra: a decentralized structured storage system, Operating Syst. Rev. 44 (2) (2010) 35–40.

[74] M. Tomasevic, V. Milutinovic, Hardware approaches to cache coherence in shared-memory multiprocessors, Part 2, IEEE MICRO (14) (6) (1994) 61–66.

[75] A. Grujic, M. Tomasevic, V. Milutinovic, A Simulation study of hardware DSM approaches, IEEE Parallel Distrib. Technol. Spring (1996).

[76] M. Tomasevic, V. Milutinovic, A Simulation study of snoopy cache coherence protocols, in: Proceedings of the HICSS-92, Koloa, Hawaii, USA, 1992, pp. 427–436.

[77] D. Gajski, V. Milutinovic, H.J. Siegel, B. Furht, Tutorial on Computer Architecture, IEEE Press, 1987.

[78] V. Milutinovic, D. Fura, W. Helbig, J. Linn, Architecture/compiler synergism in GaAs computer systems, IEEE Comput. 20 (5) (1987) 72–93.

[79] I. Ikodinovic, A. Milenkovic, V. Milutinovic, D. Magdic, Limes: a multiprocessor simulation environment for PC platforms, in: Proceedings of the Third International Conference on Parallel Processing and Applied Mathematics (PPAM'99), Kazimierz Dolny, Poland, 14–17 September 1999, pp. 398–412.

[80] V. Milutinovic, Surviving the Design of a 200 MHz RISC Microprocessor: Lessons Learned, IEEE Computer Society Press, Los Alamitos, California, USA, 1997.

[81] A. Milenkovic, V. Milutinovic, Cache Injection: A Novel Technique for Tolerating Memory Latency in Bus-Based SMPs, in: Euro-Par 2000, 2000, pp. 558–566.

[82] The QuadTree, <http://en.wikipedia.org/wiki/Quadtree>, accessed 20 January 2012.

[83] A Comet Implementation for the Google Web Toolkit, <http://code.google.com/p/gwt-comet/>, accessed 20 January 2012.

[84] A. Bröring, J. Echterhoff, S. Jirka, I. Simonis, T. Everding, C. Stasch, S. Liang, R. Lemmens, New Generation Sensor Web Enablement, Sensors 11 (3) (2011) 2652–2699.

[85] T. Berners-Lee, Design Issues: Linked Data, World Wide Web Consortium (W3C) note, July 2006, <www.w3.org/DesignIssues/LinkedData.html>, accessed 20 January 2012.

[86] H. Patni, C. Henson, A. Sheth, Linked sensor data, in: IEEE International Symposium on Collaborative Technologies and Systems, May 2010, 2010, pp. 362–370.

[87] D. Le-Phuoc, M. Hauswirth, Linked open data in sensor data mashups, in: Second International Workshop on Semantic Sensor Networks Workshop (SSN2009), 2009.

[88] K. Page, D. De Roure, K. Martinez, J. Sadler, O. Kit, Linked sensor data: restfully serving rdf and gml, in: Proceedings of the Second International Workshop on Semantic Sensor Networks (SSN09), vol. 522, CEUR 2009, pp. 49–63, 2009.

[89] J. Dean, S. Ghemawat, MapReduce: simplified data processing on large clusters, in: Proceedings of the Sixth Symposium on Operating System Design and Implementation, San Francisco, CA, 6–8 December, USENIX Association, 2004.

[90] D. Abadi, A. Marcus, S. Madden, K. Hollenbach, Scalable semantic web data management using vertical partitioning, in: VLDB, 2007, pp. 411–422.

[91] C. Weiss, P. Karras, A. Bernstein, Hexastore: sextuple indexing for semantic web data management, in: PVLDB, vol. 1, No.1, 2008, pp. 1008–1019.

[92] Apache HBase, <http://hbase.apache.org/>, accessed 20 January 2012.

[93] Apache Hadoop, <http://hadoop.apache.org/>, accessed 20 January 2012.

[94] Apache Cassandra, <http://cassandra.apache.org/>, accessed 20 January 2012.

[95] NoSQL Databases, <http://nosql-database.org/>, accessed 20 January 2012.

[96] The WebSocket Protocol, <http://tools.ietf.org/html/rfc6455>, accessed 20 January 2012.

[97] Comet, <http://en.wikipedia.org/wiki/Comet(programming)>, accessed 20 January 2012.

ABOUT THE AUTHORS

Zoran Babovic is a Ph.D. student at the School of Electrical Engineering, University of Belgrade, Serbia, where he also received his M.Sc. in electrical engineering in 2004. After graduation, he has been working on several research and software development projects, in cooperation with leading EU Institutes and US/UK companies such as IPSI Fraunhofer Institute, Germany, Storage Tek, USA, Dow Jones, USA, Maxeler, UK, in the domain of multimedia, data management, and real time software systems. Since 2006 he is working as a research associate at the Innovation Center of the School of Electrical Engineering, University of Belgrade, Serbia. He participated in four EU FP6 and FP7 research projects in the domain of sensor networks, data mining, and computer architecture, as well as in four innovation and research projects funded by Serbian Ministry of Science and Technological Development. He published several conference and journal papers, and gave numerous talks at conferences in Europe.

Veljko Milutinovic received his Ph.D. in electrical engineering from University of Belgrade in 1982. During the 80's, for about a decade, he was on the faculty of Purdue University, West Lafayette, Indiana, USA, where he co-authored the architecture and design of the world's first DARPA GaAs microprocessor. Since the 90's, after returning to Serbia, he is on the faculty of the School of Electrical Engineering, University of Belgrade, where he is teaching courses related to computer engineering, sensor networks, and data mining. During the 90's, he also took part in teaching at the University of Purdue, Stanford and MIT. After year 2000, he participated in several FP6 and FP7 projects through collaboration with leading universities and industries in the EU / US, including Microsoft, Intel, IBM, Ericsson, especially Maxeler. He has lectured by invitation to over 100 European universities. He published about 50 papers in SCI journals and about 20 books with major publishers in the USA. He is a Fellow of the IEEE and a Member of Academia Europaea.

CHAPTER THREE

Mobility in Wireless Sensor Networks

Sriram Chellappan and Neelanjana Dutta

Department of Computer Science, Missouri University of Sciences and Technology, Rolla, MO 65409, USA

Contents

Advances in Computers, Volume 90
ISSN 0065-2458, http://dx.doi.org/10.1016/B978-0-12-408091-1.00003-8

Abstract

Wireless Sensor Networks (WSNs) are poised to significantly enhance a number of missions in the military, civilian, and industrial arenas. Recently, there has been a significant interest in the design of algorithms for exploiting sensor mobility. The motivation of these designs is mainly to enhance coverage in the deployment field. Broadly speaking, there are three standard notions of coverage in sensor networks: blanket, barrier, and event coverage. Blanket coverage refers to the case where every point in the sensor network needs to be covered. Barrier coverage refers to the case where every intrusion path in the sensor network needs to be covered. Event coverage refers to the case where events in the sensor network need to be covered as and when they occur. In this chapter, we present a survey of mobility algorithms for enhancing blanket, barrier, and event coverage in wireless sensor networks. The key metrics emphasized for evaluation of these algorithms are: quality of coverage, movement distance minimization, communication overhead, and energy constraints. We also highlight open issues in mobility in wireless sensor networks, including some discussions on uncontrolled sensor mobility.

1. INTRODUCTION

A Wireless Sensor Network (WSN) is a network comprising of a number of tiny embedded devices (called sensors) with limited sensing, processing, communication, and storage ability. When deployed (typically) in large numbers in a field of interest, sensors communicate among themselves forming an ad hoc network, formally called as a Wireless Sensor Network. WSNs are emerging to be critical for a variety of military, civilian, and industrial missions and applications. Military missions like battlefield monitoring, border patrol, soldier navigation can be significantly enhanced with WSNs. In the civilian arena, applications like soil monitoring, earthquake prediction, medical sensing, and networking are all becoming increasingly feasible with WSNs. A variety of industries are also benefiting from WSNs in the realm of product tracking, equipment maintenance, etc. In the last decade, a significant amount of research has been conducted in terms of leveraging sensor networks for a variety of applications such as target tracking and surveillance [1–3], soldier navigation [4], environmental monitoring [5], industrial maintenance [6, 7]. In parallel, extensive research has also been conducted to address aforementioned critical sensor networks challenges including fault detection [8, 9], design of energy efficient network protocols [2, 10], secure, and privacy preserving sensor networking [11–13], and localization [14–16].

However, despite the significant advantages that WSNs provide us, there are certain inherent limitations with WSNs. Since a typical sensor network involves thousands of sensor nodes, cost saving becomes critical. The hardware of typical sensors is primitive, precluding the feasibility of tamper resistance, large memory, GPS chips, etc. The small physical size and primitive hardware of sensors make them prone to failures and faults. Sensors are also severely energy constrained due to their small size. This challenge becomes more critical, since a majority of sensor network applications today expect sensors to work for long times unattended (without human intervention) post deployment. Furthermore, the nature of wireless communications make it difficult to secure sensor network communications from external adversaries. This challenge is exacerbated by the fact that complex cryptographic computations are not possible by the sensor nodes, considering their energy limitations.

With advances in hardware miniaturization, a recent activity of interest in WSNs is sensor mobility. A number of miniature mobile platforms are being designed and implemented. These platforms can easily interface with a wireless sensor, hence realizing the vision of sensor mobility [17–23]. Research and application have shown that mobility brings in tremendous benefits to sensor networks. For instance, let us consider coverage of a sensor network. A point in a field is said to be covered if it is within the sensing range of at-least one sensor. Coverage of a deployment field is a canonical property of any sensor network. There are three types of coverage in WSNs:

- blanket coverage (denoting coverage of every point in the deployment field),
- barrier coverage (denoting coverage of every intrusion path in the deployment field), and
- event coverage (denoting coverage of every event in the deployment field).

Various WSN applications require and exploit these types of coverage. However, achieving desired coverage can be challenging in large scale sensor networks. When a large number of sensors are deployed in a field, manual placement of sensors at desired locations is not feasible. In such fields, sensors are randomly deployed (for example from a moving vehicle or an airplane). Not all of them will be at optimal positions for desired coverage. Under such situations, mobility can significantly help the sensors to enhance quality of coverage, and hence quality of event detection and reliability. For a desired degree of coverage, the density of mobile sensors needed is typically much lower than the density of static sensors. However, just like with static sensors, there are some constraints even with exploiting sensor mobility. Since mobility is an energy consuming operation, it is not a replenishable resource and hence cannot be wasted through inconsequential movements. Also, in hostile and rugged environments like battlefields, smooth mobility of miniature platforms is not feasible and available movement paths are likely to be constrained. Keeping all these factors in considerations, researchers have proposed different algorithms for coverage in WSNs using sensor mobility.

In this chapter, we provide a comprehensive survey of mobility in wireless sensor networks. We first provide an introduction to some recent developments in hardware support for sensor mobility. We then present several recent coverage enhancing algorithms with mobile sensors from the perspective of blanket, barrier, and event coverage. Critical metrics emphasized include quality of desired coverage, movement distance minimization, communication cost, and energy constraints. Finally, we also present some open issues from the perspective of how sensor mobility impacts network security, and emergent paradigms in mobile sensor networks where sensors are unable to control their own mobility (e.g., sensors fitted on animals, patients carrying sensors, sensors deployed in ocean beds, etc.).

This chapter is arranged as follows. In Section 2, we discuss some recently developed platforms for sensor mobility. In Section 3, we present a number of algorithms exploiting sensor mobility for blanket coverage. In Section 4, we present sensor mobility algorithms for enhancing barrier coverage. In Section 5, we present algorithms for enhancing event coverage in WSNs. We then highlight important open issues in the realm of mobile sensor networks in Section 6, and conclude this chapter in Section 8.

2. PLATFORMS FOR SENSOR MOBILITY

In this section, we illustrate recently developed miniature mobile platforms for sensors. To keep the discussions in scope, we only focus on the mobility centric aspects of the platforms, and do not focus on external issues like communication, processing, power modules, etc.

XYZ Platform: The mobility subsystem of the XYZ platform (see Fig. 1) consists of an H-bridge and a miniature geared motor from a pager device [20]. The mobility subsystem is implemented on an additional accessory board that transforms XYZ to a 2-D motion enabled sensor node that can move along a horizontal string. Two output pins of the processor control the motor direction and braking. The motor is controlled via an H-bridge

Fig. 1. The XYZ platform.

which converts a 3.3 V logic of the CPU to a 5 V DC supply necessary for supporting speed and motor power requirements. A LED/phototransistor pair focused on a four segment black and white pattern that is pasted directly onto a wheel acts as an optical encoder and is used as odometer. A transition from one segment to another, detected by the sensor, occurs when the sensor node is moving. The transition is fed directly to a counter on the sensor node, and by accumulating the counter values, a position value is determined. The maximum movement distance of the XYZ platform without recharging is about 165 m.

Robomote Platform: The wheels of the Robomote platform (in Fig. 2) have DC motors from Micromo [24, 25]. The nominal voltage of the motors is 6 V and the output power is 1.41 W. The efficiency of the motors is 71% with a no-load speed of 300 rpm and a no-load current of 30 mA. The gear ratio is 25:1 and for every revolution of the wheel, we get 150 ticks for feedback control. The motors are controlled using an H-bridge, made from discrete components, and utilizes Pulse Width Modulation (PWM) for its operation. The four signals which control the motors are PWM1, PWM2, Direction1, and Direction2. By changing the direction bits, the direction of

Fig. 2. The robomote platform.

the motors can be reversed. The robomote relies on precise odometry for movement from one location to another. Hence, the robomote incorporates optical encoders for feedback. The feedback uses IR TX/RX mechanism for sensing the number of ticks on the wheel. Every rotation of the motor shaft produces six ticks, which are then processed by the op–amps. This feedback is then fed to the counters of the Atmel Microcontroller. Motion control is triggered by velocity and distance commands from the upper layer. These commands are converted to the corresponding PWM and tick values. The lower board implements a PI controller that corrects for odometry error inherent in the motors and attempts to run the robomote straight. The PI controller is activated with a frequency of 2 Hz. It computes the difference in ticks between the left and right wheels and feeds corrections back to the PWM inputs that are applied to the motors.The controller is bypassed for turn commands and calibration to avoid additional complexity. The maximum movement distance of the Robomote platform without recharging is about 360 m.

Self Healing Minefield (SHM): The Self Healing Minefield is a platform (in Fig. 3) specifically developed by DARPA for mobility support in rugged terrains. The dimensions of the mine are 12 cm in diameter and 7.5 cm in height and it weighs less than 2 kg. The platform has an orientation sensor and an optional GPS chip. Mobility support is provided by means of a fuel ignited propulsion chamber. There are four end-mounted *pancake* rocket thrusters on either side of the mine. With fuel injection, the thrusters can propel the mine to a range of upto 10 m. The maximum number of hops in the SHM platform without recharging is about 100.

Fig. 3. DARPA Self-healing minefield platform.

Discussions: With advances in hardware miniaturization, embedded mobility platforms are increasingly becoming practical as evidenced above. In each of the aforementioned implementations, sensors of appropriate sensing modality can be interfaced with the hardware circuitry to realize mobile sensors. When such mobile sensors also communicate over the wireless medium, it is called a mobile wireless sensor network. Note that while the nature of mobility in the XYZ and Robomote platforms in Fig. 1 and 2 is smooth crawling on a surface, the mobility model of the SHM platform in Fig. 3 is hop-based mobility. The hop-based model is especially suited for battlefield line environments where their rugged nature makes smooth crawling impractical.

Note here that in each of the above implementations, the maximum mobility of the mobile platform is limited. This is the case irrespective of whether the platforms are battery powered or fuel powered. Since energy is a scarce resource in sensors, and since available energy has to be shared for sensing, processing, and communication, the available energy for mobility is clearly restricted. This problem warrants the need of considering limited mobility constraints while designing algorithms that exploit sensor mobility for practical applications.

3. ALGORITHMS FOR BLANKET COVERAGE

Blanket coverage is the simplest form of coverage, where the goal is that every point in the deployment field should be within the sensing range of one or more sensors. A point is said to be 1-covered if it is within the sensing

(a)   **(b)**

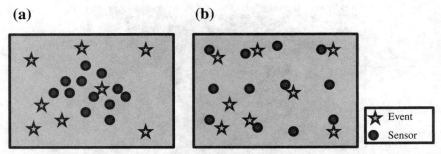

Fig. 4. (a) Instance of an initial deployment scenario and (b) deployment scenario with high degree of blanket coverage.

range of at-least *one* sensor. A point is said to be k-covered if it is within the sensing range of at-least k sensors. Starting from an initial deployment, the goal of any mobility algorithm is to relocate sensors to achieve high quality of k-blanket coverage where $k \geq 1$. Figure 4a illustrates the case of an initial deployment where the quality of blanket coverage is poor. For the same number of sensors, Fig. 4b illustrates the case of superior 1-blanket coverage Fig.4a. In the following, we detail mobility algorithms for blanket coverage in sensor networks.

3.1 Virtual Force Movement Algorithms

Wang et al. [19] designed a Virtual Force algorithm for improving 1-coverage in the network after an initial random deployment of sensors. The idea is based on sensors constructing Voronoi polygons based on their known positions. It can be noted that while sensor position estimation is not explicitly addressed, they can be computed either via GPS receivers or via known positions of a few sensors [26, 27]. The Voronoi polygon is a data structure in geometry that represents the proximity information of a set of geometric nodes.

Figure 5 illustrates the Voronoi diagram for a set of 15 points in 2-D space. Figure 6 is the construction of a Voronoi polygon for a single node. Note that line segments $V_1 - V_2, V_2 - V_3, V_3 - V_4, V_4 - V_5, V_5 - V_1$ are the perpendicular bisectors of line segments $O-A, O-B, O-C, O-D, O-E$. Each point inside the polygon $V_1, V_2, V_3, V_4,$ and V_5 is closer to Point O than to any other point on the plane. From the perspective of coverage, the Voronoi polygon is practical. In essence, if a Point p inside the Voronoi polygon of Point O (i.e., area within $V_1, V_2, V_3, V_4,$ and V_5) is not within

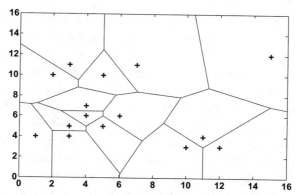

Fig. 5. Voronoi diagram for a set of 15 points (denoted by +).

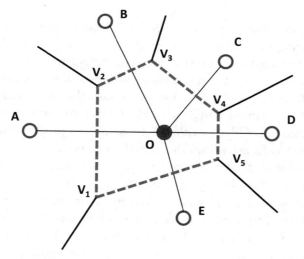

Fig. 6. Voronoi polygon for point *O*.

the sensing range of a sensor in Point *O*, then no sensor in any other point on the plane can cover Point *p*.

A number of movement algorithms are proposed in [19] leveraging from Voronoi construction. The first algorithm is called as *VECtor-based algorithm*. This algorithm is motivated by the attributes of electro–magnetic properties. Two particles close to each other are expelled apart due to repulsive forces. Assume $d(s_i, s_j)$ is the distance between two sensors s_i and s_j. Let d_{ave} be the average distance between two sensors when the sensor network is deployed for 1-coverage. In the *VEC* algorithm, the virtual force between two sensors

s_i and s_j will push them away to a distance $(d_{ave} - d(s_i, s_j))/2$. In case, a sensor covers its entire Voronoi polygon, its neighboring sensor will be pushed a distance $d_{ave} - d(s_i, s_j)$ away. Note that a number of such virtual forces will act on every sensor. The overall force on a sensor is simply the vector summation of virtual forces from all of its Voronoi neighbors. Eventually, these virtual forces will push sensors from a densely covered area to a sparsely covered area.

The second movement algorithm proposed is called the *VORonoi-based algorithm*. Unlike the *VEC* algorithm, the *VOR* algorithm is a pull-based algorithm. This algorithm pulls-sensors to their local maximum coverage holes. In the *VOR* algorithm, if a sensor detects the existence of coverage holes, it will move toward the farthest Voronoi vertex. However, to prevent a sensor from moving too far without knowledge of its neighbors positions, the movement distance traveled is half of the maximum possible movement distance.

The last algorithm proposed is called *Minimax* algorithm. Compared to *VOR* algorithm, the *Minimax* algorithm fixes coverage holes by moving closer to the farthest Voronoi vertex. However, it does not move as far as *VOR* to avoid the situation that the vertex which was originally close now becomes the new farthest vertex. *Minimax* instead chooses the target location as the point inside the Voronoi polygon whose distance to the farthest Voronoi vertex is minimum. This algorithm is based on the premise that a sensor should not be too far away from any of its Voronoi vertices when the sensors are evenly distributed. *Minimax* can reduce the variance of the distances to the Voronoi vertices, resulting in a more regular shaped Voronoi polygon, thereby utilizing the sensor's sensing circle in a more effective fashion.

Algorithms Features: The above algorithms based on virtual forces relocate sensors from areas of dense deployments to sparse areas, eventually balancing coverage across the entire area. The algorithms are purely distributed and localized. Hence they require minimal complexity in communication and computation. The key limitation of the Virtual Force algorithms is that since the mobility of sensors is based on purely local decisions, they may not be optimal in the global scenario. Therefore, it takes multiple sensor movements over multiple iterations before the algorithm converges. However, as we saw in Section 2, the maximum mobility of sensors is limited without recharging. Hence, scalability is a major issue with the Virtual Force algorithms. As the deployment fields can be very large in practice, the applicability of the Virtual Force algorithms becomes substantially limited.

More recently, there have been some works that have extended the basic idea of the Virtual Force-based algorithm. In the work of Ma et al. [28], the concept of Delaunay triangulation is coupled with virtual force techniques to design sensor mobility algorithms for coverage enhancement. The goal in this paper is to design sensor movement algorithms for positioning sensors as vertices of equilateral triangles in a plane. As we know, this is the optimal deployment pattern for full coverage of an area for sensors with circular sensing disks. In [28], each node first determines its Delaunay neighbors. With the goal to adjust the distances between two Delaunay neighbors to $\sqrt{3}r$ (where r is the sensing range of a sensor), the proposed algorithm repels closer sensors and attracts farther sensors to maintain the $\sqrt{3}r$ distance between Delaunay neighbors. In [29], Chen et al. proposed a simple extension to the basic virtual force-based approach wherein the virtual forces between sensors decreases exponentially with the distances between sensors. This approach guarantees faster convergence of the algorithm compared to the basic version.

3.2 Scan-Based Movement Algorithm

Wu and Yang in [30] address a problem similar to that in the work of Wang et al. in [19]. The sensor network considered is clustered into multiple grids and a number of sensors are deployed initially. Starting from the initial deployment, the goal is to balance the number of sensors in each grid post sensor movement. In this approach, sensors scan the grids row wise using local communication messages. The scan algorithm works from one end of the row to another (first scan) and then from the other end back to the start (second scan). The direction of the first sweep is called positive and that of the second sweep is called negative. Let us denote the number of sensors in Grid i as w_i. The first sweep calculates the prefix sum v_i, where a particular sensor in Grid i determines its prefix sum v_i by adding $v_{i-1} + w_i$ and forwarding v_i to the next grid. A sensor in the last grid determines v_n and $\bar{w} = \dfrac{v_n}{n}$ (load in a balanced state) and initiates the second scan by sending out $\bar{w}$. During this scan, sensors in each grid can determine $v_i = i\bar{w}$ (load of prefixsum in a balanced state) based on $\bar{w}$ that is passed around and its own Grid i. Knowing the load in the balanced state, each grid can easily determine its "give/take" state. Specifically, when $w_i - \bar{w} = 0$, Grid i is in the neutral state. When $w_i - \bar{w} > 0$, it is overloaded and in the *give* state. When $w_i - \bar{w} < 0$, it is underloaded and in the *receive* state. Each grid in the *give* state also needs to determine the number of sensors (load) to be sent to each direction: $\overrightarrow{w}_i$ for load in the positive direction (right), and $\overleftarrow{w}_i$ for load in the negative direction (give-left). Based on the scan procedure, we can see that,

$$\vec{w}_i = min\{w_i - \bar{w}, max\{v_i - \bar{v}_i, 0\}\}, \tag{1}$$

$$\overleftarrow{w}_i = (w_i - \bar{w}) - \vec{w}_i. \tag{2}$$

Similarly, a set of conditions can be defined for the *take* state as,

$$\vec{w}_i = min\{\bar{w} - w_i, max\{v_{i-1} - \bar{v}_{i-1}, 0\}\}, \tag{3}$$

$$\overleftarrow{w}_i = (\bar{w} - w_i) - \vec{w}_i. \tag{4}$$

This movement plan balances the number of sensors per row when sensors in each row execute the above algorithm. A subsequent column wise scan in a similar fashion, followed by movements balances the number of sensors in both rows and columns. It is proved that the number of movements in this algorithm is at most twice the number of optimal sensor movements. Figure 7 illustrates the algorithm execution with a simple example where row wise scan and column wise scan are performed on the initial deployment of sensors to minimize the variance in number of sensors in each grid.

Algorithm Features: The scan-based movement algorithm is relatively simple and incurs significantly low complexity in execution. It also has provable bounds on the number of sensor movements that are wasted. One challenge during execution of this algorithm is that it cannot handle partitions in the network partitions. Network partition is a common phenomenon in WSNs wherein one part of the network cannot communicate with another part due to loss of signal, node failure, etc. Wu and Wang [30] propose distributed suboptimal techniques to repair such partitions during initial deployment. In such cases, the algorithm executes in two stages. The first stage will repair partitions in the network while the next stage will scan the rows and columns for sensor movements.

(a)   **(b)**   **(c)**

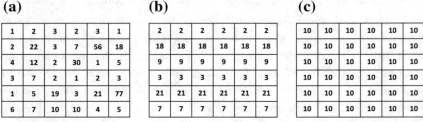

Fig. 7. (a) Execution of scan-based movement algorithm starting from an initial deployment, (b) row wise scan, and (c) column wise scan. The number in each grid is the number of sensors in the corresponding grid.

Compared to the Virtual Force-based algorithms, the Scan-based algorithm has both strengths and weaknesses. The strength of the Scan algorithm is the significantly lower number of sensor movements that it incurs compared to the Virtual Force algorithms (where sensors may have to execute several back and forth movements). The Scan-based algorithms naturally are better suited for deployment scenarios where multiple sensors are needed to cover a point, while the Virtual Force algorithms are better suited for 1-coverage only. The limitation of the Scan-based algorithm is that it always forces the sensor network to be completely load balanced. That is, the objective of this algorithm is that each grid should always have the same number of sensors after the algorithm execution. While this may seem desirable, it is not the always advantageous. In many sensor network scenarios, sensors are typically over-provisioned to compensate for faults and failures. For example, consider Fig. 7 again. Let us assume that the desired number of sensors per grid is only five. In such a case, it is enough if each grid has only five sensors. The over-provisioned sensors can stay static, and later move when sensors in other grids become faulty or fail. The Scan algorithm cannot address such scenarios. The Virtual Force algorithms, on the other hand, will converge when every point in the network is within the coverage range of at-least *one* sensor and hence any movement for load balancing is eliminated in Virtual Force algorithms.

3.3 Randomized Movement Algorithm

In [31], Liu et al., investigated a very simple mobility strategy that requires no communication, coordination, or computation strategies from the sensor network side. In this model, sensors post deployment move randomly in the network with the goal of detecting a (mobile or stationary) intruder. While this mobility model is quite simple, it does lend itself to derive interesting properties on intruder coverage with mobile sensors. The authors formally prove that overall coverage of the sensor network will improve in the case of a mobile sensor network compared to a randomly deployed all static sensor network. Along with the improvement in spatial coverage, the time taken to detect intruders naturally is lower in a mobile sensor network.

The authors model the intrusion detection process as a game played between mobile sensors and a mobile intruder. Let us assume that the sensor locations can be modeled by a stationary two-dimensional Poisson point process. Let us denote the density of the underlying Poisson point process as λ. The number of sensors located in a region R, $N(R)$, follows a Poisson distribution of parameter $\lambda ||R||$, where $||R||$ represents the area of the region.

$$P(N(R) = K) = \frac{e^{\lambda ||R||}(\lambda ||R||)^K}{k!}. \tag{5}$$

Assuming that each sensor covers a disk of radius r, the initial configuration of the sensor network can be described by a Poisson Boolean model $B(\lambda, r)$. A fundamental result derived in [31] is stated below.

Theorem 1.   *Consider a sensor network $B(\lambda, r)$ at time $t = 0$, with sensors moving according to the random mobility model at a fixed speed v_s. The optimal mobility strategy of the sensors to detect an intruder is for each sensor to choose a direction according to a uniform distribution, i.e., $f_\phi^s = \frac{1}{2\pi}$.*

It follows from Theorem 1, when sensors choose directions according to a uniform distribution, the optimal intruder mobility strategy is to stay stationary. This will maximize its detection time by sensors in the network. While the contributions of [31] are of deep theoretical interest, the practical applicability of sensors moving in a random direction in the network without stopping is limited, especially due to energy constraints among sensors.

3.4 Limited Mobility Algorithms for Blanket Coverage

In each of the sensor mobility algorithms presented above, no maximum bound is considered for the distance traveled by a sensor. In other words, while minimizing sensor mobility distance is considered, the sensors are assumed to be capable of moving any distance. As we saw in Section 2, due to energy limitations, sensors have a maximum bound on the distance they can move. When one considers such *hard* limitations in sensor mobility distance, the existing algorithms become inadequate. Figure 8 illustrates the challenges of hard sensor mobility limitations: if a sensor wishes to move from Point A

Impacts of Energy/ Distance Limitations in Controlled Sensor Mobility:

Since sensors are limited in their energy, it is very likely that there is a hard limitation on the maximum traversable distance for the sensors. This limitation will impact algorithm design for controlled sensor mobility. We illustrate with an example below.

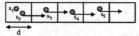

In the above figure, *five* sensors are deployed in a grid network. A grid is *covered* if a sensor is present inside it. Consider a sensor (s_2) that is redundant in its grid and it wishes to move to the empty grid on the right to improve coverage. Let the maximum distance capability of each sensor be d (due to energy limitations). As we can see, the distance limitation means that sensor s_2 cannot move to the destination by itself. To do so, s_2 may need to move to some intermediate grid towards the destination, and from then on another sensor (s_3) will move towards the destination and so on (like a chain) until a sensor finally reaches the empty grid. The presence of such a chain like mobility pattern is unique to limited mobility sensors, and is not trivial to determine in a large scale sensor network. Such a challenge does not exist when hard mobility limitations are not explicitly considered.

Fig. 8. Impacts of distance limitations in controlled sensor mobility.

in the field to Point B, it may be unable to do so if its maximum movement distance is lower than the distance to be traversed. Hence a sensor has to be dependent on other sensors to move, resulting in a chain like movement pattern triggered among multiple nodes. Identifying such a strategy in a large scale sensor network is a major challenge. In the following, we propose several movement algorithms for sensors with hard mobility limitations.

We have designed sensor mobility algorithms for enhancing blanket coverage in sensor networks in [22, 23, 32]. The fundamental contributions of our algorithms compared to the ones discussed above are twofold: (1) consideration of limitations in maximum sensor movement distance, and (2) consideration of general k-coverage scenarios. The sensor network we study is a square field of size Q with mobile sensor nodes deployed in it. It is clustered into 2-D square grids, where each grid is of size R. We denote the number of sensors in a grid, i, at time of initial deployment as n_i. The sensing area of each sensor is a circle, and a sensor present in a grid implies that the grid is completely covered. The deployment objective is for each grid to have a certain number of sensors, denoted by $\bar{k}$. At the time of initial deployment, not all grids will have $\bar{k}$ sensors. If a sensor moves from one grid to any of its adjacent neighboring grids, we consider that as *one* step made by the sensor. We denote H as the maximum number of such steps that a sensor is capable of making. In this context, our problem statement is (see Fig. 9): given a sensor network with S grids each of size R, an initial deployment of N limited mobility sensors, our goal is to determine a sequence of sensor movements such that at the conclusion of movements, (1) the variance in the number of sensors from $\bar{k}$ among all the grids in the network with less than $\bar{k}$ sensors is minimized, and (2) the overall number of steps of the limited mobility sensors is simultaneously minimized. Denoting k_i as the number of sensors in a grid i at the conclusion of sensor movements, the variance Var is,

$$Var = \frac{1}{S} \sum_{S} (\bar{k} - min(k_i, \bar{k}))^2. \tag{6}$$

Denoting h_i as the number of steps made by sensor i (where, $h_i \leq H$), and denoting N as the number of sensors initially deployed, the overall number of sensors movement steps is,

$$M = \sum_{i=1}^{N} h_i. \tag{7}$$

Our problem is to simultaneously minimize two objectives, namely Var (a non-linear function) and M.

The leftmost figure, Figure (a), shows an initial deployment of sensors in the network that is divided into imaginary grids. The number inside circles denotes the number of sensors in that region. The number in the upper left corner denotes the corresponding region ID. Let maximum number of hops H = 1, and k = 2. There are 32 sensors initially deployed. At time of initial deployment, regions 2, 3, 9, 10, 11, 14, 15 have less than k sensors. An intuitive way to minimize the variance from k is to let 8 neighboring regions locally synchronize for movement. Using local information exchanges, it is likely that the sensors move according to the sequence shown in the second Figure (b). The arrows indicate direction of movement, and the numbers beside arrows indicate number of sensors moved from that region. But the deployment in Figure (b) does not satisfy our objective to simultaneously minimize variance of number of sensors in each grid and number of hops moved by sensors. An optimal movement plan is presented in Figure (c). For optimal deployment, region 6 should move sensors to regions 10 and 15. The path to region 15 may appear long, but it is the one that makes the global variance 0 as shown in the final deployment in Figure (d). In large scale sensor networks, discovering such paths is extremely challenging.

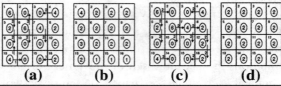

(a)   **(b)**   **(c)**   **(d)**

Fig. 9. An instance of initial deployment, intuitive movement plan, and optimal movement plan for mobile sensors.

Problem Features: Our problem is general, since we place no restriction on $\bar{k}$. If $\bar{k} = 1$, then it means a requirement of *one* sensor per grid. For applications where redundancy is important, $\bar{k}$ can be set larger than 1. An important feature of our work is that we do not minimize the variance of number of sensors among all grids from $\bar{k}$. We minimize it among only the grids that have *less* than $\bar{k}$ sensors at final deployment, which is captured by the term $min(k_i,\bar{k})$ in Eq. (6). In many cases, sensors are *over-deployed*. When the deployment objective is only $\bar{k}$ sensors per grid, the nature of the proposed solution will not let extra sensors move, when the requirement of at-least $\bar{k}$ sensors among all grids has been met. This is to preserve the mobility of sensors in such cases. Eventually, when some sensors fail (due to faults, power losses, etc.), the deficiency in $\bar{k}$ requirement can be met by the spare sensors whose limited mobility was initially preserved, effectively complementing the motivations for over-deployment.

Our Weight-Based Methodology: We now present our weight-based methodology toward designing an *optimal* algorithm for our deployment problem. We first present the premise of our approach, followed by the design of an optimal algorithm for our problem. Clearly, the overall variance is minimized (= 0), when each grid has at-least $\bar{k}$ sensors. Thus, for each grid i in the sensor network, we first create $\bar{k}$ *virtual sinks* (or simply *sinks*) in order to allocate a position (*virtually*) for each of the $\bar{k}$ sensors that are needed in each grid. Let each sink in grid i be denoted by $s_i^1, s_i^2, s_i^3, \ldots, s_i^{\bar{k}}$. For each sink $s_i^1, s_i^2, s_i^3, \ldots, s_i^{\bar{k}}$, a weight is assigned, denoted by $w_i^1, w_i^2, w_i^3, \ldots, w_i^{\bar{k}}$ respectively to prioritize movements toward larger weight sinks compared to sinks with smaller weights (with the objective being global variance minimization). The weights are defined by

$$w_i^j = 2 * j - 1 (1 \leq j \leq \bar{k}).$$ (8)

Note that sink s_i^m has more weight than s_i^n, if $m > n$. Also, $w_i^m = w_j^m$ for any two grids i and j. After sensors move toward sinks (according to their weights), some sinks will have sensors, while some do not. In order to capture the presence of a sensor in each sink among the multiple grids (after sensors move), we define the following function:

$$\phi_i^j = \begin{cases} 1 & \text{if sink } s_i^j \text{ has a sensor,} \\ 0 & \text{otherwise.} \end{cases}$$ (9)

There is a constraint for the function ϕ. If $\phi_i^j = 1$, then $\phi_i^m = 1$ for all $m > j$. We are in effect saying here that if sink s_i^j in grid i has a sensor, then each sink s_i^m in grid i with larger weights (i.e., $m > j$) should have a sensor. The function ϕ captures whether a sink contains a sensor. We define a new metric here called *Score* as follows:

$$Score = \frac{1}{S} \left(\sum_{i=1}^{S} \sum_{j=1}^{\bar{k}} \phi_i^j \times w_i^j \right).$$ (10)

The *Score* function is the summation of weights of those sinks (for all grids) that contain a sensor in them. Clearly, the *Score* is larger when there are more sinks containing a sensor. The *Score* function also considers the weight of a sink. As such, in the event that a sensor can move to more than one sink, the sensor moves to the sink with the largest weight. Therefore during sensor movements, when we attempt to maximize the *Score*, we are in effect ensuring that a sensor is contained in as many sinks as possible and that sinks with larger weight always have higher priority compared to sinks with smaller weight.

Theorem 2. *A sequence of sensor movements that maximizes Score will minimize the variance Var and vice versa.*

From Theorem 2, we can see that our original non–linear variance objective can be translated to a linear objective. In our algorithms, we create sinks for each grid depending on the number of sensors needed. Each sink has a weight associated with it, such that when sensors move, sinks with larger weights have higher priority compared to sinks with smaller weights. The goal of our algorithms is to maximize the *Score*, which according to Theorem 2 minimizes the variance *Var*. The second objective of our problem is to minimize the total number of sensor movement steps. We achieve this goal by treating sensor movement steps as costs, and minimizing such costs in our algorithms. When there are multiple sinks in other grids with same weights, our algorithms will ensure that sensors move to sinks in those grids that are closer in terms of distance to be traversed. Clearly, sinks with larger weights are still given more priority compared to sinks with smaller weights. However, with such movements, the resulting number of overall sensor movement steps is minimized, along with maximizing *Score*. If a sensor in a grid does not need to move to another grid we treat the sensor as *virtually* moving to a sink in the same grid. Such a movement incurs *zero* cost.

A Maximum Weighted Flow Algorithm: We now present our optimal algorithm to maximize the *Score* function in the sensor network, which according to Theorem 2 minimizes the variance. Algorithm 1 illustrates the pseudocode.

Algorithm 1. Pseudocode of the *OMF* algorithm

1: Collect the information on the number of sensors in each grid in the sensor network.

2: Construct a graph $G_V(V_V, E_V)$ using the above grid information, desired number of sensors per grid is $\bar{k}$ and the sensor mobility capacity H. G_V models the sensor network at initial deployment time.

3: Determine the minimum cost maximum weighted flow from source grid to weighted sinks in G_V.

4: Determine a movement plan for the sensors in the sensor network based on the above flow plan in G_V.

5: Forward the movement plan to sensors in the network.

Figure 10 shows a simple illustration of constructing virtual graph G_V that converts the sensor network into a graph structure. We have a 2×2 sensor network. We assume each sensor can move only *one* step in its top, down, right or left directions only. Let us assume that desired number of sensors per gird $\bar{k} = 3$. For each grid in the network, we create $\bar{k} = 3$ virtual sinks, and assign weights to them in accordance with our weight-based methodology. Note that vs_i^j denotes the jth virtual sink for grid i. We also create three additional vertices for each grid i, denoted by v_i^b, v_i^{out}, and v_i^{in} in order to capture the following respectively: each grid, allowable departure of sensors from a grid and allowable entry of sensors into the corresponding grid. The capacity of the edge from v_i^{in} to v_j^{out} denotes the number of sensors that can

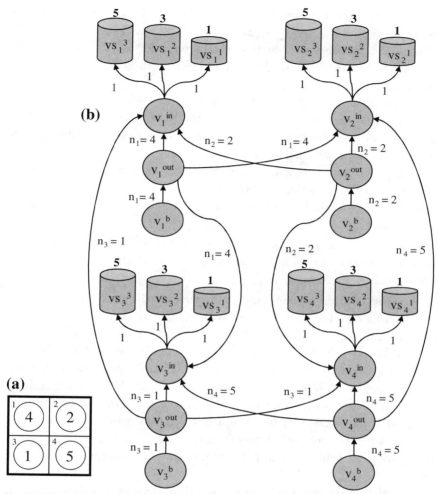

Fig. 10. (a) An instance of the initial network deployment and (b) the corresponding virtual graph G_V.

move from grid i to grid j, and is shown in G_V. Edges from v_i^b to v_i^{out} and from v_i^{out} to v_i^{in} depict internal movements within the same grid, and their capacities are simply the number of sensors in grid i initially. Since $\bar{k}$ virtual sinks are created, and since we desire $\bar{k}$ sensors per grid, the capacity of an edge from v_i^{in} to vs_i^j for any grid i is *one*. The cost of the edge between v_i^{out} to v_j^{in} denotes the minimum number of hops it takes to reach grid i from grid j. Since, the number of possible steps is limited to *one*, the cost is *one*. Clearly, other edges denote internal movements within a grid and hence have *zero* cost. Finally, we also create two additional vertices V_{source} and V_{sink}. Edges are added from V_{source} to v_i^b $\forall i$, and from vs_i^j $\forall i,j$ to V_{sink}. Based on this construction, for every feasible flow plan between v_i^{out} to v_j^{in} in G_V, there is a corresponding feasible sensor movement plan from grid i to grid j in the sensor network.

We now formally define the Maximum weighted flow problem in a graph, where each target (vertex) has a weight, and the objective is to maximize the summation of the flow amount through each target multiplied with the target weight. Mathematically, for a graph G, we want to maximize $W = \sum_{i=1}^{Z} f_i \times w_i$, where Z is the number of targets, w_i and f_i are the weight and amount of flow to Target i. Note that the maximum flow problem is a special case of this problem, where $w_i = 1$ $\forall i$. Based on the discussion so far, we now have Theorem 3.

Theorem 3.   *The Maximum Weighted Flow plan in G_V from V_{source} to V_{sink} translates to a sensor movement plan in the Network that maximizes the Score and hence minimizes the variance.*

We propose a simple technique to determine the maximum weighted flow plan in G_V. For each edge vs_i^j with weight w_i^j, we can add a cost to the edge from vs_i^j to V_{sink}, where the cost is the negative of w_i^j. However, to prevent the newly added costs from being affected by the costs already there in G_V, we multiple the new cost with an arbitrarily large number. Now the Minimum Cost Maximum Flow Plan in G_V is the Maximum Weighted Flow Plan in G_V that also minimizes overall cost. Since this plan maximizes the Score, it minimizes variance. Translating this flow plan into the network, we can say that the amount of flow from v_i^{out} to v_j^{in} is the number of sensors that move from grid i to grid j. Evidently, this plan also minimizes sensor movements.

Algorithm Features: The maximum flow algorithm proposed in [22, 23, 32] is general in the sense that it can address both 1-coverage and k-coverage problems ($k \geq 1$). In the proposed algorithm, sensors that are over-deployed do not waste their movements. They simply stay static as long as the requirement of having $\bar{k}$ sensors per grid is met. These sensors can subsequently be relocated under faults and failures of nodes in other grids. By conserving sensor mobility in this manner, the proposed algorithm improves upon both the Virtual Force and Scan-based algorithms. Note that the problem defined and the algorithm proposed are applicable for differentiated coverage when the number of sensors per grid is different for different grids. Additionally, when pure load balancing is desired (similar to the objective of the Scan-based algorithm), $\bar{k}$ can be set very large

Table 1 Comparison of different algorithms for blanket coverage.

Algorithm	Distributed Execution	Sensor Mobility Limitations Considered	Nature of Deployment Field
Virtual Force Movement	✓	✗	Unrestricted
Scan–based Movement	✓	✗	Grid only
Randomized Movement	✓	✗	Unrestricted
Optimal Maximum Flow	✗	✓	Grid only

and the maximum flow algorithm can balance sensor flows to every grid equally. Other optimization objectives like balancing mobility distance traveled among all sensors can be easily accomplished in the proposed algorithm. The proposed algorithm can also be executed suboptimally by partitioning the network into multiple large clusters and executing the maximum flow algorithm over multiple clusters.

Table 1 presents a brief comparative study of main features of the various algorithms used to achieve blanket coverage.

3.5 Theoretical Bounds for Coverage with Limited Mobility Sensors

In [33], Wang et al. extend the algorithms proposed in [22, 23, 32] for coverage with limited mobility sensor networks. In particular, the work in [33] considers the problem of deriving bounds for the amount of mobility needed to achieve k-coverage. The authors formally prove that an all mobile sensor network can provide k–coverage over a sensor field with a constant sensor density of $O(k)$, where the maximum distance a mobile sensor moves is $O(\frac{1}{\sqrt{(k)}} log^{\frac{3}{4}}(k \times L))$. The authors then propose a hybrid network where with $O(\frac{1}{\sqrt{k}})$ mobile sensors. For this network, the authors prove that k-coverage is achievable with a constant sensor density of $O(k)$, where each mobile sensor's movement is bounded by $O(log^{\frac{3}{4}} L)$. Finally, the authors propose a purely localized and distributed sensor movement algorithm that is inspired by the *maximum flow*-based sensor movement algorithms [23, 22] that can achieve the abovementioned k-coverage bounds.

4. ALGORITHMS FOR ENHANCING BARRIER COVERAGE

By definition, barrier coverage means that every intrusion path through the sensor network needs to be within the sensing range of one or more sen-

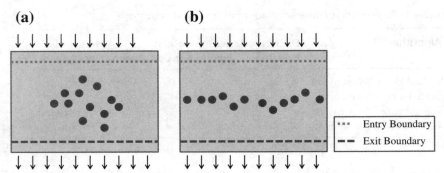

Fig. 11. (a) Instance of an initial deployment scenario and (b) deployment scenario with high degree of barrier coverage.

sors. Figure 11 illustrates the case of barrier coverage. An intrusion path is said to be 1-barrier covered if it intersects with the sensing disc of at-least one sensor. A path is said to be k-barrier covered if it intersects with the sensing disc of at-least k distinct sensors ($k \geq 1$). Starting from an initial deployment, the goal of any mobility algorithm to relocate sensors to achieve high quality of 1 or k-barrier coverage ($k \geq 1$). Figure 11a illustrates the case of an initial deployment where the quality of barrier coverage is poor. For the same number of sensors, Fig. 11b illustrates the case of superior 1-barrier coverage. In the following, we detail sensor mobility algorithms for enhancing barrier coverage in sensor networks.

4.1 Optimal Sensor Mobility Algorithms for Barrier Coverage

The issue of optimal sensor mobility algorithms for barrier coverage for belt-based deployment fields is investigated in [34] by Yang et al. In belt-based deployment, the barrier is modeled as a long belt region with two parallel sides to the belt: *entrance side* and *destination side*. In this context, Theorem 4 is formally proved for barrier without any obstructions.

Theorem 4. *Consider an intrusion path perpendicular to the source and destination barrier with a maximum intrusion speed. An optimal sensor movement strategy to maximize the coverage degree of such an intrusion is that each sensor moves in parallel to the barrier sides with maximum speed according to,*

$$f_\phi(\theta) = \begin{cases} \frac{1}{2} & \theta_s = 0 \ or \ \pi, \\ 0 & otherwise. \end{cases} \tag{11}$$

where $f_\phi(\theta)$ is the probability density function characterizing the movement of sensors.

From the above discussions, it can be stated that an intrusion equilibrium in a non–obstructed barrier is reached when: (1) each sensor moves in parallel to the destination side of barrier according to Theorem 4 and (2) the intruder crosses the barrier at the maximum intruding speed and along the path that is perpendicular to the destination side of the barrier. This is because any other intrusion yields a higher intrusion coverage degree, while any other sensor movement strategy allows the intruder to plan a better intrusion that yields a lower coverage degree. Hence, an equilibrium is reached. Unfortunately, the practicality of an algorithm that requires the sensors to move constantly is limited due to sensor mobility limitations.

4.2 Energy Efficient Algorithms for Barrier Coverage

In [35], the issue of barrier coverage with energy considerations is considered by Ban et al. The formal problem definition requires the sensors to be relocated to form 1-barrier coverage with the constraint that the overall movement distance of sensors be minimized. It is proved that this problem is NP-Hard via reduction from the Knapsack problem. The authors then design a polynomial approximation algorithm to solve this problem. The algorithm is briefly summarized as follows.

The grid barrier model, as presented in [35], is shown in Fig. 12. There are n_w rows and n_l columns of grids in grid barrier A. If a sensor is deployed in each grid in a selected row, one can construct a horizontal grid barrier in A. As a result, A is 1-barrier covered. Kumar and Lai [36] proved that by constructing horizontal grid barrier, the fewest sensors are required to achieve 1-barrier coverage. Thus the mobile sensors needed to relocate for

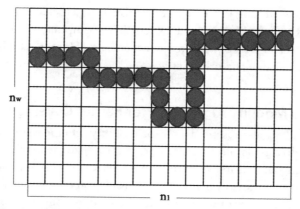

Fig. 12. Grid barrier with mobile sensors shown as circles.

1-barrier coverage by constructing horizontal grid barrier is the fewest, and the sum of moving distance in this relocation method could very likely be less than other method. Based on these observations, an approximation algorithm is proposed. This algorithm mainly has two steps: (1) Horizontal Grid Barrier Selection, which finds a row from A as a horizontal grid barrier and (2) optimal movement, which finds the optimal movement strategy for relocating mobile sensors to the selected horizontal grid barrier, subject to minimize the sum of moving distance.

1. *Horizontal grid barrier selection:* If each of the mobile sensors which construct the barrier moves to its nearest grid, the sum of moving distance is minimized. For any grid g_k, a weight is assigned to it. The weight is the distance between g_k and the nearest sensor, s_i. The sum of weights of each row is computed. The row which has the smallest weight is identified as position of the barrier.

2. *Optimal movement strategy:* On selecting the ith row as the position of horizontal grid barrier as above, the destination positions of mobile sensors needed to move are known. The destination positions are the n_l grids in ith row. Then n_l nodes from M sensors are selected to find the optimal movement strategy to relocate the selected sensors to the n_l grids in horizontal grid barrier. This problem is called as Optimal Movement Problem.

To find the optimal movement strategy subject to minimize the sum of moving distance, it is possible to get a one-to-one matching between the selected sensors and grid positions with the minimum sum of weight. Thus Optimal Movement Problem is equivalent to Bipartite Weighted Matching Problem. The Hungarian Method is known as an optimal solution to Bipartite Weighted Matching Problem (see Section 4.3), which can be used as the solution for Optimal Movement Problem. The computation complexity of Hungarian is $O(m^2 n)$ [37], where m is the size of the set which has fewer nodes, and the size of the other set is n.

4.3 Limited Mobility Algorithms for Barrier Coverage

In [38], Saipulla et al. presented a sensor mobility scheme that matches each mobile node to a grid point and attempts to minimize the maximum moving distance among all sensors when the sensors have mobility limitations. Each mobile sensor first moves vertically to its projection on a pre-defined line in the first phase. In the second phase, given the set of mobile sensors S, the grid points Y, and sensor's moving range d, the following algorithm computes whether every grid point can be occupied by a mobile sensor under the sensor mobility constraint. There are three steps in the algorithm execution:

1. Construct a bi-partite graph $G(V,E)$ ($V = X \cup Y$) as follows. Each vertex in X represents a mobile sensor, and each vertex in Y represents a grid point along the line. $E = \{(u,v),(v,u)|u \in X, v \in Y, and\ dist(u,v) < d\}$.
2. From $G(V,E)$, construct a flow graph $G^*(V^*,E^*)$ and assign capacity to each edge as follows: $\forall v \in V$, add u to V^*; $\forall (u,v) \in E$, add (u,v) to E^*. Set $capacity(u,v) = 1$ if $u \in X$ and $v \in Y$, otherwise, set $capacity(u,v) = 0$. Add a Virtual Source node S to V^* and $\forall u \in S$, add an edge (S,u) to E^*, set $capacity(S,u) = 1$; add a Virtual Sink node D to V^*, and $\forall u \in Y$ of $G(V,E)$, add an edge (u,D) to E^*, set $capacity(u,D) = 1$.
3. Use Maximum Flow algorithm (Similar to the one presented in Section 3.4) to compute and return the flow plan from S to D in G^*.

At the conclusion of the maximum flow algorithm (which executes in polynomial time), the following steps are executed. If the returned maximum flow from S to D equals the number of grid points, each grid point will be assigned a sensor and a barrier can be formed. Otherwise, if the returned maximum flow is smaller than the number of grid points, it means that there are not enough sensors to occupy all the grid points. In this case, some grid points will not be occupied by sensors.

5. ALGORITHMS FOR ENHANCING EVENT COVERAGE

In this class of movement algorithms, the objective is to move sensors starting from initial arbitrary positions toward events as and when they occur in the network. Figure 13a illustrates the case of an initial deployment where the quality of blanket coverage is poor. For the same number of sensors, Fig. 13b illustrates the case of superior 1-blanket coverage. A critical ancillary objective when sensors move for event coverage is to minimize the degradation in current coverage during sensor movements. We present some sensor mobility algorithms for event coverage below.

5.1 Voronoi-Based Movement Algorithm

Butler and Rus [39] design algorithms wherein sensors move toward events as and when they are generated. The objective is to enhance event coverage without compromising existing coverage (i.e., creating new coverage holes). After deployment, sensors discover locations of their neighbors. When events are generated in the network, each sensor predicts the movement of its

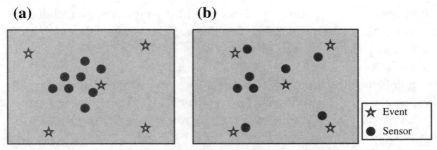

Fig. 13. An instance of initial deployment, intuitive movement plan and optimal movement plan for mobile sensors.

neighbors in order to estimate their final positions as well as its own final position. The estimation is done based on constructing voronoi polygons for the sensor itself and its neighbors. Sensors move if they can get closer to the event, and if the area that it has previously covered will still be covered by one or more neighbors.

The simplest version of the algorithm, referred to as the Complete Voronoi protocol, is also the most computationally intensive one. In this protocol, each sensor calculates the motion of every other sensor and uses this information to compute its Voronoi region after each event. This ensures the best performance, in the sense that each sensor will know exactly what area it should consider for coverage purposes. If any part of the sensor's Voronoi region is farther away than the sensing range (note that only vertices of the region need to be checked, since it is always polygonal), it knows that no other sensor is closer to this point, and it should not move away from that point. As long as the sensor maintains its Voronoi region in this way, coverage is assured.

To make this prediction correctly, note that once a sensor has stopped, it is no longer following the control algorithm that is used to predict its position. Therefore, in order for a sensor to accurately predict the state of the network, it must also know which sensors have stopped. This can be done in the following two ways.

1. If we wish to have no additional communication, then each sensor predicts whether other sensors will stop, based on the same Voronoi region calculation. However, this is a large amount of computation, and can be avoided with a small amount of communication.

2. When one sensor stops to avoid loss of coverage, it sends a broadcast message with the position at which it stopped. Other sensors can then

assume adherence to the motion algorithm unless such a message is received. Use of this communication enables a possibility that each sensor will stop only once.

This limits the accuracy of coverage in that sensors may no longer be needed in their current positions for coverage after some time has passed, and they are not allowed to move. However, if the event distribution remains constant, this is not likely to be a major concern, and having each sensor stop only once limits communication under this algorithm. To further reduce computation, one can let a sensor compute Voronoi polygons for only its neighboring sensors. This technique minimizes computation cost, but there is a slight loss in quality of coverage.

5.2 Cascading Movement Algorithm

In [18], Wang et al. proposed an algorithm for relocating mobile sensors as and when events occur, while still maintaining original sensing coverage as much as possible. In their algorithm, sensor relocation consists of two phases: identifying which sensors must move, and how to move them. For the first phase, the problem becomes finding the redundant sensors in the sensor network. The key challenge here is for sensors to independently decide who is redundant from a coverage perspective and who is not. The authors proposed a quorum based-approach for sensors to identify redundant sensors using local communication and coordination. The authors proposed a cascading algorithm (similar to the concept discussed in Fig. 8) which will be executed once events take place in the network. The metrics of interest include minimizing energy consumption and event coverage delay.

6. OTHER RESEARCH ISSUES IN MOBILE SENSOR NETWORKS

We now discuss some orthogonal issues, apart from coverage that we believe are critical in emerging mobile sensor networks.

6.1 Information Confidentiality in Mobile Sensor Networks

Secure communications is a critical requirement in many sensor network missions, especially in ones that are military related. Toward this end several challenges are present. First, since the nature of communication messages is wireless, some information leakage through the transmission of wireless signal is unavoidable. Secondly, the energy constraints of sensors imply that computationally expensive techniques like public key cryptography are infeasible for WSNs. Simply provisioning a unique key for each sensor to communicate with the base station prevents sensors from communicating with each other. On the other hand, distributing the same key to all sensors exposes all communications under node capture attacks. When sensors are randomly deployed, it is not possible to predict where nodes are likely fall in the network. Hence pre-distributing same keys to those nodes that are within communication range of each other is not possible.

The standard approach for secure communications in WSNs is called Random Key Pre-distribution (RKP) [40]. The idea of RKP-based schemes is that each sensor is pre-distributed with k distinct keys randomly chosen from a large pool of K keys, and nodes are then deployed randomly. After deployment, nodes use pre-distributed keys to establish a pairwise symmetric key with their neighbors directly or using other nodes as proxies. While this approach works fine for static sensor networks, it cannot work in the case of mobile sensor networks. This is because, when a particular sensor moves, its current neighborhood information changes. When new neighbors are discovered, the sensor has to re-establish pairwise keys with its neighbors directly or through proxies. This process incurs tremendous communication overhead and delay. In [11], Mao and Wu extend the virtual force approach discussed in Section 3.1 in order to consider coverage and *secure* connectivity. Each sensor has a certain number of keys initially predistributed, and two sensors can securely communicate if they are in the transmission range of each other *and* share a common key. To enhance both coverage and secure connectivity, weights are assigned to the virtual forces depending on keys shared. The weights ensure that sensors sharing keys do not move too far apart, while those that do not share keys move farther. In this manner coverage is enhanced among secure neighbors, and so are the chances of other sensors finding secure neighbors.

However, there are still several open challenges in the realm of secure communication in mobile sensor networks. How to ensure k-coverage and secure sensor connectivity, how to address challenges related to limited sensor mobility, how to minimize computation and communication overhead during mobility and key management are some of the open issues.

6.2 Issues in Wireless Sensor and Mobile Actor Networks

Nodes in WSNs (as pointed earlier) are small in size and limited in energy. Once sensors sense, process and communicate events of interest in a deployment field, there is very little they can do. To address this limitation, many practical deployments of wireless sensor networks today incorporate a few powerful *actors* to react according to sensed data. Examples of such actors are soldiers during border patrol, mobile robots during disaster recovery, unmanned aerial vehicles (UAVs) in hostile zones, etc. There are a number of open issues in the realm of actor mobility management in wireless sensor and actor networks.

In [41], Zhao et al. proposed that a few mobile actors can be leveraged to move in the network and assist a number of static sensors for secure communications. The approach basically allows mobile actors to move to multiple locations in the sensor network. At each location, a group of sensors are provisioned with same keys so that they can establish secure communication among themselves with high probability. The actors also ensure that across groups, a small number of same keys are provisioned so that communication can happen across groups as well. In [4], Li et al. designed distributed algorithms among sensors to navigate a few mobile actors according to events of interest in the field. In this work, events of interest are fires around which soldiers must be navigated. In [4], (virtual) potential fields are utilized by sensors. In particular, sensors repel actors away from fires that ensures soldier navigation to a desired path stays away from fires. In [42], coordination and communication problems in sensor and actors are studied by Melodia et al. A new location management scheme is proposed to handle the mobility of actors with minimal energy expenditure for the sensors. The proposed idea is based on a hybrid strategy that includes location updating and location prediction. Mobile actors broadcast location updates limiting their scope based on Voronoi diagrams, Sensors predict the movement of actors based on Kalman filtering of previously received updates. This scheme enables efficient geographical routing, and an optimal energy aware forwarding rule is designed for sensor actor communication. A variety of other algorithms are proposed to control data delivery delay based on power control, network congestion, and load balancing by letting multiple actors to be recipients for traffic generated in the event area. Issues related to detecting and defending against malicious mobile actors, handling mobility-related faults and failures, considering lifetime of mobile sensor and actor nodes are all critical open issues in this realm.

6.3 Sensor Mobility Algorithms Design for Other Area Coverage Paradigms

The second paradigm of coverage is *exploratory coverage*, wherein the objective is to move a number of sensors across a target area such that at the conclusion of sensor movements, the entire area has been explored by one or more sensors. Practical instances of exploratory coverage include law enforcement officers searching the hide-out of a potential suspect, bomb squads exploring an airport for explosives, rescue personnel searching for survivors in a disaster zone, etc. Designing mobility algorithms that can enable a number of tiny mobile sensors to replace the human element in such missions (to minimize their casualties) during exploration of target areas is a critical open problem. The core difference between blanket and exploratory coverage is that: in the latter case, once a point has been explored by a sensor, it need not be explored again by another sensors. It is worth mentioning here that in the ideal case, a single sensor with unlimited mobility can explore all areas. However, there are two critical limitations here: sensors are constrained in their mobilities and such kinds of exploration are slow. The research issue here is the design of efficient, high performing and rapidly converging sensor mobility algorithms for target area exploration, while simultaneously minimizing resulting sensor movement distances and exploration time.

6.4 Mobility Assisted Security in Sensor Networks

WSNs today are subject to a variety of attacks like Denial of Service (DoS), eavesdropping, selective forwarding, Sybil, false localization, identity replication, etc. A number of such attacks are sensor position centric. For instance, in DoS attacks, a portion of the network where sensors are positioned can be jammed with frequencies that sensors use for communication. While numerous approaches exist for defending against jamming attacks, sensor mobility provides a simple solution to this problem. It requires sensors to slightly move away from the victim zones and communicate thereon. Similarly, a host of localization attacks (that are also position centric) can be effectively detected with only a slight amount of sensor mobility, wherein a small number of verifiers are suitable to schedule sensor movements in order to validate their positions in the network. Similar techniques using mobility are also likely to provide defenses against Sybil attacks, identity replication attacks. To the best of our knowledge, such issues are yet to be addressed, Other security upsides of sensor mobility include enhancement of multi-path availabilities which can also be effective in defending against a host of attacks like packet drops, selective forwarding, blackhole attacks, etc.

We wish to point out here that sensor mobility is not always a benign resource from the perspective of security. In fact, we wish to point out that sensor mobility itself can be a double edged sword from the perspective of security. As we know, mobility is a critical resource for the sensors. Needless to say, attackers can exploit this resource as well to launch attacks and compromise sensor network performance. For instance, one naive attack model is for attackers to capture certain nodes in the network and trigger malicious movements, which has impacts ranging from coverage losses, energy depletions, cascaded movements among other sensors, etc. Furthermore, if orchestrated more efficiently, mobility centric attacks can cause advanced disruptions to the network in terms of topology corruptions, routing path losses, etc. Other possible attacks leveraging sensor mobility include the inducing of fake movements (e.g., to cover events) when actually no real movement was made. This has effects like non-detection of real events, which can cause severe performance degradation. Modeling, analyzing, and quantifying impacts of such types of mobility centric attacks to WSNs is an important open issue. Moreover, all of the sensor mobility algorithms discussed so far assume the presence of benign sensor nodes. Studying algorithms performance under the presence of a limited number of malicious mobile sensor nodes will be an interesting avenue of further research. With security being a critical focus in WSN-related research today, this avenue will yield the design of *security-aware* sensor movement algorithms for coverage. Rationales for security-aware algorithms design could be to exploit cooperation among neighboring sensors during movements to enhance movement reliability, proactive detection of malicious mobile sensors in the network, etc.

6.5 Topology Control Using Sensor Mobility

Topology control is an important component of WSN operation. Apart from coverage alone, topology refers to connectivity, sensor clustering, hierarchical role assignment, etc. Practically speaking, such requirements translate to full coverage and k connectivity among sensors (that is, at least k paths exist between each pair of sensors, where $k \geq 1$), or require a certain number of sensors to be physically present in a geographical area of the network, or some higher capacity sensors acting as masters for many slave sensors, etc. An interesting research problem is to design sensor movement algorithms to achieve such topologies with an initial arbitrary deployment. Furthermore, due to faults and failures, it may happen that the established topologies are corrupted with time. The research issue in this premise is to enable sensors to detect such corruptions (via detecting appropriate network invariants), and designing movement algorithms to dynamically correct such violations when they occur.

7. UNCONTROLLED SENSOR MOBILITY

In this section, we discuss different algorithms that consider uncontrolled sensor mobility. We will first present features of uncontrolled sensor mobility, followed by current work on mobility centric protocols design, and open research issues.

7.1 Features of Uncontrolled Sensor Mobility

In uncontrolled mobility, energy, and form factor (shape of the sensor node) limitations do not impact mobility, since the sensors cannot control their motion. What is critical is the network mission, that dictates sensor mobility and its patterns. There are several such practical instances. The mobility of sensors fitted on patients (for body monitoring) is one where each patient moves independently and within a restricted scope. The mobility of sensors fitted on zebras (for habitat monitoring) has periodic shifts in movement speeds and distances (for grazing, walking, running, etc.), with a certain degree of clustering among multiple zebras due to their social behavior. The movement of sensors in oceans (for water current and water life monitoring) has a significant interdependency because of potentially thousands of sensors moving simultaneously with each other in close contact. Also, the geographic scope of mobility is much larger here. All three mobility patterns although uncontrolled are unique. The mobility patterns have impacts to protocols design for these missions, as discussed in the next subsection.

Differences in uncontrolled sensor networks mobility and MANETs mobility: Mobility models in MANETs [43] typically characterize mobile agents (e.g., humans, animals, etc.) moving ad hoc. While there is some similarity between uncontrolled sensor networks mobility and MANETs mobility, uncontrolled sensor networks unlike typical MANETs are mission-specific. The consequences are certain unique movement patterns for the different missions in uncontrolled mobility sensor networks, which are clearly different from existing ad hoc mobility models characterizing typical MANETs.

7.2 Protocols Design in Uncontrolled Sensor Mobility

Applications within the scope of uncontrolled sensor mobility are still in their incipient stages of development. Currently, the major focus has been the design of effective data delivery protocols under uncontrolled sensor mobility. In the following, we discuss data delivery protocols in the realm of uncontrolled sensor mobility. While the protocols are also contingent on issues like mission scale, bandwidth, energy consumption, etc., we focus on those protocol features that are contingent on mobility patterns in the mission.

7.2.1 Publish-Subscribe Data Delivery Protocol for Patient Monitoring

Data delivery in the patient monitoring scenario [44] is based on a publish/subscribe framework where sensors publish data to a specific channel and end-users (i.e., medical caregivers) subscribe to channels of interest. Due to transmission energy constraints multi-hop communications among the nodes may be the only choice. However, it may also happen that both patients and caregivers are mobile. This twin mobility scenario means proactively maintaining routing paths will not be feasible, while discovering paths reactively may incur too much delay.

In [44], the data delivery protocol is based on the Adaptive Demand Driven Multicast Routing (ADMR) protocol [45] that takes a middle ground. Nodes are assigned as forwarders through a route discovery process that periodically occurs. Every node maintains a node table indexed by the publisher node ID. Each node table entry contains the shortest path cost from the publisher to the current node. While several metrics can be used for path costs, in [44], the radio's Link Quality Indicator is used as well as the previous hop in the best path from the publisher, that is updated periodically. When a subscriber wishes to receive data from a specific channel, it sends a unicast route reply message along the reverse path from itself to the publishing device, using the previous hop information in the node table. Upon receiving the route reply, each intermediate node configures itself as a forwarder for the requested channel and subsequently rebroadcast received messages for that channel. Simulations have shown that the ADMR protocol can effectively handle mobility of both the patients and care givers. The performance though depends on the periodicity of route maintenance, which again depends on how rapidly mobility compromises existing data delivery structure.

7.2.2 History-Based Protocol for Habitat Monitoring

In the habitat monitoring application in [3], the data delivery protocol is designed to specifically take advantage of the mission's mobility patterns for more efficient data delivery and energy conservation. Here, sensors placed in the collars of zebras collect information on animal movements including position, speed, temperature, etc. Data is logged by the sensors and should be periodically reported back to a sink (researchers traveling in vehicles in the habitat). Clearly, the energy limitations make broadcast type protocols unsuitable. To enable scalability, and take advantage of knowledge of movement patterns of zebras, the authors propose history-based protocols, where each sensor periodically updates its hierarchy level depending on its proximity to the sink. The closer the sensor is to the sink, higher is the hierarchy level. Since zebras are slow movers, it is likely that the sensor (and zebra) currently close to the sink, will also be close to it in the near future. The data delivery protocol here is simple where sensors forward packets greedily to sensors with higher hierarchies, thus taking effective advantage of mobility patterns of the mission.

7.2.3 Data Delivery in Ocean Monitoring Application

In ocean monitoring, thousands of sensors are deployed. The large deployment scale, coupled with large scale movements precludes the chances of scalable run-time data delivery protocols. In this mission, sensors only sense, aggregate, and store data. After the mission lifetime, the sensors will automatically float to the surface and data is then recovered individually from them.

7.3 Open Research Issues in Uncontrolled Sensor Mobility

In this section, we proceed to discuss two open research issues that we believe are critical and imminent in this area: modeling uncontrolled sensor mobilities, and protocols design for other problems.

7.3.1 Developing Sound Models for Uncontrolled Sensor Mobility Scenarios

There are a host of new applications possible where sensors have to move uncontrolled (e.g., landslide monitoring, twister monitoring, habitat monitoring, etc.). The success of such applications is clearly contingent on the ability to design efficient protocols (e.g., neighbor discovery, data delivery, localization, security, etc.) for these applications. Since, it is impractical to test protocols in real situations, they have to be thoroughly tested in simulations using sound models that characterize sensor mobility. Clearly, existing mobility models in MANETs cannot encompass all the features of sensor networks mobility. An important research issue in the future will be designing high fidelity mobility models for a wide class of sensor network scenarios, along with the design of new metrics to test such models. We point out an orthogonal development in mobile Vehicular Ad hoc Networks (VANETs) that have some similarities with uncontrolled mobility sensor networks. Recently, researchers have understood that mobility in VANETs are inherently different from mobility in MANETs, leading to works on modeling VANETs, and developing metrics for testing the models. Protocols developed for VANETs can now be tested on these models, before they become accepted in practice. We hope that this recent development provides further impetus to the development of high fidelity models and metrics for uncontrolled mobility sensor networks, which is lacking today.

7.3.2 Protocols Design for Other Problems

The acceptance of uncontrolled mobility sensor network applications will naturally result in a wide variety of application demands for which efficient protocols need to be developed. These include: efficient data delivery including resolving channel issues, neighbor discovery, routing, data aggregation, etc. (for all applications); coarse/fine grained sensor localization (for many applications), data security, and privacy (especially in sensitive habitat monitoring, medical monitoring), energy management (for all applications), etc. All issues, while having some similarity with MANETs will need a fresh treatment in uncontrolled mobility sensor networks taking into account the features of the mission and the associated mobility patterns.

8. FINAL REMARKS

In this chapter, we provided a comprehensive survey on mobility in wireless sensor networks. We presented details and insights on various sensor mobility platforms and algorithms for enhancing blanket, barrier, and event cxoverage. Several challenges related to mobile sensor networks stemming from size and energy limitations were also highlighted. The survey also included some on-going and open research issues in the realm of secure communications in wireless sensor, issues in mobile sensor and actor networks, and issues in uncontrolled sensor networks mobility.

Abbreviations

2-D	2-Dimensional
ADMR	Adaptive Demand Driven Multicast Routing
CPU	Central Processing Unit
DARPA	Defense Advanced Research Projects Agency
DoS	Denial of Service
GPS	Global Positioning System
IR	Infrared

LED	Light Emitting Diode
MANET	Mobile Ad hoc Network
OMF	Optimal Maximum Flow
PWM	Pulse Width Modulation
RX	Reception Range
SHM	Self Healing Minefield
TX	Transmission Range
VANET	Vehicular Ad hoc Network
WSN	Wireless Sensor Network

REFERENCES

[1] T. Abdelzaher, B. Blum, Q. Cao, D. Evans, J. George, S. George, T. He, L. Luo, S. Son, R. Stoleru, J. Stankovic, A. Wood, Envirotrack: an environmental programming model for tracking applications in distributed sensor networks, in: Proceedings of International Conference on Distributed Computing Systems (ICDCS), Tokyo, March, 2004.

[2] C. Gui, P. Mohapatra, Power conservation and quality of surveillance in target tracking sensor networks, in: Proceedings of ACM International Conference on Mobile Computing and Networking (MobiCom), Philadelphia, 2004.

[3] P. Juang, H. Oki, Y. Wang, M. Martonosi, L. Peh, D. Rubenstein, Energy-efficient computing for wildlife tracking: design tradeoffs and early experiences with zebranet, in: Proceedings of International Conference on Architectural Support for Programming Languages and Operating Systems (ASPLOS-X), San Jose, October, 2002.

[4] Q. Li, M. De Rosa, D. Rus, Distributed algorithms for guiding navigation across a sensor network, in: Proceedings of the 9th Annual International Conference on Mobile Computing and Networking, ACM, 2003, pp. 313–325.

[5] G. Werner-Allen, K. Lorincz, M. Ruiz, O. Marcillo, J. Johnson, J. Lees, M. Welsh, Deploying a wireless sensor network on an active volcano, Internet Computing, IEEE 10 (2) (2006) 18–25.

[6] L. Krishnamurthy, R. Adler, P. Buonadonna, J. Chhabra, M. Flanigan, N. Kushalnagar, L. Nachman, M. Yarvis, Design and deployment of industrial sensor networks: experiences from a semiconductor plant and the north sea, in: Proceedings of the 3rd International Conference on Embedded Networked Sensor Systems, ACM, 2005, pp. 64–75.

[7] V.C. Gungor, G.P. Hancke, Industrial wireless sensor networks: challenges, design principles, and technical approaches, IEEE Trans. Ind. Electron. 56 (10) (2009) 4258–4265.

[8] G. Hoblos, M. Staroswiecki, A. Aitouche, Optimal design of fault tolerant sensor networks, in: Control Applications, Proceedings of the 2000 IEEE International Conference on, IEEE, 2000, pp. 467–472.

[9] L. Prasad, S.S. Iyengar, R.L. Kashyap, R.N. Madan, Functional characterization of fault tolerant integration in distributed sensor networks, IEEE Trans. Syst., Man Cybern. 21 (5) (1991) 1082–1087.

[10] T. He, S. Krishnamurthy, J.A. Stankovic, T. Abdelzaher, et al., Vigilnet: an integrated sensor network system for energy-efficient surveillance, in: Submission to ACM Transaction on Sensor Networks (ToSN), 2004.

[11] Y. Mao, M. Wu, Coordinated sensor deployment for improving secure communications and sensing coverage, in: Proceedings of ACM Workshop on Security of Ad Hoc and Sensor Networks (SASN), Alexandria, November, 2005.

[12] D. Liu, P. Ning, Efficient distribution of key chain commitments for broadcast authentication in distributed sensor networks, in: Network and Distributed System Security Symposium (NDSS), San Diego, February, 2003.

[13] H. Chan, A. Perrig, D. Song, Random key predistribution schemes for sensor networks, in: Proceedings of IEEE Symposium on Research in Security and Privacy, May, 2003.

[14] T. He, C. Huang, B.M. Blum, J.A. Stankovic, T. Abdelzaher, Range-free localization schemes for large scale sensor networks, in: Proceedings of ACM International Conference on Mobile Computing and Networking (MobiCom), San Diego, August, 2003.

[15] C. Wang, L. Xiao, J. Rong, Sensor localization in an obstructed environment, in: Proceedings of IEEE/ACM Intl Conference on Distributed Computing in Sensor Systems (DCOSS), Marina del Rey, June, 2005.

[16] Andreas Savvides, Chih-Chieh Han, Mani B. Srivastava, Dynamic fine-grained localization in ad-hoc networks of sensors, in: Proceedings of ACM MobiCom, 2001.

[17] G. Cao, G. Kesidis, T. La Porta, B. Yao, S. Phoha, Purposeful mobility in tactical sensor networks, in: Sensor Network Operations, IEEE Press, 2005.

[18] G. Wang, G. Cao, T. La Porta, W. Zhang, Sensor relocation in mobile networks, in: Proceedings of IEEE Conference on Computer Communications (INFOCOM), Miami, March, 2005.

[19] G. Wang, G. Cao, T. La Porta, Movement-assisted sensor deployment, in: Proceedings of IEEE INFOCOM, Hong Kong, March, 2004.

[20] D. Lymberopoulos, A. Savvides, Xyz: a motion-enabled, power aware sensor node platform for distributed sensor network applications, in: Proceedings of ACM IPSN, April, Los Angeles, 2005.

[21] K. Dantu, M Rahimi, H. Shah, S. Babel, A. Dhariwal, G. Sukhatme, Robomote: enabling mobility in sensor networks, in: Proceedings of IPSN-SPOTS, Los Angeles, April 2005.

[22] S. Chellappan, W. Gu, X. Bai, B. Ma, D. Xuan, K. Zhang, Deploying wireless sensor networks under limited mobility constraints, IEEE Trans. Mobile Computing 6 (10) October, 2007.

[23] S. Chellappan, X. Bai, B. Ma, D. Xuan, Mobility limited flip-based sensor networks deployment, IEEE Trans. Parallel Distrib. Syst. 18 (2) (2007).

[24] Gabriel T. Sibley, Mohammed H. Rahimi, Gaurav S. Sukhatme, Robomote: a tiny mobile robot platform for large-scale ad-hoc sensor networks, in: Proceedings of IEEE International Conference on Robotics and Automation (ICRA), September 2002.

[25] http://alpha.micromo.com/stepper-motors-datasheets.aspx

[26] N. Bulusu, J. Heidemann, D. Estrin, Adaptive beacon placement, in: Proceedings of IEEE International Conference on Distributed Computing Systems (ICDCS), Phoenix, AZ, April, 2001.

[27] P. Pathirana, N. Bulusu, A.V. Savkin, S. Jha, Node localization using mobile robots in delay-tolerant sensor networks, in: IEEE Trans. Mobile Computing 4 (3) (2005), 285–296.

[28] M. Ma, Y. Yang, Adaptive triangular deployment algorithm for unattended mobile sensor networks, IEEE Trans. Comput. 56 (7) (2007).

[29] J. Chen, S. Li, Y. Sun, Novel deployment schemes for mobile sensor networks, Sensors 7 (11)(2007) 2907–2919.

[30] J. Wu, S. Wang, Smart: a scan-based movement-assisted deployment method in wireless sensor networks, in: Proceedings of IEEE INFOCOM, Miami, March, 2005.

[31] B. Liu, P. Brass, O. Dousse, P. Nain, D. Towsley, Mobility improves coverage of sensor networks, in: Proceedings of ACM International Symposium on Mobile Ad Hoc Networking and Computing (MobiHoc), Urbana Champaign, May, 2005.

[32] S. Chellappan, X. Bai, B. Ma, D. Xuan, Sensor networks deployment using flip-based sensors, in: Proceedings of IEEE MASS, Washington DC, November, 2005.

[33] W. Wang, V. Srinivasan, K. Chua, Trade-offs between mobility and density for coverage in wireless sensor networks, in: Proceedings of ACM International Conference on Mobile Computing and Networking (MobiCom), Montreal, September, 2007.

[34] G. Yang, W. Zhou, D. Qiao, Defending against barrier intrusions with mobile sensors, in: International Conference on Wireless Algorithms, Systems and Applications, Chicago, August, 2007.

[35] D. Ban, W. Yang, J. Jiang, J. Wen, W. Dou, Energy-efficient algorithms for k-barrier coverage in mobile sensor networks, Int. J. Comput. Commun. Contr. 5 (5) (2010) 616–624.

[36] S. Kumar, T.H. Lai, A. Arora, Barrier coverage with wireless sensors, in: Proceedings of ACM International Conference on Mobile Computing and Networking (MOBI-COM), Cologne, September, 2005.

[37] E.L. Lawler, Combinatorial optimization: networks and matroids, Dover Pubns, 2001.

[38] A. Saipulla, B. Liu, G. Xing, X. Fu, J. Wang, Barrier coverage with sensors of limited mobility, in: Proceedings of The 11th ACM International Symposium on Mobile Ad Hoc Networking and Computing (MOBIHOC), 2010.

[39] Z. Butler, D. Rus, Controlling mobile sensors for monitoring events with coverage constraints, in: IEEE International Conference on Robotics and Automation (ICRA), New Orleans, April, 2004.

[40] L. Eschenauer, V.D. Gligor, A key-management scheme for distributed sensor networks, in: Proceedings of the ACM Conference on Computer and Communication Security (CCS), November 2002, pp. 41–47.

[41] L. Zhou, J. Ni, C.V. Ravishankar, Supporting secure communication and data collection in mobile sensor networks, in: IEEE INFOCOM, April, 2006.

[42] T. Melodia, D. Pompili, I.F. Akyldiz, Handling mobility in wireless sensor and actor networks, IEEE Trans. Mobile Computing 9 (2) (2010) 160–173.

[43] T. Camp, J. Boleng, V. Davies, A survey of mobility models for ad hoc network research, Wireless Commun. Mobile Computing 2 (5) (2002) 483–502 (Special Issue on Mobile Ad Hoc Networking: Research, Trends and Applications).

[44] V. Shnayder, B. Chen, K. Lorincz, T. Fulford-Jones, M. Welsh, Sensor networks for medical care, Tech. Rep., Dept. of Electrical Engineering and Computer Science and Engineering, Harvard University, April 2005.

[45] J.G. Jetcheva, D.B. Johnson, Adaptive demand-driven multicast routing in multi-hop wireless ad hoc networks, in: Proceedings of ACM international Symposium on Mobile Ad Hoc Networking and Computing (MobiHoc), October 2001.

ABOUT THE AUTHORS

Sriram Chellappan is an Assistant Professor in the Computer Science Department at Missouri University of Science and Technology. His primary areas of interest are in Mobile Networking, Social Computing and Cyber Security. He received his PhD degree from the Department of Computer Science at The Ohio-State University in 2007. He received the NSF CAREER Award in 2013.

Neelanjana Dutta is a PhD Candidate in the Department of Computer Science at Missouri University of Science and Technology. She received her Undergraduate degree in Institute of Engineering and Management from West Bengal University of Technology. Her areas of interests are in Mobile Ad Hoc Networks and Network Security.

CHAPTER FOUR

A Classification of Data Mining Algorithms for Wireless Sensor Networks, and Classification Extension to Concept Modeling in System of Wireless Sensor Networks Based on Natural Language Processing

Staša Vujičić Stanković[*], Nemanja Kojić[‡], Goran Rakočević[†], Duško Vitas[*], and Veljko Milutinović[‡]

[*]School of Mathematics, University of Belgrade, Serbia
[†]Mathematical Institute, Serbian Academy of Sciences and Arts, Serbia
[‡]School of Electrical Engineering, University of Belgrade, Serbia

Contents

Advances in Computers, Volume 90
ISSN 0065-2458, http://dx.doi.org/10.1016/B978-0-12-408091-1.00004-X

Abstract

In this article, we propose one original classification and one extension thereof, which takes into consideration the relevant issues in Natural Language Processing. The newly introduced classification of Data Mining algorithms is on the level of a single Wireless Sensor Network and its extension to Concept Modeling on the level of a System of Wireless Sensor Networks. Most of the scientists in this field put emphasis on issues related to applications of Wireless Sensor Networks in different areas, while we here put emphasis on categorization of the selected approaches from the open literature, to help application designers/developers get a better understanding of their options in different areas. Our main goal is to provide a good starting point for a more effective analysis leading to possible new solutions, possible improvements of existing solutions, and possible combination of two or more of the existing solutions into new ones, using the hybridization principle. Another contribution of this article is a synergistic interdisciplinary review of problems in two areas: Data Mining and Natural Language Processing. This enables interoperability improvements on the interface between Wireless Sensor Networks that often share data in native natural languages.

1. INTRODUCTION

This article concentrates on two different aspects on Wireless Sensor Networks (WSNs): Data Mining (DM) in WSNs and enhancements of DM using appropriate tools, and algorithms of Natural Language Processing (NLP), which can be used to enhance the quality of DM in WSNs. Consequently, the article is organized into two parts and the presentation of the examples is preceded with two different classification/extension efforts.

The first part of the article is focused on the level of a single WSN. This part examines the approaches of embedding a distributed Data Mining algorithm into a WSN. We introduce a classification of DM algorithms. To assist application designers, our classification of DM algorithms starts from the application domain. The assumption is that an average user starts from the application that he/she has to implement and desires to see a list of implementation options that he/she can select from. Consequently, we start from the major four algorithm types for DM in WSN, with a subsequent special emphasis on optimization criteria used (energy awareness, or jointly energy and performance, etc.).

The second part of this article examines systems of multiple WSNs. We consider the case in which each one of these WSNs is used in one country and incorporates elements of the local natural language (measure systems, etc.). We will refer to one such network as the national WSN. Here we focus on approaches that can be used for interoperability and knowledge extraction across multiple national WSNs (each WSN in the system uses a different natural language). We introduce a classification extension based on Concept Modeling (CM), using the mechanisms developed for NLP.

The organization of the article is as follows. Section 2 provides the problem definition, elaboration of the problem importance, and an assessment of the problem trends. Classification methodology is discussed in Section 3. In order to be able to compare various approaches (encompassed by our classification), this research utilizes a set of performance measures, both on the technology level and on the application level, which are elaborated in details latter in Section 3. At a single WSN level, the major research issues in DM are along the following four areas: classification, clustering, regression, and association rule mining. A simple analysis of the implemented systems, using Google Scholar or a similar system, indicates that a great majority of applications is based on the above-mentioned four algorithms. Existing solutions and their drawbacks are discussed in Section 4 from the viewpoint of introduced classification, following the principles of the innovation creation methodology presented in Appendix#1. Once a set of single (for example national) WSNs is connected into a system of WSNs, the issue that comes out is that different WSNs utilize different terminologies (or even different ontologies) to refer to the same concepts, so an uniformization effort is needed. Consequently, the major research issues are related to CM, which will be discussed further in Section 5. Section 6 provides the conclusion. Finally, the authors' research effort to improve quality of the results of an autonomous WSN using knowledge from the Semantic Web is presented in Appendix#2.

2. PROBLEM STATEMENT

Issues of importance for better understanding of the basic orientation of any research, as well as for the research presented in this article, are: problem definition (*What is the problem definition?*), elaboration of the problem importance (*Why is it important?*), and an assessment of the problem trends (*Why will the importance grow?*).

The following lines elaborate these three issues briefly:

The problem of this research can be defined as Classify-and-Compare. This problem is important because it makes it possible to compare performances of various examples in different classes; it is also important because classification may offer possibilities of introducing new approaches, making improvements of the existing approaches, and hybridization of two or more different approaches. This problem will grow because sensor networks are used more and more widely in many fields.

3. CLASSIFICATION CRITERIA AND CLASSIFICATION TREE, ON THE LEVEL OF A SINGLE WIRELESS SENSOR NETWORK

Table 1 presents the set of classification criteria used here. The emphasis is on algorithm type, mobility type, and the attitude toward energy awareness.

Table 1 Classification criteria used in this research.

C1: Algorithm type	– Classification – Clustering – Regression – Association rule mining
C2: Mobility type	– Mobile (M) – Static (S)
C3: Attitude toward energy awareness	– Approaches characterized with energy efficiency awareness alone (EE) – Approaches characterized with multi-parameter efficiency optimizations, overall optimization (OO)

When the three criteria are applied, 16 classes of approaches are obtained.

According to the second and the third criterion, these can be organized into four basic groups (MEE—Mobile Energy Efficient, SEE—Static Energy Efficient, MOO—Mobile Overall Optimized, and SOO—Static Overall Optimized), as presented in Fig. 1.

Table 2 specifies one representative example for each one of the 16 classes of the classification presented here. Note that four of the classes include no examples. Something like that may happen for two reasons: (a) when the particular combination of criteria makes no sense, and (b) when the particular combination of criteria does make full sense, but either the technology, or the application, or both are not yet ready for the challenges related to the implementation of such an approach. If the case (a) is in place, the missing

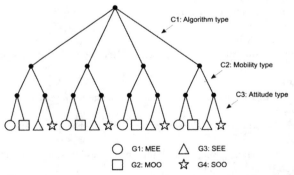

Fig. 1. Classification tree used in this research. Ci ($i = 1,2,3$)—classification criteria. C1 ϵ {classification, clustering, regression, association rule mining}, C2 ϵ {M,S}, C3 ϵ {EE,OO}. Gj ($j = 1, \ldots, 4$)—basic groups of WSNs. $Gj \epsilon$ {MEE, SEE, MOO, SOO}.

Table 2 The obtained classification and the related representative examples (full reference for each example is given in the bibliographical part of this article).

MEE (Classification)
  - "Training a support vector machine–based classifier in distributed sensor networks" Flouri et al. [1]

MEE (Clustering)
  - "DEMS: a data mining based technique to handle missing data in mobile sensor network applications" Gruenwald et al. [2]

MEE (Regression)
  - "Prediction-based monitoring in sensor networks: taking lessons from MPEG" Goel and Imielinski [3]

MEE (Association Rule Mining)
  - No representative examples found: A new challenge for researchers.

MOO (Classification)
  - "A distributed approach for prediction in sensor networks" McConnell and Skillicorn [4]

MOO (Clustering)
  - "Online mining in sensor networks" Xiuli et al. [5]
  - "K-means clustering over a large, dynamic network" Datta et al. [8]

MOO (Regression)
  - "A distributed approach for prediction in sensor networks" McConnell and Skillicorn [4]

MOO (Association Rule Mining)
  - No representative examples found: A new challenge for researchers.

SEE (Classification)
  - "Training a support vector machine–based classifier in distributed sensor networks" Flouri et al. [1]

SEE (Clustering)
  - "An energy efficient hierarchical clustering algorithm for wireless sensor networks" Bandyopadhyay and Coyle [6]

SEE (Regression)
  - "Prediction-based monitoring in sensor networks: taking lessons from MPEG" Goel and Imielinski [3]

SEE (Association Rule Mining)
  - "Estimating missing values in related sensor data streams" Halatchev and Gruenwald [7]

SOO (Classification)
  - No representative examples found: A new challenge for researchers.

SOO (Clustering)
  - "K-means clustering over a large, dynamic network" Datta et al. [8]

SOO (Regression)
  - "Streaming pattern discovery in multiple time-series" Papadimitriou et al. [9]

SOO (Association Rule Mining)
  - "Using data mining to estimate missing sensor data" Gruenwald et al. [10]

avenues represent research dead ends. If the case (b) is in place, the missing avenues represent potentially fruitful research challenges, which is the case with all four empty CLASSES of the classification presented here (when classification criteria open up new research directions, they are fully justified from the research methodology point of view). New ideas regarding the characteristics of the empty classes are discussed later on in this article.

As the conclusion to this section, we would like to stress that at the first glance it appears impossible to bring all 16 classes to the same common denominator, which enables an efficient simulation-based and/or mathematical-based comparison.

However, if the comparison is moved to both technology level and architecture level, the comparison is possible. On the technology level, the algorithms can be compared by: the number of hops to final result and the amount of energy (or whatever else relevant) used to reach the final result. On the architecture level, one can define level of accuracy and end of loop condition (one or more).

3.1 Issues on the Technology Level

The issues on the technology level are those that arise from the ways in which an algorithm interacts and uses the underlying WSN technology. The notion of "hop count" or the "number of hops" comes from the research related to routing in WSNs. A (single) hop denotes a direct transfer of a message from one WSN node to another. WSNs also allow for *multi-hop communication*. A message can be transferred from one node to another via several intermediate nodes. Obviously, such communication is more expensive in terms of energy and time. As the primary interest for examination of the communication requirements in the algorithms herein described is the energy expenditure, we argue that the amount of communication in the network should be quantified as the hop counts, rather than need for communication on the logical (algorithmic) level.

As an example, one algorithm may require only single-hop communication, where one node communicates only with all of its direct neighbors. Another algorithm may require messages to be passed to one (central) node, regardless of whether it requires multi-hop communication or not, etc.

Energy expenditure in a WSN comes from two principal sources: communication (covered above) and computation. Furthermore, as WSN nodes have a highly constrained computational capacity, one should ensure that the code to be executed is sufficiently simple and efficient. Many of the described algorithms will thus use suboptimal and heuristic approaches that will arrive at less accurate results, while making the approach feasible in a WSN.

3.2 Issues on the Architectural Level of Interest for Applications

The issues on the architectural level are those that relate to the structure of the algorithm and the correlations it can find in the data.

The level of accuracy of a DM algorithm can be defined as a percentage of departure from the correct value of the knowledge element searched for. In our classification, this relates to the percentage of the correctly classified instances. In regression, relative mean square error is commonly used. For clustering, a common approach is to look at the in–cluster similarity (the distance between points placed in one cluster). With association rule mining, the measure is how good the predictions made on the mined rules are.

The "end of DM condition" is a somewhat abstract notion that relates to the amount of time needed for a step in the algorithm operation. A number of issues fall into this category, e.g., time to convergence in the training phase (if there is one), the latency incurred when making one decision in the operation phase, etc.

3.3 Summary

The issues of DM algorithms for WSNs (the number of hops to final result, the amount of energy or whatever else relevant used to reach the final result, level of accuracy, and one or more end of loop condition) discussed in Sections 3.1 and 3.2 highly influence each other. In fact, the process of the design of an algorithm can be seen as making a set of trade-offs regarding these issues. For example, one may choose to consider only correlations valid over small areas and in small sections of the network. These will typically be easier to find, and exploiting will be simpler (and these will be less computationally intensive methods). Communication wise, such an approach would enable only single-hop communication to be required. However, the model will fail to exploit correlations (and the available data) in wider area of the network, sacrificing its overall accuracy.

4. PRESENTATION OF EXISTING SOLUTIONS AND THEIR DRAWBACKS

For presentation of representative examples, we use the presentation methodology that concentrates on six important aspects, as indicated next:

a. The seven Ws of the research (*who, where, when, whom, why, what, how*).

b. Essence of the approach (*the main strategic issues which differ from the research presented here*).

c. Details of the approach (*the main tactical issues of interest for the research presented here*).

d. Further development trends of the approach (*both technology and application issues*).

e. A criticism of the approach (*looking from the viewpoint of performance and complexity*).

f. Possible future researcher avenues (*along the lines of the innovation creation methodology presented in Appendix #1 of this article*).

For the representation of the classes from Table 2, which include no examples, we focus on two aspects: one related to innovation methodology, which provides the best method to develop a new approach, and one with guidelines for future innovators.

4.1 The MEE (Classification)—Mobile Energy Efficient Classification

The reference [1] contains one of the approaches from this solution group that was selected for illustration purpose in this article (research performed at the University of Crete, Institute of Computer Science (FORTH-ICS), and Universidad de València, Escuela Técnica Superior de Ingeniería supported by the Greek General Secretariat for Research and Technology under the program PENED).

The objective of the research was to develop an energy efficient distributed classification algorithms for large-scale WSNs. The classification is one of the most important tasks in WSN. Support Vector Machines (SVM) has been used successfully as good classification tools. SVMs are very suitable for incremental training due to sparseness representation of the decision boundary they provide. Therefore, only a small set of training examples are considered in the process of training an SVM and that is a good optimization in decision-making processes. The key idea is to preserve only the current estimation of the decision boundary at each incremental step along with the next batch of data (or part of it).

Two algorithms are described in the paper: Distributed Fixed-Partition Support Vector Machine training (DFP-SVM training) and Weighted Distributed Fixed-Partition training (Weighted DFP-SVM training). These two algorithms have in common the fact that an SVM is trained incrementally using an energy efficient clustering protocol. Sensors in a WSN are first organized into local spatial clusters. Each cluster has a cluster-head, a special sensor that receives data from all other sensors in the cluster, performs data fusion, and transmits the results to the base station. This greatly reduces the communication and thus improves energy efficiency. The SVM is trained using the training examples. In the context of DFP-SVM, the test examples are divided into batches, each of which corresponds to a single cluster. Therefore, each cluster gets its batch, and the training is started. When a hyper-plane is found, it is transmitted, along with support vectors, to the next cluster, where it is additionally adjusted.

The number of support vectors is typically relatively small compared to the number of the training examples. Hence, it makes sense to estimate separating hyper-plane through a sequence of incremental steps. Each step is performed at a given cluster. The clusters are logically ordered as a linear sequence. Hence, the data of previous clusters can be compressed to their corresponding estimated hyper-plane. Thus, instead of transmitting all the measurements to the next cluster-head, only the current estimation of the hyper-plane is transmitted, which reduces the energy spent on communication. When the estimated hyper-plane reaches the end of the cluster chain, training of the SVM is done.

However, definition of classes (to be separated) is often time- or space-varying. An SVM trained using old data may become unusable and it is necessary to refresh the definition of the separating hyper-plane. This issue is known as a concept drift and it complicates the process of training an SVM. This problem is highlighted in the context of distributed SVM training. It appears that the data in the batches of the training set can be very different. Thus, hyper-plane discovered in one cluster can be completely different from the one discovered in some other cluster. To deal with these issues, the original DFP-SVM algorithm is slightly modified by the definition of the loss functions. The loss function makes the error on old support vectors more costly than the error on the new samples. The definition of the loss function is:

$$\Phi(w,\xi)^n = \frac{1}{2}\|w\|^2 + C\left(\sum_{i \in I}\xi_i + L\sum_{i \in S}\xi_i\right), \tag{1}$$

where the parameter L increases the cost for the old support vectors, the parameter ξ_i, $i = 1, 2, \ldots n$ is a set of variables that measure the amount of violation of the constraints, the parameter C defines the cost of constraint violation, and w is a linear combination of the support vectors, which represents the separating hyper-plane.

Simulation-based experiments were performed to test accuracy and energy efficiency of the DFP and Weighted DFP algorithms compared to the centralized methods. In respect to accuracy, the approximation of the separating hyper-plane is very close to the hyper-plane obtained by the centralized approach.

Total energy consumed for training an SVM is divided into energy consumed within a cluster and energy used for data transfer between cluster-heads. The tests performed show that DFP algorithms save more than 50% energy than the centralized algorithm, which is very important in large-scale wireless networks comprised of energy-constrained sensor units.

The described algorithms required a linear pass through all the clusters in order to finish the training of an SVM. If the number of clusters is large, the hierarchical cluster could be a potential solution that would reduce the number of passes through the clusters, decrease the consumption of energy used for the training.

4.2 The MEE (Clustering)—Mobile Energy Efficient Clustering

A representative approach of this solution group is given in [2], with all relevant details (research performed at the University of Oklahoma, School of Computer Science, supported in part by DARPA, and a grant from CISCO Systems). In line with the goal of the chosen approach, Mobile WSNs were used to solve the complex problem of missing data from mobile sensors. This research presents a DM-based technique called Data Estimation for Mobile Sensors (DEMS).

In WSN applications, sensors move to increase the covered area or to compensate for the failure of other sensors. In such applications, corruption or loss of data occurs due to various reasons, such as power outage, radio interference, mobility, etc. In addition, in mobile WSNs, the energy from sensors' batteries is partially spent on moving from one place to another. Therefore, it is necessary to develop an efficient and effective technique for handling the missing data. The best way to do that is to estimate the value of missing data using the existing sensor readings and/or analyzing the history of sensors' readings.

The development of the DEMS technique was based on the framework called MASTER (Mining Autonomously Spatio-Temporal Environmental Rules). The MASTER framework is a comprehensive spatio-temporal association rules mining framework, which provides an estimation method and a tool for pattern recognition of the data in static sensor networks. This framework uses an internal data structure called MASTER-tree to store the history for each sensor, as well as the association rules among the sensors. Each node in the MASTER-tree is a sensor, except for the root node that is an artificial empty node. Association rules are represented as paths or sub-paths in the tree, starting from the root node. The number of sensors in the MASTER-tree is limited by the MASTER algorithm due to the need to reduce the complexity of maintaining a large MASTER-tree. Hence, MAS-TER groups the sensors into small clusters, and for each cluster it maintains a separate MASTER-tree. The MASTER-tree is updated after a set of sensor readings arrives. If some data are missing, than an appropriate MASTER-tree is found for a missing sensor, and the association rules stored in the MASTER-tree are evaluated to estimate the missing data.

However, MASTER approach has certain characteristics, because of which it is it not possible to apply it directly on mobile sensor networks. First, it was designed for static sensor networks and the sensor cluster is solely based on spatial attributes of the sensors. Moreover, if a sensor reading is missing, it is not enough just to estimate the sensor's value, but to predict its location too.

Therefore, DEMS solves the drawbacks and adopts the existing func-tionalities of the MASTER framework to allow data estimation in mobile sensor networks. The DEMS estimates missing data based on both spatial and temporal relations among sensor readings. First, a monitoring area is divided into hexagons. Each hexagon corresponds to a virtual static sensor (VSS) placed in the center of the hexagon. The artificial virtual static sensor does not exist physically, but it exists during the execution of the algorithm. Now, DEMS converts the real mobile sensors readings into VSS's readings, based on the real sensors' locations. Furthermore, DEMS performs cluster-ing of the virtual static sensors and creates a MASTER-tree for each created cluster.

For each missing real mobile sensor reading, DEMS performs the esti-mation through three major steps: (1) missing real sensor is mapped to its corresponding VSS, (2) MASTER-tree is consulted and the estimation is produced based on the association rules stored in the MASTER-tree, and (3) estimated VSS reading is converted into the corresponding real mobile sensor reading. It is worth mentioning that each real mobile sensor reading is accompanied by parameters of its location. Based on the spatial data, it is possible to map a real mobile sensor to the corresponding hexagon and the VSS, as well.

A VSS reports its reading in the current round if a real mobile sen-sor is present in its hexagon. If VSS is active, it reports a reading in the current round; otherwise, it is inactive. When multiple real mobile sensors are present in the hexagon, the corresponding VSS sends the average of all the real sensors' readings. A VSS is missing if one real sensor exists, or is expected to exist, in the hexagon and its reading is missing in the current round.

In DEMS, all real mobile sensors send their data to the base station. In the base station, the received readings of the real mobile sensors are mapped to the corresponding VSS readings. The mapping is done as follows: using a geometric mapping, DEMS finds the corresponding VSS for a real mobile sensor reading. If the location of the real mobile sensor is missing, DEMS predicts it. If the reading is missing, the corresponding VSS is declared missing in the current round.

The DEMS framework consists of the following two modules: MASTER-tree projection module and data estimation module. The MASTER-tree projection module maintains the MASTER-tree and up-to-data association rules between VSSs. The data estimation module estimates the missing sensors' readings using the association rules stored in the MASTER-tree. The data estimation process tries iteratively to find the best matching association rule (based on confidence and support) in which the missing (VSS) sensor is consequent.

Compared to the existing solutions, such as SPIRIT or TinyDB, DEMS has proved to be more effective in estimating the missing sensor data.

As the authors have suggested, the major challenges are solution for the case when multiple mobile sensors report data at different times and expansion of the algorithm to include multi-hop MSNs, mobile base stations, and clustered MSNs.

4.3 The MEE (Regression)—Mobile Energy Efficient Regression

The reference [3] contains one of the approaches from this solution group that we have selected for illustration purposes in this article (research performed at the Department of Computer Science Rutgers, the State University of New Jersey supported by DARPA, and a grant from CISCO Systems).

The approach is also presented as the most representative example of the class of approaches in WSNs based on regression, with emphasis on achieving energy efficiency during the monitoring operation. Energy efficiency is often achieved by prediction of sensors' readings. The prediction is an important concept for energy efficient algorithms because it reduces the amount of energy spent on transmitting the readings to the base station. The transmission of readings from sensors to the base station requires much more energy than it is spent on computation that predicts sensors' readings.

The authors showed that the concepts from MPEG might be applied to this paradigm.

In mobile sensor networks, besides complexity of an algorithm, it is always necessary to maintain the structure of the network. That is the main trade-off in mobile sensor networks between their flexibility and complexity of maintenance. This approach considers that sensors are grouped into clusters, where each cluster has its cluster-head. The configuration of clusters is fixed in a static sensor network. However, in a mobile sensor network, additional energy must be spent on maintaining the clusters.

More details can be found in the section that describes this approach in the context of static WSNs performing the regression-based monitoring operation.

4.4 The MEE (Association Rule Mining)—Mobile Energy Efficient Association Rule Mining

This class includes no representative examples, although the application of association rule mining in Mobile Energy Efficient WSNs makes lots of sense.

In the light of the methodology presented in Appendix#1, the most promising course leading to a new useful solution is Catalytic Mendelyeyevization. In this context, Catalytic Mendelyeyevization means that DM using association rule mining in MEE networks obtains better performance if a new resource is added (in hardware, in the communications infrastructure, in system software, or in the DM algorithm itself) to increase performance.

4.5 The MOO (Classification)—Mobile Overall Optimization Classification

A representative approach of this solution group is given in [4] with all relevant details (research performed at the Queen's University, School of Computing).

There are two broad kinds of sensor networks: peer-to-peer (ad hoc) and hubbed networks. The hubbed networks are in the focus of this article. In a hubbed network, the network structure is a tree. Sensors are leaves, and the root is a powerful, more substantial computational device. Nowadays, sensors become more powerful and thus capable of local computation. This opens many possibilities for training predictors in a distributed fashion. When sensors are just passive input devices, the decision-making process or classification is done at the central site/server. The centralized approach has a few drawbacks, such as intensive communication between sensors and the central server, the central server becomes a single point of failure, etc. In the centralized approach, each sensor reports its raw reading to the central place. When the readings of all sensors are finally collected, a DM algorithm is run to classify the data.

However, when sensors are capable of local computation, they can perform local prediction and determine the class of the data locally. Instead of sending the raw data to the root node, each sensor sends its locally discovered class to the root node, which determines the appropriate prediction by voting the received classes of the local predictors. The central node uses weighted or un-weighted voting.

As it was discussed, each sensor maintains its local model for prediction. In the given paper, one of the contributions is a framework for building and deploying predictors in sensor networks in a distributed way.

The communication between sensors and the central node is most often bidirectional in sensor networks, which provides some sort of feedback in such networks. Sensors send predicted classes to the central node, and the central node sends the classification results back to its sensors after determining the appropriate prediction. Upon receiving the outcome of the classification, sensors can compare their local predictions with the global predictions. If a local prediction differs from the global prediction, or the accuracy of the local prediction drops below a defined threshold, the given sensor can respond to it by relearning the local model. This mechanism significantly improves robustness of the distributed predictor. Finally, since only local predictions are communicated to the central node, this framework is also suitable for the applications where data security is concern.

4.6 The MOO (Clustering)—Mobile Overall Optimization Clustering

A representative approach of this solution group is given in [5] with all relevant details (research performed at School of Electronics Engineering and Computer Science, National Laboratory on Machine Perception, Peking University, Beijing, China, in co-operation with the Department of Computer Science, The Hong Kong University of Science and Technology, Clear Water Bay, Kowloon, Hong Kong). The chosen approach presents online mining techniques in large-scale WSNs performing data-intensive measurement and surveillance. The emphasis in this research is on discovering patterns and correlations between data arriving from sensors, which is essential for making intelligent decisions in real-time.

Development of algorithms for online mining faces the following challenges: resource constraints (battery lifetime, communication, CPU, and storage constraints), mobility of sensors increases complexity of sensor data and sensor data come in time-ordered streams. Hence, the only reasonable way to perform online mining is to process as much data as possible in a decentralized fashion. Thus, energy-costly operations, such as communication, computation, and data maintenance are highly reduced. The following three problems, along with the corresponding preliminary solutions, were identified and discussed in this research: (1) discovery of irregularities in sensor data, (2) sensor data clustering, and (3) discovery of correlations in sensor data.

Sensor data irregularities are detected in two ways: detecting irregular patterns and detecting irregular sensor data. The goal of the irregularity detection is to find what values differ a lot from the rest of the data. Regarding the pattern irregularity detection, the authors proposed a new approach called pattern variation discovery (PVD). This approach includes four steps: selection of a reference frame, definition of normal patterns, incremental maintenance of the normal patterns, and irregularity detection. The data processed in order to consider possible irregularities are often organized into matrices. Therefore, detection of irregular data involves (costly) matrix operations. In order to optimize matrix comparison, the authors proposed a technique called Singular Value Decomposition (SVD), which transforms each matrix into a singular value and then compares these values instead of the whole matrices.

Apart from the detection of irregular patterns, it is also necessary to check distribution of the data arriving from a single sensor and find out if there are values that are completely different compared to other values reported by the sensor. By nature, sensor data irregularities may be either temporal, or spatial. Historical sensor data sequences are analyzed using an appropriate model for temporal irregularities. When some value substantially affects model parameters, it is detected as an irregularity. The sliding window concept is used here to constrain the amount of sensor data being processed with the purpose of detecting temporal irregularities.

The spatial irregularities are handled by a statistical model that finds irregularities in a sensor's reading by considering readings from its neighbor sensors. For a practical reason, to reduce resource consumption, only one-hop neighbor sensors are considered for detecting the spatial sensor data irregularities.

The approach called multi-dimensional clustering was proposed for the sensor data clustering. It works as follows: first, sensors' data are clustered along each attribute (e.g., temperature, humidity, etc.). Afterwards, sensors are clustered according to their readings. Sensors clusters are formed by using the theory of bipartite graphs. Sensors clusters are populated with sensors having similar readings on corresponding attributes.

Finally, detecting correlations in sensors' readings is very important task for data analysis applications since it allows the application to estimate some values from the values of the correlated attributes. Sensor data are viewed as data streams ordered in time. Such data streams may be represented using matrix. Then correlation detection is done by performing matrix operations. Matrix operations may be simplified using the SVD technique.

The authors of this position paper presented interesting and useful techniques for real-time DM in WSNs. The main issues and challenges were identified, such as detection of irregularities, clustering and discovery of correlations in sensor data, etc. The corresponding solutions were also proposed. The most promising part of this approach that holds a lot of potential for further research is the pattern discovery. The proposed approach should be upgraded in some very important aspects of DM in sensor networks, such as energy awareness, adaptivity, and fault tolerance.

4.7 The MOO (Regression)—Mobile Overall Optimization Regression

This class includes no representative examples, although the application of regression in Mobile Overall Efficient WSNs makes lots of sense. In the light of the methodology presented in Appendix#1, the most promising avenue leading to a new useful solution is Transdisciplinarization via Mutation.

In this context, Transdisciplinarization via Mutation means that the DM algorithm can be enhanced with resources utilized when regression is used in other disciplines of science and engineering. This implies that resources used elsewhere are incorporated into the WSN environment, using analogies, but applied carefully for maximal performance and minimal complexity increase.

4.8 The MOO (Association Rule Mining)—Mobile Overall Optimization Association Rule Mining

This class includes no representative examples and conclusions are similar to the one discussed for the Mobile Overall Optimization Regression class.

4.9 The SEE (Classification)—Static Energy Efficient Classification

The reference [1] contains one of the approaches from this solution group that was selected for illustration purposes in this article (research performed at the University of Crete, Institute of Computer Science (FORTH-ICS), and Universidad de València, Escuela Técnica Superior de Ingeniería, supported by the Greek General Secretariat for Research and Technology under the program PENED).

The objective of the research was to develop an energy efficient distributed classification algorithms for large-scale WSNs. The algorithm itself is general, and can be used in context of both static and mobile sensor networks. Thus, this approach was already presented in the section on the MEE classification.

4.10 The SEE (Clustering)—Static Energy Efficient Clustering

A representative approach of this solution group is given in [6] with all relevant details (research performed at the School of Electrical and Computer Engineering, Purdue University).

The chosen approach presents a distributed, randomized clustering algorithm for organizing the sensors in a WSN into clusters and upgrading the algorithm for the generation of the hierarchy of cluster-heads.

The authors defined t units as the time required by data to reach the cluster-head from any sensor k hops away. It can be concluded that if a sensor does not receive a cluster-head advertisement within time duration t, it is not within k hops of any volunteer cluster-head, and hence becomes a forced cluster-head because the advertisement is limited by k hops.

The authors came to the conclusion that the energy savings increase with the number of levels in the hierarchy and used the results in stochastic geometry to derive solutions for the values of parameters of algorithm that minimize the total energy spent in the network when all sensors report data through the cluster-heads to the processing center.

4.11 The SEE (Regression)—Static Energy Efficient Regression

The reference [3] contains one of the approaches from this solution group that we have selected for illustration purposes in this article (research performed at the Department of Computer Science Rutgers, the State University of New Jersey supported by DARPA and a grant from CISCO Systems). The approach uses WSNs with Rene motes since the emphasis is on proposing a new paradigm for energy efficient monitoring. In this representative example, the authors described DM algorithms, the paradigm that can be visualized as a watching a "sensor movie." The authors showed that the concepts from MPEG might be applied to that paradigm.

This paper considers large-scale WSNs having non-deterministic topology. Sensors in the networks are organized in clusters, may be multiple hops away from the nearest wired node, and each cluster has its cluster-head sensor. There are a few approaches for performing monitoring operations in WSNs. A naïve one would be so-called centralized approach. Each sensor in network reports its readings to the base station which maintains the database of readings of all sensors in the network. Thus, monitoring is based on querying the centralized database. It requires a lot of energy for the communication purpose. The fact is that similar and correlated readings are unnecessarily sent to the base station and no compression is done.

Apart from this, there is one more approach for performing monitoring in WSN, called PREMON (PREdiction-based MONitoring). It is based on fact that it is more effective to have a group of sensors performing a sensing task than one powerful sensor. It is very likely that spatially proximate sensors report correlated readings. It is very important to find a mechanism for predicting sensor values based on the recent history of its readings and readings of the sensors in its neighborhood. The correlation may be spatial, temporal or spatio-temporal. Thus, the sensor needs not transmit its reading if it can be predicted by a monitoring entity.

The essence of this approach is as follows: the server maintains the current state of all the sensors involved in the monitoring operation; based on this it generates prediction models which are sent to the appropriate sensors; the cluster-head or base station may predict a set of readings that a sensor is going to see in the near future; the sensor transmits data to the monitoring entity only when the data differ from the reading given by the prediction model.

Like many approaches, this one also brings some trade-offs. That is, additional computational power is required for building the prediction models and communicating them to the cluster-heads, in favor of decrease of the number of typical transmissions. The idea hidden behind this decision is based on the fact that the transmissions require more energy than it is spent on computation and sending the prediction models.

As the authors suggested, experimental results show that the proposed solutions from this approach save energy considerably, by more than five times, increase sensor lifetimes, as well as the lifetime of WSN made of these sensors.

4.12 The SEE (Association Rule Mining)—Static Energy Efficient Association Rule Mining

The reference [7] contains one of the approaches from this solution group that we have selected for illustration in this article (research performed at the University of Oklahoma, School of Computer Science). The approach presented in this paper is performing an estimation of the missing, corrupted, or late readings from a particular sensor, by using the values available at the sensors relating to the sensor nodes the readings of which are missing, through association rule mining. This power-aware technique is called WARM (Window Association Rule Mining).

The amount of lost or corrupted data in WSNs is significant. There is a few ways to deal with this problem, such as data retransmission, data duplication, ignoring missing data, or estimating the missing data. The choice of the technique depends on the characteristics and demands of the application deployed over a WSN. However, WSNs consist of small sensors that are energy constrained. Hence, it is necessary to develop a DM algorithm that consumes as little energy as possible from sensors' batteries. The most efficient mechanism to handle the missing data is to predict them.

Sensors' readings are sent continuously to a base station or proxy sensors as data streams. Data stream comprises of tuples that exist online and their arrival rate is not strict. Data streams are potentially unbounded and might be incomplete or missing. Exploiting the sliding window concept is crucial for dealing with the unbounded data streams. Therefore, the key objective of this research is to develop a technique for dealing with missing tuples in data streams, in the presence of other data that are somehow related to the missing tuple. For estimating the values of the missing tuple, the association rule mining is used first to identify the sensors that are related to the sensors with missing tuples. When the relation is found, readings of the related sensors are used to calculate the missing values. It is all incorporated in Data Stream Association Rule Mining Framework (DSRAM). The framework generates only association rules between pairs of sensors; since researchers has found that the bottleneck in mining for association rules is the task of discovering association rules between three sensors and more. By decreasing the number of items in association rules, complexity of the algorithm is highly reduced. In addition, the representation of the simplified association rules is feasible and leads to an additional decrease of time needed for generating all applicable association rules. Evaluation of association rules is done with respect to a particular state of sensor. In general, an association rule consists of pairs of sensors with two extra parameters: minimal confidence and minimal support.

Association rule DM framework relies on certain data structures (data model), used for representing the association rules, and corresponding algorithms that maintain the data structures. The main data structures are buffer, cube, and counters. The algorithms that maintain the data structures are: checkBuffer(), update(), and estimateValue(). The essence of the proposed data model and algorithms is to generate relatively good estimation of missing data relatively fast.

The buffer is a data structure that stores data arriving from the sensors in one round of reading. It is implemented as one-dimensional array of size n, where n is the number of sensors.

The cube is a data structure aimed for tracking the correlation between pairs of sensors' according to the collected readings. By its nature, the cube is a data cube implementing the sliding window concept. The cube consists of slices, and each slice consists of nodes. A slice is a two-dimensional quadratic matrix which represents correlations between pairs of sensors after one round of readings. Dimensions of the matrix are determined by the number of sensors. Cells of the matrix are called nodes, and hold the values as follows: if sensors Si and Sj send the same reading/value, corresponding node holds that value. In case when a node corresponds to a single sensor, it holds the value reported by that sensor. Otherwise, the node is set to -1, meaning that sensors measured different values.

The counter is a data structure, the aim of which is to speed up the estimation of a missing value. Without the counter, determining association rules would be a time-consuming operation due to going through all the data stored in the cube and performing counting of the correlation parameters, such as actual confidence and actual support. Hence, the counters are stored for each pair of sensors with respect to each state that sensors can send. The counter is implemented as a three-dimensional array with size (n, n, p), where n is the number of sensors, and p is the number of possible states that a sensor can publish. Having the counter data structure, the association rule parameters actual confidence and actual support can be read very easily and fast.

The checkBuffer() algorithm checks the buffer at the predefined time interval for the presence of missing sensors' readings in the current round. If missing values found, it calls the estimateValue() algorithm, otherwise the update() algorithm is called. The purpose of the update() algorithm is to update both the cube and the counter. The cube and the counter are updated in two cases: in regular case when no missing values are encountered in the buffer, or right after the estimating missing values in the buffer. The cube is updated by discarding the oldest slice and putting the newest one at the front. When correlation between two sensors in the current round is discovered, then corresponding node in the counter is incremented. On the other hand, when the oldest slice is discarded from the back of the cube window, it is considered for the purpose of updating the nodes in the counter. If a node in the discarded slice is different than −1, than corresponding node in the counter is decremented.

The estimateValue() algorithm is performed in several steps. The essence of the algorithm is that when a missing sensor is found, then data from the cube and the counter are used to find which sensors are correlated to the missing sensor. If there are a few correlated sensors, then the most eligible sensor is found and its value is used as the estimation. The estimated value is then stored to the buffer, which is then checked again for other missing values. When a missing value cannot be estimated by the association rule mining, it is estimated using the average value of all available readings for the missing sensor.

The WARM approach was compared with other similar approaches in terms of estimation accuracy, time, and space complexity. The simulation results show that WARM requires more space and time to produce the estimation than considered alternative approaches. However, WARM produces better accuracy of the estimated data.

This approach has great potentials because it is usable and acceptable for many applications, and allows determining the association rules between sensors that produce the same readings. However, it can be enriched to discover the association rules between sensors that produce different readings. In addition, the association rules can be assigned weights, meaning that the events that happened closer to the present moment are more relevant for DM than the events that happened further into the past. The approach has to be upgraded for the case of multiple sensor failure of co-related sensors, too.

4.13 The SOO (Classification)—Static Overall Optimization Classification

This class includes no representative examples, although the application of classification in Static Energy Efficient WSNs makes lots of sense. In the light of the methodology presented in Appendix#1, the most promising avenue leading to a new useful solution is Hybridization via Synergy and Retrajectorization via Granularization.

In this context, Hybridization via Synergy means that the existing DM algorithms and ideas for classification in both mobile and static WSNs can be used for generating a hybrid DM algorithm that does overall optimization in static WSNs. In addition, Retrajectorization via Regranularization means that the existing DM algorithm used in static sensor networks which considers only energy efficiency can be enhanced with new relevant parameters to support overall optimization within a sensor network. However, each proposed idea must be applied carefully for maximal performance and minimal complexity increase.

4.14 The SOO (Clustering)—Static Overall Optimization Clustering

A representative approach of this solution group is given in [8] with all the relevant details (research performed at the Department of Computer Science and Electrical Engineering, University of Maryland). The chosen approach presents the first K-means algorithm for a large WSN. The algorithm presented in this approach is suited for the dynamic WSN without any special server nodes.

The algorithm is initiated at a single node that generates an initial set of centroids randomly along with a user-defined termination threshold and sends these to all of its immediate neighbors. A node which receives the initial centroids sends them to the remainder of its immediate neighbors and begins iteration one. Eventually all nodes will enter iteration #1 with the same initial centroids and termination threshold. The algorithm repeats iterations of a modified K-means at each node and collects (at each iteration) all the centroids and their cluster counts for iteration from its immediate neighbors. These, along with the local data, are used to produce the centroids for the next iteration. If the new centroids differ substantially from the old ones, then the algorithm goes onto the next iteration. Otherwise, it enters a terminated state.

As the authors suggested, centralizing all the data to a single machine to run a centralized K-means is not an attractive option and the algorithm ought to ensure the following: not to require global synchronization, to be communication efficient, and to be robust to network or data changes. In this approach, the achieved accuracy is relatively high, but the communication cost has to be improved in the future work.

4.15 The SOO (Regression)—Static Overall Optimization Regression

A representative approach of this solution group is given in [9] with all relevant details (research performed at the Department of Computer Science Department, Carnegie Mellon University). The essence of this research is to find a scalable and efficient mechanism for incremental pattern discovery in a large number of numerical co-evolving streams. The chosen approach presents the SPIRIT (**S**treaming **P**attern d**I**scove**R**y in mult**I**ple **T**imeseries), which can incrementally find correlations and hidden variables in the numerical data streams, for example, in sensor network monitoring problem.

The correlations and the hidden variables summarize key trends in the stream collection. Summarizing the key trends is done quickly, without buffering of the streams and without comparing the pairs of streams. The hidden variables compactly describe the key trends and highly reduce the complexity of further data processing.

Thus, main characteristics of the SPIRIT approach are:

- It is scalable, incremental and any time. Requires little memory and processing time.
- It scales linearly with the number of streams.
- It is adaptive and fully automatic.
- Does not require the sliding window concept, and thus does not need to buffer any stream of data.

The SPIRIT framework exploits auto-regression due to its simplicity, but it is possible to incorporate any other algorithm. The main task of the SPIRIT algorithm is to find an appropriate and minimal set of hidden variables that can express the current trend of data in the streams. In each incremental step, the SPIRIT processes one vector of the stream. Each value in the vector is given an appropriate weight (w), according to the current state of the hidden variables (y). Then the existing hidden variables are adjusted accordingly. Some of them may disappear, or some new hidden variables may appear after processing of the current vector. In addition, the hidden variable represents the hypothesis function that is represented by the following equation:

$$y_{t,i} = w_{i,1}x_{t,1} + w_{i,2}x_{t,2} + \cdots + w_{i,n}x_{t,n}, \tag{2}$$

where t is a time tick, the symbol n is the number of the measured values, and $x_{t,i}$ denotes a measured value at time t.

Given a collection of n co-evolving, semi-infinite streams, producing a value $x_{t,j}$, for each stream $1 \leq j \leq n$ and for each time tick $t = 1, 2, \ldots$, SPIRIT does the following:

- Adapts the number k of hidden variables necessary to explain/summarize the main trends in the collection.
- Adapts the participation weights $w_{i,j}$ of the jth stream on the ith hidden variable ($1 \leq i \leq k$ and $1 \leq j \leq n$), so as to produce an accurate summary of the stream collection.
- Monitors the hidden variables y_{ti}, for $1 \leq i \leq k$. Keeps updating all the above efficiently.

The authors presented great results from evaluation processes of the SPIRIT method on several datasets where it discovered the hidden variables. It is recognized as a good method for interpretation in various applications. The SPIRIT was tested using performance and accuracy tests. The performance tests gave the following results: SPIRIT requires limited space and time, scales linearly with respect to the number of streams, and the number of the hidden variables, and executes several times faster than other methods. Regarding the accuracy, the SPIRIT produces the results that are very close to the ideal results. However, solutions that give the ideal results require much more resources than SPIRIT does.

4.16 The SOO (Association Rule Mining)—Static Overall Optimization Association Rule Mining

A representative approach of this solution group is given in [10] with all relevant details (research performed at the School of Computer Science, University of Oklahoma). In this paper, a data estimation technique for missing, corrupted, or late readings from one or more sensors in a WSN at any given round, Freshness Association Rule Mining—FARM, is presented. The major contribution of FARM is to incorporate the temporal factor that is inherent to most data stream applications.

Sensors that monitor some environment send their readings as continuous flows of data, called data streams. The amount of lost or corrupted data is significant. There exist a few well-known mechanisms for dealing with this problem, such as data retransmission, data duplication, ignoring missing data or estimating the missing data. Since WSNs consist of small energy-constrained sensors, it is necessary to develop a DM algorithm that consumes as little energy as possible from sensors' batteries. The most efficient mechanism to handle missing data is to estimate them with respect to the readings from the other sensors in the network.

In order to estimate missing data, it is necessary to extract some knowledge from the data streams. The FARM approach uses association rules to represent the knowledge extracted from the data streams. The rounds of readings in the data streams are not treated equally and do not contribute equally in the process of estimating missing data. There is the difference in importance between recent and old rounds.

The crucial concept of the FARM approach is the data freshness. This concept is implemented in a data freshness framework. The freshness framework is aimed to incorporate the temporal aspect into the association rules and the estimation, to store data streams in a compact form allowing maintenance of large history, and to provide retrieval of the original data from the compact form unambiguously.

Each round of data readings is given a different weight, based on relative recentness. The weight parameter is calculated by the following recursive function:

$$w(1) = 1, \tag{3}$$
$$w(n) = p \cdot w(n-1), \tag{4}$$

where $p \geq 1$, input to w is the round order, and w is a function that returns the weight of a given round. An equivalent definition is:

$$w(n) = p^{n-1}, \tag{5}$$

where the parameter p is referred to as the damping factor, which represents the relative importance of a round comparatively with the previous round.

The weight reflects freshness of a data round. The more recent the data are, the higher the assigned weight is, which contributes in DM with higher importance.

Association rules represent relation between pairs of sensors since that provides the best space-time performances. The association rule parameters are calculated with respect to a particular reported state. The actual weight support is calculated as sum of the weights of the rounds where both sensors in the rule reported the same state. The actual weight confidence is a sum of round weights where both related sensors reported the same state divided by the sum of round weights where the antecedent sensor reported the given state.

The FARM relies on certain data structures (data model) used for representing the association rules and corresponding algorithms that maintain the data structures. The two main data structures are the Buffer and the two-dimensional Ragged Array. The algorithms that maintain the data structures are: checkBuffer(), update(), and estimateValue(). The essence of the proposed data model and algorithms is to generate relatively good estimation of missing data relatively fast.

The buffer is a data structure that stores round data (with a special value for missing/corrupted values). It is implemented as a one-dimensional array of size n, where n is the number of sensors.

The ragged array is viewed as an upper triangular part of a quadratic matrix (each row/column corresponds to a single sensor; a row/column is denoted as S_i, where i takes values from one to the number of sensors). An element of the array (in the intersection of the row S_i and the column S_j) is an object that holds the history of round information for a given pair of sensors. The object contains one-dimensional array of s entries, where s is the number of states that sensors can send. Each element in the array holds the sum of all round weights in which both sensors reported the same state (weight support). Compacted report history of a particular sensor is located in corresponding diagonal entry of the ragged array. It is possible to recover the order of rounds in which the sensor reported the given state, since the weight sum values are not redundant. Each weight sum value is formed in a unique way. It is all about determining which "digits" form the weight sum in a number system with base p. However, the practical issue for implementation is that the weight counter cannot increment indefinitely, because it leads to the overflow problem. These data structures are maintained by the algorithms which are described in the following paragraph.

The checkBuffer() algorithm is the main procedure that checks the buffer for any existing missing values. If there are some missing values, it invokes estimateValue() method which is to estimate the missing values. When the buffer check is finished (all missing values are estimated) this procedure invokes the procedure update() which updates the ragged array.

The update() procedure checks if the identical readings exist in the buffer. For each pair of sensors that reported the same state this procedure updates the ragged array object by adding the current weight to the value in the ragged array object that corresponds to the given pair of sensors and given state.

The estimateValue() algorithm examines the association rules to find antecedent sensors for the missing sensor. It first determines eligible sensors' states for estimation the actual support of which is larger than the minimum user-defined support. In addition, it is necessary to determine the eligible sensors, too. The eligible sensors are found by using a temporary data structure called StateSet. The StateSet is created per each state that sensors can report. It can be viewed as a hash table, where the keys are the sensor states and the values are the sets of sensors. Then the procedure examines rules between the missing sensor and each sensor from the StateSet separately. If the actual weight confidence of a single rule is larger than the user-defined minimum weight confidence, the antecedent sensor in the rule is declared as the eligible sensor. The contribution weights are calculated and compared for each eligible state, with respect to the association rules between the eligible sensors and the missing sensor. Finally, the missing value is estimated by weighted averaging the readings of the eligible sensors.

The FARM approach was compared with a few similar approaches for estimating missing values. According to the performed tests, the response time for FARM was not longer than one millisecond, compared to the results of other approaches. On the other hand, this method is the best in the estimation accuracy and its root mean square error was 20–40% better than the error of the other approaches.

The authors tested the FARM with data from climate sensing and traffic monitoring applications. In these approaches, the achieved estimation accuracy is relatively high, but the cost may be improved in the future work, which makes the FARM a good candidate for real-time applications.

4.17 Summary

For easier understanding of the major achievements of the twelve existing approaches, Table 3 summarizes the ways in which the major technological and application issues were treated in the presented examples; namely: hop count, optimization focus, the level of accuracy of a DM algorithm, and the end of loop condition of the applied DM algorithm.

These parameters are selected for comparison of the representative approaches/solutions of the given classes. The hop count parameter describes time-complexity of a solution (number of iterations that lead to the result). The optimization-focus parameter tells whether a solution incorporates some sort of optimization in Data Mining (energy awareness, performances, etc.). The level of accuracy parameter describes precision of the results produced by a given solution. The end condition parameter tells about condition that is to be satisfied in order to finish the process of Data Mining in a WSN.

Table 3 Summary of the technological domain and application domain solutions implemented in the surveyed examples of DM in WSN.

Category	Parameters	Hop count	Optimization focus	Accuracy level	End condition
	Classification	Depends on the number of the linearly organized clusters.	Energy consumption. Requires 50% less energy than the centralized approach. Hyper-plane is obtained incrementally, in a distributed fashion	The separating hyper-plane approximation is very close to the one obtained by the centralized approach	Algorithm finishes when the hyper-plane approximation reaches the end of the cluster "chain"
MEE	Clustering	Depends on the number of sensor clusters in a network. Each physical sensor communicates directly to the base station	Energy consumption. Missing data estimation	Accuracy of the estimated data is quite high, compared to other solutions	Algorithm works continuously. Data estimation is done iteratively, by searching for a best matching value
	Regression	The same as for the SEE Regression.	The same as for the SEE Regression	The same as for the SEE Regression	The same as for the SEE Regression
	Association Rule Mining		No representative solutions found		

(continued)

Table 3 Continued.

Category	Parameters	Hop count	Optimization focus	Accuracy level	End condition
	Classification	The same as for the MEE Classification	The same as for the MEE Classification	The same as for the MEE Classification	The same as for the MEE Classification
	Clustering	Hop count is a user-defined parameter	Energy consumption. Hop count minimization from a sensor to a base station through the chain of hierarchical cluster-heads	Accuracy is not an applicable parameter for this approach	The end condition comprises of the maximum number of allowed hops from a sensor to its cluster-head and the probability of becoming a cluster-head
SEE	Regression	The key complexity is related to building of the prediction model. Implicitly depends on the size of a network and the number of sensor clusters in it	Energy consumption. Prediction of missing data. Error tolerance. Delay tolerance	Accuracy is relatively good, but the authors proposed some ideas about how to make it better	Algorithm works continuously. There are no applicable end conditions
	Association Rule Mining	Updating the association rules hides the essential complexity of the approach	Energy consumption. Space consumption (using window concept). Prediction of missing data	Approach achieves relatively high accuracy, compared to other solutions	Algorithm works continuously. In each iteration, one data stream tuple is processed

(continued)

Table 3 Continued.

Category	Parameters	Hop count	Optimization focus	Accuracy level	End condition
	Classification	Each sensor communicates directly to the central sensor node. The hop count is one. A sensor and the central node communicate iteratively, until a prediction model is stable	Energy consumption. Performances. Data security	The achieved accuracy level is relatively high	The model construction is done until the central node's decision is the same as the local sensor' decision
MOO	Clustering	The hop count parameter is not explicitly applicable to this approach	Energy consumption. Detection of correlations in the data to improve decision-making performance. Fault tolerance	There is a trade-off between accuracy and consumed energy. The accuracy depends on the needs for the energy efficiency	Algorithm works continuously. There is no applicable end condition
	Regression		No representative solutions found		
	Association Rule Mining		No representative solutions found		

(continued)

Table 3 Continued.

Category	Parameters	Hop count	Optimization focus	Accuracy level	End condition
	Classification		No representative solutions found		
	Clustering	Depends on the size of the network. Each node sends its centroids to its immediate neighbors and waits for feedback. It collects centroids back from its neighbors and derives the new ones. If they differ substantially from the old ones, the new iteration is started.	Scalability. Energy consumption	The achieved accuracy is relatively high. The error is less than 3% per node	Executes until the new centroids do not differ substantially from the old ones
SOO	Regression	Scales linearly with the number of streams and the number of hidden variables. Scales linearly with the stream size (the size of one tuple in the stream)	Energy consumption. Space (memory), execution time. Provides good performances	The achieved accuracy is very close to the ideal accuracy. Implemented in forecasting applications	Algorithm works continuously. In each cycle, one data stream tuple is processed until all the participation weights and the hidden variables are updated
	Association Rule Mining	Online data stream processing. One processing cycle involves: buffer check, association rules update and data estimation	Energy consumption. Data estimation	Data estimation accuracy is high. Achieves better accuracy for 20–40% than the similar data estimation approaches	Algorithm works continuously. A processing cycle is done when all pairs of sensor readings from the buffer are examined

Apart from the given parameters that are used for comparison of the approaches, all of the approaches have in common the strategy of collecting the sensor data readings. One of the essential principles in engineering has been used here, the "Divide and conquer" principle. Namely, sensor readings are not collected and processed at one place. Instead, each approach proposes the sensor data processing in a distributed fashion. Therefore, sensors are logically clustered (whether on the spatial, or the temporal basis) and most of the Data Mining is done within clusters. That way, only small set of partial conclusions is transmitted from clusters to a central place (a base station), where the final decision is made. This approach highly reduces energy-consuming communication between sensors and the base station, increasing the lifetime of the sensors and the WSN.

5. CLASSIFICATION EXTENSION TO CONCEPT MODELING IN SYSTEMS OF WIRELESS SENSOR NETWORKS BASED ON NATURAL LANGUAGE PROCESSING AND NON-UNIFORM SEMANTICS

5.1 Ongoing Research Milestones

This section sheds light on a technique that can be used to convert statements of a natural language into the statements of a highly reduced topic-oriented language, the weather forecast sublanguage (a language that a WSN can understand—a language needed by a WSN to obtain information from the Internet).

Based on the classification presented above, for a particular application area of WSN, one can select a DM algorithm that gives the best results. The next step for performance improving is to enable the WSN to consult data from the Internet. Data from the Internet are most often given in an unstructured form. The goal is to adapt these data to a form suitable for use in DM algorithms for WSNs. This problem will be addressed in a follow–up study of the same authors, in the domain of weather forecast. Therefore, it is necessary:

1. To create multi–lingual corpuses of weather forecasts.
2. To analyze weather forecast texts in different natural languages from these corpuses, from different sources on the Internet, and to make sublanguages (formal descriptions of expressions used in the particular natural weather forecast language).
3. To create weather forecast Conceptual Model suitable for the problem of communication in the Systems of WSNs at the international level.

The main goal is to provide that related concepts from different natural languages could be mapped into the same concept.

4. To develop the Information Extraction (IE) mechanism for the natural language in which a text is written and to map the extracted information into the appropriate concepts.
5. Additionally, the problem of using different metrics and a large number of different abbreviations in weather forecast texts in different languages has to be solved, as well as automatic conversion of the measured values from one system to another, and to determine the exact time for which the forecast was generated.

The problems of IE and CM will be further discussed hereinafter, with special emphasis on problems of NLP of the texts in Serbian. More detailed information about sublanguages can be found in [11].

5.2 Information Extraction Consideration from the Viewpoint of Ongoing Research with Special Review of the Problem in the Serbian Language Processing

IE is one of the most significant problems of NLP. It is generally a problem of great complexity, but especially for Slavic languages. For the purpose of our research, Serbian is the natural language of interest.

Named Entity Recognition (NER) [12] is one of the tasks of IE. The main issue of the NER is to identify proper names in text documents and to classify them in some of the predefined categories: the ENAMEX category (persons, organizations, and locations), the TIMEX category (temporal expressions), or the NUMEX category (numeric expressions) [13].

The material for analysis is organized in a corpus of weather forecasts gathered from various on-line newspapers and other weather forecast services. There are at least two types of weather forecasts. The first one is so-called telegraphic form, where the data are given in a tabular form and is much more suitable for processing. The second form is a free form, which is more similar to the regular speech form. An example of weather forecast in the Serbian language:

SRBIJA, PROGNOZA VREMENA ZA: 14.01.2012.

Ujutro hladno sa umerenim, lokalno i jakim mrazem. Pre podne umereno oblačno i uglavnom suvo. Od sredine dana na severu, a uveče i noću i u ostalim krajevima pretežno oblačno, mestimično sa slabim snegom uz neznatno povećanje. Vetar slab i umeren, na planinama povremeno i jak, zapadni i severozapadni. Najniža temperatura od −14 °C do −2 °C, u planinskim predelima i na visoravnima i do −20 °C. Najviša temperatura od −2 °C do 3 °C.

(*SERBIA, weather forecast: 14.01.2012.*

In the morning cold with moderate, locally heavy frost. The morning moderately cloudy and mostly dry. From the middle of the day in the north, and in the evening and night in other parts, too, mostly cloudy, with snow in places with a slight increase. Weak and moderate wind, in the mountains occasionally strong, from the west and northwest. The lowest temperature from −14 °C *to* −2 °C, *in the mountains and uplands, to* −20 °C. *Maximum temperature from* −2 °C *to* 3 °C.)

Proper names and their categories from the above example would be: the ENAMEX category (location *Srbija*), the TIMEX category (temporal expression: *14.01.2012.*, *Ujutro* (*In the morning*), *Pre podne* (*Morning*), *Uveče i noću* (*In the evening and night*), etc.), and the NUMEX category (numeric expressions: −14, −2, −20, 3). The main goal is to construct an IE system to produce the output, for example, in the form:

DATE_TIME: 14.01.2012.
REGION: SRBIJA
MIN_TEMP:
    FROM: −14 °C TO: −2 °C
MAX_TEMP:
    FROM: −2 °C TO 3 °C

Numerous techniques and services were developed for NER in English and Western European languages, but there is still plenty of room for development for the Slavic languages (typically morphologically rich languages). This problem is addressed in several ways for Serbian: through the set of electronic morphological dictionaries based on finite automata, the algorithms based on statistical methods, and by using the GATE [14] and the Unitex [15] systems.

Problems of the named entities' recognition, as essential part of IE, are extremely complex in the texts of the contemporary Serbian language (as discussed in [16, 17]). These problems stem from several sources rooted in the fundaments of Serbian. For example, Cyrillic and Latin alphabets are both official alphabets for texts in Serbian, but the transliteration is not unified. For example, the toponym *New York* in the Cyrillic alphabet could be represented as *Hjyjopk* or *њyjopk*, while in the Latin alphabet it is represented as *Njujork* (or even *NJujork*). Furthermore, the orthography of Serbian does not give precise definition how to treat foreign names that inevitably occur in texts, such as the names of countries, cities, and so on. For example, the *Microsoft* Company takes the forms *Mikrosoft* and *Majkrosoft*.

Another problem is that the inflectional and derivational morphologies of Serbian are very rich. Serbian has seven cases and three values for numbers—singular, plural, and paukal [18]. Serbian Grammar dictates that numeral one agrees with a noun in gender, number, and case, numerals greater than or equal to five do not inflect and they agree with a noun in the genitive plural, while numerals two, three, and four either inflect and agree with a noun, or they do not inflect. If the latter is the case, they agree with a noun in so-called "paukal," a special kind of grammatical number used with selected small values (2, 3, and 4). Not all grammarians agree with that; some of them argue that in the case of these small values, the noun agrees in genitive singular since, in most cases, the forms are the same. However, electronic dictionaries for Serbian use the notion of "paukal" since it better explains a numerous agreement phenomena that are not within the scope of this article (as analyzed in [19]).

Another great problem are compounds, too, because each compound as a whole, or just some part of it, can be inflected. For example, in the compound *Novi Sad,* both units are inflected: *Novom Sadu,* while in the compound *Sant Petersburg* only second unit inflects: *Sant Petersburgu.* Additionally, for instance, proper names may have a number of derived forms, adjectives or adverbs.

More details about these characteristics, typical for Slavic languages, can be found in [20], while the detailed analysis for the Serbian language can be found in [21].

5.2.1 Overview of Resources Developed for the Processing of the Serbian Language

Numerous resources that can be used for the purposes of our research were developed for processing of Serbian, but a great number of them has to be modified or improved. Most of these resources were developed in the Unitex system [22], while some of them were adapted for the GATE system [23].

The Unitex system is an open-source system, developed by Sébastien Paumier at the Institut Gaspard-Monge, University of Paris-Est Marne-la-Vallée, in 2001. It is a corpus processing system based on automata-oriented technology that is in constant development. The system is used all over the world for NLP tasks, because it provides support for a number of different languages and for multi-lingual processing tasks.

One of the main parts of the system are electronic dictionaries of the DELA type (Dictionnaires Electroniques du Laboratoire d'Automatique Documentaire et Linguistique or LADL electronic dictionaries), which is presented in Fig. 2. The system consists of the DELAS (simple forms DELA) and the DELAF (DELA of inflected forms) dictionaries. The DELAS

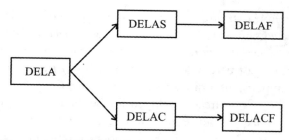

Fig. 2. The DELA system of electronic dictionaries.

dictionaries are the dictionaries of simple words, non-inflected forms, while the DELAF dictionaries contain all of simple words' inflected forms. On the other side, the system contains dictionaries of compounds DELAC (DELA of compound forms) and dictionaries of inflected compound forms DELACF (DELA of compound inflected forms).

The morphological dictionaries in the DELA format were proposed in the Laboratoire d'Automatique Documentaire et Linguistique under the guidance of Maurice Gross. The DELA format of the dictionaries is suitable for resolving problems of the text segmentation and morphological, syntactic, and semantic text processing. More details about the DELA format can be found in [24].

The morphological electronic dictionaries in the DELA format are plain text files. Each line in these files contains a word entry and the inflected form of the word. In other words, each line contains the lemma of the word and some grammatical, semantic, and inflectional information.

An example entry from the DELAF dictionary in English is "*tables, table. N+Conc:p.*" The inflected form *tables* is mandatory, *table* is the lemma of the entry, while the *N+Conc* is the sequence of grammatical and semantic information (*N* denotes a noun, and *Conc* denotes that this noun is a concrete object), *p* is an inflectional code, which indicates that the noun is plural.

These kinds of dictionaries are under development for Serbian by the NLP group at the Faculty of Mathematics, University of Belgrade. According to [21], the present size of the DELAS Serbian morphological dictionary (of simple words), contains 130,000 lemmas. Most of the lemmas from the DELAS dictionary belong to general lexica, while the rest belong to various kinds of simple proper names. The DELAF dictionary contains approximately 4,300.000 word forms with assigned grammatical categories. The size of DELAC and DELACF dictionaries are approximately 10,500 and 54,000 lemmas, respectively.

Similar example entry from the Serbian dictionary of simple word forms with appropriate grammatical and semantic code is *padao,padati*V+IMPER F+ IT+IR EF:GMS, where the word form *padao* is singular (S) masculine gender (M) of the active past participle (G) of the verb (V) *padati* "to fall" that is imperfective (Imperf), intransitive (It), and ireflexive (Iref).

Another type of resources developed for Serbian are different types of finite-state transducers. Finite-state transducers are used to perform morphological analysis and to recognize and annotate phrases in weather forecast texts with appropriate XML tags such as ENAMEX,TIMEX, and NUMEX, as we have explained before.

An example of the finite-state transducer graph for recognition of temporal expressions and their annotation with TIMEX tags is presented in Fig. 3. This finite-state transducer graph can recognize the sequence "*14.01.2012.*" from our weather forecast example text, and annotate it with TIMEX tag, so it can be extracted in the form "DATE_TIME: 14.01.2012."

Another system that is more suitable for solving the IE (and CM) problem is open-source free software GATE (General Architecture for Text Engineering). The GATE system or some of its components are already used for a number of different NLP tasks in multiple languages. The GATE system is architecture and a development environment for NLP applications. GATE is in development by the University of Sheffield NLP Group since 1995.

The GATE architecture is organized in three parts: Language Resources, Processing Resources, and Visual Resources. These components are independent, so the different types of users can work with the system. Programmers can work on development of the algorithms for NLP, or customize the look of visual resources for their needs, while linguists can use the algorithms and the language resources without any additional knowledge about programming.

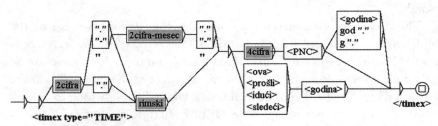

Fig. 3. Finite-state transducer graph for extracting and annotating temporal expressions.

Visual Resources, graphical user interface, will remain in its original form for the purpose of this research. It will allow the visualization and editing of Language Resources and Processing Resources. Language Resources for this research involve corpuses of weather forecast texts in multiple languages and weather forecast Concept Model that will be built. The required modification of Processing Resources, especially modifications for application to the processing of Serbian texts are presented below.

The IE task in GATE is embedded in the ANNIE (A Nearly-New Information Extraction) System. Detailed information about ANNIE can be found in [25]. The ANNIE System includes the following processing resources: Tokeniser, Sentence Splitter, POS (part-of-speech) tagger, Gazetteer, Semantic Tagger, and Orthomatcher. Each of the listed resources produces annotations that are required for the following processing resource in the list:

- Tokeniser splits text into tokens (words, numbers, symbols, white patterns, and punctuation). Tokeniser can be used to process texts in different languages with a little or no modifications.
- Sentence Splitter segments the text into sentences using cascades of finite-state transducers. It is also application and language-independent.
- POS Tagger assigns a part-of-speech tag (lexical category tag, e.g., noun, verb) in the form of annotation to each word. English version of POS Tagger included in the GATE system is based on the Brill tagger. It is application-independent, but language-dependent resource, and has to be completely modified for Serbian.
- Another language-dependent, but application-dependent, resource is Gazetteer that contains lists of cities, countries, personal names, organizations, etc. Gazetteer uses these lists for annotating the occurrence of the list items in the texts.
- Semantic Tagger is based on the JAPE (Java Annotations Pattern Engine) language [26]. JAPE performs finite-state processing over annotations based on regular expressions and its important characteristic is that it can use Concept Models (ontologies).
  Semantic Tagger includes a set of JAPE grammars, where each grammar consists of a set of phases and each phase represent a set of rules. Furthermore, rules contain Left-Hand Side and Right-Hand Side. Left-Hand Side (LHS) of the rule describes the annotation pattern to be recognized usually based on the Kleene regular expression operators. Right-Hand Side (RHS) of the rule describes the action that has to be taken after

the LHS recognize the pattern, e.g., new annotation creation. It is an application-and language-dependent resource.

- Orthomatcher identifies relations between named entities found by the Semantic Tagger. It produces new annotations based on relations between named entities. It is an application-and language-independent resource.

The main goal is to develop language-or application-dependent resources (Gazetteer, POS Tagger, and Semantic Tagger) for Serbian. The way that we chose for solving this problem is to use previously described resources developed for the Unitex system and adapt them for usage in the GATE system. Modifying the Gazetteer lists is a simple process of translation from one language to the other. Building JAPE grammars with ontology support for weather forecast domain requires the initial development of appropriate sublanguage and Concept Model, which will be discussed in the following subsection, as the subject of the authors' ongoing research. The problem of creating an appropriate POS Tagger is highly complex and will not be presented here in details.

Briefly, we made the wrapper for Unitex, so it can be used directly in the GATE system to produce electronic dictionaries for given weather forecast texts and a mechanism for generating appropriate POS Tagger annotation for each word. This solution of the problem, although showed a few disadvantages, could represent a good foundation for building Semantic Taggers based on Concept Models and IE systems in general.

5.3 Concept Modeling Consideration from the Viewpoint of Ongoing Research

During the process of text analyses written in a natural language such as Information Retrieval, IE, Document Classification, etc., one can face numerous problems. Some of these problems stem from the nature and the language specifics. However, there are a number of general issues that are not strictly related to the structure of a language, but to the great complexity of the human thinking process. People are usually not aware of the fact that their complicated way of thinking, connecting different facts, and deducting, as is reflected in [27–29]. Some of the general problems are merely finding matches based on keywords without taking into consideration different ways of expressing the same idea in other words (or in another language), synonyms, or the meaning of words in a given context. As one of the proposed solutions to these problems is organization of entities into concepts with defined relationships.

The concepts are naturally involved in communication and in people expression. All types of real things and different abstractions, such as, for example, ideas or moods, are represented with concepts. Although the concepts are ubiquitous, there is no precise or unique definition of that term. According to WordNet [30], concept is defined as "*conception, construct (an abstract or general idea inferred or derived from specific instances).*" An overview of different approaches to defining the concepts is given below.

Certainly the concepts themselves do not carry great importance, as long as it does not take into account their grouping and relating in a proper way. The concepts with appropriate relationships form Ontology (a Concept Model).

For the purpose of this research, the analysis of multi-lingual corpuses, i.e., collections of texts in different natural languages, is significant. The main goal is to recognize expressions presented in different languages and to link them to the appropriate concepts, which gives the ability of performing language-independent analyzes in various applications.

Tim Berners-Lee, who invented World Wide Web, also proposed a Semantic Web [31]. He realized that data on the WWW are not equally suitable for computer and for people interpretation. The WWW was made in the way that it is reasonable for people, but the data has to be well defined for the computers to perform interpretation. Therefore, beside the entities, i.e., concepts from the WWW, the SW contains relations between them, represented as metadata.

In Concept Models, the concepts and relations between them are presented in the form:

$$SUBJECT < predicate > OBJECT,$$

which is called the *triple*. For example,

$$Lightening < causes > Thunder.$$

According to survey paper [32], in CM, basic issues of importance are definition and organization.

5.3.1 Concept Definition
There is no formal definition of concepts, as discussed above, but the concepts can be defined according to domain of usage. Possible approaches for definition are explicit and implicit (Fig. 4).

In explicit definition of concepts approach, the definitions depend of the area in which they will be used. For example:

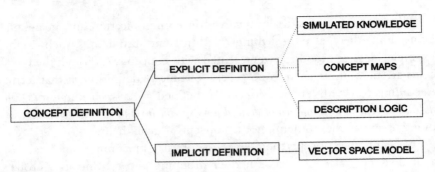

Fig. 4. Possible approaches to concept definition.

- In Simulated Knowledge, the concepts are the entities with language-independent, but of syntactically and semantically interdependent meaning.
- In Description Logic, the concepts are defined as classes, sets of objects, operations, and relations between them.
- In Concept Maps (CMAPs), the concepts are defined as objects or events with certain regularities between them that can be labeled as will be discussed below in the Concept Presentation subsection.

In implicit definition of concepts approach, the concepts are recognized as "good" index terms. Vector Space Model (VSM) is the technique that is used also in Information Retrieval, Document Classification, and Document Clustering.

In VSM, a set of documents is represented as vectors of index terms that can be keywords or longer phrases. If $D = \{d_1, d_2, \ldots, d_n\}$ is a set of n text documents, and $T = \{t_1, t_2, \ldots, t_j\}$ is a set of j relevant index terms, then each indexed document from the set D is represented as a j-dimensional vector (Fig. 5). We can denote $\vec{V}(d_i) = (v_{i1}, v_{i2}, \ldots, v_{ij})$, where $d_i \in D$, as the vector for the document d_i with one component in the vector for each index term from the set T, i.e., v_{il} is the number of occurrences of the term t_l in the document d_i.

The similarity measure between two documents d_1 and d_2 is taken as cosine similarity of their vector representation $\vec{V}(d_1)$ and $\vec{V}(d_2)$:

$$\text{sim}(d_1, d_2) = \frac{\vec{V}(d_1) \cdot \vec{V}(d_2)}{|\vec{V}(d_1)||\vec{V}(d_2)|},$$

where the numerator represents inner product of the vectors $\vec{V}(d_1)$ and $\vec{V}(d_2)$:

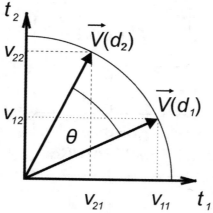

Fig. 5. Vector Space Model where: t_1 and t_2 represent two relevant index terms $\vec{V}(d_1) = \{v_{11}, v_{12}\}$ and $\vec{V}(d_2) = \{v_{21}, v_{22}\}$ represent vectors for the documents d_1 and d_2, respectively, with one component v_{ij} in the vector for each index term, where v_{ij} is the number of occurrences of the term t_l in the document d_j.

$$\vec{V}(d_1) \cdot \vec{V}(d_2) = \sum_{i=1}^{j} (v_{1i}v_{2i})$$

and the denominator is the product of their Euclidean lengths:

$$\vec{V}(d) = \sqrt{\sum_{i=1}^{j} v_j^2}.$$

Thus, as the cosine similarity measure is greater the documents are more similar, and appropriate "good" index terms, that increase similarity between the documents, can be recognized as concepts.

5.3.2 Concept Organization

As far as organization, possible approaches are organization in standard database, and organization in Knowledge Rich Data Base (KRDB).

Organization in database implies concepts in the form of data and, if needed, appropriate metadata, and their relationships. As mentioned before, human way of thinking and interconnecting knowledge about different subjects is very complex, and for now on, we can only attempt to emulate it throw techniques such as Object-oriented approaches, the Unified Modeling Language (UML), or Entity Relationship model. The main goal in all

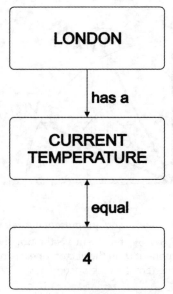

Fig. 6. Illustration of the sentence *"Current temperature in London is* 4 °C." shows relationship *has a* between concepts *London,* and *Current temperature* that has value (is *equal*) 4.

of these approaches is to express the great number of different relationships between concepts and their attributes.

For example, the sentence *"Current temperature in London is* 4°C," at a glance, describes a simple relationship represented in Fig. 6, between London and its Current temperature of 4 °C.

This sentence, however, conceal much more complex relationships between concepts and their attributes, such as that *London* is the name of the city, the city has a *current temperature* with value 4, the value of the temperatures are measured in degrees, the unit of degrees are Celsius, the Celsius degrees has an acronym C, and the symbol °. These relationships can be presented as in Fig. 7.

Organization in the Knowledge Rich Data Bases (KRDB) implies the presentation of the concepts as a set of entities with attributes and their relationships. More about KRDB one can find in [33].

5.3.3 Concept Presentation
Some of the possible concept presentations are graphical, textual, and visual presentation, as presented in Fig. 8.

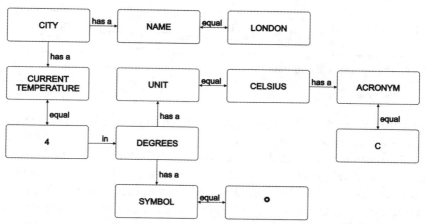

Fig. 7. Illustration of more complex relationships between concepts and their attributes from the sentence *"Current temperature in London is 4 °C."*

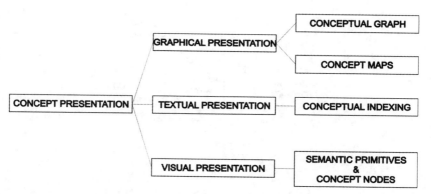

Fig. 8. Possible approaches to concept presentation.

5.3.3.1 Graphical Presentation

Conceptual Graph (CG) is a formal language developed by John F. Sowa, in 1976, for knowledge representation. CGs are directed graphs of two kinds of nodes: concepts and relations between them.

Example sentence *"Current temperature in London is 4 °C."* is presented in the CG notation in Fig. 9, where the concepts *Current temperature, London,* and *Degree value* are presented by rectangles and conceptual relations are presented by circles. Every conceptual relation must have at least one arc that belongs to it in CG. In the example sentence: *Current temperature* has an

Fig. 9. The Conceptual Graph for the example sentence "*Current temperature in London is* 4 °C."

attribute (Attr) which is *Degree value* 4. The conceptual relation (In) relates a *Current temperature* to a *city London*.

Concept mapping was developed by Joseph D. Novak and his research team at Cornell University in the 1970s [34]. It is a technique for graphical representation of the hierarchical structure of concepts and relationships among them. CMAP is a kind of diagram for representing knowledge and its organization.

The concepts are usually represented as boxes or circles, while the relationships are represented as labels on the arrows between them. In the

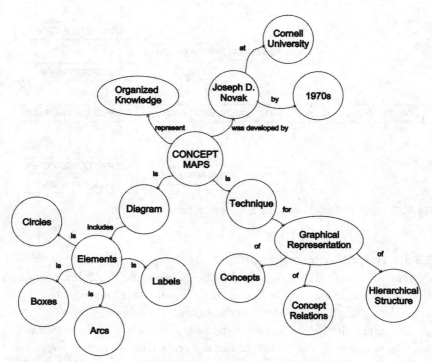

Fig. 10. Example of the concept map graphical presentation, where concepts are presented in ellipses, and relationships between them are presented with arcs, labeled with the relationship names.

hierarchical structure, the most general concepts are presented at the top of the Concept Models, and the less general concepts are arranged hierarchically below. The relationships between concepts from different parts of the Concept Models are called cross-links. Cross-links represent the way in which two concepts from a different domains of knowledge represented in the Concept Model are related.

A CMAP example is presented in Fig. 10.

5.3.3.2 Textual Presentation

In textual presentations, there is no formal definition of the concepts. The concepts are created in the context of their occurrences in the documents. Users mark parts of documents as the appropriate concepts and possible relationships between them. In this case, relationships could denote grouping concepts into a new one, or just relation between two closely associated concepts without their grouping into a new one.

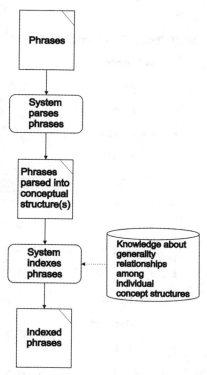

Fig. 11. Process of indexing phrases in textual presentation.

In general, the phrases from the document are indexed based on the conceptual structures. The process of indexing is presented in Fig. 11. Each phrase is parsed automatically by the system into one or more conceptual structures. Based on the knowledge about the relationships' generality between the concept structures, the phrases are indexed.

Thesaurus is one practical implementation of a Conceptual Indexing (CI) textual presentation. In Fig. 12, an excerpt from the CI taxonomy related to text document about weather forecast is presented.

5.3.3.3 Visual Presentation

Visual presentation is primarily oriented on image retrieval. An example of image retrieval system based on concepts is presented in [35]. In this approach, every image is associated with appropriate Semantic Primitives and Concept Nodes. The Semantic Primitives represents basic terms from a particular domain, which builds Concept Nodes.

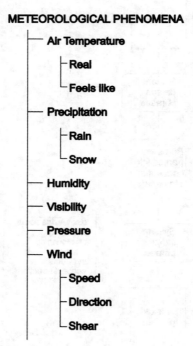

Fig. 12. Excerpt from the Conceptual Indexing taxonomy related to the weather forecast domain.

5.4 Synergy of Data Mining and Concept Modeling in Wireless Sensor Networks

One of the basic advantages of WSNs is their ability to interpret correctly the current state of the covered environment. At the same time, this is a drawback of WSNs, because, often times, information from the global environment can influence both, the current decisions of WSN as well as the adaptability to future decisions that a WSN has to make.

The above-mentioned drawback is cured if the WSN has ability to read appropriate data from the Internet, which helps in two domains: current decisions are more accurate, and future correct decisions are reached with less delay. However, linking a WSN and DM implies a crucial problem: How to understand the essence of data on the Internet. Data on the Internet are typically given in a natural language, while WSN can understand only a simple Domain Specific Language (DSL). This problem is overcome with a specialized Natural Language Processor tuned for the subject matter and embedded into a nearby Internet Server.

6. CONCLUSION

There is almost no area of modern human lives in which WSNs do not contribute heavily. To gather and process data relevant to the user, whether it is data from the single WSN or the system of WSNs, for the sake of the need for further analysis and use, it is necessary to involve automatic processing. Humans have become powerless over an enormous amount of data that is available. Long-term research efforts showed that one of the most suitable mechanisms for solving these problems was incorporating DM algorithms in the automatic process.

On the other hand, SW was created as an attempt to resolve the problems of finding relevant information among the vast amount of information available on the Web more effectively. The required information is defined and linked with additional knowledge in a way that is understandable to machines, not only for the purpose of displaying, but also for use in various applications.

The main goal of this study is to present research efforts in DM algorithms incorporation in WSNs, and their recent efforts to integrate the semantic content and data from WSNs in order to invent new and improve existing hybrid methods of combining DM and SW to provide benefit from various heterogeneous sources.

Two different aspects of DM in WSNs are analyzed in this research: with and without additional semantic analysis-oriented support. A novel classification is presented, together with a thorough presentation of selected examples, and possible extension to the usage of NLP in order to improve performance and results on the level of a System of National WSNs. The major contribution of this research is a comprehensive view of current achievements in this field, and in its opening of new research avenues, which was induced by the proposed classification and its extension.

Some of the classes of the proposed classification include no examples, but do make lots of sense, and therefore represent a challenge for researchers. For the future, we could freely say that with semantically enhanced sensor data, we could advance the state-of-the-art of the modern science.

APPENDIX#1: AN INNOVATION CREATION METHODOLOGY

Based on the previous experience of the authors in solving complex problems, which is described for example in [36], we came up to the idea to write an innovation creation methodology. This appendix defines four major directions that can be used to create the innovations in science and engineering:

a. Mendelyeyevization.
b. Hybridization.
c. Transdisciplinarization.
d. Retrajectorization.

Each one of these directions includes two subdirections, as indicated next:

Mendelyeyevization: Catalyst Versus Accelerator

If one of the classification classes includes no examples, it first has to be checked why is that so. If it is so because it makes no sense, an appropriate explanation is in place. If it is so because the technology or the applications are not yet ready for such an approach, one can act in the same way as the famous chemists Mendeleyev: empty positions in any classification are potential avenues leading to new inventions. As indicated in Fig. 13, these inventions sometimes need a catalyst (a resource that makes an invention happen) or an accelerator (a resource that turns a known invention without potentials into an invention with potentials). We refer to such an approach as Mendelyeyevization.

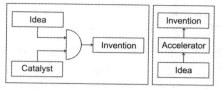

Fig. 13. Catalyst versus accelerator (Mendelyeyevization).

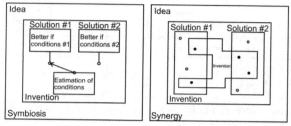

Fig. 14. Self-explanatory symbolic representation of hybridization innovation approach: symbiosis versus synergy.

Hybridization: Symbiosis Versus Synergy

Sometimes two classification classes can be combined in order to obtain a hybrid solution (hybridization). Hybrid solutions can be symbiotic (measuring the conditions in the environment and switching from one approach to the other, so that each approach is active all the time, while the conditions are such that it provides better performance compared to the other approach) or synergistic (creating a new approach, which, for each particular solution element, takes a better solution element of the two different approaches). This is shown in Fig. 14. The assumption here is that one solution is better under one set of conditions, and the other solution is better under another set of conditions. Another assumption is that solution elements of one solution are better in one domain and that solution elements of another solution are better in another domain.

Transdisciplinarization: Modifications Versus Mutations

Often, good new ideas are generated if algorithms, procedures, ways of thinking, or philosophies of thinking can be ported from one field to another, along the lines of transdisciplinary research methodologies (Transdisciplinarization). As indicated in Fig. 15, for an idea to work better in

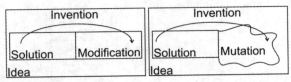

Fig. 15. Self-explanatory symbolic representation of Transdisciplinarization innovation approach: modification versus mutation.

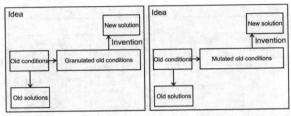

Fig. 16. Self-explanatory symbolic representation of retrajectorization innovation approach: reparametrization versus regranularization.

the new field, either smaller modifications or larger mutations have to be introduced.

Retrajectorization: Reparametrization Versus Regranularization

Sometimes it is simply the best to take a research trajectory different (even opposite) compared to what others take (retrajectorization). The different (opposite) research trajectory makes sense either if a more detailed set of parameters is in place (due to technology changes), or because parameters of the environment have changed permanently (due to application changes), as indicated in Fig. 16. The two alternatives are referred to as a reparametrization and regranularization.

APPENDIX#2: SYMBIOTIC HYBRIDIZATION OF DATA MINING AND SEMANTIC WEB

This appendix describes research efforts of the authors. The work is based around distributed classification algorithms, while observing the WSN as a vertically distributed data system.

Three different case studies are presented:

1. A hybrid method that combines DM and SW, allowing for use of data from various, heterogeneous sources.

2. A method for detecting events through large WSN systems, with an emphases on situations when the effects are visible in only a subset of sensors' readings.
3. An approach for exploiting interaction information from data collected from sensors located at different nodes.

All three of the algorithms start from an approach similar to the one described as the representative example of the MOO classification class. Each node in the network builds a local classifier/predictor based on a labeled set of previous local readings. These local predictors can be built using any kind of a classifier. In the research presented in this section, unpruned C4.5 trees were used. The reason for not pruning the trees was that a single sensor node typically only contains a few sensors, resulting in a low number of features. Therefore, the trees are not likely to grow too large and overtrain, even if pruning is not used. On the other hand, as each node builds its own tree, finding an optimal amount of pruning would need to be done for each node individually, leading to a large overhead.

In the operation phase, the nodes periodically take sensor readings and use the locally trained models to reach decisions regarding the target value. These local decisions are then forwarded to a central location, where majority logic is used to make global estimate of the target value. The simplest form of reaching the global decision is the simple or un-weighted voting. The global estimate of the target value is taken to be the value that was chosen by the highest number of local predictors (and thus received the most "votes"). An alternative form of reaching the global estimates is to allow the votes to be weighted, and thus to place a greater emphasis on the local decisions coming from the nodes in which we are more confident. One choice for the weighting scheme is to weight with the per-class accuracy (the percentage of times in the past the mode made a correct estimate when choosing the particular class value).

Hybrid Wireless Sensor Network—Semantic Web in Data Mining

The basic notion behind this approach is that a WSN can give precise and fine-grain information regarding the (limited) area it covers, but fails to capture a broader context and large-scale global trends, observable when viewing a much larger area. On the other hand, the Web (or in this case a SW, as the data are assumed to contain enough semantic information to be used) contains an abundance of information from various sources.

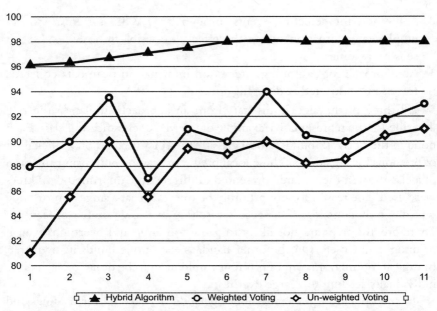

Fig. 17. Hybrid approach accuracy versus the un-weighted and weighted voting schemes based only on WSN data.

These information are often not precise or specific to the area of interest to the WSN, but still allow for a detection of global phenomena on a coarse grain level. The hybrid approach allows for predictions from the WSN to be used, unless there is a strong prediction out of the data from the Web that is not in line with the WSN results.

The WSN part of the algorithm remains unchanged. Each node builds a local predictor, and the global decision is reached as a (weighted or un-weighted) majority of these decisions. A second global predictor is made from the data available through SW. The semantic information is used to place this second decision into the same context as the WSN decision. The two global decisions are than compared based on the confidence assigned to them (precisely, a weighted voting procedure is performed, with only the two sources of votes, the WSN decision and the SW decision). Figure 17 presents the results of a simulation study. The hybrid approach can reach more accurate decisions, or can reach the correct decision earlier, before the effects of the global trends become apparent in the local patterns present on the data taken from the sensors.

Mining from Large Disperse Networks

In a large, disperse WSN, the location of a sensor node plays an important role in the patterns observable in the data taken from the node's sensors. Let us assume that the goal is to detect and categorize an event-taking place in the area covered by a WSN. When an event occurs, it produces effects directly observable through the readings of the sensors. As we move further away from the event's location, these effects will diminish in their intensity, the patterns picked up by individual sensors become "weaker," and decisions made by the nodes become less accurate. An un-weighted scheme has no means by which to consider this phenomenon, as votes from all nodes are treated equally. The above present weighted scheme based on accuracy is better, as it will assign a bigger weights to the nodes closer to the event (which will have higher accuracy, since they have a "better view," and in turn a clearer pattern to detect the specific event at the specific location). However, as the networks grow larger, for each given event the vast majority of the nodes will be too far for their sensor to pick up any of the effects of the event. These sensors will then be making random guesses (possibly based on the environmental noise). While the accuracy of random guesses may be expected to be low, it will be a non-zero value. Since the number of random-guessing nodes is very large, they will often overpower the few highly accurate nodes. Perhaps the clearest example demonstrating this is one where the event occurrence is rare. Majority of the network will decide that there was no event. Since most of the time there really is no event, their accuracy for making this decision will be high, even if they are wrong whenever there is an event they cannot observe.

To resolve this issue, an alternative weighting scheme was proposed. The scheme is based around using the Cohen's Kappa Statistic instead of the per-class accuracy. Figure 18 presents an overview of the results obtained when using the Kappa Statistic-based votes versus the un-weighted scheme and the per-class accuracy weighted voting.

Exploiting Interaction Information from Data Collected from Sensors Located at Different Nodes

A sensor node is a small, low-powered device with a limited sensory range and precision and a modest processing capability. In some cases, the information that is locally available at any given node in the network is not sufficient to make clear decision regarding the state in the environment. This issue is typically tackled by a set of techniques, known as collaborative sensing.

However, the above-described DM algorithms first make decisions only on locally available data, and then use these to reach a global decision. In applications where collaborative sensing is necessary, such approaches would lead to an unacceptable loss of information. One example is the problem when the target is a XOR function of two sensed variables. If these are sensed by sensors located at different nodes, neither node is able to make a better-than-random decision. On the other hand, if the two variables are available at the same node, the pattern defining the target value can easily be detected. On the other hand, moving the data around WSN consumes a considerable amount of energy, a problem among the core issues that WSNs are supposed to tackle.

A proposed solution is to modify the WSN DM algorithm to include detection of variables that carry large amounts of interaction information (information about the target value that can only be inferred if the variables are observed together). In the training phase, the nodes build predictors both on the local data and on the combination of local data and the data received from other nodes. If the combined predictor preforms significantly better, it is used in the operation phase. Otherwise, only the local predictor is used and the raw data are not communicated. For further reduction of the communication overhead, a node is limited to receiving only the data from the nodes in its immediate neighborhood (those it can communicate directly with).

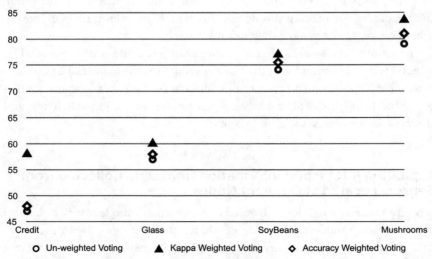

Fig. 18. System accuracy of Kappa Statistic-based voting versus the un-weighted scheme and the per-class accuracy weighted voting.

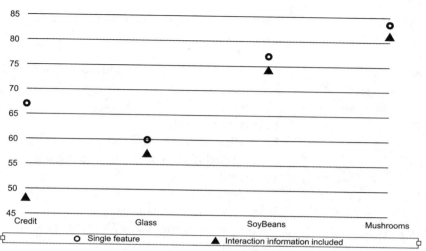

Fig. 19. System accuracy when the interaction information is included versus a system based only on local predictor built from data available at individual nodes.

Figure 19 presents an overview of the simulation results obtained with a modified version of the algorithm that includes interaction information mining versus the same algorithm built only on local data.

ACKNOWLEDGMENT

The work presented here was supported by the Serbian Ministry of Education and Science through the projects 178006 and III 47003.

Abbreviations

ANNIE	A Nearly-New Information Extraction
CG	Conceptual Graph
CI	Conceptual Indexing
CM	Concept Modeling
CMAP	Concept Maps
DELA	Dictionaires Electroniques du LADL or LADL electronic dictionaries
DELAC	DELA of compound forms
DELACF	DELA of compound inflected forms
DELAF	DELA of inflected forms
DELAS	Simple forms DELA
DEMS	Data Estimation for Mobile Sensors

DFP–SVM	Distributed Fixed–Partition Support Vector Machines
DM	Data Mining
DSL	Domain Specific LanguageDSRAM—Data Stream Association Rule Mining
EE	Energy Efficiency
FARM	Freshness Association Rule Mining
GATE	General Architecture for Text Engineering
IE	Information Extraction
JAPE	Java Annotations Pattern Engine
KRDB	Knowledge Rich Data Base
LADL	Laboratoire d'Automatique Documentaire et Linguistique
LHS	Left–Hand Side
M	Mobile
MASTER	Mining Autonomously Spatio–Temporal Environmental Rules
MEE	Mobile Energy Efficient
MOO	Mobile Overall Optimized
NER	Named Entity Recognition
NLP	Natural Language Processing
OO	Overall optimization
POS	Part–of–speech
PREMON	PREdiction based MONitoring
PVD	Pattern variation discovery
RHS	Right–Hand Side
S	Static
SEE	Static Energy Efficient
SOO	Static Overall Optimized
SVD	Singular Value Decomposition
SVM	Support Vector Machines
SW	Semantic Web
UML	Unified Modeling Language
VSM	Vector Space Model
VSS	Virtual static sensor
WARM	Window Association Rule Mining
WSN	Wireless Sensor Networks

REFERENCES

[1] K. Flouri, B. Beferull-Lozano, P. Tsakalides, Training a support vector machine-based classifier in distributed sensor networks, in: 14th European Signal Processing Conference (EUSIPCO '06), Florence, Italy, September, 2006, pp. 4–8.

[2] L. Gruenwald, S. Sadik, R. Shukla, H. Yang, DEMS: a data mining based technique to handle missing data in mobile sensor network applications, in: DMSN '10, Singapore, 2010.

[3] S. Goel, T. Imielinski, Prediction-based monitoring in sensor networks: taking lessons from MPEG, in: ACM Computer Communication Review, 2011.

[4] S. McConnell, D. Skillicorn, A distributed approach for prediction in sensor networks, in: First International Workshop on Data Mining in Sensor Networks, 2005 SIAM Conference on Data Mining, Newport Beach, CA, April, 2005.

[5] M. Xiuli, Y. Dongqing, T. Shiwei, L. Qiong, Z. Dehui, L. Shuangfeng, Online Mining in Sensor Networks, Lecture Notes in Computer Science, vol. 3222, 2004, pp. 544–550.

[6] S. Bandyopadhyay, E.J. Coyle, An Energy Efficient Hierarchical Clustering Algorithm for Wireless Sensor Networks, in: INFOCOM 2003. Twenty-Second Annual Joint Conference of the IEEE Computer and Communications. IEEE Societies, vol. 3, 2003, pp. 1713–1723.

[7] M. Halatchev, L. Gruenwald, Estimating missing values in related sensor data streams, in: International Conference on Management of Data, Baltimore, Maryland, June, 2005.

[8] S. Datta, C. Giannella, H. Kargupta, K-means clustering over a large, dynamic network, in: Proceedings of 2006 SIAM Conference on Data Mining, Bethesda, MD, April, 2006.

[9] S. Papadimitriou, J. Sun, C. Faloutsos, Streaming pattern discovery in multiple time-series, in: Proceedings of the 31st VLDB Conference, Trondheim, Norway, 2005.

[10] L. Gruenwald, H. Chok, M. Aboukhamis, Using data mining to estimate missing sensor data, in: Seventh IEEE Conference on Data Minig, Omaha, NE, October 2007, pp. 207–212.

[11] R. Kittredge, J. Lehrberger (Eds.), Sublanguage—Studies of Language in Restricted Semantic Domains, De Gruyter, Berlin, 1982.

[12] S. Sekine, E. Ranchhod, Named Entities: Recognition, Classification and Use, John Benjamins Publishing Company, Amsterdam, Philadelphia, 2009.

[13] N. Chinchor, Named entity task definition, in: MUC-7. Fairfax, Virginia, 1998.

[14] H. Cunningham, D. Maynard, K. Bontcheva, V. Tablan, N. Aswani, I. Roberts, G. Gorrell, A. Funk, A. Roberts, D. Damljanovic, T. Heitz, M.A. Greenwood, H. Saggion, J. Petrak, Y. Li, W. Peters, Text Processing with GATE (Version 6), <http://tinyurl.com/gatebook,2011>.

[15] S. Paumier, Unitex 2.1 User Manual, <http://www-igm.univmlv.fr/~unitex/UnitexManual2.1.pdf.2008>.

[16] C. Krstev, D. Vitas, I. Obradović, M. Utvić, E-Dictionaries and Finite-State Automata for the Recognition of Named Entities, in: Andreas Maletti, Matthieu Constant (Eds.), Proceedings of the 9th International Workshop on Finite State Methods and Natural Language Processing, FSMNLP 2011, Blois, France, July 12-15, 2010, Association for Computational Linguistics, ISBN 978-3-642-14769-2, 2011, pp. 48–56.

[17] S. Gucul-Milojević, Personal Names in Information Extraction, INFOtheca 11, no. 1 (April 2010), 53a—63a, 2010, pp. 47–58.

[18] Z. Stanojčić, Popović, Lj, Gramatika srpskoga jezika, in: Zavod za udžbenike i nastavna sredstva, Beograd, 2002.

[19] C. Krstev, D. Vitas, The treatment of numerals in text processing, in: Pozna Poland (Ed.), Proceedings of third Language & Technology Conference, October 5–7, 2007, Zygmunt Vetulani, pp. 418–422, IMPRESJA Widawnictwa Elektroniczne S.A., Pozna, 2007.

[20] A. Przepiórkowski, Slavonic information extraction and Partial Parsing, in: Balto-Slavonic Natural Language Processing, Association for Computational Linguistics (ACL'07), Prague, 2007, pp. 1–10.

[21] C. Krstev, Processing of Serbian—Automata, Texts and Electronic Dictionaries, Faculty of Philology, University of Belgrade, Belgrade, 2008.

[22] Unitex homepage: <http://www-igm.univ-mlv.fr/~sunitex/>.

[23] GATE homepage: <http://gate.ac.uk/>.

[24] B. Courtois, M. Silberztein, Dictionnaires électroniques du français, in: Langue française 87, Larousse, Paris, 1990.

[25] H. Cunningham, GATE, A General Architecture for Text Engineering, Comput. Humanities 36 (2) (2002) 223–254.

[26] H. Cunningham, D. Maynard, K. Bontcheva, V. Tablan, GATE: A framework and graphical development environment for robust NLP tools and applications, in: Proceedings of the 40th Anniversary Meeting of the Association for Computational Linguistics (ACL'02), 2002.

[27] D. Dou, D. McDermott, P. Qi, Ontology translation by ontology merging and automated reasoning, Yale University, New Haven, 2004.

[28] W.J. Frawley, G. Piatetsky-Shapiro, C.J. Matheus, Knowledge discovery in databases: An overview, Artificial Intelligence Magazine 13 (3) (1992) 57–70.

[29] J. Han, Y. Huang, N. Cercone, Y. Fu, Intelligent query answering by knowledge discovery techniques, IEEE Trans. Knowl. Data Eng. Archive 8 (3) (1996) 373–390.

[30] WordNet homepage: <http://wordnet.princeton.edu/>.

[31] T. Berners-Lee, Weaving the Web, Orion Business Books, 1999.

[32] S. Omerovic, Z. Babovic, Z. Tafa, V. Milutinovic, S. Tomazic, Concept Modeling: From Origins to Multimedia, Springer, NY, USA, 2011.

[33] H. Fujihara, D. Simmons, Knowledge conceptualization tool, IEEE Trans. Knowl. Data Eng. Archive 9 (2) (1997) 209–220.

[34] J. Novak, A. Cañas, The theory of underlying concept maps and how to construct them, Technical Report, Florida Institute for Human and Machine Cognition CmapTools 2006–01, USA, 2005.

[35] T. Chua, H. Pung, G. Lu, H. Jong, A concept-based image retrieval system, in: Proceedings of the Twenty-Seventh Hawaii International Conference on System Sciences, vol. 3, Information systems: decision support and knowledge-based systems, Wailea, Hawaii, USA, 4–7 (Jan) 1994, 590–598, 1994.

[36] V. Milutinovic, Surviving the Design of a 200 MHz RISC Microprocessor: Lessons Learned, IEEE Computer Society Press, Los Alamitos, California, USA, 1997.

ABOUT THE AUTHORS

Staša Vujičić Stanković is a teaching assistant and also a PhD Student at the Department of Computer Science and Informatics, University of Belgrade, Faculty of Mathematics, in Serbia. She is a former student of the Mathematical Grammar School, a unique school in Serbia, specialized for students talented in mathematics, physics and computer science. She has graduated at Faculty of Mathematics in Belgrade, Serbia, in Computer Science with very high average grade. One of her main interests and the topic she researches as a part of her PhD studies is the natural language processing, and in particular information extraction in Serbian using the lexical resources for Serbian developed from the Natural Language Processing Group at the Faculty of Mathematics, University of Belgrade, whose member she is. Her current research interests also include the semantic web, information retrieval and web search, formal languages and automata theory, and databases. She published several conference and journal papers, and gave numerous talks at conferences in Europe till now.

Nemanja Kojić is a teaching assistant at the University of Belgrade, School of Electrical Engineering, Department of Computer Science and Engineering since 2010. He graduated from the University of Belgrade, School of Electrical Engineering as one of the best students in generation, where currently is doing his PhD. One of his main interests and the PhD research topics is Model-Based Engineering, Model-Driven Development Based on Executable UML and Data Mining in Wireless Sensor Networks. He participated in several important industrial and research projects since 2005 and published several conference and journal papers.

Goran Rakočević graduated from the School of Electrical Engineering, University of Belgrade in 2007. In 2008 he enrolled in the PhD studies at the same school. Since, he has been working on industrial and research projects at the University. Since 2011 he is also an assistant researcher with the Mathematical Institute of the Serbian Academy of Sciences and Arts. His research interests include AI in ubiquitous computing, data mining and machine learning in highly distributed systems and sensor networks, as well as applications of machine learning to bio- and neuro-informatics.

Duško Vitas is a professor at the Department of Computing, Faculty of Mathematics, University of Belgrade, Serbia since 1994. Mr. Vitas received his Bachelor degree in Informatics in 1973, Magister degree in 1977, and Ph.D. degree in 1993, all in Mathematics at Faculty of Mathematics, Belgrade. Since 1991 he is employed at the Faculty of Mathematics, Belgrade. He published more than 120 scientific and professional papers.

Veljko Milutinović received his Ph.D. in electrical engineering from University of Belgrade in 1982. During the 80's, for about a decade, he was on the faculty of Purdue University, West Lafayette, Indiana, USA, where he co-authored the architecture and design of the world's first DARPA GaAs microprocessor. Since the 90's, after returning to Serbia, he is on the faculty of the School of Electrical Engineering, University of Belgrade, where he is teaching courses related to computer engineering, sensor networks, and data mining. During the 90's, he also took part in teaching at the University of Purdue, Stanford and MIT. After year 2000, he participated in several FP6 and FP7 projects through collaboration with leading universities and industries in the EU/US, including Microsoft, Intel, IBM, Ericsson, especially Maxeler. He has lectured by invitation to over 100 European universities. He published about 50 papers in SCI journals and about 20 books with major publishers in the USA. Professor Milutinovic is a Fellow of the IEEE and a Member of Academia Europaea.

CHAPTER FIVE

Multihoming: A Comprehensive Review

Bruno Sousa*, Kostas Pentikousis†, and Marilia Curado*

*CISUC, University of Coimbra, Polo II, Pinhal de Marrocos, 3030-290 Coimbra, Portugal
†Huawei Technologies, Carnotstrasse 4, 10587 Berlin, Germany

Contents

Advances in Computers, Volume 90
ISSN 0065-2458, http://dx.doi.org/10.1016/B978-0-12-408091-1.00005-1

Abstract

IP multihoming is a networking concept with a deceptively simple definition in theory. In practice, however, multihoming has proved difficult to implement and optimize for. Moreover, it is a concept, which, once adopted in the core Internet architecture, has significant impact on operation and maintenance. A trivial definition of multihoming would state that an end-node or an end-site has multiple first-hop connections to the network. In this chapter, we survey and summarize in a comprehensive manner recent developments in IP multihoming. After introducing the fundamentals, we present the architectural goals and system design principles for multihoming, and review different approaches. We survey multihoming support at the application, session, transport, and network layers, covering all recent proposals based on a locator-identifier split approach. We critically evaluate multihoming support in these proposals and detail recent developments with respect to multihoming and mobility management.

1. INTRODUCTION

Multihoming and multiaccess in Internet Protocol (IP) networks have been lately fostered by the exponential growth in availability of devices with multiple built-in communication technologies. Paradigms where hosts have access to various networks are not new, of course. Multihoming has long been adopted to increase resilience, dependability, and performance in high-end servers. At the other end of the network node spectrum, mobile phone manufacturers have been integrating different cellular radio access technologies into "multi-band" cell phones to realize global reachability and ease of migration. Nonetheless, multiaccess network selection is currently rudimentary and automation is not implemented. Today, efficient multihoming and multiaccess support in heterogeneous networks is still inhibited by mechanisms that rely mainly on presets and static policies, and require user input as well.

Nodes with multiple network interfaces have the potential of connecting to different networks and capitalizing on heterogeneous network resources and, in the process, enable their users to enjoy high-performing, ubiquitous communication. On the other hand, multiaccess and multihoming lead to more intricate application and protocol configurations in order to meet the challenging goals of reliability, ubiquity, load sharing, and flow distribution. These communication system properties are tightly coupled with the multihoming concept. For instance, the Stream Control Transport Protocol (SCTP) [1] natively uses a *primary-backup* model to deal with failures in active paths, over and above the path failure recovery mechanisms provided by the network layer. Still, multiaccess and multihoming are yet to become prevalent in network deployments despite years of research and development in the area. Indeed, the corresponding support is often missing from state-of-the-art protocols. For example, modern mobility management protocols, such as Mobile IPv6 (MIPv6) [2] have been only recently extended in [3, 4] to support multiple address registration and flows configuration per address. In addition, protocols like the Session Initiation Protocol (SIP) [5] have limited support for all types of applications. SIP is tailored for User Datagram Protocol (UDP) applications, nonetheless with MIPv6 it has wider multihoming support for applications [6].

Over the years, different solutions to enable multihoming have been put forth, depending of whether they are designed for end-host or end-site multihoming. Despite such distinction, recent solutions combine features of both types. Hybrid proposals may also target multihoming support at different layers of the TCP/IP protocol stack, namely, at the application, transport, and network layers. Furthermore, in some proposals new layers are introduced, such as the Host Identity Protocol (HIP) [7] or Site Multihoming by IPv6 Intermediation (SHIM6) [8]. These newly introduced layers perform specific functionalities and aim at reducing the ensuing complexity in existing layers due to the lack of multihoming mechanisms in the original protocol stack.

From an end-site perspective, routing scalability is a concern that is driving research toward novel proposals such as the Routing Architecture for the Next Generation Internet (RANGI) [9]. RANGI aims for incremental deployment and can be even employed by single end-nodes or nodes with routing and forwarding functions, such as the Identifier Locator Network Protocol (ILNP) [10]. These proposals rely on a locator-identifier split approach but differ on how identifiers are set.

Hybrid proposals include support for both end-host and end-site multihoming. The intrinsic disadvantage with such proposals is that end-hosts, as well as intermediate nodes in the network (e.g., routers) need to be modified. That said, multihoming support can also be more efficient, if all nodes are synchronized to meet the multihoming goals. For instance, LISP-Mobile Node [11] is such an example, where the functions of the Locator Identifier Separation Protocol (LISP) [12] are being extended, to enable end-hosts to support mobility and multihoming at a greater extent.

This chapter provides a comprehensive survey of protocols supporting end-host, end-site, and hybrid multihoming. Implementation details, an overview of multihoming support in operating systems and applications are detailed. In addition hybrid multihoming proposals are surveyed, which establishes the distinction with our previous work on this topic [13]. Thus, to the best of our knowledge, this chapter is the first to present an in-depth and up-to-date survey on multihoming protocols, by including more recent trends (hybrid approaches) and by detailing the status of the respective protocol implementations in simulators and operating systems. We capitalize upon the taxonomy of multihoming goals fulfillment (i.e., resilience, ubiquity, load sharing, and flow distribution) we introduced in [13], to analyze the different protocols, and their respective multihoming support. This approach is more objective than other approaches that use cost as the sole metric [14]. Last but not least, this chapter includes not only the most recent, but also multihoming proposals that have been the base for others, as opposed to previous overviews on the matter [15–17] which focused only on a subset of multihoming protocols.

The remainder of this chapter is organized as follows. Section 2 introduces multihoming definitions and related terminology. Section 3 presents design considerations for multihoming solutions. Multihoming support of operating systems and applications is discussed in Section 4. Following a top-down approach, Section 5 presents multihoming at the transport layer, while Section 6 discusses multihoming in mobility management protocols. Specific multihoming proposals are discussed in Sections 7, 8 and 9 for end-host, end-site, and hybrid multihoming, respectively. Finally, Section 10 provides an outlook on future research directions in the area of multihoming management and concludes the chapter.

2. MULTIHOMING TYPES AND CONCEPTS

This section clarifies concepts related with multihoming, such as multiaddressing, multiaccess, and overlapping networks and provides an objective definition of multihoming. In addition, three different types of multihoming are characterized, namely end–host, end–site, and hybrid multihoming types.

2.1 Concepts

Multihoming is lately associated with other concepts, including multiaddressing, overlapping networks, multiple interfaces, and overlay routing. Multiaddressing, for example, corresponds to a configuration in which multiple addresses are assigned to a given host based on prefixes advertised in different connections [18]. Overlapping networks correspond to networks that are configured in a way that there is a common area of coverage. Typically, mobile and wireless end-nodes connecting to these (overlapping) networks must have multiple interfaces, each one specific to the technology sustaining the respective network [19]. Overlay routing is associated with inter-domain routing techniques that improve fault tolerance, and is only applied in an end-site context. Thus we consider Multihoming according to Definition 1 to avoid disambiguity.

Definition 1.   Multihoming is an entity (host or network) configuration that has several first-hop connections to a given destination. Such connections can be accommodated through single or multiple (physical or logical) network interfaces.

Alternative definitions consider multihoming as the availability of two or more connectivity providers to offer fault tolerance and traffic engineering capabilities [18]. Or simply, a host is considered multihomed if it has multiple IP addresses [20]. Wang et al. [21] explain that multihoming support in a given protocol can follow different approaches. In the ownership approach, the entity owning the Home Agent (HA) and mobile routers, and providing Internet access to multihomed network elements plays a key role. If these network elements are controlled by a single entity, this is called the Internet Service Provider (ISP) model, otherwise it is referred to as the Subscriber/Provider model. On the other hand, the configuration-oriented approach considers parameters such as the number of Home Agents or the prefixes advertised.

2.2 End-Host Multihoming

```
List 1. Example of IPv6 aliases configuration
for FreeBSD
ifconfig  if1  inet6  2001:db8:1::1/48  alias
ifconfig  if1  inet6  2001:db8:1::2/48  alias
```

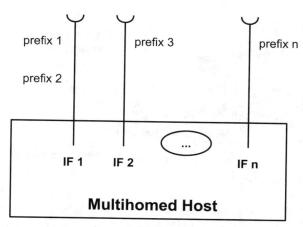

legend: *IF - interface*

Fig. 1. Multihomed host.

A multihomed host, on which different interfaces (logical or physical) exist, is depicted in Fig. 1. In addition, each interface can have different network prefixes configured. For instance, interface *IF 1* has been assigned two prefixes, namely *prefix 1* and *prefix 2*. Moreover, the host can have multiple physical interfaces which have been associated with a single prefix, as is the case of *IF 2* and *IF n* with *prefix 3* and *prefix n*, respectively. This configuration is possible when virtual interfaces are assigned to a physical interface, as depicted in List. Note that here we use the terms prefix and address interchangeably. From an *end-host* perspective, a multihomed host has multiple prefixes configured on the links it connects to, thus having the possibility to explore several paths to reach a peer, as each prefix is normally advertised by different access routers.

2.3 End-Site Multihoming

Figure 2 illustrates a multihomed site, which has connections to two service providers. A multihomed network can have multiple routers, such as, for example, *MR 1* connecting to Service Provider 1 and *MR 2* connecting to Service Provider 2. Moreover, a single router can have several external interfaces that connect to the same or different service providers, as the example of *MR 1*.

End-site multihoming, where a site uses multiple connections to the Internet to meet objectives such as increasing network reliability or improving performance [22, 23], is a network configuration quite typical for large

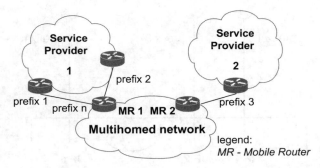

Fig. 2. Multihomed network.

deployments. Day recalls [24] that *end-site* multihoming first came up in the context of ARPANet back in 1972 due to the desire to have redundant network connections, thus allowing for more robust network operation. Recently, and within a wireless mobile context, a multihomed mobile network may have several points of attachment to the Internet and multiple prefixes available.

Different perspectives can be followed to consider a mobile network as multihomed [25–27]. First, the **ownership-oriented** approach takes into account the ownership of the Home Agent (HA) and Mobile Routers. A mobile router is defined as an entity providing Internet access to the multihomed network, as mentioned above. If these network elements are controlled by a single entity, this is called the ISP model, otherwise it is referred to as the Subscriber/Provider model. Second, the **problem-oriented** approach considers the number of Home Agents and network prefixes advertised. Finally, the **configuration-oriented** approach considers different parameters such as the number of Home Agents, the number of prefixes available and the number of Collocated Care of Address (CCoA) prefixes.

2.4 Hybrid Multihoming

Hybrid Multihoming mixes both end-host and end-site characteristics, but requires the participation of end-host and network entities (e.g., servers) for full multihoming support. The hybrid multihoming type corresponds to the most current proposals that target issues on networks, such as routing scalability, but at the same time also address drawbacks of the current TCP/IP architecture, such as the dual role of IP address (identifier and locator). According to Fig. 3, MH1 is a multihomed host, but multihoming management requires

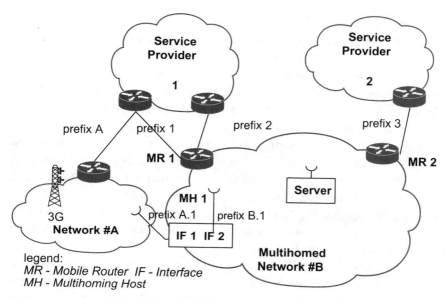

Fig. 3. Hybrid multihoming scenario.

support from the network (server) to maintain the location information, so that other end-hosts in the Internet can communicate with MH1.

3. DESIGNING FOR MULTIHOMING

This section introduces the overall goals that current and future multihoming solutions ought to pursue. We then present open problems in this research area and briefly summarize the current solution space.

3.1 Goals

Multihoming has gained attention over the last few years [28], mainly due to the potential benefits. In particular, multihoming solutions aim to achieve the following goals: **R**–Resilience, **U**–Ubiquity, **L**–Load balancing/sharing and **F**–Flow distribution [13].

The diversity of multiple interfaces/paths can improve *resilience* as upon a failure of one interface/path, another one can be employed to provide connectivity. For instance, as mentioned above, a *primary-backup* model is adopted by SCTP [1]. That is, if the primary path fails, the backup path can be used seamlessly without causing any application-layer service interruption.

Multiple network interfaces, in particular when used in a mobile and wireless network environment, enable *ubiquitous access* to the Internet over different media.

Load sharing goes one step further than the primary-backup model, as multiple interfaces/paths can be used simultaneously to improve throughput. For example, Iyengar et al. [29] describe how one can perform concurrent multiple transfers using SCTP.

Flow distribution, or flow stripping, offers even finer granularity than load sharing. For many, flow distribution is the ultimate goal to achieve, as it implicitly means that all previous goals are also attained. Flows are stripped, perhaps even dynamically, according to policies and preferences aiming to reduce cost, optimize bandwidth use, and minimize the effect of bottlenecks to delay-sensitive applications, among others. Such policies can be defined by users or service providers [30].

Multihoming support could potentially be added at any layer of the protocol stack. The designer's choice, of course, comes with certain pros and cons, and one needs to consider thoroughly the trade-offs as well as the complexity of each solution [31]. Deployment considerations need also to be addressed early on. There are two possible approaches for introducing multihoming. On the one hand, a multihoming proposal may be completely transparent to upper layers, in such a way that there is no disruption to ongoing sessions. On the other hand, the solution may not be transparent [32], but allows upper layers to participate in multihoming management and operation. Other concerns may arise, as solutions should target end-hosts, mobile networks, or both.

3.2 Open Issues

As multihoming aspects are introduced in current specifications of the IP architecture, there are still several issues that need to be addressed. Previous work identifies these open problems [19, 33], as detailed below.

The first problem relates to **default gateway mechanisms**. Current specifications use a default gateway to assure connectivity to the network. Such a mechanism introduces limitations in the exploration of multiple connections, as flows cannot be forwarded across different connections to meet user requirements (e.g., load balancing). A simple solution is to use static routes, on a flow or destination granularity, but this type of approach is not scalable and it is difficult to manage in practice.

A second issue is related with **configuration parameters**. Network nodes, running IPv4 or IPv6, receive specific configurations for each active connection via the Dyanamic Host Configuration Protocol (DHCP), Router Advertisement (RA) [34] or other mechanisms. In these scenarios, issues such as split Domain Name System (DNS) might occur since there is no binding mechanism between the resolution name and the destination. Split DNS refers to the case of getting different name resolution results depending on which of the available network interfaces is used to issue the DNS lookup. Solutions to overcome these issues rely on merging interface-specific to node configurations to avoid conflicting result sets, as is the case with name resolution in private networks [19].

Failure detection also poses restrictions on multihoming support. Current failure detection mechanisms do not perform well as they may rely on timers. For instance, existing Router Advertisements do not detect failed links on the failure event, but only on the failure of an event advertisement, which relies on timers. A solution to mitigate such problem is to use cross-layer information, such as link layer events to detect network attachment [35] and loss of connectivity.

Path exploration mechanisms introduce performance constraints limiting multihoming support. Reachability between pairs of addresses must be reactive, and reduce the overhead of signaling procedures. For instance, one strives to reduce the number of messages (and payload size) necessary to detect that a path is congested (e.g., by detecting high Round Trip Time (RTT) values) or is not reachable at all [36].

Another problem with multihoming is related with **path selection** mechanisms. As available and working paths are identified, upper-layers (e.g., applications) should become aware of such path diversity. The introduction of multiple addresses raises source address selection issues, as upper layers need to select the right source address to deliver data to the corresponding path. A standard solution to perform source address selection is still missing [19]. **Ingress filtering** requires compatibility with other mechanisms, such as source-address selection. If the source address is not properly assigned to the respective link, existing filtering processes will discard these packets. Solutions to overcome this limitation include source-based routing mechanisms, or routing based on interface-scoped sets, instead of node-scoped [19]. In the former, routing is based on the source address and not on the traditional destination address. In the latter, routing is performed based on the interface characteristics to meet the application requirements.

Rehoming corresponds to the process of diverting existing sessions from one path to another. Existing flows need to be redirected to a new path or, if such flow redirection is not supported, new sessions must be established.

Protocols like SHIM6 [37] or SCTP [38] provide mechanisms that introduce support for rehoming.

Mobility management protocols are being extended [3, 4] to accommodate different requirements that lead to a more efficient multihoming support. For instance, the registration of multiple care of addresses obtained from the distinct interfaces of a mobile node, or even the synchronization between mobile agents responsible to assist mobile node and Network Mobility (NEMO) [25] in the mobility process, such as Home Agents and Mobile Routers.

Locator-identifier split approaches extend multihoming support by separating the roles of an IP address. Nevertheless, such approaches are not devoid from multihoming issues. Mechanisms to efficiently select a locator can be hard to implement or even introduce incompatibility in the fulfillment of multihoming goals (e.g., resilience and load balancing). If these approaches do not support dynamic capabilities negotiation they may not adapt to mobile environments or end up with scalability issues. Reliable schemes must also assure identity uniqueness and stability. Locator-identifier split approaches have also associated mapping issues. A flexible, and stable mapping service can be hierarchical such as the Domain Name System (DNS), or can be distributed using a Distributed Hash Table (DHT) architecture. Each has its own advantages and disadvantages; see Information-Centric Networks (ICN) [39] for more details.

Security is another important issue in multihoming architectures, as they introduce new security threats, like "time-shifting" attacks, which affect proposals that adopt the locator-identifier split approach [40]. As locators change during communications, an attacker does not need to be always present in the path between a source and a destination host. This kind of attack is similar to the man-in-the-middle one, as the attacker can inform a destination host that the real source can be found at a location different than the legitimate one and controlled by the attacker.

3.3 Multihoming Design Considerations

Architecture proposals for multihoming addressing issues such as failure detection, security, path selection and default gateway choice [19, 32], should consider different design guidelines to meet one or more of the multihoming goals. Briefly, design considerations include adopting a locator-identifier split approach for end-host, end-site, and hybrid multihoming. Moreover, support at the network level, by modifying site exit routers is required for end-site and hybrid multihoming approaches.

The first guideline that should be considered relates to the **locator-identifier split**. Conventional IP architectures assume that the transport layer endpoints are the same entities as those used by the network layer. Thus, multihoming support based on a locator–identifier split requires that the transport layer identity is decoupled from the network layer locator in order to allow multiple forwarding paths to be used by a single transport session. Different approaches can be considered [16], either by modifying an existing protocol or by introducing a new layer. With the latter approach, upper layer protocols (e.g., applications) use endpoint identifiers to uniquely identify a session while the lower layer protocols (e.g., network) employ locators. If this approach is used, a mapping between an identifier and a locator is necessary. In a multihoming context, the locator–identifier mapping must be assured by a dynamic process so that a session can include different features, such as invariant endpoint identifiers throughout the session lifetime, and modification of locators to maintain end-to-end reachability.

In principle, this mapping can be maintained at any layer of the protocol stack. One reasonable choice is to place this functionality between the transport and the application layers, so that applications would interface with the endpoint identity protocol stack element through an Application Programming Interface (API). A second approach is to place a new layer between the transport and the network layers. With the modified layer approach, an existing layer can be adapted to perform the mapping between identifiers and locators. For instance, if the transport layer functionalities are modified, a set of locators can be bound to a session, and the locator is communicated to a remote entity. On the other hand, if the network layer is modified, there are two ways to achieve the desired functionalities. The first is by rewriting the packet header and the second is by using encapsulation to perform packet header transformation.

Another consideration for end-site and hybrid multihoming includes the **modification of a site exit-router**. End-site multihoming can be assured by a network element. For instance, an exit-router can perform packet rewriting for a given locator of a correspondent node. Nevertheless, this type of approach raises security concerns, which might be difficult to overcome. Redirection attacks are such an example, which may compromise routing, since packets for a destination can be redirected to any location [16, 17]. Thus, the host should always be able to perform the endpoint-to-locator mapping on its own.

Scalability is of essence in any network architecture and multihoming is not an exception. Multihoming architectures should be scalable and need to strive to minimize the impact on routers and end-hosts. Basic connectivity must be always provided. If any modification is required it should be in the form of logically separating added functions from existing ones [28].

Security is also paramount for future architectures. Multihoming proposals should not introduce new security threats. For instance, multihoming solutions should be resilient to redirection attacks that compromise routing, new packet injection attacks (malicious senders can inject bogus packets into the packet stream between two communicating peers) and flooding attacks, which are normally associated with Denial of Service attacks [17].

4. OPERATING SYSTEMS AND APPLICATIONS

This section is devoted to the support of multihoming in applications. We focus on proposals acting at the application layer and support multihoming. For instance, the name-based sockets proposal represents a change of paradigm on how applications see the information of layers bellow. Moreover, as presented in Section 4.2, server applications incorporate mechanisms to support multiple interfaces or multiple paths.

4.1 Protocols at Application Layer

This subsection discusses two application-layer protocols, namely Session Initiation Protocol (SIP) and Name Based Sockets (NBS).

4.1.1 Session Initiation Protocol (SIP)

Session Initiation Protocol (SIP) [5] is a session protocol that enables mobility at the application layer. SIP employs a Universal Resource Identifier (URI) to represent the user identity connected to a SIP domain. Sessions, therefore, are bound to the URI and not to an IP address. On mobility events, the user sends a binding update message that renews the mapping in the SIP server (URI to IP address). The communication proceeds, as the URI is used to identify the user during the entire session. One drawback of SIP is that it is intended for UDP applications. Thus TCP applications can not have the support of SIP in mobility events [41], as the change of IP address leads to the termination of connections. Some proposals mitigate this issue by combining SIP with Mobile IP [6].

Another drawback of SIP relates to the privacy of the user IDs, which is provided in the clear. PrivaSIP [42] is a proposal that enables the protection of caller and caller's IDs by the use of cryptography. Further, the media multihoming proposal [43] combines SIP with SCTP, enhancing multihoming support, for instance, resilience support (e.g., recovery is possible in failures of middle nodes). Nonetheless, this last proposal is very recent and needs further details to enable its implementation.

4.1.2 Name-Based Sockets (NBS)

The Name Based Sockets (NBS) proposal [44] introduces a novelty that in a sense facilitates multihoming. Applications only use domain names, while IP addresses (e.g., selection, discovery) are managed by the operating system. Such functionality is proposed as an extension to the socket API through the introduction of a new familly AF_NAME. Nodes communicating with each other, initially exchange names, in a piggyback scheme. The first packets convey the name on an IP-Option/IPv6 extension header. A receiver node, upon detecting such option, adds its name in the reply packets. The name can be based on a Fully Qualified Domain Name (FQDN), on ip6.arpa (host interface address) or nonces (session identifiers). The ports rely on service keywords attributed by the Internet Assigned Numbers Authority (IANA) (e.g., http for port 80).

The Name Based Sockets proposal can be combined with other protocols, such as SHIM6 to enable mobility [45]. Nevertheless, it requires node modifications and removes the possibility of applications to use multiple addresses according to their own requirements. For instance, to use all addresses simultaneously to support resilience. This proposal did not attain enough support in IETF standardization. Nonetheless, it has the advantage of not requiring new infrastructure to be deployed [46].

Table 1 summarizes multihoming support in application-layer protocols. SIP enjoys widespread implementation, efficient mobility support, and can be extended to also support resilience. Such extension relies on the combination

Table 1 Multihoming support in application-layer protocols.

Protocol	Multihoming Goals				Strengths	Weak Aspects	Implementation	
	R	U	L	F			Simulators	OS
SIP	X	√	X	X	Widely available. Resilience can be supported	No flow distribution capabilities	Yes	Yes
NBS	X	√	X	X	Resilience can be supported.	Not standardized	–	Linux [46]

of SIP and SCTP. The same logic applies to NBS, that can support resilience if combined with SHIM6. But, in contrast to SIP, NBS represents a new concept and introduces modifications that may hinder its widespread implementation.

4.2 Operating Systems and Server Applications

Although most mobile devices have very rudimentary mechanisms for heterogeneous network access selection and management, modern operating systems have started to introduce connection managers to select the best path for applications based on preference sets (e.g., cost, bandwidth) [47]. Others explore techniques similar to *IP aliasing* to support multiple IP addresses due to the different (physical/virtual) network connections [48]. IIP network multipathing (IPMIP) [49] extends the functionality of IP aliasing techniques by providing interface failure detection and by offering load sharing in systems with multiple interfaces.

Linux supports multipath routing by allowing the specification of multiple next hops for a given destination. The motivation for multipath routing can include tolerance to failures (using a backup route) or load sharing to increase throughput [50]. While simple reliability can be based on the specification of several routes with different weights, load balancing requires more advanced mechanisms that can be based on identical weights such as the implemented Equal Cost Multipath (ECMP) algorithm. The distribution of traffic, under multipath configuration, is based on routing cache entries to distribute traffic according to different algorithms, such as *Weighted Round Random*. In FreeBSD 8.0, the routing infrastructure was modified to split L2 and L3 information [51]. This split introduces benefits that facilitate the utilization of parallel computing and introduce support for ECMP.

Server applications such as DHCP and File Transfer Protocol (FTP) can be configured according to the sets of each subnet a host can connect to. For instance, *vsftpd*, an FTP daemon, can be configured for multiple FTP domains [52]. Both approaches have drawbacks, since this kind of configuration requires IP addresses for each FTP domain and a multihomed DHCP server can perform differently for each network [53]. Apache, a web server, provides support for multihoming via *virtual hosts* [54] that give the possibility of hosting several domains on a single physical machine. Domains can be identified on a name or IP configuration basis. In the last approach, a virtual host is configured based on a server IP address. A clear distinction between Apache and *vsftpd* is that configuration is centralized and not split on a domain basis.

5. MULTIHOMING AND TRANSPORT PROTOCOLS

An overview on multihoming support at the transport layer is presented in this section. This overview includes proposals standardized by Internet Engineering Task Force (IETF), and non-standardized proposals. Proposals like Transport Connection Protocol (TCP) Multi-Home Options [55], Multiple TCP Fairness [56], among others, are grouped in a subsection and are included in this overview primarily for historical reasons, as many of these proposals have been pioneers in the introduction of multihoming support in transport protocols. Other proposals like Proxy-based Inverse Multiplexer (PRISM) [57] include a complete architecture to support multihoming, but changes act at the transport layer. Standardized solutions include Multipath Transport Control Protocol (MPTCP) [58, 59], Stream Control Transport Protocol (SCTP) [38] with respective extensions and Datagram Congestion Control Protocol (DCCP) [60].

5.1 Non-Standard TCP-Based Proposals

With **TCP Multi-Home Options** [55], Transport Connection Protocol (TCP) peers first negotiate the multihoming permitted option. During connection establishment, the path based on the current address is marked as the primary path. As the primary path is established, the multihoming *Add* and *Delete* options may be used to convey local address information from the sender to the destination. Then, on the reception of a multihoming option, all paths that can be created are registered. If the option corresponds to *Delete*, paths are unregistered after a certain amount of time. Although the proposed scheme attempts to enhance TCP with multihoming support, it mainly focuses on increasing resiliency to path failures, by capitalizing on the availability of different network interfaces. The scheme does not enable bandwidth sharing between different paths or applications [61].

Standard TCP does not have default mechanisms for explicitly exploring multiple paths. However, with the **Multiple TCP Fairness** proposal [56] an application may employ multiple TCP instances to stripe packets across all available paths. The issue with this approach resides on the independency of each path. For instance, it is hard to guarantee that the multiple TCP instances do not displace more bandwidth on a single link as a single TCP instance over the path would take. In other words, a "fairness" issue arises as greedy applications employing more than one TCP connection in parallel receive a larger portion of what is their fair share of network resources. The Multiple

TCP Fairness proposal allows multiple TCP instances but ensures that an application does not take a disproportionate share of the available bandwidth. As such, the proposal introduces bi-level congestion control mechanisms which feature a single "master" congestion control mechanism to determine the overall sending rate and appropriate it to different number of subflows, which run their own congestion control procedures. Thus, "TCP fairness" with respect to other TCP variants is assured by the bi-level congestion control mechanism. Using simulation the authors evaluate their proposal and find that there is a certain degree of increased overhead in TCP operation.

FAST TCP [62] is a TCP variant that significantly improves the protocol's performance especially over high-speed long-distance connections. FAST TCP employs a delay-based congestion algorithm. Arshad and Mian [63] propose an extension to FAST TCP to support multihoming and improve end-to-end throughput. Multihoming support is based on different functionalities, which include sender and receiver mechanisms and Selective Acknowledgments (SACKs). At the sender, for each available path, there is a window control mechanism to estimate RTT and keep track of sent and acknowledged packets. The window control mechanisms are required on a per interface basis, since different bandwidth and delay conditions may exist. The receiver maintains and controls a single buffer for receiving. This buffer is shared by all flows, allowing the sender to divide the globally advertised window among all available paths, proportionally to the congestion window size. SACKs are used in FAST TCP to estimate RTT more accurately. A drawback with the FAST TCP multihoming mechanism is its susceptibility to throughput problems, namely, on network congestion situations on the path from destination to source. One-way congestion measurement is proposed to avoid erroneous RTT estimates [63]. Moreover, different paths can have different RTT values leading to unfair share of resources [64].

TCP Extension for Using Multiple Network Interfaces Simultaneously (TCP EUMNIS) [65] extends TCP to support simultaneous connections on heterogeneous interfaces. This extension modifies the TCP connection setup, to allow multiple addresses. In addition, it introduces a new TCP option, to maintain compatibility with existing TCP proposals.

5.2 Proxy-Based Inverse Multiplexer (PRISM)

The Proxy-based Inverse Multiplexer (PRISM) [57] is a proposal to improve TCP performance over wireless networks by capitalizing on collaborative multihomed mobile nodes. In such an environment, TCP performance can

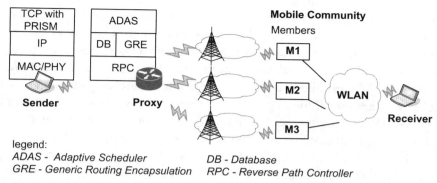

legend:
ADAS - Adaptive Scheduler   *DB - Database*
GRE - Generic Routing Encapsulation   *RPC - Reverse Path Controller*

Fig. 4. PRISM architecture.

often be dramatically degraded due to packet reordering and the hetero-geneity of wireless links.

PRISM, illustrated in Fig. 4, uses a proxy for routing, and is responsible to stripe each TCP flow over multiple links. In addition, the server (proxy) includes congestion control mechanisms to avoid packet loss. Besides the TCP mechanisms, mobile nodes can be organized in a community-like net-work in order to share connections.

Although PRISM may have great potential, the reliance on a gate-way/proxy node can be a concern. For example, despite providing support for simultaneous use of different paths, PRISM requires nodes to trust on the proxy server, which rises security issues in this community-supported network architecture. Moreover, upon a proxy failure, nodes cannot employ the advanced mechanisms provided by PRISM. Also as resources are shared between nodes in a community, mechanisms to guard against malicious or abusive users must be put in place, but this is not addressed in [57].

5.3 MultiPath TCP

Multipath Transport Control Protocol (MPTCP) [58, 59] allows the simul-taneous use of diverse paths that can exist between a sender and a receiver. MPTCP represents the most recent efforts that the Internet Engineering Task Force (IETF) is promoting to enhance the TCP capabilities to handle multiple addresses. The goals of MPTCP include throughput and resilience improvement by performing resource pooling, on which multiple addresses can be joined transparently to applications. MPTCP divides the transport layer into two sublayers, the MPTCP sublayer providing ordering of appli-cation data and reliability, congestion control and path management (detect multiple paths), and the subflow sublayer that assures reliable delivery of data, working as standard TCP. Initially MPTCP, establishes a connection setup and if multiple addresses exist, additional subflows are added for these addresses to the initial established connection. Moreover, connections are terminated by transmitting the *FIN* packet of the connection and of the last subflow. When establishing a connection, peers exchange their capabilities in terms of MPTCP support and, in addition, specific options are introduced to allow the creation of subflows or to inform about new configured addresses.

The Multipath TCP API [66] allows MPTCP-aware applications to control MPTCP. Through the API, applications can activate or deactivate MPTCP for certain data transfers, can query MPTCP regarding the addresses used on the MPTCP subflows, obtain the connection identifier and restrict MPTCP binding to a set of addresses. Nevertheless, the proposed API does not allow management of paths or scheduling of data.

5.4 Stream Control Transport Protocol and Extensions

The Stream Control Transport Protocol (SCTP) is a connection–oriented protocol designed to assure reliable signaling and transport [38]. SCTP distinguishes itself from earlier proposed transport protocols due to its native support for multihoming, which allows, for instance, hosts to use all available IP addresses.

The multihoming support of SCTP is based on several mechanisms [67]. First, address management at association setup, during which a node informs its peers about its IP addresses in the address parameters of the *INIT* chunk (type of message exchange to start the association setup). Besides IP addresses, host names can also be used. The associations include information from the verification tag field of the SCTP common header and a checksum field, which allows the verification of the association a packet belongs to. Second, path and peer monitoring so–called *HEARTBEAT* chunks are employed to monitor peers and path status (active or inactive). Finally, for path selection, as the association setup proceeds, an active path is chosen as the primary path. SCTP uses Selective ACKs (SACKs) mechanisms to improve RTT estimation. The detection of a path failure is based on timeout and retransmission approaches [68].

The SCTP API [69] allows associating an SCTP endpoint with multiple addresses. The SCTP API includes support for connection-less features (e.g., as UDP) to allow the control of multiple associations (*a one-to-many* mode), and support for connection–oriented features (e.g., as TCP). These modes are not compatible leading to the specification of different methods. Applications can get information from the SCTP data (associations, addresses and status of each association) by using the data structures that are filled upon calling specific methods. Another option, is that applications can subscribe to events and notifications. For instance, they can be notified when an association is established, or when there is a modification in the addresses of an association.

Mobile SCTP (mSCTP) [70] extends SCTP to support mobile environments. mSCTP allows dynamic address reconfiguration by modifying IP addresses that were negotiated during the SCTP association setup. Such support is specified with new message types that contain the IP address and parameters to indicate the operation to perform, namely add, remove or modify the primary address. mSCTP can be employed by fault–intolerant applications, which require fast recovery. Different proposals extend mSCTP to allow different metrics for network selection [36]. Mobile SCTP (mSCTP) [36] extends SCTP to mobile environments. mSCTP allows dynamic address reconfiguration by modifying IP addresses that were negotiated during the SCTP association setup. Such support is specified with new message types that contain the IP address and parameters to indicate the operation to perform, namely add, remove or modify the primary address.

Concurrent Multipath Transfer (CMT) [29] adds simultaneous data transfer capabilities across multiple paths to SCTP. CMT addresses some performance issues of SCTP, such as unnecessary fast retransmission at the sender and increased ACK traffic due to fewer delayed ACKs. If the available paths have unbalanced delay or bandwidth, an SCTP receiver can experience packet reordering, which will consequently lead to fast retransmission at the sender. CMT mitigates these issues by introducing modifications in the SCTP specification. A receiver delays the ACKs, instead of immediately acknowledging out-of-order packets. Packet loss measurement, besides considering *SACKs*, also employs historical information. Moreover, the connection window, *cwnd*, is updated according to the path conditions. CMT still needs to mitigate RTT issues due to the different paths characteristics. For instance, SACKs on faster return paths will be delivered before preceding SACKs sent over slower paths.

5.5 Datagram Congestion Control Protocol

The Datagram Congestion Control Protocol (DCCP) [60] is an unreliable transport protocol that can employ different, so-called pluggable, profiles to control data congestion, also known as Congestion Control IDentifier (CCID) profiles. For instance, CCID2 is a profile that exhibits a TCP-like behavior [71], while CCID4 [72] can be used by applications that want to follow a TCP-friendly rate control but are bound to use small packets. Although DCCP is a recently proposed transport protocol supporting different congestion algorithms according to the different kinds of applications, it does have multihoming features [73].

A multihoming extension to DCCP has been proposed [74], although it did not advance within the IETF standardization track. The extension introduces multihoming and mobility support by grouping multiple transport connections into a single application level entity (also called generalized connection). While applications only see one socket, transport connections can be transferred from one address to another. This requires extra information during the handshake. First the generalized connection identifiers are set between the peers and, on at a second stage, transport connections are added to the generalized connection, via the DCCP request message. Nonetheless, DCCP multihoming and mobility support is limited, since there is no support for simultaneous movements or load sharing between the different connections, as discussed in [16].

Table 2 summarizes the main characteristics of the aforementioned transport protocols support for multihoming, listing the respective strong and weak aspects and evaluates the attainment of the multihoming goals of TCP, SCTP, and DCCP derived proposals. DCCP and UDP, due to their unreliable nature, do not support multihoming efficiently or have limited support.

Standard TCP is being extended by Multipath TCP (MPTCP) to support multiple paths using centralized congestion control mechanisms. Despite the plurality of proposals to enhance TCP features for better multihoming support, only MPTCP advanced in the IETF standardization track. TCP Multi-Home Options [55] introduces new TCP options in messages to add and remove addresses, that can be used to reach a particular destination, employing a primary-backup model. TCP Fairness [56] introduces support for multi-priority flows and specific congestion control mechanisms using a bi-level congestion control framework under the management of a master process. Different control mechanisms enable the support of multiple paths, nevertheless with a considerable delay in the probing of the different paths (e.g., in terms of RTT). The FAST TCP multihoming approach [62] introduces sender and receiver mechanisms (specific congestion control) and Selectective Acknowledgments (SACKs). The concentration of mechanisms at the sender and receiver sides poses some issues with heterogeneous links. TCP EUMNIS [65] is an extension that enables the concurrent usage of paths in TCP, but has not entered in the standardization track. PRISM [57] introduces a network element, acting as a proxy that stripes flows over

Table 2 Multihoming support in transport protocols.

Protocol	Multihoming Goals				Strengths	Weak Aspects	Implementation	
	R	U	L	F			Simulators	OS
UDP	X	X	X	X	Fast and widely available	No multihoming support	Yes	Yes
TCP	X	X	X	X	Reliable and widely available	No multihoming support	Yes	Yes
MPTCP	√	X	√	X	Being standardized compatible with TCP	Introduces security concerns	In ns2 [75], htsim [76]	In Linux [77]
TCP Multihome Options	√	X	X	X	Simple implementation to assure reliability	Not standardized.	In OMNet++ [61]	–
TCP Fairness	√	X	√	X	Support multiple paths independently	Introduces overhead in the probing process. Implementation not publicly available	In ns2 [56]	–
FAST TCP Multihoming	√	X	X	X	Implementation available	Issues with heterogeneous paths	In ns2 [78]	–

(continued)

Table 2 Continued.

Protocol	Multihoming Goals			Strengths	Weak Aspects	Implementation	
	R	U	L	F			Simulators	OS

Protocol	R	U	L	F	Strengths	Weak Aspects	Simulators	OS
TCP EUMNIS	√	X	X	X	Simultaneous paths	No mobility support	–	–
PRISM	√	X	√	√	Performs flow distribution according to link characteristics	Security issues. Requires support from the network	In ns2 [57]	In Linux [57]
SCTP	√	X	X	X	Supports multiple paths natively	No mobility support.	In ns2, in OMNet++ [79]	In multiple [80]
mSCTP	√	√	X	X	Advanced mobility support.	Does not allow simultaneous use of paths	–	In FreeBSD [80]
CMT	√	X	√	X	Supports load sharing with simple mechanisms	Issues with heterogeneous paths. Not publicly available	In ns2 [80]	In FreeBSD [80]
DCCP Generalized connection	√	√	X	X	Supports multiple addresses	Limited mobility support.	In ns2 [81]	Only DCCP

multiple links. Such an approach, however, does not work if the proxy experiences a failure, introduces security issues, and does not support mobility.

Another transport protocol with native multihoming is SCTP [38] that supports multiple IP addresses which are negotiated during the association phase, establishing primary and secondary paths. Notwithstanding, SCTP does not support dynamic update of addresses that occur on mobility events. Mobile SCTP [70] addresses such limitation. Others, such as CMT [29], break the primary-backup model of SCTP and allow the simultaneous use of different paths.

To complement the ideas herein introduced, we recommend that readers interested in further protocol details consider the following references: [16, 67, 82].

6. MULTIHOMING AND MOBILITY MANAGEMENT

This section overviews multihoming support in IPv6-based protocols, namely Mobile IPv6 [2], Proxy Mobile IPv6 (PMIPv6) [2] and respective extensions. IPv4-related protocols are left out of scope as their solutions for multihoming are less scalable and not forward-looking (e.g., future support for mobility with IPv4 is limited).

6.1 Mobile IPv6

MIPv6 [2] is to a large degree the archetypical mobility management protocol for IPv6 networks. Maintaining established communications while moving is similar to preserving established communications through outages in the multihoming context. MIPv6 maintains established communications while a mobile node moves across networks. However, current MIPv6 does not fully support multihoming, as it assumes that the home address does not change during the mobility management process. With such an assumption, whenever there is a change in the home address, e.g., a node with multiple prefixes in the home network, MIPv6 does not support new addresses acting as the home address. Even if binding update messages convey information in advance about alternative prefixes [16], this may not be enough to enable session survivability, as MIPv6 procedures fail, since they rely on a single address.

6.2 Proxy Mobile IPv6

Proxy Mobile IPv6 (PMIPv6) [2] is a network mobility management protocol designed to assist IPv6 mobile nodes that do not have functionality to support mobility management. PMIPv6 introduces two entities, namely the Local Mobility Anchor (LMA), which acts as the Home Agent of the MN; and the Mobile Access Gateway (MAG) which is an access router capable of managing the signaling for a mobile node attached to its link.

PMIPv6 supports multihoming according to the configuration of prefixes and addresses, as detailed in [83]. The configuration scenarios can include a unique prefix per interface, a unique address or a shared address across interfaces [84]. The most efficient configurations are the dedicated prefixes/addresses per interfaces, as they allow the mobile node to use simultaneously both connections, nevertheless they have issues associated, such as multi-link subnet issues. The shared address configuration has limited multihoming support, as only one IP address is visible to applications.

Recently different extensions have been proposed to enhance the multihoming support of PMIPv6. The Logical interface specification [85], allows to perform handovers between heterogeneous technologies more efficiently.

6.3 Multiple Care of Addresses and Flow Bindings

The Multiple Care of Address (MCoA) proposal [86] extends MIPv6 to allow the registration of multiple Care of Addresses. With several Care of Addresses the mobile node can maintain concurrent paths with its correspondent nodes [87]. The mobile node is always reachable at a unique permanent IPv6 address (employed as an identifier) while several temporary addresses (Care of Addresses) are used as locators to reveal the current network location of the node. Since locators change over time, each path is identified with a Binding Unique Identification (BID) number. Moreover, multiple registrations can be conveyed in a single message to reduce overhead. The enhanced multihoming support of MIPv6, empowered by MCoA registration, lacks a specification on how multiple registered addresses can be used. For instance, if the addresses can be used simultaneously, or if an address is chosen based on the link characteristics. Nevertheless, a non-standard mechanism may lead to non-interoperable MCoA implementations [88].

The specification of flow bindings [4, 89] extends MIPv6 and MCoA specifications defining how multiple flows can be exchanged between two nodes, in a multihoming context. This enables to bind a particular flow to a Care of Address and use another address to receive information from other flows. The flow bindings specification permits conveying policies between the mobile node and other mobility agents (e.g., home agents) [89]. Whilst the flow bindings specification deals with the transfer of policies, the way they can be generated or mapped to user preferences (e.g., link with higher bandwidth) is left out of scope. Due to its specificity, PMIPv6 is being extended to support flow bindings on a distinct proposal [90].

6.4 Network Mobility

Network Mobility (NEMO) is a protocol [99] that manages the mobility of a network of nodes typically moving in tandem. NEMO Basic Support extends MIPv6 procedures, through the addition of the Mobile Router (MR) entity. Each Mobile Network Node is connected to MR, and all together they form the mobile network. A mobile network (NEMO) is considered multihomed when a MR has multiple egress interfaces connecting to the Internet, or when there are multiple MRs or multiple global prefixes on the network [21]. Each of the multihoming goals has different requirements for NEMO multihoming support [21]. In order to achieve permanent and ubiquitous access, at least one bi-directional tunnel must be available. For reliability, both inbound and outbound traffic must be transmitted over another bi-directional tunnel once the active one fails. Moreover, multiple simultaneous tunnels must be maintained to assure load sharing and load balancing. Multihoming support in NEMO can also be classified based on the number of Mobile Routers, number of prefixes and the number of Collocated Care of Address (CCoA)-prefixes, instead of resorting to the number of Home Agents [27]. Multihoming models are based on a packet flow classification, which is divided into three segments. First, the segment between CN and HA, which is affected by the number of prefixes available. Second, the segment between HA and MR, which depends on the number of CCoAs, and finally the segment between MR and the MNNs.

NEMO Extended Support (NEMO-ES) [100] enables route optimization and policy based routing. Multihoming support is improved, as care is taken with the choice of the router that will route packets in a nested mobile network. Nested mobile networks (sub-NEMO) are introduced in [101]. They are networks that obtain access to the Internet via another mobile network (parent-NEMO). For example, consider the case of a mobile network of devices of a group of colleagues (sub-NEMO) on board a train en route to a meeting (parent-NEMO). The sub-NEMO has been established prior to embarking on the train in order to share documents and a cellular connection to the Internet. One can imagine that several more mobile networks (used in a similar fashion by families, for example) can also board the train, which also offers high-speed connectivity on board via a Wireless Local Area Network (WLAN). In this type of topology, if there is no route optimization, multiple tunnels will exist, and quite likely, at least one for each mobile network. Mobile routers can be organized into several hierarchical levels. By introducing route optimization mechanisms, it is possible to significantly reduce the multiple tunnels overhead and the cost introduced of using several paths through multiple Home Agents. Only one tunnel is employed between the root Mobile Router and the correspondent router. That said, such route optimization mechanisms do not come for free. The process of establishing hierarchical mobile networks introduces delay, which is proportional to the number of nested levels, and increases with the number of levels. Therefore, the use of balanced nested configurations is preferable.

Table 3 compares and contrasts the protocols presented in this section. Moreover, the support of multihoming goals **R**-Resilience, **U**-Ubiquity, **L**-Loach Sharing, and **F**-Flow distribution, is also listed.

With respect to MIPv6, the main restrictions for multihoming include the assumption that the home address does not change during the mobility management process and the use of a single binding between a care of address and the home address [102]. MCoA [3] and flow binding [4] proposals overcome the last restriction of MIPv6. Protocols like Fast Mobile IPv6 (FMIPv6) [103] and Hierarchical Mobile IPv6 (HMIPv6) [104], despite their improved mobility support when compared with MIPV6, have not been discussed as they share the same limitations of MIPv6 regarding multihoming support.

Multihomed nodes with no MIPv6 compatibility can be assisted by the network on mobility events. PMIPv6 [105] is a protocol that provides mobility–assistance to nodes which are not Mobile IP (MIP)–aware. Different configurations are possible within multihomed nodes: a unique prefix per interface, a unique address per interface and a shared address across interfaces. Nonetheless support from the network (e.g., context transfer capabilities between access routers) and configuration–tuning on nodes (logical interfaces) may be required.

The multihoming support analysis in NEMO [106] can follow the configuration approach, depending on the number of Mobile Routers, advertised Mobile Network Prefixes, and Home Agents. Moreover, NEMO can be associated with other protocols, such as HIP [107] to overcome the non-optimized routing performance in NEMO and to enhance security and multihoming support.

On the implementation front, the Nautilus6 project [93] enhances and maintains the main implementations of MIPv6 and NEMO protocols in GNU/Linux and BSD systems.

We recommend the following references on this topic: [87, 90, 100].

Table 3 Multihoming support in mobility management protocols.

Protocol	Multihoming Goals				Strengths	Weak Aspects	Implementation	
	R	U	L	F			Simulators	OS
MIPv6	X	✓	X	X	Supports global mobility	Limited multihoming support	Mobiwan for ns2 [91] and xMIPv6 for OMNet++[92]	Nautilus6 project [93] for BSD and Linux
MCoA	X	✓	✓	X	Supports multiple bindings	No standard mechanism to enable load sharing	MCoA for OMNet++ [94]	Draft version in Nautilus6 project [93]
Flow Bindings	X	✓	✓	✓	Enables distribution of policies	No standard mechanism to define local policies	–	ANEMONE project [95] for Linux
PMIPv6	X	✓	X	X	Easier implementation when compared to MIPv6	Logical interfaces, to hide the specificity of physical interfaces	Hyon for ns2 [96]	OpenAir project [97] for Linux
NEMO	X	✓	X	X	Supports network mobility	Limited multihoming support	xMIPv6 project for OMNet++ [92]. No public extensions for ns-2 [98]	Nautilus6 project [93] for BSD and Linux

7. END-HOST MULTIHOMING

This section overviews protocols and architectures tailored for end-host multihoming support. We review proposals that only require modifications on end-hosts, or are designed specifically for end-nodes. For instance, without modifications, these proposals do not enable multihoming support for networks, only for end-nodes. Proposals like SHIM6, Host Identify Protocol (HIP) constitute the standardized ones, while others, such as Name Address and Route System (NAROS), or Practical End-host Multihoming (PERM) have not reached standardization.

7.1 Site Multihoming by IPv6 Intermediation

SHIM6 [8] is a multihoming protocol that adds a shim layer in the IP stack of end-hosts. SHIM6 brings the advantage of assuring transport layer communication survivability, as the identity and location functions are split. For instance, the switch between address pairs is transparent to applications, since the identifier is only used to identify endpoints, while the locator is used to perform routing. In this split, SHIM6 provides the mapping function between Upper Layer Identifier and locator at the receiver and sender end-hosts.

SHIM6 uses failure detection and recovery mechanisms described in the Reachability Protocol (REAP) [108], which work independently from upper layer protocols. Failure detection can be based on keep-alive mechanisms or using information from upper layers (e.g., TCP control features). Recovery mechanisms rely on the exploration of available addresses, so that in the end an operational pair can be found and used.

As stated in [8], SHIM6 can use different protocols to prevent hijacking attacks. Cryptographically Generated Addresses (CGA) [109] correspond to IPv6 addresses on which the interface identifier is built based on public key mechanisms. Hash-Based Address (HBA) [110] employs symmetric key cryptographic mechanisms with smaller computational requirements when compared to CGA. The interface identifiers of the addresses in HBA are generated as hashes of the available prefixes and on random numbers.

Despite providing fault tolerance, SHIM6 breaks the functionality of some protocols, such as Internet Control Message Protocol (ICMP), since routers on the path cannot see the host identifier. Notwithstanding, SHIM6, when compared to other multihoming solutions, for instance HIP, has the advantage of an easier deployment in the Internet [23], since

SHIM6-compatible hosts can communicate with other nodes that are not SHIM6-aware.

SHIM6 is accompanied by a socket API [111, 112] that allows applications to access information about failure detection and path exploration. Moreover, through this API applications can turn on/off shim layer functionality, and obtain or set preferred source and destination locator(s). Applications can also employ the API to inform the shim layer about the status of the communication or even control the frequency on which the REAP mechanism is executed.

7.2 Host Identify Protocol and Extensions

HIP [7] is a protocol that adopts a locator–identifier split approach and supports multihoming natively. HIP introduces a new host identity namespace and a new host identity layer between the network and the transport layers. In addition, HIP decouples identifiers (used by transport layer protocols) from locators (used for routing purposes). In short, the transport layer sockets and the IP security associations are bound to host identifiers, which in the end are tied to IP addresses.

Multihoming support in HIP is based on two approaches: *LOCATOR* parameter and *RendezVous* service [113]. Using the *LOCATOR* parameter approach, a HIP host can notify a correspondent peer about alternate addresses through which it is reachable. With the HIP *RendezVous* service, each HIP host publishes its host identifier with a *RendezVous* Server. The *RendezVous* Server maintains the mapping between the host identifiers and the locators, with limited support for mobility. HIP may raise issues with firewalls and middleboxes that need to inspect packet contents. Also, multihoming support does not include traffic engineering or policy address selection schemes.

The HIP API [114] relies on the SHIM6 API for different functionalities. HIP API introduces the socket family AF_HIP and protocol family PF_HIP. Using the HIP API applications can open sockets based on Host Identification Tags (HITs) solely, can start communications with unknown peer identifiers and can perform explicit locator-identifier mapping. Functions like getaddrinfo () allow the application to query about local HITs, and choose a source HIT, associating the same to the socket via the bind () function. The client can also use the setsocket () function to indicate the HIT preference on the socket binding (for instance, if prefers public HITs).

HIP-based Simultaneous Access [30, 115] introduces a policy system based on HIP to allow simultaneous multiaccess. The proposal extends HIP by allowing flows to use different paths independently of each other, since HIP does not support load sharing. To enable flow distribution support, flows are identified by source and destination ports and by HIT. The *RendezVous* Server, specified in [116], is extended to include the storage of flow policies. Then, *POLICY UPDATE* messages are employed to negotiate policies between peers during the HIP association lifetime. Whilst these policies define the usage rules of the available interfaces, the proposal does not detail policy specification (e.g., rules actions, interface priority, and cost).

7.3 Name Address and Route System (NAROS)

The Name Address and Route System (NAROS) [117] is a mechanism that decouples traffic engineering from routing. Such decoupling does not require routing manipulation to support traffic engineering. The NAROS architecture includes a server that holds the appropriate source address for a given host. This way, a host before communicating with a peer must query the NAROS server to obtain the correct source address. Such selection of source address is ruled by traffic engineering policies. NAROS supports traffic engineering for unequal load balancing distribution, without impacting the routing system. The drawback of this approach is the required modification of clients [117–119]. Also, NAROS does not preserve traffic flows across address changes. Integration with DNS can reduce overhead, as clients in

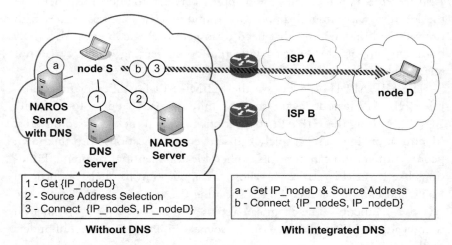

Fig. 5. NAROS with and without integrated DNS.

one operation can obtain the best source–destination address pair, as depicted in Fig. 5.

7.4 Practical End-Host Multihoming

Practical End–host Multihoming (PERM) [120] enables flow scheduling in multihomed hosts. This framework extends the Linux socket API to allow a host to explore different paths on a flow-level basis. PERM also introduces the concept of collaborative multihoming in which users share their Internet connection with others. PERM includes different functions to allow this collaboration. For instance, besides the connection manager and the monitor, the incentive manager creates incentives to share Internet access, based on policies (e.g., user shares when the connection is idle). The hybrid flow scheduling algorithm in PERM considers flow volume, load of a link and the respectively associated RTT. For instance, a flow with light volume is scheduled on the connection with the smallest RTT, while others are scheduled based on the predicted flow volume and current load of each link. Nevertheless, optimal performance is obtained with prediction information which depends on particular scenarios.

7.5 Strawman Architecture

Strawman [121] is an architecture performing flow striping at the session layer to improve the performance of applications in nodes with multiple interfaces. The Strawman architecture aims to allow striping over multiple connections, to maximize throughput and minimize delay, jitter and loss. Moreover, it also supports multimedia applications by allowing in-order delivery but without transport guarantees. To achieve such goals, different functionalities are included in the architecture. First, connection establishment employs secure mechanisms, such as Secure Socket Layer (SSL) or Transport Layer Security (TLS) [122]. Second, path evaluation, which evaluates the service on a path based on network metrics (e.g., round–trip delay, throughput, and packet loss) or application feedback. Third, connection management, on which the transport protocol is selected based on the application preferences and requirements. Finally, data delivery, on which algorithms (e.g., round robin based) are applied to schedule flows between the different paths.

Implementing this architecture requires modifications to the sockets API, preferably in kernel space, to allow for efficient interaction with all transport protocols. This API must be available between the session layer and applications. In addition, the strawman architecture does not follow a locator-identifier approach, which in a sense limits its potential for mobility support and requires modification of applications. Moreover, to the best of our knowledge, the code implementing the aforementioned API has not become publicly available.

7.6 Forwarding Directive, Association, and Rendezvous Architecture (FARA)

Forwarding directive, Association, and Rendezvous Architecture (FARA) [123] is a location/identifier split proposal that optimizes end-host mobility support by using rendezvous mechanisms [124]. FARA includes different components such as the entities that are the mobile end-nodes, the association corresponding to the communication between entities and the communication substrate that is the network communication subsystem responsible for addressing and routing packets of FARA associations.

Associations are identified by an identifier, moreover entities communicating with each other need forwarding directives that are obtained from the FARA directory service. The mentioned service works similarly to the way DNS does, by mapping forwarding directives and rendezvous information used to establish the association IDs during the initial communication. Such mapping is required as no global namespace exists in FARA, instead the association IDs, the entity names and the end system address are used to establish communication between entities. FARA has good support for mobility, as the forwarding directive management system keeps the forwarding directives updated, namely, when location changes due to mobility events. As such, a static rendezvous point is associated to each mobile event.

FARA is very generic and does not provides too much details that foster its implementation [125], despite including its early implementation in a tesbed. Moreover, the proposed architecture requires modification in end-nodes and on the network side to enable mobility support [126].

7.7 Layered Naming Architecture (LNA)

Layered Naming Architecture (LNA) [127] is a proposal that implements changes in end-hosts and on the naming resolution system. LNA introduces a three-level name resolution: user-level descriptors to service identifiers (SIDs), SIDs to end-point identifiers (EIDs) and EIDs to IP addresses. Applications bind to SIDs that are host-independent names, and transport protocols bind to EIDs; the network layer resolves EIDs to IP addresses. The resolution infrastructure for both SIDs and EIDs is based on flat names using DHT mechanisms.

SIDs can be compared to URLs that can be obtained by search engines, while directory services map SIDs to human-readable names. With LNA, an end-host (*e*) has also the ability to delegate to another host packet-receiving. When the delegated host receives packets for *e* it forwards the packet to the ultimate destination, by using the destination EID that is present on the packet. Such delegation system is performed on the resolution infrastructure and enables middleboxes (e.g., NAT or firewalls) to stand-up on behalf of other entities.

LNA introduces two types of mapping that can cause overhead in initial communications as well as on updates due to mobility (location update and rebinding to SIDs needs to take place). Flat names can pose scalability issues [126].

The pros and cons of the reviewed proposals for end-host multihoming support are summarized in Table 4, according to the multihoming goals fulfillment.

End-host multihoming proposals can follow different approaches. The Locator-Identifier (Loc/ID) split is one of the approaches aiming to break the dual role of IP addresses. SHIM6 [37] is a locator-identifier multihoming approach that adds a shim layer between the network and transport layers. SHIM6 uses REAP [132] to perform the detection of invalid locators and recover in an application-independent fashion. SHIM6 also includes security mechanisms to enable the protection of the identity of nodes. Nevertheless, SHIM6 must be combined with other protocols, such as MIPv6, to provide mobility support.

HIP [7] is an identity protocol that also decouples identifiers from locators. Its multihoming support relies on two approaches, one that resorts to the inclusion of new options in the HIP messages, that is, the *LOCATOR* parameter, and another that employs a *RendezVous* Server that maintains the mapping between identifiers and locators. Extensions to HIP [30] introduce load sharing and flow distribution support. The *RendezVous* servers are updated to store flow policies and HIP messages are updated to convey policies. This proposal extends the HIP4BSD implementation [133], but is not publicly available.

NAROS [117] explores a routing/TE decoupling approach by implementing a server that holds the information of the appropriate source address a multihomed host must use when communicating with a certain peer. This approach alleviates the changes on the routing systems (network part) but stresses the modification on the host part, as each node must query the server

Table 4 Comparison of end-host multihoming proposals.

Protocol	Approach	Multihoming Goals				Strengths	Weak Aspects	Implementation	
		R	U	L	F			Simulators	OS
HIP	Loc/ID split	✓	X	X	X	IP family agnostic; security	Complicated implementation and deployment	HIPSim++ [128]	InfraHIP [129]
HIP SIMA	Loc/ID split	✓	✓	✓	✓	Security	Limited policy specification	–	–
SHIM6	Loc/ID split	✓	X	X	X	Easier deployment than HIP	Mobility and security issues	REAP in OPnet [130]	LinShim6 [131]
NAROS	Routing/TE decouple	✓	X	✓	X	Load sharing for unequal paths	No LoC/ID split support	–	–
PERM	Flow Strip	✓	X	✓	✓	Security	No LoC/ID split support; requires application modification	–	–
Strawman	Flow strip	✓	X	✓	✓	Security	No LoC/ID split support; requires application modification	–	–
LNA	Loc/ID split	✓	X	X	X	Delegation on other hosts	Overhead with updates	–	–
FARA	Loc/ID split	✓	✓	X	X	Supports mobility		–	–

for each new communicating peer. Unfortunately, no public implementation is available.

The strawman architecture [121] and PERM [120] explore flow stripping mechanisms. Whilst such approaches have fine-grained capabilities (e.g., support of flow distribution according to policies), they require applications to be modified to support multihoming. These proposals are implemented by extending the functionalities of the Linux sockets API.

Further information can be found in [7, 8].

8. END-SITE MULTIHOMING

End-site multihoming includes proposals that are tailored for networks and groups of nodes sharing common resources (e.g., medium addressing schemes, etc). End-site multihoming has gained more attention than end-host multihoming, mainly due to the routing scalability problems that the Internet is facing (e.g., high growth in the core routing). We classify end-site multihoming approaches in three major types: First, address rewriting approaches, which change addresses in packets; Second, hierarchical approaches, which structure networks to address scalability; Third, mapping and encapsulation approaches, which implement the locator-identifier (Loc/ID) split paradigm, and as such, require mapping facilities to retrieve locator from identifiers, or vice versa. Before detailing the different types of approaches an introduction regarding the locator-identifier paradigm is provided. We state also that this section does not provide an overview on routing protocols, such as the Border Gateway Protocol (BGP) [134], as these are part of current IP routing architectures in Internet, and do not support Loc/ID paradigm.

8.1 Locator-Identifier (Loc/ID) Overview

In the context of a Loc/ID implementation, different approaches can be pursued, namely the so-called *map-and-encap* and *address rewriting*. The map-and-encap approach, as depicted in Fig. 6, is based on the mapping and encapsulation processes as follows. A source host, on a domain sending a packet to a destination, inserts the source Endpoint Identifier (EID) and the destination EID in the packet header (Fig. 6:1). When the packet arrives at the border router of the same domain, the Ingress Tunnel Router (ITR) performs the mapping between the destination EID and the Routing Locator (RLOC) (Fig. 6:2—mapping phase). After the successful mapping, the ITR encapsulates the packet and sets the destination address to the RLOC

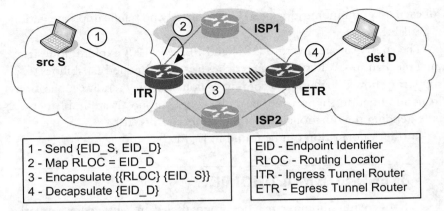

Fig. 6. *Map and encap* approach.

retrieved in the mapping phase (Fig. 6:3—encapsulation phase). Finally, the packet arrives at the destination domain, on which a border router, the Egress Tunnel Router (ETR), performs the decapsulation and the delivery to the destination EID (Fig. 6:4). The advantages of this approach are support of both IPv4 and IPv6, leaving end-hosts unchanged, and minimizing the modifications in the routing system.

In the address rewriting approach, the 128 bits of an IPv6 address are split, where the 64 most significant bits are used as the routing locator and the 64 least significant bits are used as the endpoint identifier. Figure 7 illustrates the

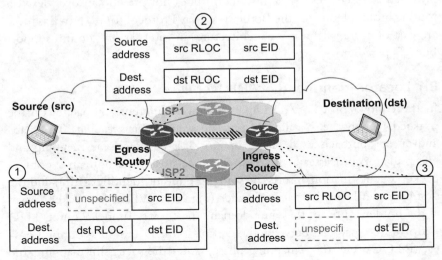

Fig. 7. Address rewriting approach.

process of address rewriting. The routing locator information is not known by the end nodes (source and destination). Whilst this approach supports IPv6 only, it allows for consistency between prefix assignment and physical network topology.

8.2 Address Rewriting Approaches

This subsection details address rewriting approaches, which implement Loc/ID split by changing addresses.

8.2.1 Global Locator Local Locator and Identifier Split (GLI-Split)

The Global locator Local locator and Identifier Split (GLI-Split) [135] is a locator-identifier addressing and routing architecture. GLI-Split implements a global locator, local locator and identifier split, that is, it distinguishes locators for local routing (e.g., inside a domain) from those used for global routing. To allow compatibility with IPv6 protocols, locators and identifiers are coded as IPv6 addresses. GLI-split works by performing address rewriting carried out by the GLI-gateway with the assistance of the mapping systems. Moreover, GLI-split introduces two types of mapping systems. The local one is restricted to a domain, while the global mapping system is used for the global routing domain (e.g., Internet backbone). GLI-split supports mobility, but requires modifications to protocols like Dynamic Host Configuration Protocol (DHCP) to support multihoming.

8.2.2 4 + 4

The 4 + 4 proposal [126, 136] extends the NAT architecture to enable end-to-end host transparency. 4 + 4 uses two name spaces in DNS: one is the private IP addresses of the end-host and the other is the public IP address of the NAT router responsible for the end-host. Thus the 4 + 4 address is formed by concatenating two IPv4 addresses, the public and the private one. As such, 4 + 4 introduces a new header that is encapsulated in IPv4 to allow compatibility with standard IPv4 routers. As routing occurs, 4 + 4 routers (NAT gateways) perform swapping of addresses to assure that private IPv4 addresses are never used outside the network they belong. The proposal allows end-hosts to have more than one address, and provides support for incremental deployment. Nevertheless, in only applies to IPv4 and may represent security concerns as private addresses are exposed in packets forwarded in public networks.

8.2.3 IP Next Layer (IPNL)

The IP Next Layer (IPNL) [137] is an earlier proposal that also extends NAT
by adding a new layer between IP and TCP. It is different from 4 + 4 as it
introduces new paradigms regarding the identification of a host. In IPNL
the end-host is identified by the FQDN, and the IPNL address is the locator.
The IPNL address corresponds to the gateway address, the realm number and
the host address triplet. Thus for each communication, peers must use the
FQDN, obtaining the IPNL address in the initial packet exchange. The host
itself does not know all the possible addresses it has (when behind several
routers) since it is only aware of its name. This type of design introduces
overhead in packet processing; for instance, NAT routers need to maintain
FQDN records per host [136].

8.2.4 Translating Relaying Internet Architecture Integrating Active Directories (TRIAD)

Translating Relaying Internet Architecture integrating Active Directories
(TRIAD) [138] is a proposal that also uses names as identifiers and introduces a new paradigm for routing that is based on content, with the goal
of reducing the access time to content. A content layer and content routers
holding mapping information are introduced to allow the access to specific content identified in the form of an URL. A host contacts a content
router that answers to a request with the next content router. At the end
the content router next to the destination content server replies with the
preferred address of the server. With such approach, a client gets the best
path to the content server. Although the content approach of TRIAD is
interesting, TRIAD has some implementation issues, since modifications are
required in the end-hosts and routers with NAT or gateway functionalities.
Details to promote implementation are missing, as well. For instance, how
one identifies and recovers from network failures.

8.2.5 Pluralistic Network Architecture (Plutarch)

Plutarch [139] is a proposal that introduces contexts to suppress the need of
global names to identify hosts [126]. The context identifies the end-host on
which the host is connected, and the communication between the different
contexts occurs by the aid of dedicated functions (e.g., Addressing, Naming,
Routing, and Transport). Moreover, Plutarch argues that naming and addressing should be handled by end-to-end systems and not hierarchical, domain-
based system such as DNS. The dedicated functions are assured by context
borders (e.g., NAT routers) to assure end-to-end service. Despite including

some implementation primitives, Plutarch specification is not ready for a global adoption in the Internet as items such as failure notification or intrinsic function discovery are not specified.

8.3 Hierarchical Approaches

Hierarchical approaches organize the network in a logical way, in order to overcome limitations (scalability) and overhead of flat networks. For instance, alternatives to BGP routing are proposed where convergence is enhanced, and the support of policies is improved. This subsection details proposals that include multihoming support by through a hierarchical architecture [140].

8.3.1 hiPv4

Hierarchical IPv4 (hiPv4) [9] is a framework that splits the core address space (ALOC) from the edge address space (ELOC). ALOC is globally unique, while ELOC is only used for routing and forwarding purposes inside local domains. With ALOC and ELOC split, there is a hierarchical organization of addresses, in the sense that the ALOC can correspond to the AS. hiPv4 introduces a Locator Swap router to perform the change between the prefixes and the introduced locator header that includes information about the ELOC and ALOC elements. Additionally a host identifier scheme is introduced to avoid locator renumbering at security nodes (e.g., firewalls). hiPv4 requires modifications to DNS, nodes, routers and security elements (e.g., firewalls) that do not facilitate its implementation. In addition, hiPv4 may break the functionality of other protocols, such as Mobile IP, since the IPv4 header is changed. Finally, efficient multihoming requires multi-path transport protocols, such as SCTP or MPTCP.

8.3.2 AIS or Evolution

Aggregation with Increasing Scopes (AIS) or evolution [141], is a locator-identifier split approach in which prefixes are aggregated in different steps and according to their scope. The first step aggregates prefixes with the same next hop. A second step configures a router as an Aggregation Point Router (APR) that aggregates prefixes as a virtual prefix. Other routers, not acting as APRs, store only routes announced on the virtual prefixes. Aggregation leads to reduction in the mapping sizes, nevertheless may also lead to route traffic through non-optimal paths since they must traverse the APR. AIS has no support for mobility and does not include failure notification mechanisms to enable multihoming.

8.3.3 IRON-RANGER

IRON-RANGER [142] implements an overlay network, where specific routers manage virtual prefixes, from which provider independent prefixes are leased to end-nodes (e.g., customer sites). This proposal introduces serving routers, clients in end-user networks, and relay routers. Serving routers perform forwarding and mapping services, while the clients connect end user networks to the overlay network, via tunnels. The relay routers connect the IRON network to the rest of the Internet, and also perform the function of advertising virtual prefixes. The hierarchical organization of IRON-RANGER makes it scalable and facilitates deployment. IRON-RANGER supports mobility and also enables end-hosts to register multiple locators. Nonetheless, there are no public implementations.

8.3.4 eFIT

Enabling Future Internet Transit (eFIT) [143] divides the network into user networks and transit wire. To accommodate heterogeneous user networks, under an administrative authority, eFIT introduces a mapping service to translate user network addresses into transit wire addresses. Transit wire addresses are structured with the provider ID (globally unique); location ID containing the continent ID, country ID and metropolitan area ID; and the subnet ID and interface ID (current IP address). This structure of the transit wire addresses allows organizing the network in a hierarchical fashion. eFIT requires changes to protocols, such as BGP to include support for the new address structure. In addition, the specification lacks details regarding the mapping service (e.g., implemented via DNS or distributed hash tables). eFIT includes resilience support and mobility without update mechanisms.

8.3.5 IPv6 Dual Homing (V6DH)

The IPv6 Dual Homing (v6DH) [144] introduces an addressing convention where all addresses are routable and are specified in a primary secondary form. For instance, Provider Aggregatable (PA)-A is primary and PA-B is secondary. When a failure occurs on a certain PA, another PA can be used. For such, non working PAs are identified based on ICMP. Moreover, V6DH keeps information of unreachable links instead of maintaining all the links in the routing table, while scalability can be assured with this approach (less routes), it requires a change in the behavior of BGP [145].

8.4 Map and Encapsulation Approaches

This subsection details mapping and encapsulation approaches.

8.4.1 LISP

The Locator-Identifier Separation Protocol (LISP) is a map-and-encap protocol [12] aiming to improve site multihoming, decouple site addressing from provider addressing, and reduce the overhead associated with routing tables (e.g., size and latency lookup operations). To implement such goals, LISP specifies the data plane on which the mapping and encapsulation processes take place, and the control plane to manage the EID-RLOC mapping system. Since LISP only defines the messages for querying data and receiving information from the mapping system, it adopts a flexible design that allows different solutions for a mapping system. The proposals to perform EID-RLOC mapping under standardization include LISP Alternative Topology (LISP-ALT) [12] and LISP Map Server (LISP-MS). LISP-ALT uses existing protocols to build an alternative topology in order to manage the mapping. LISP-MS includes MAP-Servers that accept Map-requests from ITRs and resolve the EID-to-RLOC mapping using a database, which is filled with the authoritative EID-to-RLOC mappings provided by ETRs.

8.4.2 IvIP

The Internet Vastly Improved Plumbing (IvIP) Architecture [146] is a core-edge split proposal implementing a map-and-encap approach. IvIP uses a fast-push mapping scheme, where all mapping information is kept on query database servers. Ingress tunnel routers query database servers to determine the correct egress tunnel router, to which traffic must be routed. IvIP works for IPv4 and IPv6 and supports mobility through extensions. Nevertheless, the mapping requires real-time reachability monitoring of egress routers, and in addition, it has scalability issues.

8.4.3 A Practical Transit Mapping Service (APT)

The Practical Transit Mapping Service (APT) [147] is a proposal that aims to reduce the number of nodes that must be modified, or that require additional resources. For instance, APT introduces the encapsulation/decapsulation routers that maintain a reduced cache of mappings to perform capsulation of packets. Only the default mappers, new elements, have all the maps, and are used by the encapsulation routers when no match is found in their respective cache. The full mapping is obtained from a specific BGP instance, which introduces more overhead. In addition, as no reachability is preserved on the mapping, APT relies on external protocols (IGP or BGP) to detect failures on mappings. APT also supports mapping priorities that can enhance multihoming support, but requiring routing policies to be configured on default mappers. In comparison to LISP, APT has some advantages since no modifications are performed at the edge sites [145]. Nonetheless, APT has not been standardized and no specifications for incremental deployment have been produced. Finally, introduces overhead due to the high number of tunnels.

8.4.4 Core Router-Integrated Overlay (CRIO)

CRIO [148] aims at mitigating the trade-off between path length and routing table size. CRIO decouples address hierarchy from physical topology and is suitable for global and VPN routing, as it relies on tunnels to forward data and on virtual prefixes to reduce routing tables size. CRIO also supports mapping weights that establish the preference of entries over another in a multihoming context. Nevertheless, weights need a complementary policy mechanism. CRIO in some cases does not provide the shortest path in the mapping. The mapping distribution relies on BGP protocols and it has not reached standardization despite not requiring new hardware and supporting non continuous networks due to the aggregation of virtual prefixes [145].

8.4.5 IP with Virtual Link Extension (IPvLX)

IPvLX [145, 149] aims to allow IPv6 and IPv4 coexistence. IPvLX recommends to employ IPv6 as identifiers and IPv4 addresses as locators, although this is not a rigid rule. IPvLX uses DNS for mapping, thus requiring changes on DNS systems, and implements a "site-local" resolution system to hold records of nodes that are more dynamic. IPvLX has not reached standardization and is more suitable to be employed with IPv4 to IPv6 transition solutions.

8.4.6 Tunneling Route Reduction Protocol (TRRP)

TRRP [145, 150] relies on GRE tunnels to forward traffic. It uses DNS for mapping and introduces new records that establish how traffic is forwarded on IPv4 or IPv6 tunnels. As such, by having multiple entries in DNS with the respective preference, multihoming is supported, since a destination can be reached by several addresses. Nevertheless, routers must be modified to accommodate several records in the lookup operation. The TRRP specification describes an implementation plan that includes different phases; nevertheless, no mobility support is stated.

8.4.7 Intentional Naming System (INS)

The Intentional Naming System (INS) [153] introduces a new paradigm regarding naming resolution. INS is a wide-area inter-domain and an intra-domain self-configuring resolver network. The domain space resolvers (DSR) hold a list of active Intentional Name Resolvers (INR). INS provides resource discovery and service location by using names not tied to network locations, but rather to the intention that applications have on accessing data. INS forms an application level overlay network of name resolvers to enable the binding between application intent to services and service location. INS is a proponent of late bindings, as message forwarding is integrated with the name resolution. For instance, if an application wants to send data it sends messages to the resolvers that forward messages to the respective names (destination). This form of binding supports mobility, as resolvers have an updated view of the location of nodes. For such update resolvers use a discovery protocol that frequently sends name information or uses triggered updates (e.g., due to events). To support scalability, names are organized hierarchically, similarly with DNS. INS employs virtual spaces, where a resolver is responsible for a specific virtual space [126]. INS also supports service and node mobility. Nevertheless the proposal targets intra-domain deployment [153] and has not been significantly advanced since its original publication.

8.4.8 Virtual Aggregation (ViAggre)

ViAggre [154] is a proposal that also aims to reduce the routing table size by aggregating routes into virtual prefixes and using such virtual networks inside the ISP. Virtual prefixes have no topological meaning and can be obtained by aggregating IPv4 addresses into 128 bit addresses. A router acting as an aggregation point only maintains routes for the virtual prefixes that it is aggregating. When there is need to send packets to external routers, then MPLS tunnels are employed to avoid loops inside the ISP network.

One advantage of ViAggre includes the possibility of incremental deployments as no changes are required in the routers or network protocols, and it is transparent between ISPs [145]. For instance, if an ISP adopts ViAggre, it can still communicate with other non-ViAgree compliant networks. Nevertheless, ViAggre requires ISPs to use MPLS to enable encapsulation between aggregation points and introduces management overhead inside the ISP network, as configuration of aggregation points is needed, as well as the placement in the network, and the choice of virtual prefixes. ViAggre has no public implementation available, although the authors published evaluation results from a real testbed.

Although there are several proposals based on the locator–identifier split idea, implementation requirements may determine, in part, the respective success of each proposal (see also Table 5). For instance, GLI-Split [135] maintains compatibility with IPv6 but requires changes to protocols like DHCP.

Mapping and encapsulation approaches have the advantage of facilitating deployment. LISP [12] is expected to decrease the size of routing tables in the core network when deployed due to the core-edge separation and the flexibility to implement the mapping system following different guidelines. Implementations for LISP are already available, such as OpenLisp (see http://gforge.info.ucl.ac.be/projects/openlisp). Others, such as, IvIP [146] do not address mobility natively. APT [147] has deployment concerns, since it aims to reduce the number of nodes that require modification. For instance, it does not require modifications on end-sites like LISP does, nonetheless it introduces overhead with tunnels. In the same line of deployment concern, Core Router-Integrated Overlay (CRIO) [148] does not require new hardware, as aggregation of prefixes is employed, but it does not provide the shortest path. Some proposals, like IPvLX [149] are tailored for IPv4-to-IPv6 transition, and as such, have limited multihoming support. Tunneling Route Reduction Protocol (TRRP) [145] requires changes on DNS to allow the retrievement of multiple records, corresponding to the multiple addresses of an end-host. Without the wide adoption that the current Internet architecture enjoys, Intentional Naming System (INS) [153] enhances multihoming capabilities inside a single domain by mapping the intention that end-hosts have on data. ViAggre [154] is one of the proposals that enable ViAggre-compliant nodes to communicate with standard nodes (deployment concerns), but relies on MPLS to avoid loops inside a domain.

hiPv4 [9] is a hierarchical proposal that requires changes to protocols like DHCP to enable multihoming support. Similarly, eFIT [143] requires changes to BGP. Aggregation with Increasing Scopes (AIS) [141] is another hierarchical proposal that has routing scalability concern. As such, AIS avoids non-optimal paths. IRON-RANGER [142] introduce parallel networks to introduce benefits on a first one.

Some proposals build upon current practices in the Internet architecture and implement extensions to NAT, to allow the support of multihoming and enable end-to-end communication. For instance, 4 + 4 [136] supports multiaddressing, but raises security concerns since it exposes private addresses in packets. Others, such as IP Next Layer (IPNL) [137] address security but disable the multihoming information on end-hosts (e.g., hosts do not know

Table 5 Comparison of end-site multihoming proposals.

Protocol	Approach	Multihoming Goals				Strengths	Weak Aspects	Implementation	
		R	U	L	F			Simulators	OS
LISP	Map encapsulation	✓	X	✓	X	Flexible mapping	Encapsulation overhead		In FreeBSD [151]
GLI-Split	Address rewrite	✓	✓	✓	X	Security	Requires nodes changes	–	–
4 + 4	NAT extension	X	X	X	X	Facilitates deployment	Only for IPv4	–	In Linux [152]
IPNL	NAT extension	✓	✓	X	X	Supports mobility	Hosts are not aware of their multihoming condition	–	In Linux [137]
TRIAD	NAT extension	X	X	X	X	Optimized access to content	Weak multihoming approach	–	–
Plutarch	NAT extension	X	X	X	X	Routing based on context	Weak multihoming approach	–	–
hiPv4	Hierarchical	✓	✓	✓	X	Hierarchical organization	Impacts other protocols	–	–
AIS	Hierarchical	X	X	X	X	Address aggregation done by scope	Unclear multihoming support	–	–
IRON-RANGER	Hierarchical	✓	✓	✓	✓	Follows a business model.	Relies on an overlay network	–	–

(continued)

Table 5 Continued.

Protocol	Approach	Multihoming Goals				Strengths	Weak Aspects	Implementation	
		R	U	L	F			Simulators	OS
eFIT	Hierarchical	✓	✓	X	X	Supports mobility	Requires changes to BGP	–	–
IvIP	Map encapsulation	✓	X	✓	✓	Mobility supported with extensions	Scalability issues	–	–
APT	Map encapsulation	✓	X	✓	✓	Mobility supported with extensions	Scalability issues. Not standardized	–	–
CRIO	Map encapsulation	✓	X	✓	✓	Policies support	No mobility support. Not standardized	–	–
IPvLX	Map encapsulation	✓	✓	X	X	For IPv4 to IPv6 transition	Not standardized	–	–
TRRP	Map encapsulation	✓	X	X	X	Works with existent protocols	Requires changes in routers	–	–
INS	Map encapsulation	✓	✓	X	X	Support mobility	For intra-domains	–	–
ViAggre	Map encapsulation	✓	✓	X	X	Allows incremental deployments	Requires MPLS. Introduces overhead	–	–
V6DH	Hierarchical	✓	X	X	X	Requires changes in DNS	Facilitates deployment	–	–

if they have multiple addresses). Translating Relaying Internet Architecture integrating Active Directories (TRIAD) [138] introduces the concept of routing by content, but requires many modifications to the actual Internet architecture. Also Plutarch [139] uses the context to enable identification and puts emphasis on end-hosts functionalities. Nonetheless, Plutarch does not include failure detection mechanisms.

V6DH [144] introduces a primary–backup protection model by requiring the specification of a primary and a backup address. This introduces enhanced resilience support at the cost of mandating changes in current protocols (e.g., BGP) to convey information of multiple addresses.

9. HYBRID MULTIHOMING

Proposals implementing hybrid multihoming can support both end-host and end-site multihoming. Hybrid multihoming solutions can enable multihoming support on a single host or network, without requiring any modification or amendment to the specification.

This section describes hybrid multihoming approaches in three distinct categories: First, content/service-centric approaches include solutions that focus on information [155]; Second, locator–identifier split approaches enable the separation of the dual-role (location and identification) in IP addresses; Third, new architectures and routing–centric approaches that enable multihoming by providing scalable and efficient routing mechanisms.

9.1 Content-Centric and Service-Centric Approaches

This subsection includes proposals that specify an architecture that relies on data/information and not on IP addresses, such as Content-Centric Networks (CCNs). For instance, Name Data Networking (NDN) [156] performs routing based on the interest that a node has on certain (named) data. Nonetheless, NDN is still at an early stage of development. Another proposal is the Architecture for Services Integration, controL, and Optimization for the Future Internet (SILOS) [157] that has multihoming support but lacks failure-tolerance mechanisms. SILOS, in comparison to NDN, has the disadvantage of not supporting mobility, while it incorporates cross–layer schemes that facilitate adding new functionalities. The Service-Centric End-to-End Abstractions for Network Architecture [158] approach specifies the data service to forward information. To enable such transfer, functionalities are added on routers or other nodes closest to end-hosts. Nonetheless, no support for flow distribution or mobility is provided. With limited multihoming support NetServ [159] is an architecture that virtualizes services to facilitate adding new functionalities. Services have also associated resilience mechanisms that allow efficient failure detection. Nonetheless advanced features, such as mobility or flow distribution are only supported if specific services enable these features.

Proposals supporting multihoming more efficiently are detailed next.

9.1.1 Networking Named Content (NNC)

NNC [160] introduces an architecture where all operations focus on data and, as such, data protection is supported. Nodes request content by using interest packet types and NNC nodes (e.g., ISP routers) use distinct tables to inspect the Interest packets. For instance, if the requested content is found on their cache (Content store table), the nodes reply immediately with Data packets, otherwise they forward packets to nodes. Both packet types do not carry any information regarding location, but rather the content name with a hierarchical structure. Mobility is supported in NNC, since there is no binding to IP addresses. Also, NNC includes mechanisms for automatic failover, which enable resilience [161]. NNC can be deployed incrementally and supports flow distribution. Implementation of this proposal is at a very early stage, but basic code is publicly available at www.ccnx.org.

9.1.2 Data-Oriented Network Architecture (DONA)

DONA [162] proposes a new clean-state architecture, where names are generated based on public key mechanisms, routing is based on names and name resolution relies on specific handlers that reply to clients in the presence of "find" packets. The transport layer binds to names and not to IP information. DONA also assures that the shortest path is found for certain data, as packets are forwarded to the data servers closest to the node requesting the data. In addition, DONA includes failure detection mechanisms and supports concurrent use of multiple connections. Unfortunately, no public code is available.

9.1.3 Multiaccess Network Information (NetInf)

Multiaccess Netinf [163] is an information-centric proposal that allows the creation, distribution and retrieval of information using infrastructure primitives. NetInf includes different components. The name resolution service enables the resolution of local and global (e.g., outside local domain) resources. The notification service informs applications about the domains their are connected (e.g., the availability of a new access point). One of the advantages of NetInf includes mobility and multihoming support, as objects are decoupled from their storage location. In addition objects are classified in different types, for instance Information objects provide meta-information and references to Data objects that relate with Bit level objects; for more details on NetInf interested readers are referred to [164, 165]. The NetInf proposal has already a public implementation [166], where well-known applications, such as Firefox and Thunderbird have been adapted to work under the NetInf architecture.

Table 6 summarizes information–centric proposals where routing/ forwarding is based on names and not on current IP addresses. With such characteristics, there is no compatibility with current TCP/IP architectures, which constitutes a disadvantage regarding near-term deployment. For instance, SILOS [157] focuses on services and their interaction with other layers and nodes and has no multihoming support. Data Oriented Network Architecture (DONA) [162] and Network Named Content (NNC) [160] support all multihoming goals. Other proposals, like Service-Centric End-to-End Abstractions [158] and Name Data Networking (NDN) [156] are not mature as they miss details in their specifications. NetServ [159] brings virtualization into services, that is, services are virtualized per application request. However all these proposals fail to provide a mature implementation that can practically demonstrate the advantages of routing by data/information on a large scale.

9.2 Address Rewriting Approaches

Hybrid multihoming proposals implement the Loc/ID split paradigm through address rewriting.

The Identifier Locator Protocol (ILNP) [10] is a proposal that implements a locator-identifier split by employing address rewriting. The locator is used to route traffic, while the identifier is employed as a node identifier without topological significance. The identifier is obtained in a IEEE EUI-64 bit format, while locators correspond to the 64 bit prefix of an IPv6 address. Applications bind their sessions to the identifier and not to the locator. If the identifier is globally unique, procedures like Duplicate Address Detection (DAD) are not necessary, which improves mobility support. ILNP requires modifications to DNS in order to allow nodes to update their locator records.

RANGI [9] introduces a host identifier layer between the network and transport layers. The host identifier has an organizational structure to allow easier mappings between locators and identifiers. The locators are based on IPv4 addresses embedded in IPv6 addresses, in such a way that the domain

Table 6 Comparison of content-centric multihoming proposals.

Protocol	Approach	Multihoming Goals				Strengths	Weak Aspects	Implementation	
		R	U	L	F			Simulators	OS
NDN	Content network	✓	✓	✓	✓	Routing by names	Issues with privacy	ccnSim for Omnet++[167]	CCNx for Linux [168]
NNC	Content network	✓	✓	✓	✓	Routing by names	No public implementation available	–	–
DONA	Content network	✓	✓	✓	✓	Routing by names	No public implementation available	–	Linux [162]
NetInf	Information network	✓	✓	✓	✓	Routing by Information	Security aspects of information objects	OpenNetInf [166]	Linux [163]
Service-Centric	Content network	✓	X	X	X	Routing by information	Specification with open issues	–	–
SILOS	Functional blocks	X	X	X	X	Includes cross-layer mechanisms	Not compatible with current architectures	–	–
NetServ	Functional blocks	✓	X	X	X	Mobility and flow distribution can be added	Not compatible with current architectures	–	–

Table 7 Comparison of address rewriting multihoming proposals.

Protocol	Approach	Multihoming Goals				Strengths	Weak Aspects	Implementation	
		R	U	L	F			Simulators	OS
ILNP	Loc/ID split	✓	✓	✓	✓	Supports end-host multihoming	Requires changes to DNS	–	–
RANGI	Loc/ID split	✓	✓	X	X	Facilitates IPv4 to IPv6 migration	Requires changes to hosts	–	–

identifier is a 96-bit prefix (assigned by the provider) and the remaining 32 bits correspond to a private or public IPv4 address. In the address rewriting approach of RANGI, the mapping between domain name and host identifiers is done via DNS, while the mapping between identifiers and locators is performed on a distributed mapping system. RANGI allows incremental deployment and facilitates the migration from IPv4 to IPv6 networks. Although no procedures are specified for handling mobility updates and the lack of a publicly available implementation, RANGI, through the use of proxies, allows its interoperation with standard IPv4 and IPv6 nodes.

Both ILNP and RANGI require changes to DNS or to hosts, as summarized in Table 7, which can limit their adoption rate. Nonetheless ILNP offers better multihoming support, as all multihoming goals are supported. RANGI has also the advantage of facilitating the migration from IPv4 to IPv6 networks.

9.3 Hierarchical Approaches

Hybrid proposals implement the Loc/ID paradigm by organizing the network into hierarchies. The motivation for hierarchal approaches can be diverse and proposals like the Hierarchical Routing Architecture (HRA) [169] aim to mitigate routing scalability issues. HRA extends routing protocols, such as BGP, to allow the hierarchical organization of the network. Moreover, extensions to BGP are also required to enable support of the Loc/ID split paradigm. Nonetheless, multihoming support in HRA is limited, as no flow distribution and load sharing are supported. Other proposals organize the network as a tree instead of implementing a hierarchy through administrative domains like HRA. The Node ID Internetworking Architecture (NIIA) [170] organizes the network as a tree. Routing inside domains uses locators and between domains it employs Node ID or default routes to parent nodes in the tree. NIIA also supports multiple registration on the tree, to accommodate nodes with multiple interfaces. NIIA has been evaluated in a testbed, but a public implementation is not available.

9.3.1 Less-IS-More Architecture (LIMA)

The Less-IS-More Architecture (LIMA) [171] is a locator-identifier split approach that enables inter-domain routing. LIMA proposes a hierarchical scheme, on which addresses are composed by a globally unique provider AS number, a provider local stub AS number and deploys a stub-local intra-domain address (IDA). LIMA borders routers, which implement two routing tables: one for provider numbers and another for stub networks. With this, routers no longer need to perform longest prefix match or have information about stubs. The operation of LIMA requires changes to DHCP and DNS. For instance, DNS must maintain intra-domain mappings as well as provider number and stub numbers. LIMA supports multiaddressing with the aid of transport protocols such as SCTP or MPTCP. LIMA also includes Name-Based Sockets to perform translation between names and addresses at the end-nodes. Finally, LIMA supports policies and mobility via dynamic DNS mechanisms.

9.3.2 iMark

iMark [172] uses global identifiers to enable end-to-end communication. iMark employs virtual networks to distinguish between infrastructure providers and service providers (providing virtual resources), as these can be different entities. Virtual networks are organized hierarchically, where controllers are the elements that provide name resolution and address location inside a network, while adapters are responsible for protocol/address translation between virtual networks. iMark supports simultaneous connections, even on heterogeneous networks, by using distinct global identifiers. iMark also distinguishes the type of mobility, in order to manage the respective updates; at the micro-level updates occur inside a virtual network, while at the macro-level end-users connect to a different virtual network. The iMark specification lacks some details, namely how identifiers are generated and in what form they are provided (e.g., FQDN). The evaluation in a testbed demonstrates the scalability of the proposal, but the respective code is not publicly available.

9.3.3 HiiMap

HiiMap [173] is a locator–identifier split approach that uses DHT to perform mapping between identifiers and locators. The novelty of HiiMap is the introduction of a region prefix (RP) in the unique identifier (UID). By employing RP, networks can be organized hierarchically and deploy trust relations between the global authority (GA) and local authorities of the different regions (countries). Addresses in HiiMap include the UID that is a flat, and randomized worldwide unique 128 bit address and is attributed by the GA. The region prefix identifies the region where mapping the UID to the corresponding locator is performed (can be compared to the home network in Mobile IP). HiiMap has an implementation in a testbed but no public code is available. Nonetheless, migration plans are provided. HiiMap supports mobility between networks and between regions, since locators are updated in the home region. It also includes security mechanisms to provide authentication of the identity of end–nodes.

9.3.4 Scalable and Secure Identifier-to-Locator Mapping Service (SILMS)

Scalable and Secure Identifier-to–Locator Mapping Service (SILMS) [174] is a hybrid approach that introduces modifications in end-hosts and in the network. SILMS is a locator–identifier split approach that optimizes lookups on the mapping services by caching the most frequent maps in all service nodes. The most important maps are determined via Bloom filters (probabilistic data structures) and with management servers that collect statistics about mapping data. The identifier in SILMS follows the same logic of HIP, and the locator corresponds to an IPv6 address. SILMS supports flow distribution by introducing a hierarchical architecture, where policy and management servers are responsible for flow policies, while border routers manage local mappings and run a mapping propagation protocol. However, there is no efficient mobility support and no public implementation is available.

9.3.5 MILSA

The Mobility and Multihoming support Identifier Locator Split Architecture (MILSA) [175] is a locator–identifier split proposal that introduces different hierarchies in the network, namely the Real-Zone Bridging Server (RZBS) hierarchy and the Realm Hierarchy. The Realm Hierarchy corresponds to a logical concept, in which the trust relationships between different groups of objects are maintained. The RZBS Hierarchy contains an overlay network of RZBS servers which map identifiers to locators. MILSA does not affect DNS and includes support for mobility. Enhanced MILSA (EMILSA) [176] avoids global routing and improves MILSA with respect to mobility and multihoming. EMILSA does not affect DNS as the Loc/ID-based proposal introduces different hierarchies in the network. In addition, a specific sublayer is added in the network layer to perform the separation between identifiers and locators. Nevertheless, the (E)MILSA architecture remains at an early stage of development and no code for simulation or real testbed is publicly available.

9.3.6 TurfNet

TurfNet [177] is a locator–identifier split approach and aims to enable the communication between autonomous and heterogeneous networks that may use different address schemes. A new host identity namespace is introduced, and the network is composed vertically (relation between ISP and customer) and/or horizontally (between peer networks), denominating the composed networks by turfs. Registration and lookup services enable inter-turf communication and announce the reachability of end–nodes outside their local turfs. Gateways keep soft-state of the communications of the local turf-nodes and inter-turf gateways perform locator and protocol translation for packets traversing different turfs. The TurfNet proposal supports mobility, even when end–nodes move between heterogeneous domains, since nodes are required to register with the lookup service. The proposal is evaluated empirically [178] to demonstrate its scalability performance. Nonetheless, no public implementation is available.

9.3.7 Postmodern Internet Architecture (PoMo)

Postmodern Internet Architecture (PoMo) [179] is a new architecture that enables the control of flows by users and operators. This architecture is based on a locator–identifier split approach and enables applications to obtain information about the status of network (e.g., cross-layer information). PoMo organizes the network hierarchically and includes motivation functionalities. Motivations include the reasons to proceed with forwarding. Nevertheless in PoMo extra-information in packets is needed to convey information to enable such mechanism [161]. PoMo supports flow distribution, mobility and resilience mechanisms, but has no public implementation.

9.3.8 Hierarchical Architecture for Internet Routing (HAIR)

HAIR [180] introduces different levels of hierarchy with the goals of supporting mobility, traffic engineering and reducing the size of routing tables. The hybrid nature of this proposal relies in the fact that some functionalities are removed from the core of the network and are placed on end-nodes. In this case, end-nodes have the function of translating identifiers and locators, while functions to assure scalability are placed in the network. The mapping service is distributed at the authorities owning such mapping. The hierarchical organization of HAIR includes edges, where hosts are attached, intermediate with routers to allow routing between edges and core, and finally the core. Intermediate routers are responsible to manage locators and mappings in the intermediate network mapping. When a node needs to communicate with another, it first retrieves the identification of the destination (e.g., via DNS) and then it needs to find the respective location. For such, a query is performed on the mapping system. One of the drawbacks of HAIR is that it does not include specification on the format of identifiers [145]. Nevertheless, HAIR has an implementation for demonstration purposes [181].

9.3.9 Hierarchical Inter-Domain Routing Architecture (HIDRA)

The Hierarchical Inter-Domain Routing Architecture (HIDRA) [145] is a proposal with two concerns, the first one is to reduce the size of routing tables at core networks and the second is related with deployment concerns. HIDRA is a hierarchical network architecture that uses mapping and encapsulation, and also employs IPv4 addresses for location and identification purposes, to maximize the compatibility with existent approaches. HIDRA uses BGP as a proactive mapping system (with the overhead of transmitting routes that may not be necessary), nevertheless the mapping devices are placed at the edges, near end-nodes. In an optimized HIDRA mode, end-nodes can perform encapsulation before transmission. In a reactive mapping mode, HIDRA adds more information to the mapping (e.g., priority) enabling traffic engineering. As one of the concerns in HIDRA is deployment, detailed steps are provided to enable migration from existing architectures to HIDRA. For instance, a default route must be installed to send all traffic to an encapsulation point. An implementation in a Linux testbed is used to test HIDRA. Nevertheless, reactive mapping optimizations are not specified.

Hybrid proposals rely on the locator-identifier split paradigm, nonetheless, some organize the network in an hierarchical way to facilitate deployment and management. The Node ID Internetworking Architecture (NIIA) [170] organizes the network as a tree, and employs default routes to parent nodes to enable inter-domain routing. In addition, NIIA supports multiple registration of nodes in the tree (useful when there are multiple interfaces). Notwithstanding, no implementations are available, as summarized in Table 8. Less-Is-More Architecture (LIMA) [171] uses a hierarchical structure to enable efficient inter-domain routing and relies on transport protocols such as SCTP and MPTCP to enable multiaddressing configurations. iMark [172] includes support for simultaneous connections between heterogeneous networks. Nonetheless, details to enable its implementation are missing, such as the mechanism to generate identifiers. HiiMap [173] organizes the network according to a region prefix, allowing trust relationships with authorities. MILSA [175] has the advantage of not introducing changes on DNS, or even relying on this service to support mobility.

Hierarchical Architecture for Internet Routing (HAIR) [180] is a hierarchical proposal that aims to enable traffic engineering and puts emphasis on the role of end-hosts by moving core functionalities to end-hosts. Nonetheless, it lacks details regarding identifiers. Hierarchical Inter-Domain Routing Architecture (HIDRA) [145] is also a proposal that aims to foster deployment. For instance, it relies on existing routing protocols such as BGP to allow a proactive mapping system. Proposals, like Hierarchical Routing Architecture (HRA) [169] support mobility by extending HIP and BGP protocols. SILMS [174] has the limitation of only supporting IPv6.

Instead of aiming compatibility, other proposals pursue a security-oriented paradigm. PoMo [179] and Node ID Internetworking Architecture (NIIA) [170] include native security mechanisms, aiming to protect the identity of nodes.

9.4 Map and Encapsulation

This subsection details proposals that implement the locator-identifier split paradigm through mapping and encapsulation mechanisms. The Internet Indirection Infrastructure (I3) [182] is among the first Loc/ID split approaches, where packets contain data and identifiers. A server holds the role of mapping identifiers to locators. The namespace is based on DHTs, and I3 employs the concept of triggers to announce services (e.g., web-service). Nonetheless, I3 is prone to security issues, namely, denial-of-service attacks. With this in mind, secure-i3 [183] has been proposed, with the principle of hiding end-node addresses. Host identity indirection infrastructure (Hi3) [184] combines secure-i3 and HIP and introduces better multihoming support by introducing identifier layers for service and hosts. The Dynamic Recursive Unified Internet Design (DRUID) [185] is an architecture where the data, control, management and security planes are unified, so that different planes can act coordinated in the presence of events (attacks, failures, etc).

Table 8 Comparison of hierarchical multihoming proposals.

Protocol	Approach	Multihoming Goals				Strengths	Weak Aspects	Implementation	
		R	U	L	F			Simulators	OS
LIMA	Loc/ID split	✓	✓	✓	✓	Includes protocols supporting multihoming	Requires changes to DHCP and DNS	–	–
iMark	Loc/ID split	✓	✓	✓	✓	Support concurrent connections	Specification not complete	–	–
HiiMap	Loc/ID split	✓	✓	X	X	Support security	No public implementation available	–	–
HRA	Loc/ID split	✓	✓	X	X	Scalable and supports mobility	Does not support flow distribution	–	–
SILMS	Loc/ID split	✓	X	X	✓	Supports flow distribution	Only for IPv6	–	–
MILSA	Loc/ID split	✓	✓	✓	✓	Supports flow distribution	No public implementation	–	–
TurfNet	Loc/ID split	✓	✓	X	X	Supports mobility	No public implementation	–	–
NIIA	Loc/ID split	✓	✓	X	X	Includes security	No public implementation	–	–
PoMo	Loc/ID split	✓	✓	✓	✓	Includes security	Extra-information on packets	–	–
HAIR	Routing architecture	✓	✓	✓	✓	Hierarchical network organization	Missing details on implementation	–	In Linux [181]
HIDRA	Routing architecture	✓	✓	✓	✓	Includes deployment concerns	Optimize mode not specified (e.g., reactive)	–	In Linux [145]

But DRUID is rather a conceptual architecture that relies on trust between different components and supports neither mobility nor flow distribution. Another proposal with enhanced security support but with limited multi-homing support is the Split Naming/Forwarding (SNF) architecture [186] that includes three namespaces: the Fully Qualified Domain Name (FQDN) acting as identifiers, locators based on IP addresses, and ephemeral correspondent identifier (ECI) used to identify packets, which avoid sending identifiers. SNF in comparison to DRUID supports mobility but has no resilience built-in mechanism. Some proposals, like the HIP Mobile Router (HIP-MR) [187] extend protocols to enable hybrid multihoming support. For instance, in HIP-MR the mobile router maintains bindings of the mobile nodes, so that on mobility events peers can be updated with the location of mobile nodes. Nonetheless, this type of solution is limited to nodes supporting the extended protocol, in the case of HIP-MR, HIP nodes. General Internet Signaling Transport (GIST) Overlay Networking Extension, or GONE [188], also combines multiple protocols such as GIST, SCTP, and HIP to enable support for multihoming and resilience against failures and DoS attacks. GONE in comparison to HIP-MR supports all multihoming goals, but has the disadvantage of introducing signaling overhead. Some proposals focus on supporting multiple technologies. For instance, Spontaneous Virtual Networks (SpotVNet) [189] supports Bluetooth and others by employing cross-layer mechanisms. However, such characteristic does not enhance multihoming support, as no flow distribution or load sharing features are supported.

9.4.1 LISP Mobile Node

LISP-MN [11] is a version of LISP that targets mobile nodes. Some of the functionalities of Ingress and Egress Tunnel routers of LISP are placed on the mobile node. As such, the node has capabilities of handling mobility without the assistance of servers in the network. LISP Mobile Nodes behave as a LISP site, updating locators in the associated mapping system when performing handovers. The identifiers (EID), also employed in LISP, do not change and are used in all the connections of the LISP Mobile Node.

As pictured in Fig. 8, LISP Mobile Node (node S), receives a new Routing Locator (RLOC), when connecting to ISP2. Afterwards, the respective mappings need to be updated. For such, the MN sends a Solicit-Map-Request (SMR) message, which is intercepted by next-hop LISP routers which, in turn, forward the message as Map-Request to the mapping server, which replies with a Map-Reply message. Nodes need to be compliant with the

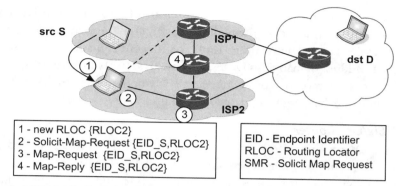

1 - new RLOC {RLOC2}
2 - Solicit-Map-Request {EID_S,RLOC2}
3 - Map-Request {EID_S,RLOC2}
4 - Map-Reply {EID_S,RLOC2}

EID - Endpoint Identifier
RLOC - Routing Locator
SMR - Solicit Map Request

Fig. 8. LISP Mobile Node handover.

LISP Mobile Node specification, nevertheless, a mapping server can be employed to allow the communication with non LISP nodes. Moreover, the proposal has an implementation available.

9.4.2 Unmanaged Internet Architecture (UIA)

UIA [190] is compatible with current IP architecture and can be incrementally deployed. UIA targets personal devices and specifies a transport protocol—Structure Stream Transport (SST) to enable efficient transport of streams. SST has the advantage of supporting transactions like HTTP, nevertheless it does not have multihoming features like SCTP does (e.g., primary-backup model). UIA integrates a routing architecture that enables peer devices to communicate in an ad hoc way. Moreover, security and privacy are included natively. Distributed hash tables are employed to hold the mappings of locators and identifiers.

9.4.3 Delegation-Oriented Approach (DOA)

DOA [191] focuses on the specification on middleboxes (e.g., NAT, firewalls) to eliminate their side-effects (e.g., alter or hinder end-to-end communication between peers) and to facilitate implementation, as middleboxes are commonplace nowadays. DOA does not eliminate middleboxes, but as a locator-identifier split approach, it provides identifiers to hosts and means to end-nodes to perform delegation (if packets should be/or not sent off-path boxes). The Entity Identifier (EID) identifies the end-node, while the IP address is employed as a locator. EIDs, acting as global identifiers, are generated with public keys and are placed into each packet (DOA introduces modifications in packet headers). A mapping infrastructure is also needed.

Mappings can be in the tuple EID, IP address or EID to a list of EIDs. The latter one reflects the nodes on which the packet goes through the delegated nodes before reaching destination [126]. The Erecord contains the mappings and the IP address of mappings DOA implements security mechanisms, since EIDs can only be modified by the respective end-nodes. Nevertheless, it does not include mechanisms to update locators in mobility events [126].

9.4.4 Six/One Router

The Six/One router [192] introduces the translation between provider-independent and provider-dependent addresses. Six/One router has some similarities with Shim6 as it uses one of the locators for the node identity during the session and only targets IPv6 networks. The translation of addresses is assured by specific hardware that performs translation of network source and destination addresses. If the mapping holds records for source and destination addresses, Six/One can support multihoming and mobility, nevertheless mapping must be assured by an external specification such as DNS. One major advantage of Six/One is communicating with non Six/One routers [145] and the reduced size of the routing table and the update frequency. Flow diversity is enabled in Six/One with the extended proposal [193] that adds monitoring features and inform upper layers (e.g., TCP) on the best performant paths.

Locator-identifier proposals support mobility and allow incremental deployments. End-host and end-site multihoming approaches tend to merge into one approach that enables both types of multihoming—hybrid multihoming, as Table 9 summarizes. LISP-MN [11] extends LISP [12], an end-site multihoming approach, to enhance mobile nodes capabilities, regarding mobility and multihoming support. HIP Mobile Router [187] extends HIP to support end-site multihoming. Such support relies on the delegation that end-hosts perform on mobile routers, to manage mobility. Proposals like Six/One Router [192], have a limitation, as they only apply to IPv6.

Dynamic Recursive Unified Internet Design (DRUID) [185] unifies data, management, control and security planes to allow a unified coordination in the presence of events. Despite following Loc/ID split paradigm, DRUID fails to be a complete specification (e.g., mapping system details), which limits its deployment. Tailored for events, the Indirection Infrastructure (I3) [182] introduces the concept of triggers, which end-hosts must use to indicate their interest in certain data (e.g., web-service). The concept relies on triggers (data), which enable native multicast or anycast support, useful when there is more than one node interested in a certain data type. I3 has security issues, but has been extended to improve its security [183].

Table 9 Comparison of map and encapsulation multihoming proposals.

Protocol	Approach	Multihoming Goals				Strengths	Weak Aspects	Implementation	
		R	U	L	F			Simulators	OS
LISP-MN	Loc/ID split	✓	✓	X	X	Mobility support	No load sharing	–	LISPMob [194]
HIP MR	Loc/ID split	✓	✓	X	X	Security	For HIP-aware nodes only	–	In Linux [195]
DRUID	Loc/ID split	✓	X	X	X	Includes trustiness.	No mobility support	–	–
I3	Loc/ID split	✓	✓	X	X	Supports multicast/anycast services	Security issues	–	In Linux [196]
DOA	Loc/ID split	✓	X	X	X	Includes security mechanisms	No mobility support	–	–
Six/One Router	Loc/ID split	✓	✓	✓	✓	Can support flow distribution	Only for IPv6	–	–
SNF	Loc/ID split	X	✓	X	X	Includes security	Limited resilience support	–	–
SpotVNet	Loc/ID split	✓	✓	X	X	Incremental deployment	No advance Multihoming mechanisms	–	–
GONE	Loc/ID split	✓	✓	✓	✓	Good multihoming support	Signaling overhead	–	In Linux [197]

SNF [186] introduces translation gateways to enable communication between domains, and supports security but, similarly to Delegation Oriented Approach (DOA) [191], it does not support mobility. Some proposals aim to allow incremental deployments, as such, for example, [189] which support incremental deployments. Unfortunately, multihoming support for current architectures is not very advanced. For instance, there is no support for resilience or flow distribution. Other proposals, like GONE [188], for an efficient multihoming support combine several protocols, which however may introduce significant signaling overhead.

9.5 New and Routing-Centric Architectures

New routing architectures try to combine the positive aspects of standards that enable services used worldwide. For instance, the Switched Internet Architecture (SIA) [198] combines aspects of the IP architecture and the telephone architecture, where addresses are organized hierarchically including a network ID and a host ID. The network ID is formed based on the geographical information (e.g., country) and organization code. The host ID corresponds to a numeric identifier, similar to a cellular number. But such kind of architecture needs to be evaluated in order to assess its benefits [161].

Other proposals for new architectures stand by a hierarchical organization of the network. For instance, Internet 3.0 [199] divides the network into multiple tiers, where the first tier corresponds to the infrastructure, the second to resources or hosts and the final tier to data and users. Internet 3.0 supports mobility, flow distribution mechanisms and resilience mechanisms. Once again, such approach needs to be evaluated in order to determine if all the tenets support security and enable scalability.

9.5.1 New Internet Routing Architecture (NIRA)

NIRA [200] is a policy-based network architecture that allows user-specified routes, and mitigates the routing problems in different components, such as route discovery, route availability discovery, route representation and packet forwarding, and provider compensation. Route discovery is performed via a dedicated protocol that divides the task of discovery between source and destination, where the first finds topological information on the domains it is connected and queries a lookup service, while the destination performs the same operations on the respective domains it is connected. On route discovery, source and destination nodes can optimize routes by sharing information between them. One drawback of the route discovery mechanism is the initial delay to establish connections. The dedicated protocol for router discovery also includes mechanisms to identify the availability of routes. NIRA employs source routing as the route representation and packet forwarding mechanism. Provider compensation relies on contractual agreements with the users and on policy checking mechanisms to prevent illegitimate route usage.

The main concern with NIRA is that it introduces too many modifications that do not facilitate deployment [145].

9.5.2 User-Controlled Routes

User-Controlled Routes [201] is a proposal to enable source routing. Users or end-hosts can select routes according to their preferences. The architecture is modular, and each module has different functionalities. For instance, one can detect the routes that are available, while another implements controls to detect failures (connectivity issues). The detection of routes requires their advertisement from operators, which advertise routes according the service level agreements. The Name-to-Route Lookup Service (NRLS) is a service that performs mapping of hosts into route maps, and is assured by the network.

Source routing is a mechanism that enables multihoming support in terms of flow distribution, but has issues, such as ingress filtering. Moreover, this proposal does not have a publicly available implementation nor mechanisms for mobility management.

9.5.3 eXpressive Internet Architecture (XIA)

XIA [202] introduces the eXpressive Internet Architecture (XIA) to enable interaction between different principals, such as users, content and services. Principals are identified by the respective identifiers. It is up to XIP communication between components placed on different hosts. XIP replaces IP, and consequently includes all the procedures to allow communication and packet structure. For instance, a XIP packet may contain information of multiple paths to a destination. XIA supports mobility, resilience, and flow distribution but no public implementation is available.

The current Internet architecture has evolved, despite the associated drawbacks (recall the dual-role of the IP address). As such, other solutions do not target the current model of Internet, but introduce new architectures that require bootstrapping (e.g., start from zero). Table 10 summarizes proposals introducing new architectures or modifying existent ones to accommodate new functionalities.

In a future vision of services, successor of Web 2.0, Internet 3.0 [199] introduces multiple tiers to support security and policies between the

Table 10 Comparison of new and routing-centric multihoming proposals.

Protocol	Approach	Multihoming Goals			Strengths	Weak Aspects	Implementation	
		R	U	L	F			Simulators	OS
NIRA	Routing architecture	√	X	√	√	Supports policies	Initial round trip time to establish connections	–	–
Internet 3.0	New architecture	√	√	√	√	Strong security support	Not implemented	–	–
User-Controlled	Routing architecture	√	X	√	√	Supports flow distribution	No implementation	–	–
Switched Internet	Routing architecture	√	√	X	X	Security support	No implementation	–	–
XIA	Routing architecture	√	√	√	√	Security support	No implementation	–	–

different entities. As such, multihoming support is high in the research agenda but no implementation is available to assess such enhancement regarding multihoming and support for future services. The Switched Internet Architecture [198] merges aspects of the IP architecture and telephone systems to improve location and identification in the Internet. Nonetheless, the benefits of such merge are not clear [161]. eXpressive Internet Architecture (XIA) [202] is also a proposal that includes an architecture where the components are the users, content and services. With such concepts, a packet may contain information of multiple paths to a destination, but a public implementation is not available.

Proposals, such as New Internet Routing Architecture (NIRA) [200], and User-Controlled Routes [201], have the drawback of introducing high delay in address configuration, or have a limited mobility support, but enable the support of flow distribution.

The best approach for an efficient hybrid multihoming support is not clear, as each one has its own advantages and disadvantages. Content-centric proposals focus their specification on content/information, which is nowadays the main usage of current architectures (e.g., access, update, share information). Solutions that consider the goal of information transfer might be a good paradigm to follow. The address of a packet is not relevant, what really matters is its content. Questions arise regarding the representation of such content, how to disseminate it and how to assure privacy [161].

Locator-identifier split approaches break the dual-role of current IP addresses. This is an advance regarding multihoming support. But this characteristic by its own is not enough to meet multihoming, mobility challenges. The way the locator-identifier split paradigm can be explored includes hierarchical organization of networks, efficient and scalable mapping systems (e.g., map identifier to locator), or new architectures that break the compatibility with the current IP architecture. Current solutions do extend, or include HIP functionalities, to enable identification of nodes. For instance, HIP Mobile Router [187] and GONE [188] incorporate HIP to allow unique and secure identities. Another aspect to consider is the placement and type of mapping systems. If centrally organized, they can represent a point-of-failure or have scalability issues. When distributed, they can scale better, but lookups might not be efficient [174].

Proposals, where implementation must be done from scratch, must have their benefits validated, as the price to pay for deployment is high. New architectures fall into this type of proposals. The native security support is an attractive point, others can also be pointed as the bleeding edge, such as the ability to coordinate path selection between users and service operators.

Further details can be found on the following references: [9, 41, 126, 145, 161].

10. OUTLOOK AND CONCLUSIONS

As we have seen, multihoming may require support from all layers in the Internet protocol stack, including applications. Of course, the decision to place the bulk of multihoming support at any particular layer comes with its own advantages and drawbacks. Typically, one resorts to the utilization of different paths according to preference sets, for instance, based on bandwidth and delay estimates. An application which supports multihoming may be better suited to control its flows with much finer granularity than what is possible, say, for example, with HIP and a set of static policies. On the other hand, in the absence of scalable source routing mechanisms, applications cannot be assured that their preferences will always be attended to with the current crop of transport protocols. Furthermore, presently there is no standard mechanism for sharing network path information with the applications. As such, advanced applications usually employ active and passive measurement mechanisms and/or participate in overlay networks in order to obtain a better view of network performance across different paths.

From an end-host perspective we find that there is lack of standard mechanisms for address selection, taking into consideration upper-layer requirements, such that, for instance, real-time applications require faster paths while data applications require paths with more bandwidth. We argue that an efficient multihoming protocol cannot be coupled with a single layer, but instead it must be the result of cooperation between multiple layers, which act in a concerted manner to meet the same goals. Earlier research in this area [203, 204] laid the groundwork, but much more needs to be done. Applications can share information, in a cross-layer fashion and enforce decisions according to their requirements via protocol APIs. Care should be taken, so that the functions belonging to a layer do not overlap with others, or that applications do not take decisions that break the functionality of layers below.

From an end-site perspective, multihoming proposals should not focus only on routing scalability. Instead they should incorporate support for the diverse multihoming goals natively, rather than relying on extensions. For instance, improved resilience support should not come at the expense of mobility support. Going a step further, hybrid multihoming gives us the possibility of employing protocols, both as end-host and end-site solution. The advantages of having protocols at the end-host cooperating to achieve a goal can be extended to the network domain, where different hosts in an end-site cooperate to achieve efficient multihoming support in future networks. Hybrid multihoming has some issues that include the choice of nodes to hold particular functionalities. For instance, if mapping should be kept at nodes closer to end-hosts, or even if nodes should cooperate to enable distributed mappings. In addition, how nodes can cooperate in this matter is an issue that deservers further research. End-site and hybrid multihoming proposals can have issues with mapping systems. While DNS is the standard nowadays, it has limited support for mobility and security. In the future, perhaps dynamic hash tables will enable distribution of mapping data, and support security to a greater extent.

Other architectures, somehow compliant with the Loc/ID split paradigm, have been proposed. For instance, routing can be based on names, which translate the interest that a certain node has to data, or to a service. Such architectures may break compatibility with the current Internet protocol stack. When deployment concerns arise, such can be an issue.

Another important aspect to consider is the analysis of forthcoming solutions. Scalability, security, implementation, compatibility or disruption with existing architectures constitute a more appropriate set of criteria to consider. Software-defined networking [205] enable testing in current devices (e.g., simple switches). OpenFlow is, therefore, a new tool to consider when evaluating the aforementioned criteria for multihoming solutions.

ACKNOWLEDGMENTS

Bruno Sousa would like to acknowledge the support of the PhD Grant SFRH/BD/61256/2009 from Ministério da Ciência, Tecnologia e Ensino Superior, FCT, Portugal. This work has also been supported by CoFIMOM project PTDC/EIA-EIA/116173/2009 and TRONE project CMU-PT/RNQ/0015/2009.

Acronyms

AIS	Aggregation with Increasing Scopes
API	Application Programming Interface
BGP	Border Gateway Protocol
CCID	Congestion Control IDentifier
CCN	Content-Centric Network
CCoA	Collocated Care of Address

CGA	Cryptographically Generated Addresses
CMT	Concurrent Multipath Transfer
CRIO	Core Router-Integrated Overlay
DCCP	Datagram Congestion Control Protocol
DHCP	Dynamic Host Configuration Protocol
DHT	Distributed Hash Table
DNS	Domain Name System
DOA	Delegation Oriented Approach
DONA	Data Oriented Network Architecture
DRUID	Dynamic Recursive Unified Internet Design
ECMP	Equal Cost Multipath
FMIPv6	Fast Mobile IPv6
FQDN	Fully Qualified Domain Name
FTP	File Transfer Protocol
HA	Home Agent
HAIR	Hierarchical Architecture for Internet Routing
HBA	Hash Based Address
HIDRA	Hierarchical Inter-Domain Routing Architecture
HIP	Host Identity Protocol
HIT	Host Identification Tag
HMIPv6	Hierarchical Mobile IPv6
HRA	Hierarchical Routing Architecture
I3	Internet Indirection Infrastructure
IANA	Internet Assigned Numbers Authority
ICN	Information-Centric Network
IETF	Internet Engineering Task Force
ILNP	Identifier Locator Network Protocol
INS	Intentional Naming System
IP	Internet Protocol
IPMIP	IP network multipathing
IPNL	IP Next Layer
IPvLX	IP with Virtual Link Extension
LIMA	Less-Is-More Architecture
LISP	Locator Identifier Separation Protocol
Loc/ID	Locator-Identifier
MIP	Mobile IP
MIPv6	Mobile IPv6
MPTCP	Multipath Transport Control Protocol
mSCTP	Mobile SCTP

NAROS	Name Address and Route System
NBS	Name Based Sockets
NDN	Name Data Networking
NEMO	Network Mobility
NetInf	Network Information
NIIA	Node ID Internetworking Architecture
NIRA	New Internet Routing Architecture
NNC	Networking Named Content
PERM	Practical End-host Multihoming
PRISM	Proxy-based Inverse Multiplexer
RA	Router Advertisement
RTT	Round Trip Time
SACKs	Selective Acknowledgements
SCTP	Stream Control Transport Protocol
SIA	Switched Internet Architecture
SIP	Session Initiation Protocol
SHIM6	Site Multihoming by IPv6 Intermediation
SNF	Split Naming/Forwarding
SSL	Secure Socket Layer
TCP	Transport Connection Protocol
TLS	Transport Layer Security
TRIAD	Translating Relaying Internet Architecture integrating Active Directories
TRRP	Tunneling Route Reduction Protocol
UDP	User Datagram Protocol
UIA	Unmanaged Internet Architecture
URI	Universal Resource Identifier
ViAggre	Virtual Aggregation
WLAN	Wireless Local Area Network
XIA	eXpressive Internet Architecture
XIP	eXpressive Internet Protocol

REFERENCES

[1] L. Budzisz, R. Ferrús, A. Brunstrom, K.-J. Grinnemo, R. Fracchia, G. Galante, F. Casadevall, Towards transport-layer mobility: evolution of SCTP multihoming, Computer Commun. 31 (5) (2008) 980–998.

[2] K.-S. Kong, W. Lee, Y.-H. Han, M.-K. Shin, H. You, Mobility management for All-IP mobile networks: Mobile IPv6 vs. Proxy Mobile IPv6, Wireless Commun. 15 (2) (2008) 36–45.

[3] R. Wakikawa (Ed.), Multiple Care-of Addresses Registration, IETF RFC: 5648, October 2009.

[4] G. Tsirtsis, H. Soliman, N. Montavont, G. Giaretta, K. Kuladinithi, Flow Bindings in Mobile IPv6 and Nemo Basic Support, IETF RFC: 6089, January 2011.

[5] J. Rosenberg, H. Schulzrinne, G. Camarillo, A. Johnston, J. Peterson, R. Sparks, M. Handley, E. Schooler, SIP: Session Initiation Protocol, IETF RFC: 3261, June 2002.

[6] N. Seta, H. Miyajima, L. Zhang, All-SIP mobility: session continuity on handover in heterogeneous access environment, in: Proceedings of the VTC2007-Spring, IEEE, April 2007, pp. 1121–1126.

[7] A. Gurtov, Host Identity Protocol (HIP): Towards the Secure Mobile Internet, Wiley Series, 2008.

[8] A. Garcia-Martinez, Marcelo, Bagnulo, I. Van Beijnum, The Shim6 architecture for IPv6 multihoming, Commun. Mag. 48 (9) (2010) 152–157.

[9] T. Li, Recommendation for a Routing Architecture, IETF RFC: 6115, February 2011.

[10] R. Atkinson, S. Bhatti, S. Hailes, Evolving the internet architecture through naming, J. Sel. Areas Commun. 28 (8) (2010) 1319–1325.

[11] D. Farinacci, D. Lewis, D. Meyer, C. White, LISP Mobile Node, IETF Draft: draft-meyer-lisp-mn (work in progress), October 2012.

[12] M. Dave, The locator identifier separation protocol (LISP), Internet Protocol J. 11 (1) (2008) 23–36.

[13] B. Sousa, K. Pentikousis, M. Curado, Multihoming management for future networks, Mobile Networks Appl. (MONET) 16 (2011) 505–517.

[14] T. Moore, D. Pym, C. Ioannidis, Internet Multi-Homing Problems: Explanations from Economics, first ed., Springer, 2010, pp. 67–78 (Chapter 5).

[15] S. Shinta, K. RyoJi, O, ToshiKane, A Comparative analysis of multihoming solutions, Inform. Processing Soc. Jpn (IPSJ) 120 (2006) 209–216.

[16] C. De Launois, M. Bagnulo, The Paths Toward IPv6 Multihoming, Commun. Surveys Tuts 8 (2) (2006) 38–51.

[17] G. Fekete, T. Hämäläinen, State of host-centric multihoming in IP networks, in: Proceedings of the NTMS '09, IEEE, December 2009, pp. 1–5.

[18] M. Bagnulo, A.G. Martinez, A. Azcorra, C. de Launois, An incremental approach to IPv6 multihoming, Computer Commun. 29 (5) (2006) 582–592.

[19] M. Blanchet, P. Seite, Multiple Interfaces and Provisioning Domains Problem Statement, IETF RFC: 6418, November 2011.

[20] R. Braden (Ed.), Requirements for Internet Hosts—Communication Layers, IETF RFC: 1122, October 1989.

[21] Q. Wang, R. Atkinson, J. Dunlop, Design and evaluation of flow handoff signalling for multihomed mobile nodes in wireless overlay networks, Comput. Networks 52 (8) (2008) 1647–1674.

[22] J. Abley, B.Black, V.Gill, Goals for IPv6 Site-Multihoming Architectures, IETF RFC: 3582, August 2003.

[23] A. Dhraief, N. Montavont, Toward mobility and multihoming unification-the Shim6 protocol: a case study, in: Proceedings of the WCNC '08, IEEE, March–April 2008, pp. 2840–2845.

[24] J. Day, Patterns in Network Architecture: A Return to Fundamentals, Prentice Hall PTR, 2008.

[25] C. Ng, T. Ernst, E. Paik, M. Bagnulo, Analysis of Multihoming in Network Mobility Support, IETF RFC: 4980, October 2007.

[26] T. Ernst J. Charbon, Multihoming with NEMO basic support, in: Proceedings of the ICMU '04, IPSJ, January 2004.

[27] Younghwan Choi, Bongsoo Kim, Sang-Ha Kim, Minkyo In, Seungyun Lee, A Multihoming mechanism to support network mobility in next generation networks, in: Proceedings of the APCC '06, IEEE, August 2006, pp. 1–5.

[28] Jorge Espi, Robert Atkinson, Ivan Andonovic, John Dunlop, Proactive route optimization for fast Mobile IPv6, in: Proceedings of the VTC 2009-Fall, vol. 6, IEEE, September 2009, pp. 1–5.

[29] J. Iyengar, P. Amer, R. Stewart, Concurrent multipath transfer using SCTP multihoming over independent end-to-end paths, IEEE/ACM Trans. Network 14 (5) (2006) 951–964.

[30] S. Pierrel, P. Jokela, J. Melen, K. Slavov, A policy system for simultaneous multiaccess with host identity protocol, in: Proceedings of the ACNM '07, IEEE, May 2007, pp. 71–77.

[31] V. Ishakian, I. Matta, J. Akinwumi, On the cost of supporting mobility and multihoming, in: Proceedings of the GLOBECOM '10, No. 1, IEEE, December 2010, pp. 310–314.

[32] Upendra Rathnayake, Henrik Petander, Maximilian Ott, Aruna Seneviratne, Protocol support for bulk transfer architecture, in: Proceedings of the WCNIS '10, IEEE June 2010, pp. 598–602.

[33] N. Montavont, R. Wakikawa, T. Ernst, C. Ng, K. Kuladinithi, Analysis of Multihoming in Mobile IPv6, IETF Draft: draft-ietf-monami6-mipv6-analysis (work in progress), May 2008.

[34] S. Hagen, IPv6 Essentials, O'Reilly Media, Inc., 2006.

[35] S. Krishnan (Ed.), Link-Layer Event Notifications for Detecting Network Attachments, IETF RFC: 4957, August 2007.

[36] J. Fitzpatrick, S. Murphy, M. Atiquzzaman, J. Murphy, Using cross-layer metrics to improve the performance of end-to-end handover mechanisms, Computer Commun. 32 (15) (2009) 1600–1612.

[37] E. Nordmark, M. Bagnulo, Shim6: Level 3 Multihoming Shim Protocol for IPv6, IETF RFC: 5533, June 2009.

[38] R. Stewart (Ed.), Stream Control Transmission Protocol, IETF RFC: 4960, September 2007.

[39] Kostas Pentikousis, Distributed Information Object Resolution, in Proceedings of the ICN '09, IEEE, March 2009, pp. 360–366.

[40] M. Bagnulo, A.G. Martinez, A. Azcorra, C. de Launois, An incremental approach to IPv6 multihoming, Computer Commun. 29 (5) (2006) 582–592.

[41] R. Jain, S. Paul, Future wireless networks: key issues and a survey (ID/locator split perspective), Int. J. Commun. Network Distrib. Syst. 8 (1/2) (2012) 24–52.

[42] G. Karopoulos, G. Kambourakis, S. Gritzalis, E. Konstantinou, A framework for identity privacy in SIP, J. Network Comput. Appl. 33 (1) (2010) 16–28.

[43] Rohit Verma, Media Multihoming in SIP Sessions, IETF Draft: draft-rverma-media-multihoming-over-sctp (work in progress), January 2012.

[44] J. Ubillos, M. Xu, Z. Ming, C. Vogt, Name-Based Sockets Architecture, IETF Draft: draft-ubillos-name-based-sockets (work in progress), September 2010.

[45] Mingwei Xu, Zhongxing Ming, Javier Ubillos, Christian Vogt, Name Based Sockets—Shim6, IETF Draft: draft-xu-name-shim6 (work in progress), September 2010.

[46] Zhongxing Ming, Javier Ubillos, Mingwei Xu, Name-based Shim6: a name-based approach to host mobility, SIGMOBILE Mob. Comput. Commun. Rev. 15 (4) (2012) 46–48.

[47] W. Wasserman, P. Seite, Current Practices for Multiple Interface Hosts, IETF RFC: 6419, November 2011.

[48] IBM, iSeries TCP/IP Configuration and Reference Version 5 (SC41-5420-04), May 2001.

[49] Sun, System Administration Guide: IP Services, April 2009.

[50] C. Benvenutti, Understanding Linux Network Internals, O'Reilly, December, 2005.

[51] Q. li, K. Macy, Optimizing the BSD routing system for parallel processing, in: Proceedings of the PRESTO '09, ACM, August 2009.

[52] RedHat, Starting and Stopping vsftpd, <https://access.redhat.com/knowledge/docs/en-US/RedHatEnterpriseLinux/6/html/DeploymentGuide/s2-ftp-vsftpd-start.html>, (accessed 30.11.2012).

[53] RedHat, Configuring a Multihomed DHCP Server, <https://access.redhat.com/knowledge/docs/en-US/RedHatEnterpriseLinux/6/html/DeploymentGuide/sect-ConfiguringaMultihomedDHCPServer.html>, (accessed 30.11.2012).

[54] A.S. Foundation, Apache Virtual Host documentation, <http://httpd.apache.org/docs/2.2/vhosts/>, (accessed 30.11.2012).

[55] A. Matsumoto, M. Kozuka, K. Fujikawa, Y. Okabe, TCP Multi-Home Options, IETF Draft: draft-arifumi-tcp-mh (work in progress), October 2003.

[56] R. Tse, TCP fairness in multipath transport protocols, Bachelor Thesis, Department of Computer Science, Brown University, May 2006.

[57] K.-H. Kim, K.G. Shin, PRISM: improving the performance of inverse-multiplexed TCP in wireless networks, IEEE Trans. Mobile Comp. 6 (12) (2007) 1297–1312.

[58] A. Ford (Ed.), Architectural Guidelines for Multipath TCP Development, IETF RFC: 6182, March 2011.

[59] A. Ford (Ed.), TCP Extensions for Multipath Operation with Multiple Addresses, Internet Draft: draft-ietf-mptcp-multiaddressed (work in progress), October 2012.

[60] E. Kohler, M. Handley, S. Floyd, Congestion Control Protocol (DCCP), IETF RFC: 4340, March 2006.

[61] M. Qureshi, M. Saleem, Simulation and visualization of transmission control protocol's (TCP) flow-control and multi-home options, in: Proceedings of the IBCAST '07, IEEE, January 2007, pp. 139–146.

[62] D.X. Wei, C. Jin, S.H. Low, S. Hegde, FAST TCP: motivation, architecture, algorithms, performance, IEEE/ACM Trans. Network 14 (6) (2006) 1246–1259.

[63] M.J. Arshad, M.S. Mian, Issues of Multihoming Implementation Using FAST TCP: A Simulation Based Analysis, Proc. IJCSNS 8 (9) (2008) 104–114.

[64] S. Belhaj, M. Tagina, VFAST TCP: an improvement of FAST TCP, in: Proceedings of the UKSIM '08, IEEE, April 2008, pp. 88–93.

[65] I. Valdovinos, J. Diaz, TCP extension to send traffic simultaneously through multiple heterogeneous network interfaces, in: Proceedings of the ENC '09, IEEE, September 2009, pp. 89–94.

[66] M. Scharf, A. Ford, MPTCP Application Interface Considerations, IETF Draft: draft-ietf-mptcp-api (work in progress), October 2012.

[67] F. Siddiqui, S. Zeadally, SCTP multihoming support for handoffs across heterogeneous networks, in: Proceedings of the CNSR '06, IEEE, May 2006, pp. 8–250.

[68] S. Charoenpanyasak, B. Paillassa, SCTP multihoming with cross layer interface in ad hoc multihomed networks, in: Proceedings of the WiMOB '07, IEEE, October 2007, p. 46.

[69] R. Stewart, K. Poon, M. Tuexen, V. Yasevich, P. Lei, Sockets API Extensions for Stream Control Transmission Protocol (SCTP), IETF RFC: 6458, December 2011.

[70] R. Stewart, Q. Xie, M. Tuexen, S. Maruyama, M. Kozuka, Stream Control Transmission Protocol (SCTP) Dynamic Address Reconfiguration, IETF RFC: 5061, September 2007.

[71] S. Floyd, E. Kohler, Profile for Datagram Congestion Control Protocol (DCCP) Congestion Control ID 2: TCP-like Congestion Control, IETF RFC: 4341, March 2006.

[72] S. Floyd, E. Kohler, Profile for Datagram Congestion Control Protocol (DCCP) Congestion ID 4: TCP-Friendly Rate Control for Small Packets (TFRC-SP), IETF RFC: 5622, August 2009.

[73] Y. Lai, DCCP: transport protocol with congestion control and unreliability, Internet Comput. 12 (5) (2008) 78–83.

[74] E. Kohler, Generalized Connections in the Datagram Congestion Control Protocol, IETF Draft: draft-kohler-dccp-mobility (work in progress), June 2006.

[75] Y. Nishida, MPTCP Implementation on NS-2, <http://www.jp.nishida.org/mptcp/>, (accessed 30.11.2012).

[76] Networks Research Group—UCL, htsim—MultiPath TCP Simulator, 2012.

[77] INL—IP Networking Lab, UCL, MultiPath TCP—Linux Kernel Implementation, 2012.

[78] C.D. of Electrical and E.E.U. of Melbourne, FAST TCP Simulator Module for ns-2, <http://www.cubinlab.ee.unimelb.edu.au/ns2fasttcp/>, (accessed 30.11.2012).

[79] INET, INET Framework—Implemented Protocols, <http://inet.omnetpp.org/index.php?n=Main.Status>, 2012 (accessed 30.11.2012).

[80] K.F. e.V., SCTP, <http://www.sctp.de/sctp.html>, (accessed 30.11.2012).

[81] E. Dedu, Wireless DCCP patch in NS2, <http://lifc.univ-fcomte.fr/home/ededu/ns2/>, (accessed 30.11.2012).

[82] A. Ford, C. Raiciu, M. Handley, S. Barre, J. Iyengar, Architectural Guidelines for Multipath TCP Development, IETF RFC: 6182, March 2011.

[83] H. Kim, S. Choi, A method to support multiple interfaces a mobile node in next generation wireless network, in: Proceedings of the NCM '10, IEEE, August 2010, pp. 276–281.

[84] V. Devarapalli, N. Kant, H. Lim, C. Vogt, Multiple Interface Support with Proxy Mobile IPv6, IETF Draft: (work in progress), March 2009.

[85] T. Melia and S. Gundavelli, Logical Interface Support for Multi-Mode IP Hosts, IETF Draft: draft-ietf-netext-logical-interface-support (work in progress), October 2012.

[86] J.-Y. Pan, J.-L. Lin, K.-F. Pan, Multiple care-of addresses registration and capacity-aware preference on multi-rate wireless links, in: Proceedings of the AINA '08, IEEE, March 2008, pp. 768–773.

[87] K. Mitsuya, R. Kuntz, S. Sugimoto, R. Wakikawa, J. Murai, A policy management framework for flow distribution on multihomed end nodes, in: Proceedings of the MobiArch '07, ACM, August 2007, pp. 1–7.

[88] B. Sousa, M. Silva, K. Pentikousis, M. Curado, A multiple care of addresses model, in: Proceedings of the ISCC '11, IEEE, June–July 2011, pp. 485–490.

[89] U. Toseef, A. Udugama, C. Goerg, C. Fan, F. Pittmann, Realization of multiple access interface management and flow mobility in IPv6, in: Proceedings of the MOBIL-WARE '08, ICST, February 2008, pp. 1–8.

[90] C.J.B. (Ed.), Proxy Mobile IPv6 Extensions to Support Flow Mobility, IETF Draft: draft-ietf-netext-pmipv6-flowmob (work in progress), October 2012.

[91] T. Ernst, MobiWan: NS-2 Extensions to Study Mobility in Wide-Area IPv6 Networks, <http://www.inrialpes.fr/planete/mobiwan/> (accessed 30.11.2012).

[92] F.Z. Yousaf, C. Bauer, xMIPv6, <http://www.kn.e-technik.tu-dortmund.de/en/forschung/ausstattung/xmipv6.html>, (accessed 30.11.2012).

[93] Nautilus, Nautilus6 Project Overview—Deployment of the Mobile Internet, <http://www.nautilus6.org/> (accessed 30.11.2012).

[94] B. Sousa, Multiple Care of Address Registration in OMNet++, <http://mcoa.dei.uc.pt/> (accessed 30.11.2012).

[95] A. Boutet, B. Le Texier, J. Montavont, N. Montavont, G. Schreiner, Advantages of flow bindings: an embedded mobile network use case, in: Proceedings of the TRIDENT-COM '08, ICST, March 2008, pp. 1–5.

[96] H. Choi, Proxy Mobile IPv6 for NS-2, <http://commani.net/pmip6ns/> (accessed 30.11.2012).

[97] OpenAir3, <http://www.openairinterface.org/openairfiles/documents/papersandppt presentations/Nutshell.pdf>(accessed 30.11.2012).

[98] R. Kong, The Simulation for network mobility based on NS2, in: Proceedings of the CSSE, '08, vol. 4, IEEE, December 2008, pp. 1070–1074.

[99] R. Kuntz, Deploying reliable IPv6 temporary networks thanks to NEMO basic support and multiple care-of addresses registration, in: Proceedings of IEEE the SAINT '07, January 2007, p. 46.

[100] A. Deleplace, T. Ernst, T. Noel, Multihoming in nested mobile networks with route optimization, in: Proceedings of the SAINT '07, IEEE, January 2007, p. 49.

[101] C. Ng, P. Thubert, M. Watari, F. Zhao, Network Mobility Route Optimization Problem Statement, IETF RFC: 4888, July 2007.

[102] D. Johnson, C. Perkins, J. Arkko, Mobility Support in IPv6, IETF RFC: 6275, July 2011.

[103] R. Koodli, Mobile IPv6 Fast Handovers, IETF RFC: 5268, June 2008.

[104] Hesham Soliman, Claude Castelluccia, Karim ElMalki, Ludovic Bellier, Hierarchical Mobile IPv6 (HMIPv6) Mobility Management, IETF RFC: 5380, October 2008.

[105] S. Gundavelli, K. Leung, V. Devarapalli, K. Chowdhury, B. Patil, Proxy Mobile IPv6, IETF RFC: 5213, August 2008.

[106] V. Devarapalli, R. Wakikawa, A. Petrescu, P. Thubert, Network Mobility (NEMO) Basic Support Protocol, IETF RFC: 3963, January 2005.

[107] S. Nováczki, L. Bokor, G. Jeney, S. Imre, Design and evaluation of a novel HIP-based network mobility protocol, J. Networks 3 (1) (2008) 10–24.

[108] A. de la Oliva, I. Soto, A. Garca-Martnez, M. Bagnulo, A. Azcorra, Analytical characterization of failure recovery in REAP, Computer Commun. 33 (4) (2010) 485–499.

[109] T. Aura, Cryptographically Generated Addresses (CGA), IETF RFC: 3972, March 2005.

[110] M. Bagnulo, Hash-Based Addresses (HBA), IETF RFC: 5535, June 2009.

[111] M. Komu, M. Bagnulo, K. Slavov, S.S. (Eds.), Socket Application Program Interface (API) for Multihoming Shim, IETF RFC: 6316, July 2011.

[112] G. Fekete, Network Interface Management in Mobile and Multihomed Nodes, Ph.D. Dissertation, Faculty of Information Technology, University of Jyväskyla, June 2010.

[113] A. Gurtov, M. Komu, R. Moskowitz, Host identity protocol: identifier/locator split for host mobility and multihoming, Internet Protocol J. 12 (1) (2009) 27–32.

[114] M. Komu, T. Henderson, Basic Socket Interface Extensions for Host Identity Protocol (HIP), IETF RFC: 6317, July 2011.

[115] G. Camarillo, A. Kera nen, S. Pierrel, Automatic flow-specific multi-path management for the host identity protocol (HIP), in: Proceedings of the WCNC '10, IEEE, April 2010, pp. 1–6.

[116] J. Laganier, L. Eggert, Host Identity Protocol (HIP) Rendezvous Extension, IETF RFC: 5204, April 2008.

[117] C.D. Launois, O. Bonaventure, M. Lobelle, U.C.D. Louvain, The NAROS approach for IPv6 multihoming with traffic engineering, in: Proceedings of the QoFIS '03, Springer-Verlag, October 2003, pp. 112–121.

[118] P. Savola, T. Chown, A survey of IPv6 site multihoming proposals, in: Proceedings of the ConTEL '05, vol. 1, IEEE, June 2005, pp. 41–48.

[119] M. Dunmore, N.T. Borch, T. Chown, O. Kramer, P. Savola, Deliverable D4.5.3 Evaluation of Multihoming Solutions, <http://www.6net.org/publications/deliverables/D4.5.3.pdf>, February 2005 (accessed 30.11.2012).

[120] N. Thompson, G. He, H. Luo, Flow Scheduling for End-Host Multihoming, in Proceedings of the INFOCOM '06, IEEE, April 2006, pp. 1–12.

[121] A. Habib, N. Christin, J. Chuang, Taking Advantage of multihoming with session layer striping, in: Proceedings of the INFOCOM '07, IEEE, April 2007, pp. 1–6.

[122] T. Dierks, E. Rescorla, The Transport Layer Security (TLS) Protocol Version 1.2, IETF RFC: 5246, August 2008.

[123] David Clark, Robert Braden, Aaron Falk, V. Pingali, FARA: reorganizing the addressing architecture, SIGCOMM Comput. Commun. Rev. 33 (4) (2003) 313–321.

[124] Craig A. Shue, Minaxi Gupta, An internet without the internet protocol, Comput. Network 54 (18) (2010) 3232–3245.

[125] Bengt Ahlgren, Lars Eggert, B. Ohlman, J. Rajahalme, Andreas Schieder, Names, addresses and identities in ambient networks, in: Proceedings of the DIN '05, ACM, August–September 2005, pp. 33–37.

[126] Subharthi Paul, Jianli Pan, Raj Jain, A survey of naming systems: classification and analysis of the current schemes using a new naming reference model, Department of Computer Science & Engineering—Washington University, Technical Report, October 2009.

[127] H. Balakrishnan, K. Lakshminarayanan, S. Ratnasamy, S. Shenker, I. Stoica, M. Walfish, A layered naming architecture for the internet, SIGCOMM Comput. Commun. Rev. 34 (4) (2004) 343–352.

[128] Laszlo Bokor, Host Identity Protocol (HIP) Simulation Framework for INET/OMNeT++, <http://www.ict-optimix.eu/index.php/HIPSim>, (accessed 30.11.2012).

[129] Andrei Gurtov, InfraHIP Infrastructure for HIP, <http://infrahip.hiit.fi/>, (accessed 30.11.2012).

[130] S. Khan, OPNET Application and Network Performance, <https://enterprise1.opnet.com/tsts/4dcgi/MODELSFullDescription?ModelID=873>, (accessed 30.11.2012).

[131] INL, LinShim6, <http://inl.info.ucl.ac.be/LinShim6>, (accessed 30.11.2012).

[132] J. Arkko, I. van Beijnum, Failure Detection and Locator Pair Exploration Protocol for IPv6 Multihoming, IETF RFC: 5534, June 2009.

[133] Pekka Nikander, HIP for Internet Project, <http://hip4inter.net/>, (accessed 30.11.2012).

[134] I. van Beijnum, BGP—Building Reliable Networks with the Border Gateway Protocol, O'Reilly Media, 2002.

[135] M. Menth, M. Hartmann, D. Klein, Global Locator, Local locator, identifier split (GLI-split), Institute of Computer Science, University of Würzburg, Technical Report 470, April 2010.

[136] Z. Turányi, A. Valkó, A.T. Campbell, 4 + 4: an architecture for evolving the internet address space back toward transparency, SIGCOMM Comput. 33 (5) (2003) 43–54.

[137] Paul Francis, Ramakrishna Gummadi, IPNL: a NAT-extended internet architecture, SIGCOMM Comput. Commun. Rev. 31 (2001) 69–80.

[138] M. Gritter, D.R. Cheriton, An architecture for content routing support in the internet, in: Proceedings of the USITS '01, USENIX Association, March 2001, pp. 4–4.

[139] Jon Crowcroft, Steven Hand, Richard Mortier, Timothy Roscoe, Andrew Warfield, Plutarch: an argument for network pluralism, SIGCOMM Comput. Commun. Rev. 33 (4) (2003) 258–266.

[140] Lakshminarayanan Subramanian, Matthew Caesar, Cheng Tien Ee, Mark Handley, Morley Mao, Scott Shenker, Ion Stoica, HLP: A next generation inter-domain routing protocol, EECS Department, University of California, Berkeley, Technical Report UCB/CSD-04-1357, October 2005.

[141] V. Khare, D. Jen, X. Zhao, Y. Liu, D. Massey, L. Wang, B. Zhang, L. Zhang, Evolution towards global routing scalability, J. Sel. Areas Commun. 28 (8) (2010) 1363–1375.

[142] F. Templin, The Internet Routing Overlay Network (IRON), IETF RFC: 6179, March 2011.

[143] D. Massey, L. Wang, B. Zhang, NeTS-FIND: Enabling Future Internet innovations through Transit wire (eFIT), <http://www.nets-find.net/Funded/eFIT.php>, 2009 (accessed 30.11.2012).

[144] Brian Dickson,V6DH: Incremental IPv6 Dual-Homing Approach for addressing end-site reliability needs (per RADIR problem statement), IETF Draft: draft-dickson-rrg-v6dh (work in progress), 2008.

[145] B. Clevenger, HIDRA: hierarchical inter-domain routing architecture, Ph.D. Dissertation, Faculty of California Polytechnic State University San Luis Obispo, 2010.

[146] W. Zhang, X. Yin, J. Wu, W. Zhang, S. Huang, Real aggregation for reducing routing information base size, JCIT 5 (6) (2010) 1–7.

[147] D. Jen, M. Meisel, D. Massey, L. Wang, B. Zhang, L. Zhang, APT: A Practical Transit Mapping Service, IETF Draft: draft-jen-apt-01 (work in progress), November 2007.

[148] Xinyang Zhang, Paul Francis, Jia Wang, K. Yoshida, Scaling IP routing with the core router-integrated overlay, in: Proceedings of the ICNP '06, IEEE, November 2006, pp. 147–156.

[149] F. Templin (Ed.), The IPvLX Architecture, IETF Draft: draft-templin-ipvlx-08 (work in progress), November 2007.

[150] William Herrin, Tunneling Route Reduction Protocol (TRRP), <http://bill.herrin.us/network/trrp.html>, (accessed 30.11.2012).

[151] OpenLisp, The OpenLisp Project, <http://www.openlisp.org/>, (accessed 30.11.2012).

[152] Zoltán Turányi, András Valkó, Andrew T. Campbell, 4+4: an architecture for evolving the Internet address space back toward transparency, SIGCOMM Comput. Commun. Rev 33 (5) (2003) 43–54.

[153] W. Adjie-Winoto, E. Schwartz, H. Balakrishnan, J. Lilley, The design and implementation of an intentional naming system, SIGOPS Oper. Syst. Rev. 34 (2) (2000) 22.

[154] Hitesh Ballani, Paul Francis, T. Cao, Jia Wang, Making routers last longer with ViAggre, in: Proceedings of the NSDI '09, USENIX symposium, April 2009, pp. 453–466.

[155] Kostas Pentikousis, Prosper Chemouil, Kathleen Nichols, George Pavlou, Dan Massey, Information-centric networking, Commun. Mag. 50 (7) (2012) 22–25.

[156] L. Zhang, D. Estrin, J. Burke, V. Jacobson, J.D. Thornton, D.K. Smetters, B. Zhang, G. Tsudik, D. Massey, C. Papadopoulos, L. Wang, P. Crowley, E. Yeh, Named Data Networking (NDN) Project, <http://www.named-data.net/techreport/TR001ndn-proj.pdf>, October 2010 (accessed 30.11.2012).

[157] Rudra Dutta, G.N. Rouskas, I. Baldine, A. Bragg, D. Stevenson, The SILO architecture for services integration, control, optimization for the future internet, in: Proceedings of the ICC '07, IEEE, June 2007, pp. 1899–1904.

[158] T. Wolf, Service-centric end-to-end abstractions in next-generation networks, in: Proceedings of the ICCCN '06, IEEE, October 2006, pp. 79–86.

[159] Henning Schulzrinne, Srinivasan Seetharaman, Volker Hilt, Collaborative Research: FIND: NetSerV? Architecture of a Service-Virtualized Internet, <http://www.nets-find.net/Funded/Netserv.php>, (accessed 30.11.2012).

[160] V. Jacobson, D. Smetters, J. Thornton, Networking named content, in: Proceedings of the CoNEXT '09, ACM, December 2009, pp. 1–12.

[161] S. Paul, J. Pan, R. Jain, Architectures for the future networks and the next generation internet: a survey, Computer Commun. 34 (1) (2011) 2–42.

[162] M. Chawla, B. Chun, A. Ermolinskiy, A data-oriented (and beyond) network architecture, SIGCOMM Comput. Commun. Rev. 37 (4) (2007) 181–192.

[163] Kostas Pentikousis, Teemu Rautio, A multiaccess network of information, in: Proceedings of the WoWMoM '10, IEEE, June 2010, pp. 1–9.

[164] Christian Dannewitz, Kostas Pentikousis, Rene Rembarz, Éric Renault, Ove Strandberg, Javier Ubillos, Scenarios and research issues for a network of information, in: Proceedings of the MobiMedia '08, ICST, May 2008.

[165] Bengt, Ahlgren, Matteo D'Ambrosio, Marco Marchisio, Ian Marsh, Christian Dan-
       newitz, Börje Ohlman, Kostas Pentikousis, Ove Strandberg, René Rembarz,Vinicio
       Vercellone, Design considerations for a network of information, in: Proceedings of the
       CoNEXT'08, ACM, 2008, pp. 66:1–66:6.
[166] Christian Dannewitz, NetInf—Network of Information, <http://www.netinf.org/
       home/home/>, (accessed 30.11.2012).
[167] Giuseppe Rossini, Dario Rossi, Raffele Chiocchetti, ccnSim, <http://perso.telecom-
       paristech.fr/~drossi/index.php?n=Software.ccnSim>, (accessed 30.11.2012).
[168] Giuseppe Rossini, Dario Rossi, Raffele Chiocchetti, CCNx team, <http://www.
       ccnx.org/software-download-information-request/download-releases/>, (accessed
       30.11.2012).
[169] Xiaohu Xu, Dayong Guo, Hierarchical routing architecture (HRA), in: Proceedings
       of the NGI '08, IEEE, April 2008, pp. 92–99.
[170] S. Schütz, H. Abrahamsson, B. Ahlgren, M. Brunner, Design and implementation of
       the node identity internetworking architecture, Comput. Networks 54 (7) (2010)
       1142–1154.
[171] J. Li, M. Manley, M. Veeraraghavan, R. Williams, A Less-is-more architecture (LIMA)
       for a future internet, in: Proceedings of the INFOCOM '12, IEEE, March 2012, pp.
       55–60.
[172] N. Chowdhury, F. Zaheer, R. Boutaba, iMark: an identity management framework for
       network virtualization environment, in: Proceedings of the IM '09, IEEE, June 2009,
       pp. 335–342.
[173] O. Hanka, G. Kunzmann, C. Spleiss, J. Eberspacher, A. Bauer, HiiMap: hierarchical
       internet mapping architecture, in: Proceedings of the ICFIN '09, IEEE, October 2009,
       pp. 17–24.
[174] Jie Hou, Liu Yaping, Gong Zhenghu, SILMS: a scalable and secure identifier-to-locator
       mapping service system design for future internet, in: Proceedings of the WCSE '09,
       vol. 1, IEEE, October 2009, pp. 54–58.
[175] J. Pan, S. Paul, R. Jain, M. Bowman, MILSA: a mobility and multihoming supporting
       identifier locator split architecture for naming in the next generation internet, in:
       Proceedings of the GLOBECOM '08, IEEE, November–December 2008, pp. 1–6.
[176] J. Pan, R. Jain, S. Paul, M. Bowman, S. Chen, Enhanced MILSA architecture for
       naming, addressing, routing and security issues in the next generation internet, in:
       Proceedings of the ICC '09, IEEE, June 2009, pp. 1–6.
[177] S. Schmid, L. Eggert, M. Brunner, Tur fNet: an architecture for dynamically composable
       networks, in: Proceedings of the DIN '05, ACM, September 2005, pp. 28–32.
[178] J. Pujol, S. Schmid, L. Eggert, M. Brunner, J. Quittek, Scalability analysis of the turfnet
       naming and routing architecture, in: Proceedings of the DIN '05, ACM, September
       2005, pp. 28–32.
[179] B. Bhattacharjee, K. Calvert, J. Griffioen, Postmodern Internetwork Architecture,
       <http://profusion.ittc.ku.edu/publications/documents/Bhattacharjee2006_Postmod_
       Arch.pdf>, The University of Kansas, Technical Report 2006 (accessed 30.11.2012).
[180] Anja Feldmann, Luca Cittadini, Wolfgang Mühlbauer, Randy Bush, O. Maennel,
       HAIR: hierarchical architecture for internet routing, in: Proceedings of the ReArch
       '09, ACM, 2009, pp. 43–48.
[181] Anja Feldmann, Luca Cittadini, Wolfgang Mühlbauer, Randy Bush, O. Maennel,
       Hairarchsite, <http://sites.google.com/site/hairarchsite/>, 2012 (accessed 30.11.
       2012).
[182] I. Stoica, Daniel Adkins, Shelley Zhuang, Scott Shenker, S. Surana, Internet indirection
       infrastructure, IEEE/ACM Trans. Network 12 (2) (2004) 205–218.
[183] D. Adkins, K. Lakshminarayanan, A. Perrig, Towards a More Functional and
       Secure Network Infrastructure, <http://www.eecs.berkeley.edu/Pubs/TechRpts/

2003/6241.html>, EECS Department, University of California, Berkeley, Technical Report UCB/CSD-03-1242, 2003 (accessed 30.11.2012).

[184] A. Gurtov, D. Korzun, A. Lukyanenko, Hi3: an efficient and secure networking architecture for mobile hosts, Comput. Commun. 31 (10) (2008) 2457–2467.

[185] J. Touch, I. Baldine, R. Dutta, G.G. Finn, B. Ford, S. Jordan, D. Massey, A. Matta, C. Papadopoulos, P. Reiher, A dynamic recursive unified internet design (DRUID), Comput. Networks 55 (4) (2011) 919–935.

[186] A. Jonsson, M. Folke, B. Ahlgren, The split naming/forwarding network architecture, in: Proceedings of the SNCNW '03, ACM, September 2003.

[187] J. Ylitalo, J. Melén, P. Salmela, H. Petander, An experimental evaluation of a HIP based network mobility scheme, in: Proceedings of the WWIC '08, Springer, May 2008, pp. 139–151.

[188] X. Fu and J. Crowcroft, GONE: an infrastructure overlay for resilient, DoS-limiting networking, in: Proceedings of the NOSSDAV '06, ACM, May 2006, pp. 18:1–18:6.

[189] Roland Bless, Christian Hbsch, Christoph P. Mayer, Oliver P. Waldhorst, SpoVNet: an architecture for easy creation and deployment of service overlays, River Publishers, 2011, (Chapter 2).

[190] B.A. Ford, UIA: a global connectivity architecture for mobile personal devices, Ph.D. Dissertation, Massachusetts Institute of Technology, September 2008.

[191] Michael Walfish, Jeremy Stribling, Maxwell Krohn, Hari Balakrishnan, Robert Morris, Scott Shenker, Middleboxes no longer considered harmful, in: Proceedings of the OSDI '04, USENIX Association, December 2004, pp. 15–15.

[192] C. Vogt, Six/one router: a scalable and backwards compatible solution for provider-independent addressing, in: Proceedings of the Mobiarch '08, ACM, August 2008, pp. 13–18.

[193] S. Paul, R. Jain, J. Pan, An identifier/locator split architecture for exploring path diversity through site multi-homing—a hybrid host-network cooperative approach, in: Proceedings of the ICC '10, IEEE, May 2010, pp. 1–5.

[194] D. Farinacci, D. Lewis, D. Meyer, C. White, LISPMob—a Deployable Network Layer Mobility Implementation for Linux, <http://lispmob.org/>, October 2011 (accessed 30.11.2012).

[195] OpenHIP, OpenHIP, <http://www.openhip.org/>, (accessed 30.11.2012).

[196] Daniel Adkins, Internet Indirection Infrastructure (i3), <http://i3.cs.berkeley.edu/>, 2006 (accessed 30.11.2012).

[197] Jan Demter and Xiaoming Fu, GONE—GIST Overlay Networking Extension, <http://user.informatik.uni-goettingen.de/fu/gone/>, (accessed 30.11.2012).

[198] V.P.N. Shenoy, Switched Internet Architecture, <http://www.nets-find.net/Funded/SWA.php>(accessed 30.11.2012).

[199] S. Paul, R. Jain, J. Pan, Multi-Tier Diversified Service Architecture for Internet 3.0: The Next Generation Internet, <http://www.cse.wustl.edu/~jain/papers/ftp/multitier.pdf>, Washington University—Department of Computer Science & Engineering, Technical Report 314, June 2010 (accessed 30.11.2012).

[200] X. Yang, D. Clark, A.W. Berger, NIRA: a new inter-domain routing architecture, IEEE/ACM Trans. Network 15 (4) (2007) 775–788.

[201] X. Yang, An Internet Architecture for User-Controlled Routes, <http://www.nets-find.net/Funded/InternetArchitecture.php>, 2006 (accessed 30.11.2012), pp. 1–15.

[202] A. Anand, F. Dogar, D. Han, B. Li, H. Lim, M. Machado, W. Wu, A. Akella, D.G. Andersen, J.W. Byers, S. Seshan, P. Steenkiste, XIA: an architecture for an evolvable and trustworthy internet, in: Proceedings of the HotNets-X '11, ser. HotNets-X, ACM, November 2011, pp. 2:1–2:6.

[203] Raffaele Giaffreda, Kostas Pentikousis, Eleanor Hepworth, Ramón Agüero, Alex Galis, An information service infrastructure for ambient networks, in: Proceedings of the PDCN'07, ACTA Press, February 2007, pp. 21–27.

[204] K. Pentikousis, R. Agero, J. Gebert, J.A. Galache, O. Blume, P. Pkknen, The ambient
       networks heterogeneous access selection architecture, in: Proceedings of the M2NM
       '07, IEEE, October 2007, pp. 49–64.
[205] N. McKeown, Tom Anderson, H. Balakrishnan, G. Parulkar, Larry Peterson, Jennifer
       Rexford, Scott Shenker, J. Turner, OpenFlow: enabling innovation in campus networks,
       SIGCOMM Comput. Commun. Rev. 38 (2) (2008) 69–74.

ABOUT THE AUTHORS

Bruno Sousa received his Licentiate and M.Sc. degrees from Institute Polithenic of Leiria,
Portugal in 2005, and University of Coimbra , Portugal in 2008. Currently he is finishing
his PhD at the University of Coimbra with the thesis on "Multihoming Aware Optimization
Mechanism". Master Bruno has participated in several projects, Combating Fire with mul-
tihoming and mobility (CoFIMOM), Trustworthy and Resilient Operations in a Network
Environment (TRONE), WiMAX Extensions to Isolated Research Networks (WEIRD),
among others. He has contributed to standardization in IETF, inside the 16ng working group.
His research is currently focusing on optimization mechanisms for multi-homed nodes.

Kostas Pentikousis is a senior research engineer at Huawei Technologies in Berlin, Germany and a standards delegate to IETF. Before that, he was a senior research scientist at VTT
Technical Research Center of Finland working on information-centric networking (ICN).
As an expert in this emerging area, he served as the lead guest editor for the IEEE Communications Magazine feature topic on ICN. Kostas received his B.Sc. and M.Sc. degrees in
computer science from Aristotle University of Thessaloniki, Greece (1996; summa cum laude;
ranked first) and State University of New York at Stony Brook, USA (2000), respectively. He
received his Ph.D. degree in computer science from Stony Brook University for his thesis on
"ECN, power consumption, and error modeling in TCP simulation studies" (2004) and was
an ERCIM Fellow in 2005. During his graduate studies, he interned at Computer Associates
in Islandia, NY, developing network management software. He co-authored more than 90
journal articles, conference papers and book chapters, and presented well-attended tutorials
on energy-efficient networking at IEEE ICC and IEEE VTC-Spring (2010). Dr. Pentikousis
conducts research on Internet protocols and network architecture and is known for his work
on mobile networks and management. His contributions have ranged from system design and
implementation to performance evaluation. At Huawei he worked on 3GPP EPC research
topics beyond Rel. 12 and has been awarded four patents in this area. His research is currently
focusing on carrier-grade software-defined networking (SDN) and network virtualization.

Marilia Curado is an Assistant Professor at the Department of Informatics Engineering of
the University of Coimbra, Portugal, from where she got a PhD in Informatics Engineering
on the subject of Quality of Service Routing, in 2005. Her research interests are Quality of
Service, Quality of Experience, Energy efficiency, Mobility, and Routing. She has ben general
and TPC chair of several conferences and belongs to the editorial board of Elsevier Computer
Networks. She has participated in several national projects, in Networks of Excellence from
IST FP5 and FP6, in the IST FP6 Integrated Projects, EuQoS and WEIRD, and on ICT
FP7 STREPs MICIE, GINSENG and COCKPIT. She acts regularly as an evaluator for EU
projects and proposals.

CHAPTER SIX

Efficient Data Analytics Over Cloud

Rajeev Gupta, Himanshu Gupta, and Mukesh Mohania
IBM Research, New Delhi, India

Contents

Abstract

Many industries, such as telecom, health-care, retail, pharmaceutical, financial services, etc., generate large amounts of data. Such large amount of data needs to be processed quickly for gaining critical business insights. The data warehouses and solutions built around them are unable to provide reasonable response times in handling expanding data volumes. One can either perform analytics on big volume once in days or one can

Advances in Computers, Volume 90
ISSN 0065-2458, http://dx.doi.org/10.1016/B978-0-12-408091-1.00006-3

perform transactions on small amounts of data in seconds. With the new requirements, one needs to ensure the real-time or near real-time response for huge amount of data. In this chapter we cover various important aspects of analyzing big data. We start with challenges one needs to overcome for moving data and data management applications. over cloud. For *big data* we describe two kinds of systems: (1) NoSQL systems for interactive data serving environments; and (2) systems for large scale analytics based on MapReduce paradigm, such as Hadoop, The NoSQL systems are designed to have a simpler key-value-based data model having inbuilt *sharding*, hence, these work seamlessly in a distributed cloud-based environment. In contrast, one can use Hadoop-based systems to run long running decision support and analytical queries consuming and possible producing bulk data. We illustrate various middleware and applications which can use these technologies to quickly process massive amount of data.

1. INTRODUCTION

Recent financial crisis has changed the way businesses think about their finances. Organizations are actively seeking simple, lower cost, and faster to market alternatives about everything. Clouds are cheap allowing businesses to off-load computing tasks while saving IT costs and resources. In cloud computing applications, data, platform, and other resources are provided to users as services delivered over the network. The cloud computing enables self-service with no or little vendor intervention. It provides utility model of resources where businesses only pay for their usage. As these resources are shared across a large number of users, cost of computing is much lower compared to dedicated resource provisioning. In this chapter we are discussing the use cases and issues arising out of data management over cloud.

Many industries, such as telecom, health care, retail, pharmaceutical, financial services, etc., generate large amounts of data. For instance, in 2010, Facebook had 21 PB of internal warehouse data with 12 TB new data added every day and 800 TB compressed data scanned daily [34]. These applications need to process data having:

- Large *volume*—an Indian Telecom company generates more than 1 Terabyte of call detail records (CDRs) daily;
- High *velocity*—twitter needs to handle 4.5 Terabytes of video uploads in real-time per day;
- Wide *variety*—data can be structured, semi-structured, or unstructured which needs to be integrated together; and
- Different *veracity*—data needs to be cleaned before it can be integrated.

Gaining critical business insights by querying and analyzing such massive amounts of data provides differentiated business values to these companies—a telecom company wants customer life-time value (CLV), a bank wants to manage its risk, a retail store wants to increase revenues through targeted marketing. However, getting these insights is too slow and difficult—it costs too much in time and resources. Traditionally, data warehouses have been used to manage the large amount of data. The 4 V's of big data—*volume, velocity, variety*, and *veracity*—makes the data management and analytics challenging for the traditional data warehouses. One requires new expertise in the areas of data management and systems management—who understand how to model the data and prepare them for analysis, and understand the problem deep enough to perform the analytics. The warehouses and solutions built around them are unable to provide reasonable response times in handling expanding data volumes. One can either process data having big volume in days or one can process small amounts of data in seconds. With the new requirements, one needs to ensure the real-time or near real-time response for huge amount of data. Using flexible cloud resources one can perform real-time analytics without owning large resources.

In this chapter, we cover various aspects of data management over cloud—need for cloud data management, benefits of it, various technologies proposed for distributed cloud data management, data models, methods of efficiently querying data over cloud, middleware for cloud data management, and illustrative applications. Aim of this chapter is to provide survey of cloud data management so that a user gets a good idea of concepts and issues involved in cloud data management, with suggestions for further readings to augment the content of this chapter. Here is the outline of this chapter: in the next section, we describe the factors which are important for enterprises to have cloud-based data analytics solutions. We cover the benefits of moving from an in-house solution to a cloud-based out-sourced solution. Section 3 addresses various technologies for massive scale data processing, especially Hadoop [4, 5], which is a popular open source distributed data processing technology. Hadoop processes data stored over distributed file system which can be implemented over virtualized cloud resources. For each data management application, one may need to write custom code to do the required processing over Hadoop. To avoid writing custom code for every data processing application, there are various SQL like query languages proposed. We discuss these languages in Section 4. In Section 5, we outline various middleware for cloud data management. Specifically we cover *database as a service* which can be used for on-demand databases over cloud. Section 6 is intended to introduce enterprise applications which illustrate the issues one needs to consider for designing cloud-based enterprise data management applications. Specifically, we consider applications in telecom and financial services domain. We conclude by outlining various research challenges in data management over cloud in Section 7.

2. CLOUD COMPUTING AND DATA MANAGEMENT

As discussed in the previous section, cloud computing can be used for performing massive scale data analytics in a cost effective and scalable manner. In this section we discuss the interplay of cloud computing and data management, specifically, what are the benefits of cloud computing for data management; and the factors one should consider while moving from a dedicated data management infrastructure to a cloud-based infrastructure. There are three main purposes for which data processing is required—data management, data integration, and data analytics. We specifically consider data analytics for cloud–based data processing.

2.1 Benefits of Cloud Computing

It is very difficult to manage the large volume of data using traditional relational database management systems. With the cloud-based data management, enterprises get the following benefits:

1. **Scalability:** As organizations use larger and larger data warehouses for data processing needs ranging from business analytics, regular reporting of complex event processing, and data mining; the need for performance continues to outpace the capabilities of the traditional approaches. The cloud-based approach offers a means for meeting the performance and scalability requirements of the enterprise data management providing agility to the data management infrastructure.

2. **Utility-based pricing:** As with other cloud environments, data management in the cloud benefits end-users by offering a pay-as-you-go (or utility based) model. Cloud frees up enterprises from the need to purchase additional hardware and to go through the extensive procurement process frequently. The cost-saving potential of cloud computing is enormous; previously, companies needed servers with hosting contracts and had to pay for expensive database licenses; the hardware and software involved could add crippling costs to smaller businesses and could leave many businesses using out-of-date software since they could not afford the constant upgrades. Cloud-based applications are user friendly, allowing companies to save tens of thousands in technician salaries every year.

3. **Efficient resource usage:** The data management, integration, and analytics can be offloaded to public and/or private clouds. By using public

cloud, enterprises can get processing power and infrastructure as needed, whereas with private-cloud enterprises can improve the utilization of existing cloud infrastructure. NoSQL technologies including Hadoop [4, 5] help in providing efficient query processing capabilities as will be discussed in the next section. As data volumes continue to increase these alternative approaches to support data applications will become increasingly established as platform of choice for massive scale database systems.

4. **Separation of concerns:** Cloud computing enables enterprises to more effectively handle the wide ranging data management requirements with minimum effort, thus allowing it to focus on its core work rather than getting bogged down with the infrastructure. In cloud, software upgrades are made automatically and seamlessly; thus applications can be made available anywhere anytime without any botheration for the end-user.

5. **Unified data service:** Cloud data management can be used to process a variety of data. This data can be structured, semi-structured, or unstructured. Examples of structured data include call detail records in a telecom company, graphical data is an example of semi-structured data, whereas product reviews on twitter are an example of unstructured data. Cloud provides alternative to the traditional data warehouse for processing structured relational data. As cloud data model is flexible it can be used to process semi-structured, hierarchical, and textual data as well. Further, by virtue of its ability to process different kinds of data, a single cloud data application can be defined to process mixed data format [17, 36]. This ability to contextually integrate different data formats at large scale is unmatched.

Despite all these benefits, decision to move from dedicated infrastructure to the cloud-based data processing in not easy. Next we consider the factors which an enterprise should consider before deciding to move to cloud computing-based data management.

2.2 Moving Data Management to Cloud

There are various factors which an organization should consider while moving away from privately owned computing resources toward cloud computing [1]. A data management system has to consider all the stages of data lifecycle management such as data ingestion, ETL (extract–transform–load), data processing, data archival, and deletion. Before moving one or more stages of data lifecycle to the cloud, one has to consider the following factors:

1. **Availability guarantees:** Depending on criticality of the data, one needs to decide which data and which part of its lifecycle can be offloaded to

the cloud. Each cloud computing provider can ensure a certain amount of availability. For example, transactional data processing requires quick real-time answers whereas for data warehouses long running queries are used to generate reports. Hence, one may not want to put its transactional data over cloud but may be ready to put the analytics infrastructure over the cloud.

2. **Reliability and quality of service:** Data management can be one of the core operations of an enterprise. Before offloading data management to cloud, enterprises want to ensure that the cloud provides required level of reliability for the data services. Providing reliability involves that the cloud service should be available and provides the correct answer to the enterprise users. In a cloud computing environment, availability and integrity are typically ensured by providing redundancy into the resource provisioning. By creating multiple copies of application components the cloud can deliver the service with the required quality of service.

3. **Security:** Data that is bound by strict privacy regulations, such as medical information covered by the Health Insurance Portability and Account-ability Act (HIPAA), will require that users log into be routed to their secure database server.

4. **Maintainability:** As mentioned previously, data management involves various stages of data lifecycle. Database administration is a highly skilled activity which involves deciding how data should be organized, which indices and views should be maintained, etc. One needs to carefully eval-uate whether all these maintenance operations can be performed over the cloud data.

Cloud has given enterprises the opportunity to fundamentally shift the way data is created, processed, and shared. This approach has been shown to be superior in sustaining the performance and growth requirements of ana-lytical applications and, combined with cloud computing, offers significant advantages. In the next section, we consider various data management tech-nologies which are used with cloud computing such as NoSQL, Hadoop, associated data models, etc.

3. TECHNOLOGIES FOR MASSIVE DATA PROCESSING

Big data is data that *exceeds the processing capacity of conventional database systems*. It implies that the data count is too large, and/or data values change too fast, and/or it does not follow the rules of conventional database management systems (e.g., consistency). To gain value from this data, one must choose an alternative way to process it. For using cloud computing to process big data we need different data management techniques which can utilize the massive distributed resources provided by the cloud to provide scalability and performance for data management applications. With the distributed resources we need techniques for efficiently storing and querying the massive data. We start with NoSQL (*not only SQL*) technologies which encompass a number of techniques for processing data which cannot be analyzed using traditional databases. It enables efficient capture, storage, search, sharing, analytics, and visualization of the massive scale data.

3.1 NoSQL

The term NoSQL was first used in 1998 for a relational database that does not use SQL. Currently it is used for all the alternative data management technologies which are used for solving the problems for which relational databases are a bad fit. Main reason of using NoSQL databases is the scalability issues with relational databases. With the data sizes growing rapidly, databases are required to provide much higher data throughput which can be provided by the traditional relational databases. For example, Google is required to process more than 20 petabytes of data daily [54]. In general, relational databases are not designed for horizontal scaling (distributed implementation). There are two technologies using which databases can be made scalable: replication and sharding. In the replication technology, distributed databases can be scaled using a master-slave architecture where reads can be performed at any of the replicated slave whereas writes are performed at the master. Each write operation results in writes at all the slaves, imposing a limit to scalability. Further, even reads may need to be performed at master node as previous write may not have been replicated at all the slave nodes. Although the situation can be improved by using multiple masters, but this can result in conflicts among masters whose resolution is very costly [28]. Partitioning (sharding) can also be used for scaling writes in relational databases, but applications are required to be made partition aware. Further once partitioned relations need to be handled at the application layer (e.g., modifying the queries accordingly), defeating the very purpose of relational databases. NoSQL databases overcome these problems of horizontal scaling.

An important difference between traditional databases and NoSQL databases is that the NoSQL databases, in general, do not support updates and deletes. There are various reasons for this. Many of the applications do not need update and delete operations; rather, different versions of the same data are maintained. For example, in Telecom domains, older CDRs are required for auditing and data mining. In enterprise human resource databases, employee's records are maintained even if an employee may have left the organization. These updates and deletes are handled using insertion with version control. For example, Bigtable [33] associates a timestamp with every data item. In these append-only databases, when the data gets too large, they are archived. We present an efficient archival middleware in the later parts of this chapter. Further, one needs customized techniques for implementing efficient Joins over massive scale data in distributed settings. Thus, Joins are avoided in NoSQL databases. Denormalization of databases, as explained in Section 3.3, is used so that Join queries are not required.

Relational databases provide ACID properties (Atomicity, consistency, integrity, and durability) which may be more than necessary for various data management applications and use cases. Atomicity of modification of more than one record is not required in most of the applications. Thus, single key atomicity is provided by NoSQL databases. In traditional databases, strong consistency is supported by using conflict resolution at write time (using read and write locks) which leads to scalability problems. As per [26], databases cannot ensure three CAP properties simultaneously: Consistency, Availability, and Partition tolerance (i.e., an individual operation should complete even if individual components are not available). Among consistency and availability, availability is given more importance by various NoSQL databases, e.g., giving service to a customer is more important. Consistency can be ensured using *eventual consistency* [27] where reconciliation happens asynchronously to have eventually consistent database. Similarly, most applications do not need *serialization isolation* level (i.e., to ensure that operations are deemed to be performed one after the other). *Read committed* (i.e., lock on writes till the end of transaction) with single key atomicity is sufficient. Durability is ensured in traditional relational databases as well as NoSQL databases; however, traditional databases provide durability by using expensive hardware whereas NoSQL databases provide that with cluster of disks with replication and other fault tolerance mechanisms. An alternative of ACID for distributed NoSQL databases is BASE (Basic Availability, Soft-state, and Eventual consistent). By not following the ACID properties strictly, query processing is made faster for massive scale data.

Another important reason of popularity of NoSQL databases is their flexible data model. They can support various types of data models and most of these are not strict. In relational databases, data is modeled using relations and one defines schema before one starts using the database.

But NoSQL databases can support key–value pairs, hierarchical data, geo-spatial data, graphical data, etc., using a simple model. Further, in new applications of databases, there is a need to frequently keep modifying schema, e.g., a new service may require an additional column or complex changes in data model. In relational databases, schema modification is time consuming and hard. One needs to lock the whole table for modifying any index structure. We categorize NoSQL databases using the models they use to store and query the data. Specifically, we describe three data models, namely, key–value stores, document stores, and column families.

- **Key–value stores:** In a key–value store read and write operations to a data item are uniquely identified by its key. Thus, no primitive operation spans multiple data items. (i.e., it is not easy to support range queries). Amazon's *Dynamo* [29] is an example of popular key–value store. In *Dynamo*, values are opaque to the system and they are used to store objects of size less than 1 MB. *Dynamo* provides incremental scalability; hence, keys are partitioned dynamically using a hash function to distribute the data over a set of machines or nodes. Each node is aware of keys handled by its peers allowing any node to forward a key's read or write operation to the correct set of nodes. Both read and write operations are performed on a number of nodes to handle data durability, and availability. Updates are propagated to all the replicas asynchronously (eventual consistency). Kai [25] is open source implementation of key–value store.

- **Document stores:** In document stores, value associated with a key is a document which is not opaque to the database; hence, it can be queried. Unlike relational databases, in a document store, each document can have a different schema. Amazon's *SimpleDB* [30], *MongoDB* [32], and Apache's *CouchDB*, [31] are some examples of NoSQL databases using this data model. In *CouchDB*, each document is serialized in JSON (Java Script Object Notation) format, and has a unique document identifier (*docId*). These documents can be accessed using web-browser and queried using a JavaScript. This database does not support any delete or update; hence, in each read operation multiple versions are read and the most recent one is returned as the result. *CouchDB* supports real-time document transformation and change notifications. The transformations can be done using user provided *map* and *reduce* JavaScript functions (explained later in the chapter).

- **Column family stores:** Google's BigTable [33] pioneered this data model. BigTable is a sparse, distributed, durable, multi-dimensional sorted map (i.e., sequence of nested key–value pairs). Data is organized into

Table 1 Comparison of NoSQL databases with traditional relational databases.

Product/feature	Dynamo	CouchDB	BigTable	Traditional Databases
Data model	Key value rows	Documents	Column store	Rows/relational
Transaction model	Single tuple	Multiple documents	Single and range	Range, complex
Data partition	Random	Random	Ordered by key	Not applicable
Consistency	Eventual	Eventual	Atomic	Transactional
Version control	Versions	Document version	Timestamp	Not applicable
Replication	Quorum for read and write	Incremental replication	File system	Not applicable

tables. Each record is identified by a row key. Each row has a number of columns. Intersection of each row and column contains time-stamped data. Columns are organized into column families or related columns. It supports transactions under a single row key. Multiple row transactions are not supported. Data is partitioned by sorting row-keys lexicographically. BigTable can serve data from disk as well as memory. Data is organized into Tablets of size 100–200 MB by default with each tablet characterized by its start-key and end-key. A tablet server manages 10s of tablets. Metadata tables are maintained to locate tablet server for a particular key. These metadata tables are also split into tablets. A chubby file is root of this hierarchical metadata, i.e., this file points to a root metadata tablet. This tablet points to other metadata tablets which in turn points to user application data tablets. HBase [18] is an open source implementation of BigTable.

Table 1 provides comparison of these different types of NoSQL databases with traditional relational databases. MapReduce, a generic framework to write massive scale data applications is presented next. This framework is mainly used to process decision support queries.

3.2 Hadoop MapReduce Method for Data Processing

Google introduced MapReduce [6] framework in 2004 for processing massive amount of data over highly distributed cluster of machines. This framework involves two types of user defined generic functions: *map* and *reduce*. A master node takes the input data and the processing problem, divides it into smaller data chunks and subproblems (tasks), and distributes them to worker nodes. A worker node processes one or more chunks using the task assigned to it. Specifically, each *map* process, takes a set of {*key,value*} pairs as input and generate one or more intermediate {*key,value*} pairs for each input key, independent of other pairs. In the *reduce* step, intermediate key-value pairs are combined to produce the output of the input problem. Each *reduce* instance takes a *key* and an array of *values* as input and produces output after processing the array of *values*:

```
Map (k1,v1) → list (k2,v2)
Reduce (k2, list (v2)) → list (v3)
```

Figure 1 shows an example MapReduce implementation for a scenario where one wants to find the list of customers having total transaction value more than $1000.

Hadoop [4] is the most popular open source implementation of MapReduce framework. It is used for writing applications processing vast amount

```
void map(String rowId, String row):
  // rowId: row name
  // row: a transaction recode
  customerId= extract customer-id from row
  transactionValue= extract transaction value from row
    EmitIntermediate(customerId, transactionValue);

void reduce(String customerId, Iterator partialValues):
  // customerId: Id to identify a customer
  // partialValues: a list of transaction values
  int sum = 0;
  for each pv in partialValues:
    sum += pv;
  if(pv > 1000)
  Emit(cutsomerId, sum);
```

Fig. 1. Example *MapReduce* code.

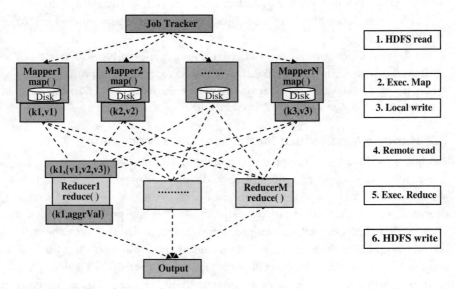

Fig. 2. MapReduce framework.

of data in parallel on large clusters of machines in a fault-tolerant manner. Machines can be added and removed from the clusters as and when required. In Hadoop, data is stored on Hadoop Distributed File System (HDFS) which is a massively distributed file system designed to run on cheap commodity hardware. In HDFS, each file is chopped up into a number of blocks with each block, typically, having a size of 64 MB. As depicted in Fig. 2, these blocks are parsed by user-defined code into {*key,value*} pairs to be read by *map* functions. The *map* functions are executed on distributed machines to generate output {*key,value*} pairs which are written on their respective local disks. The whole *key* space is partitioned and allocated to a number of reducers. Each *reduce* function uses HTTP GET method to pull {*key*, *value*} pairs corresponding to its allocated key space. For each key, a reduce instance processes the *key* and array of its associated *values* to get the desired output. HDFS has master-slave architecture. An HDFS cluster, typically, has a single master, also called *name node*, and a number of slave nodes. The name node manages the file system name space, dividing the file into blocks, and replicating them to different machines. Slaves, also called *data nodes*, manage the storage corresponding to that node. Fault tolerance is achieved by replicating data blocks over a number of nodes. The master node monitors progress of data processing slave nodes and, if a slave node fails or it is slow, reassigns the corresponding data-block processing to another slave node. In Hadoop, applications can be written as a series of MapReduce tasks also.

3.3 Writing Efficient MapReduce Code

As explained in previous section, MapReduce can be used to perform various data processing tasks by writing custom *map* and *reduce* functions for a given analytic task. This area has seen a flurry of activities in last few years and various algorithms have been proposed to carry out a number of analytic tasks like computing different classes of joins [36, 37, 39, 40, 45], log processing [38], computing wavelet histogram [41], spatial query processing [42], graph processing [43], duplicates detection, and removal [44], etc. In all these studies there are two common features used to design efficient MapReduce algorithms:

1. As discussed, *map* function of the MapReduce framework converts data into intermediate {*key*, *value*} pairs. More the number of intermediate pairs, more the communication among the cluster nodes. The first principle while designing an efficient MapReduce algorithm is to minimize the number of intermediate {*key*, *value*} pairs generated.

2. The intermediate {*key*, *value*} pairs for a given key are communicated to a common reducer though a reducer gets {*key*, *value*} pairs for multiple keys. The reducer then processes these {*key*, *value*} pairs to generate final output. The second principle while designing a MapReduce algorithm is load balancing among reducers, i.e., to ensure that all reducers get roughly similar number of {*key*, *value*} pairs to process. If it so happens that some reducers get disproportionately high number of {*key*, *value*} pairs to process, these reducers will run for a large period of time while other machines may lie idle. This results in an inefficient utilization of cluster resources thereby resulting in an inefficient MapReduce implementation.

We take example of Join processing to illustrate how efficient MapReduce algorithm can be written using aforementioned principles. In this example the join condition is expressed as $R.a \leq S.b$; i.e., for two input sets (e.g., database tables) R and S, the output should contain the records where value of the attribute a of R is less than or equals to value of the attribute b of S. Such inequality join is inherently difficult for MapReduce as it is not obvious how to generate intermediate $\{key, value\}$ pairs so that reducers can calculate the output records. These are some of the possibilities:

1. Let $[l, u]$ be the range of the values of attributes $R.a$ and $S.b$. Let the number of reducers be r with their indices being in a set $[1, r]$. We can divide the range $[l, u]$ in r equal sized partitions (of size $(u - l)/r$ each) with each partition denoted by index $1 \leq j \leq r$. We write map function such that a data record s in S with value of join attribute b in range partition j is communicated to the jth reducer. Similarly every record from R with value of attribute a in range partition j is communicated to all the reducers with index greater or equal to j. This ensures that a record of set R joins with any record of set S with a greater or equal join attribute value. This approach may suffer from the problem of load imbalance with the reducers with higher value of index getting disproportionate number of records to process. It can be seen that the reducer with index r will get all the records from the set R. Thus the reducer with larger index values are likely to run longer compared to the other reducers. We correct this imbalance using an approach proposed next.

2. In the second approach we divide the value range $[l, u]$ in m equal sized partitions (of size $(u - l)/m$ each) where $m^2 = r$, the number of reducers. A reducer is denoted by indices (i, j) such that $1 \leq i \leq m, 1 \leq j \leq m$. We write map function such that every record s in S with value of b is mapped to reducers with indices $(i, b^*m/(u-l))$ for each $i \leq b^*m/(u-l)$. Similarly, every record of R with value of join attribute a is mapped to $(a^*m/(u-l), j)$ for each $j \geq a^*m/(u-l)$. Thus, m reducers with $j = m$ receive $1/m$ fraction of R and S records. As a result the skew in the number of pairs received by every reducer is much smaller for this approach compared to the previous approach.

MapReduce is designed to fetch process a data chunk independently of other data chunks, hence, does not have a built-in support for executing join operations. Although these algorithms can be used to implement join over massive data, but it is always advisable to avoid joins (as done in NoSQL databases described in Section 3.1). In the next section, we present various data models, which can be used for storing data over HDFS.

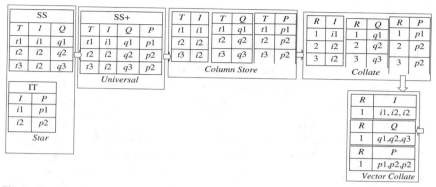

Fig. 3. Data storage options.

Using performance evaluation it shows that avoiding joins even at the cost of increasing data sizes is useful.

3.4 Data Model for HDFS Data

In traditional databases, data is usually stored as a series of rows where each individual row is stored and accessed atomically. In comparison, for cloud database technologies like NoSQL, data is mostly stored using column oriented [10], or a combination of column and row oriented schemes. The column–oriented architecture provides a combination of architectural simplicity and the ability to configure the data in a way that can reduce the physical amount of data that must be accessed. This further reduces data access latency and improves use of network bandwidth. Besides, column-oriented approach also results in efficient join processing [9]. Figure 3 shows example TPC-DS (Decision support benchmark from transaction processing performance council) data [12], which is a popular workload generator for data warehouses, in various data models. TPC-DS depicts data schema for a typical retail chain in the form of fact and dimension tables. The data can be stored in the following formats:

1. **Star schema:** This is the typical way in which data is stored in relational databases. Figure 3 shows two tables SS (*store_sales* fact table) and IT (*item*, a dimension table).

2. **Universal schema:** In this schema all the tables are de–normalized using primary key foreign-key relationships, i.e., all the columns from the dimension table are stored in place of the corresponding foreign key. The use of universal schema [11] helps in avoiding join which would have been otherwise required between the fact table and the dimension tables.

SS+ in Fig. 3 shows the example universal table for SS and IT tables of the star schema.

3. **Column store:** In this schema, all columns of the universal schema are stored as separate tables themselves. It reduces the amount of data that is required to be read (for processing any query over Hadoop) as a typical query accesses only few columns from the fact and/or dimension tables. This ensures that only the columns that are needed to compute the query answers are read, which significantly reduces the data read, and hence, the query evaluation times. Each column store table has two columns—one for the primary key (e.g., *row-id*) and another for the attribute value.

4. **Data collation:** The problem with column store is the way one typically executes multi way Joins to collect multiple required columns for query processing. The multiple joins are carried out as a sequence of two-way joins. However a sequence of two-way joins is clearly a redundant computation for column store because of two reasons: (a) column tables have a common attribute namely primary key and (b) there is only one row in each table with one primary key value and hence one row in any column table can join with only one row in another column-table. Hence rather than carrying out a sequence of two-way joins, we can join all the required columns in one pass. Data collation is an operation that takes rows with identical primary keys from all the column store tables and puts them together. In this case one stores the data in a manner similar to the column store (i.e., individual columns in separate tables), but instead of primary key one stores the *row-id* for every row in the table. This *row-id* is usually a counter starting from 1. Using a counter generally results in the reduction of the size of the data as the counter is a simple integer whereas a primary key may take more space. For processing the query, instead of joining tables corresponding to columns, one can simply collate all the values having the same *row-id*. A simple MapReduce-based implementation can be used for data collation: keep the *row-id* as key of the *map* output and *reduce* can just concatenate all the values for the same key. Figure 3 shows the example data in this case with *row-id* stored as column R.

5. **Vector collation:** The performance of simple data collate operation can be further boosted by observing that when we break any table into multiple column tables, every column table will contain the column values in exactly the same order as was present in the original table. In other words the column values of ith tuple in the original table will be found in the ith row of each column table. Hence to construct back the ith

tuple, we can put together ith rows of all the column values. We hence do not need to store a separate *row-id* for every row. We can rather store a *row-id* with a set of values, i.e., one *row-id* is associated with multiple column values. Specifically for the *vector* size B, values from *row-id*s in the range $[B^*i, B^*(i+1) - 1]$ are stored as a single value with *row-id* (key) as B^*i. Figure 3, shows how we store the *column store* data using *vector* collation ($B = 3$). Each *row-id* is associated with three column values ($v1, v2, v3$). A *map* function can read the data in vector collate format and generates the {*key,value*} pairs where the *key* is the *row-id* while the value is the vector associated with this *row-id*. The *reducer* collects the vectors with the identical keys and then iterates over these vectors to generate the final collation output, i.e., each reducer just stitches together the vectors obtained for every *row-id*. It is easy to see that the vector collate will significantly reduce the storage space requirement as not all the *row-ids* are stored. A smaller data implies a smaller reading time and hence, an overall improvement over the performance of simple collate.

Figure 4 gives the space requirements for all the aforementioned schemes as number of *store_sales* records (of TPC-DS) are varied between 3 million and 15 million. Specifically, results are shown for the following combinations of schemes:

1. **Star:** This represents the typical schema used in the data warehouses.

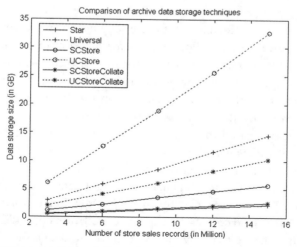

Fig. 4. Data storage requirements for various schemes.

2. **Universal:** It involves creating a single universal table after de-normalizing the star schema. For TPC-DS data used, this universal relation has 161 columns.
3. **UCStore:** In this scheme all the columns of the universal relation are stored as separate tables, i.e., this scheme has 161 tables.
4. **SCStore:** This scheme combine's star schema with column store technique, i.e., schema is the same as the star schema but each column of every table in the star schema is stored as separate table in this scheme.
5. **UCStoreCollate:** This scheme uses the universal schema—with *column store* and *vector collate*—for efficient data storage and processing.
6. **SCStoreCollate:** This scheme is similar to the previous scheme except that we do not *de-normalize* the schema.

As expected, with the increasing number of columns and decreasing number of rows in dimension tables, *Star* schemas are more efficient compared to their corresponding *Universal* schemas from space utilization point of view. All the schemes with *Universal* schema require approximately four times space compared to the *Star* schema. The *UCStore* schema consumes almost double the space compared to *Universal*. This happens because in the column store we store primary key with each of the columns. By using *vector collate* one keeps the storage requirement of the *UCStoreCollate* at almost the same level as the *Universal*. To reduce the storage requirement of schemes with universal schema further, one can use a compression technique in which the repetitive values of a column need not be stored. As many column values in *UCStore* and *UCStoreCollate* will be repetitive, this reduces the storage space by 37% while keeping almost the same query response time.

Query response performance of these schemes for representative TPC-DS queries is given in [21]. For simple *select project* queries, *Star* performs better than *Universal*. However, *Star* performs worse compared to *Universal* for queries involving two or more joins. In *Star* schema the query evaluation cost is dominated by the join costs whereas in the *Universal* schema, query cost is dominated by the read cost. With increasing data sizes, read cost increases faster compared to the join cost, hence, *Universal* performs worse compared to *Star*. *Column store* reduces the read cost but increases the join cost, thus depending on number of records, *Universal* can perform better, or worse compared to *UCStore*. In general, for larger data sizes (when read cost dominates) *UCStore* performs better than *Universal*. Since collate operation further reduces the read cost (at the expense of collation cost), *UCStoreCollate* performs better than *UCStore* which validates that *column store* model with *vector collation* can lead to efficient query processing with very large amount of data. While using these data storage mechanisms on cloud, one needs to consider the fact that cloud storage is cheaper and highly available whereas one should strive the match the query response time obtained from a typical in-house data warehouse installation. By using column store techniques with efficient column stitching (collate) one can achieve these objectives.

4. QUERYING DATA OVER CLOUD

There are three ways in which data can be processed over Hadoop: (a) writing a native MapReduce code, (b) writing a script in a high level query language, and (c) using a GUI-based tool to develop a visual representation of a processing task. In Section 3, we discussed how we can write *map* and *reduce* functions to process any analytical query. A MapReduce program can be written in various programming languages such as Java, python, Ruby, etc. But this approach of writing custom MapReduce functions for each application has these problems:

1. Writing custom MapReduce jobs is difficult, time consuming, and requires highly skilled developers.
2. For each MapReduce job to run optimally, one needs to configure a number of parameters, such as number of *mappers* and *reducers*, size of a data block each *mapper* will process, etc. Finding suitable values for these parameters is not easy.
3. An application may require a series of MapReduce jobs. Hence, one needs to write these jobs and schedule them properly.
4. As explained in Section 3.3, for efficiency of MapReduce jobs one has to ensure that all the reducers get a similar magnitude of data to process. If certain reducers get a disproportionate magnitude of data to process, these reducers will keep running for a long period of time while other reducers are sitting idle. This will hence in turn impact the performance of the MapReduce program.

Thus, instead various high level query languages have been developed in the literature so that one can avoid writing low level MapReduce programs. Queries written in these languages are in turn translated into equivalent MapReduce operations by the compiler and consequently executed on Hadoop. Three of these languages Hive [7, 20], Jaql [13, 14], and Pig [16] are the most popular languages in Hadoop Community. An analogy here would be to think of writing a MapReduce program as writing a Java program to process data in a relational database. While using one of these high level languages is like writing a script in SQL. We next briefly outline the key features of these three high level query languages to process the data stored in HDFS.

4.1 Hive

Hive [7, 20] provides an easy entry point for data analysts, minimizing the effort required to migrate to the cloud-based Hadoop infrastructure for distributed data storage and parallel query processing. Hive has been specially designed to make it possible for analysts with strong SQL skills (but meager Java programming skills) to run queries on huge volumes of data. Hive supports queries expressed in a SQL-like declarative language. Hive provides a subset of SQL, with features like *from* clause subqueries, various types of *joins, group-bys, aggregations*, *"create table as select"*, etc. All these features make Hive very SQL-like. The effort required to learn and to get started with Hive is pretty small for a user proficient in SQL.

Hive structures data into well-understood database concepts like tables, columns, rows, and partitions. The schema of the table needs to be provided up-front. Just like in SQL, a user needs to first create a table with a certain schema and then only the data consistent with the schema can be uploaded to this table. A table can be partitioned on a set of attributes. Given a query, Hive compiler may choose to fetch the data only from certain partitions, and hence, partitioning helps in efficiently answering a query. It supports all the major primitive types: *integer, float, double*, and *string*, as well as complex collection types such as *map, list* and *struct*. Hive also includes a system catalog, a meta store, that contains schemas and statistics, which are useful in data exploration, query optimization, and query compilation [20]. Hive can be extended using UDFs (user defined functions) that enable users to define their own custom functions. Hive also supports JDBC interface which can be used to issue Hive queries within a Java program. The methodology of issuing and executing a query is identical to that of issuing a SQL query from a Java program. One first opens a connection, creates a statement object, and then executes the desired query. The result of executing a query is a Java *ResultSet* object which can be iterated to obtain the results. Hive has found usages in diverse scenarios e.g., log processing, text mining, document processing etc. The biggest success story of Hive is Facebook where it is used for different kind of data processing tasks on a warehouse of size approximately 700 TB [20].

4.2 Pig

Pig is a high level scripting language developed by Yahoo to process data on Hadoop and aims at a sweet spot between SQL and MapReduce.

Pig combines the best of both worlds, the declarative style of SQL and low level procedural style of MapReduce. A Pig program is a sequence of steps, similar to a programming language, each of which carries out a single data transformation. However the transformation carried out in each step is fairly high level e.g., filtering, aggregation, etc., similar to SQL. Programs written in Pig are firstly parsed for syntactic and instance checking. The output from this parser is a logical plan, arranged in a directed acyclic graph, allowing logical optimizations, such as projection pushdown to be carried out. The plan is compiled by a MapReduce compiler, which is then optimized once more by a MapReduce optimizer performing tasks such as early partial aggregation. The MapReduce program is then submitted to the Hadoop job manager for execution.

Pig has a flexible, fully nested data model and allows complex, non-atomic data types such as set, map, and tuple to occur as fields of a table. A *bytearray* type is supported, to facilitate unknown data types and lazy conversion of types. Unlike Hive, stored schemas are strictly optional. A user can supply schema information on the fly or choose not to supply it at all. The only capability required is to be able to read and parse the data. Pig also has the capability of incorporating UDFs. A unique feature of Pig is that it provides a debugging environment. The debugging environment can generate a sample data to help a user in locating any error made in a Pig script.

4.3 Jaql

Jaql is a functional data query language, designed by IBM and is built upon JavaScript Object Notation (JSON) [8] data model. Jaql is a general purpose data flow language that manipulates semi-structured information in the form of abstract JSON values. It provides a framework for reading and writing data in custom formats, and provides support for common input/output formats like CSVs, and like Pig and Hive, provides operators such as filtering, transformations, sort, group-bys, aggregation, and join. As the JSON model provides easy migration of data to- and from- some popular scripting languages like JavaScript and Python, Jaql is extendable with operations written in many programming languages.

JSON data model supports atomic values like numbers and strings. It also supports two container types: *array* and *record* of name value pairs, where the values in a container are themselves JSON values. Databases and programming languages suffer an impedance mismatch as both their computational and data models are so different. JSON has a much lower impedance mismatch (with respect to Java), than XML, but has much richer data types than relational tables. Jaql comes with a rich array of built-in functions for processing unstructured or semi-structured data as well. For example, Jaql provides a bridge for *SystemT* [14] which can be used to convert natural language text into a structured format. Jaql also provides a user with the capability of developing *modules*, a concept similar to Java *packages*. A set of related functions can be bunched together to form a module. A Jaql script can import a module and can use the functions provided by the module. UDFs can be implemented both in Jaql as well as general purpose languages like Java. Jaql's operations like filter, group-by, etc., can be applied at top level or at any nested hierarchical level unlike Pig and Hive which provide little support for manipulating nested structures without prior un-nesting.

4.4 Comparative Analysis of Hive, Pig and Jaql

Authors of [15, 24] provide a comparison between Hive and Pig. These languages are compared using select, aggregation, and join queries on a data of size 100 GB. The data comprises of three relational tables. The authors find that Hive performs better than Pig on all three benchmarks. Authors of [3] provide a comparison of Hive, Pig, and Jaql on various dimensions. The authors write scripts for three tasks word counting, joining two relations, and weblog processing. The experiments are run across various dimensions, e.g., increasing the workload while keeping the cluster-size identical, increasing the workload with a proportionate increase in the cluster size, etc. All three languages were found to be equally concise, i.e., the script sizes for various processing tasks were found to be roughly similar. All three languages were found to be scaling well with respect to input data sizes. However, Hive was found to be the most efficient for relational processing over structured data. It is again more likely due to the fact that the input schema is flat and as discussed above, Hive has got special constructs (like partitions, schema handling, etc.) to be able to process flat data efficiently. Pig performs best when the data contains skewed key distribution because of the built-in optimization to handle the same. Pig is also able to exploit increased availability of reducer resources better as compared to Jaql and Hive. Jaql however is more computationally powerful than both Pig and Hive. It provides all the operators found in relational algebra and all of the aggregation functions found in SQL. Crucially Jaql supports recursion as well, and hence, Jaql is Turing Complete (i.e., it contains conditional constructs, recursion capable of indefinite iteration, and a memory architecture that emulates an infinite memory model [3]). Further, Jaql has more extensibility with features to read any arbitrarily formatted data, defining Jaql and Java UDFs, embedding

Table 2 Comparison of Hive, Pig, and Jaql.

Feature	Hive	Pig	Jaql
Developed by	Facebook	Yahoo	IBM
Specification	SQL like	Data flow	Data flow
Schema	Fixed schema	Optional schema	Optional schema
Turning completeness	Need extension using Java UDF	Need extension using Java UDF	Yes
Data model	Row oriented	Nested	JSON, XML
Diagnostics	Show, describe	Describe, Explain commands	Explain
Java connectivity	JDBC	Custom library	Custom library

MapReduce programs in the script, etc. Table 2 gives a summary of comparison between these three scripting languages.

4.5 GUI tools

Apart from writing native MapReduce code or writing a script in high level query languages, efforts are underway to develop GUI-based tools which can be used to define MapReduce job-flows over Hadoop. Such tools are already present for defining ETL processing tasks over relational databases. IBM Infosphere DataStage [46] and Informatica [47] are two examples of such tools. These tools are especially useful for users who find writing scripts using query languages a difficult task. Such tools offer a GUI—a drag-and-drop approach—which can be used to create a job-graph. The tools provide visual representations (e.g., buttons) for all data processing operations (e.g., filter, join, etc.). A user can *drag-and-drop* these buttons on a canvas and create the job-graph. Similarly, Dyrad [35] allows a user to specify an arbitrary directed acyclic graph to describe an application with vertices of the graph being any MapReduce programs. The vertices in this graph summarize what operations need to be carried out; what are the inputs; whereas output schema and the edges determine the sequential order of these operations. The graph thus defined is read by these tools and is converted into equivalent instructions to be executed over Hadoop. These tools hence allow users to totally bypass the need of learning any high level query language. Debugging time of the MapReduce data flows is also reduced as a user does not need to worry about correct query syntax. These tools provide many other convenient features. For example, a user can create a new custom operation. Thus, in case of log processing, a user can define a new operation *parseLog* which takes a log record as an input, parses the records, and returns a set of attribute-value pairs. A user can then use this new operation like any other regular *drag-and-drop* operation. In this way, the functionalities of these GUI-based tools can be extended. These tools can also record various kinds of metadata regarding the job-flow. For example, how many records were processed by each operation; how much time did each operation take; were there any errors encountered; etc. All this enables a user to maximize speed, flexibility, and effectiveness in building, deploying, and managing a MapReduce application.

Figure 5 illustrates an example graph developed in IBM InfoSphere DataStage. In this example data flow graph, one reads *Customer debit data* (represented by a file *Cust_debits*) and its output is fed to a filter *Filter_year_2010* through the link *DSLink2*. Output of the filter contains customer data for the year 2010. The resultant data (on *DSLink16*) is hierarchical, with each

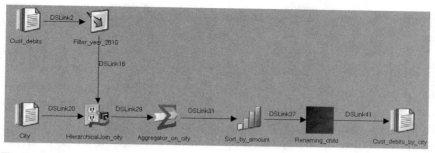

Fig. 5. An example job-graph on Hadoop.

debit record containing *city-id*. This data is joined with *City* data, fed through *DSLink20*. Hierarchical join is represented by the node named *Hierarchi-calJoin_City*. The join output is aggregated on *city* for each customer and output is sorted on debit amount. Output is stored in a file, represented by *Cust_debits_by_city*, in the user specified manner. Once this application is designed, a compiler converts the GUI specification into equivalent MapReduce jobs and the cloud runtime dynamically maps the logical jobs to the underlying cloud infrastructure for efficient distributed execution.

There are some other types of tools in Hadoop space which aid the users in developing MapReduce tasks. FlumeJava [48], PACT programming model [49], and Cascading project [50] are three such initiatives. PACT programming model is a generalization of MapReduce programming model and aims to carry out data processing tasks which are hard to represent or cannot be represented as MapReduce tasks. FlumeJava, a Java library, handles pipelines of *map* and *reduce* functions and makes them easy to develop, test, and run efficiently. Cascading is a library of Java APIs used for defining and executing MapReduce workflows on Hadoop without having to think in MapReduce. Next we present data management middleware's which use these technologies while providing higher level APIs to the users.

5. CLOUD DATA MANAGEMENT MIDDLEWARE

In this section we describe two middleware in the space of cloud data management. These technologies are *Database as a Service* and *Active archival over cloud*. *Database as a Service* outlines the challenging issues in hosting a database service on cloud whereas *Active archival* can be used to archive infrequently used data over cloud. These middleware's can be used across various industry verticals. These are developing concepts in the Hadoop community and we may get to see more of them in the future as these technologies mature.

5.1 Database as a Service

Database as a service (DBaaS) is a framework in which an organization can outsource data management to a cloud-based service provider. The vision of DBaaS is that users should have access to database functionality without worrying about provisioning hardware and configuring software [19]. DBaaS is a web service that makes it easy to set up, operate, and scale a relational database in the cloud. In DBaaS, management of database is handed over to cloud; one can request database service as and when needed; and pay the costs on the use basis. Computing power and resources (such as computing powers, database tables, etc.) can be added on-demand. Service providers in turn can manage several databases without dedicating hardware and administrators to each database.

A DBaaS provider needs to tackle multiple challenges while designing a DBaaS service. First and foremost is the issue of data privacy. As the data resides on the premises of the database service provider, the service provider needs to provide sufficient isolation and security measures to guard the data privacy. To address this problem various ways of encrypting and querying encrypted data have been developed [19–23].

Second key issue is the performance. A DBaaS needs to support databases and workloads of different sizes. The challenge arises when a database work-load exceeds the capacity of a single machine. A DBaaS must therefore support scale-out, where the responsibility for query processing (and the corresponding data) is partitioned among multiple nodes to achieve higher throughput. Hence, DBaaS needs to determine best way to partition databases for scaling out transparently. Workload aware partitioning schemes have been developed to handle this issue [22]. A DBaaS also needs to determine, given a set of databases and workloads, what is the best way to serve them from a given set of machines. To achieve this, DBaaS provider needs to understand various issues like the resource requirements of individual workloads, how they combine when co-located on one machine, the temporal variations of each workload to maximize resource utilization, etc. Another challenge is the development of a user friendly interface. The interface must be easy to use and powerful enough to allow ease in developing applications [19, 23]. Amazon, Google, IBM, Microsoft, Oracle, Saleforce.com, etc. as well as small innovators such as EnterpriseDB, LongJump, Elastra, etc., are all targeting the DBaaS market. Although most of today's DBaaS solutions are very simple, in the next few years, more sophisticated offerings will evolve to support larger, and more complex applications.

5.2 Active Data Archival

As per one scenario, enterprises can continue with the data warehouse architectures for processing their operational data while using low-cost cloud storage for storing ever increasing old, infrequently used data. Governments and industry bodies are imposing various data retention regulations such as Sarbanes-Oxley [51], HIPAA [52], Basel II [53], etc. These regulations have led to industries like law, healthcare, and retail banking to look for large data management issues. With the increase in the amount of data, the old and inactive data starts to become a burden on the warehouse and starts impacting the warehouse performance. Data archiving is the process of moving data that is no longer actively used to a separate data storage device for long-term retention. Much of the operational content in enterprises is structured data that resides in a data warehouse and, hence, the archival solutions tend to lower the cost by moving the data to cheaper tapes and optical drives. Rather than old fashioned archival over tapes, *active archival on cloud* has many desirable features, such as:

a. Archived data is kept on low-cost storage maintained by cloud.

b. A user can request and release the needed resources on cloud, hence, the burden of maintaining the require infrastructure is shifted to the service provider.

c. Archived data can be queried without bringing it back to the warehouse (we call this method of archiving as *active archiving*).

d. The archival service can be configured to fetch the infrequently used data from the warehouse based on user defined policies making the archival process *intelligent*.

A more critical need arises when business analysts want to run ad hoc queries to extract patterns and rules to understand the usage trends, buying patterns, etc. Given that archival is done by database administrators, and not the analysts, one cannot expect analysts to be aware of which part of the data resides in the warehouse and what has been migrated to the archive. It is desirable if the user can query the archived data while at the same time being oblivious to the fact that s/he is querying the archived data. As part of providing the active archival service on the cloud, the service provider needs to provide the resources required for the archival, method to convert the warehouse data into the data model suitable for the archive, and seamless access to the archived data. Figure 6 shows the block diagram

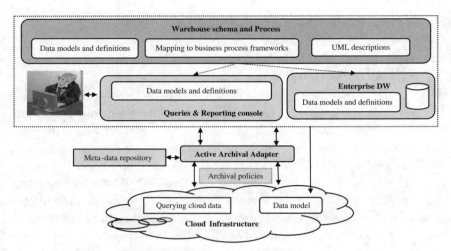

Fig. 6. Active archival architecture.

of an active archival solution. Part of the figure in the dotted rectangle gives the architecture of the data warehouse system as it exists today. *Data warehouse schema and processes* are used to generate data models, tables and views, and relationships between them. They are also used to generate the queries and reporting interface which a user can use to pose ad hoc queries or generate periodic reports. *Enterprise data models and definitions* represent the data schema whereas *Queries and Reporting Console* module gives a way to execute queries and getting results using the derived data model. *Meta-data repository* stores the metadata about the archived data. The metadata include identifiers of data in the archive, temporal attributes which can be used to identify the archived data (e.g., transaction date, delivery-date, etc.), etc. In this system the user can seamlessly query the operational data as well as archival data using a single interface i.e., the user is oblivious to the fact that the data may reside in the warehouse or in the archive. *Active archival adapter* provides a query federation system which decides whether the input query is for the operational data, archived data, or both. *Active archival adaptor* uses the *metadata repository* to derive three subqueries of any input query—the first subquery is to get the required archived data and store that in a temporary table; the second sub-query gets the data from the data warehouse and stores in the same temporary table; and the third subquery is executed over the data in the temporary table. Result of the third subquery is presented to the user. *Archival policies* module represents the policy used to archive the data from time to time. For example, one may want to archive transactional data every month, but archive images every week. As the archival system is implemented on Hadoop-based system, one may use the column–based data storage model as explained in Section 3.3. More details on query federation and performance can be seen in [21].

6. BRINGING LARGE SCALE DATA MANAGEMENT APPLICATIONS OVER CLOUD

In this Section, we consider two example applications where large scale data management over cloud can be used. These two are specific use case examples in telecom and finance domains: in the telecom domain, massive amount of *call detail records* can be processed to generate near real–time network usage information; whereas in finance domain we describe a credit card fraud detection application.

6.1 Network Infrastructure Usage Dashboard

Telecom Infrastructure operators are interested in building a dashboard that would allow the analysts and architects to understand the traffic flowing through the network along various dimensions of interest. The traffic is captured using *call detail records* (CDRs) whose volume runs into terabytes per day. The key dimension of interest is the usage of a cell site— a term used for denoting a site where antennas and electronic communications equipment are placed on a radio mast or tower to create a cell in a network. Monitoring of traffic flowing through the sites would help the operator to determine congested regions. The telecom regulatory authority also imposes fines for service providers whose networks are highly congested. Adding new cell sites is the obvious solution for congestion reduction. However, each new site costs approximately 20,000 USD to setup. Therefore, determining the right spot for setting up the cell site and measuring the potential traffic flowing through the site will allow the operator to measure the return on investment. Other uses of the dashboard include determining the cell site used most for each customer, identifying whether users are mostly making calls within cell site and for cell sites in rural areas identifying the source of traffic i.e., local versus routed calls. Given the huge and ever growing customer base and large call volumes, the above mentioned task cannot be handled by solutions designed to exploit the warehouse. A typical CDR generated by switches on the operator's network contains 81 attributes out of which about 22 attributes give useful information about the subscriber, the network, billing details and call details. The dashboard has to create various aggregates around combinations of the 22 attributes for helping the analysts. Furthermore, it had to be projected into future based on trends observed in the past. These CDRs can be loaded periodically over cloud data management solution. As cloud provides flexible storage, depending on traffic one can decide on the storage required. These CDRs can be processed using various mechanisms described in the chapter to get the required key performance indicators.

6.2 Credit Card Fraud Detection

Popularity of online shopping is growing by day. More than one-tenth of world's population is shopping online [2]. Credit card is the most popular mode of online shopping payments. As the number of credit card trans-actions rise, the opportunities for attackers to steal credit card details and commit fraud are also increasing. As the attacker only needs to know some details about the card (card number, expiration date, etc.), the only way to detect online credit card fraud is to analyze the spending patterns and detect any inconsistency with respect to the usual spending patterns. Various credit card companies compile a consumer profile for each and every card holder based on purchases s/he makes using his/her credit card over the years. These companies keep tabs on the geographical locations where the credit card transactions are made—if the area is far from the card holder's area of residence, or if two transactions from the same credit card are made in very distant areas within a relatively short timeframe,—the transactions are potentially fraud transactions. Various data mining algorithms are used to detect patterns within the transaction data. Detecting these patterns requires the analysis of large amount of data. For analyzing these credit card trans-actions one may need to create tuples of transaction for a particular credit card. Using tuples of the transactions, one can find the distance between geographic location of two consecutive transactions, amount of these trans-actions, time difference between transactions, etc. By these parameters, one can find the potential fraudulent transactions. Further, data mining based on a particular user's spending profile is required to ascertain whether the transaction is indeed fraudulent.

As number of credit card transactions is huge and the kind of processing required is not a typical relational processing (hence, warehouses are not optimized to do such processing), one can use Hadoop-based solution for this purpose. Using Hadoop one can handle petabytes of transactions to create customer profile as well as create matrices of consecutive transactions to decide whether a particular transaction is a fraud transaction. As one needs to find the fraud within some specified time, cloud-based processing can help.

By employing massive resources for analyzing potentially fraud transactions one can meet the response time guarantees.

7. RESEARCH PROBLEMS, DISCUSSION, AND CONCLUSION

In this chapter, we presented the data management and analytics aspects of cloud computing framework. Specifically we presented need for processing large amount of data having high variety and veracity at high speed, different important technologies for distributed processing over virtualized cloud resources such as NoSQL, Hadoop, Pig, Jaql, Hive, etc., and customer use cases. There are various advantages in moving to cloud resources from dedicated resources for data management and analytics. But some of the enterprises and governments are still skeptical about moving to cloud as they are uncomfortable with their data being located on systems on which they do not have full control. Further, data needs to be compliant with certain regulations such as Sarbanes–Oxley and HIPPA which customers want to ensure on their own. More work is required for cloud security, privacy, and isolation areas to alleviate these fears. Some large enterprises are used to having fully customizable environments. With cloud computing, they need to choose from the available packages. All these issues need to be resolved for accelerating adoption of cloud-based services.

Various applications involve huge amount of data and may require real-time processing, one needs tools and resources for bulk processing of huge amount of data, real-time processing of streaming data, and method of interaction between these two processing modes. For example, in credit card fraud detection application, user profiles can be created using bulk processing whereas each transaction can be evaluated against the user profile using stream processing. One needs to design such applications so that they can provide the required response time with sufficient accuracy. More research is required for facilitating such systems.

In this chapter, we also presented active archival service that makes use of a cloud-based distributed data storage mechanism given by Hadoop and HDFS to archive the infrequently used data. Such a solution should be designed to seamlessly co-exist with the data warehouse implementation existing on dedicated resources. We explained how the column oriented data storage model with efficient column collation method can be used to reduce data storage requirements with the required query processing capabilities. This approach is domain independent and can cater to all types of businesses, be the large enterprises with data centers or the small businesses that can only use a few machines for archiving. Specific details about exposing the archival as service, efficient methods to convert huge amount of warehouse data to suitable column oriented data model, etc., require more efforts.

 Acronyms

ACID	Atomicity, Consistency, Integrity, Durability
BASE	Basic Availability, Soft-state, Eventually consistent
CDR	Call Detail Records
CLV	Customer Life-time Value
CSV	Comma Separated Values
ELT	Extract Load Transform
ETL	Extract Transform Load
HDFS	Hadoop Distributed File System
HIPAA	Health Insurance Portability and Accountability
JAQL	JSON Query Language
JDBC	Java Database Connectivity
JSON	Java Script Object Notation
NoSQL	Not only SQL
TPC-DS	Decision Support database from Transaction Processing performance Council
UDF	User Defined Functions

REFERENCES

[1] A. Avizienis, et. al. Basic concepts and taxonomy of dependable and secure computing. IEEE Trans. Depend. Secure Comput. 1 (1) (2004) 11–33.
[2] A. Srivastava, A. Kundu, S. Sural, and A. Majumdar. Credit Card Fraud Detection using Hidden Markov Model. IEEE Trans. Depend. Secure Comput. 5 (1) (2008) 37–48.
[3] R. Stewart, P. Trinder, H.-W. Loidl, Comparing high level MapReduce query languages, in: Proceedings of the ninth International Conference on Advanced Parallel Processing Technologies (APPT'11), 2011.
[4] Apache Foundation, Hadoop. <http://hadoop.apache.org/core/>.
[5] Amr Awadallah, Hadoop: an industry perspective, in: International Workshop on Massive Data Analytics Over Cloud, 2010.
[6] J. Dean, S. Ghemawat, MapReduce: simplified data processing on large clusters. Commun. ACM 51 (1) (2008).
[7] Hive- Hadoop wiki. <http://wiki.apache.org/hadoop/Hive>.
[8] JSON. <http://www.json.org>.
[9] K. Palla, A Comparative Analysis of Join Algorithms Using the Hadoop Map/Reduce Framework, MS Thesis, School of Informatics, University of Edinburgh, 2009.

[10] M. Stonebraker et al. C-STORE: a column-oriented DBMS, in: Proceedings of Very Large Databases (VLDB), 2005.

[11] M. Vardi. The universal-relation data model for logical independence. IEEE Softw. 5 (2) (1988).

[12] M. Poess, R.O. Nambiar, D. Walrath, Why you should run TPC-DS: a workload analysis, in: Proceedings of Very Large Databases (VLDB), 2007.

[13] Jaql Project Hosting. <http://code.google.com/p/jaql/>.

[14] K.S. Beyer, V. Ercegovac, R. Gemulla, A. Balmin, M. Eltabakh, Carl-Christian Kanne, F. Ozcan, E.J. Shekita, Jaql: a scripting language for large scale semi-structured data analysis, in: Proceedings of Very Large Databases (VLDB), 2011.

[15] Liveland: hive vs. Pig <http://www.larsgeorge.com/2009/10/hive-vs-pig.html>.

[16] Pig. <hadoop.apache.org/pig/>.

[17] T. Venkatesan, Chakaravarthy, Himanshu Gupta, Prasan Roy, Mukesh Mohania. Efficiently linking text documents with relevant structured information, in: Proceedings of Very Large Databases (VLDB), 2006.

[18] HBase. <hbase.apache.org/>.

[19] C. Curino, Evan P.C. Jones, R.A. Popa, N. Malviya, E. Wu, S. Madden, H. Balakrishnan, N. Zeldovich. Realtional cloud: a database-as-a-service for the cloud, in: Proceedings of Conference on Innovative Data Systems Research (CIDR), 2011.

[20] A. Thusoo, J. Sen Sarma, N. Jain, Z. Shao, P. Chakka, N. Zhang, S. Anthony, H. Liu, R. Murthy, Hive—a petabyte scale data warehouse using Hadoop, in: Proceedings of Internation Conference on Data Engineering (ICDE), 2010.

[21] R. Gupta, H. Gupta, U. Nambiar, M. Mohania, Enabling active archival over cloud, in: Proceedings of Service Computing Conference (SCC), 2012.

[22] Eugene We, Samuel Madden, Yang Zhang, Evan Jones, Carlo Curino, Relational cloud—the case for a database service, Technical Report. <http://hdl.handle.net/1721.1/52606>.

[23] Hakan Hacigumus, Sharad Mehrotra, Balakrishna R. Iyer, Providing database as a service, in: Proceedings of Internation Conference on Data Engineering (ICDE), 2002.

[24] Zheng Shao, Yuntao Jia, A benchmark for hive, Pig and Hadoop, Technical Report, July 2009.

[25] Kai. <http://sourceforge.net/apps/mediawiki/kai>.

[26] Armando Fox, Steven D. Gribble, Yatin Chawathe, Eric A. Brewer, Paul Gauthier, Cluster-based scalable network services, in: Proceedings of the 16th ACM Symposium on Operating Systems Principles (SOSP), 1997.

[27] Hiroshi Wada, Alan Fekede, Liang Zhao, Kevin Lee, Anna Liu, Data consistency properties and the trade-offs in commercial cloud storages: the consumers' perspective, in: Proceedings of Conferenceon Innovative Data Systems Research (CIDR), 2011.

[28] Jim Gray, Pat Helland, Patrick E. O'Neil, Dennis shasha: the dangers of replication and a solution, in: Proceedings of ACM International Conference on Management of Data, 1996.

[29] G. DeCandia, D. Hastorun, M. Jampani, G. Kakulapati, A. Lakshman, A. Pilch, S. Sivasubramanian, P. Vosshall, W. Vogels, Dynamo: Amazon's highly available key-value store, in: 21st Symposium on Operating Systems Principles (SOSP), 2007.

[30] M. Habeeb, A Developer's Guide to Amazon SimpleDB, Pearson Education.

[31] Jan Lehnardt, J. Chris Anderson, Noah Slater, CouchDB: The Definitive Guide. O'Reilly, 2010.

[32] Kristina Chodorow, Michael Dirolf, MongoDB: The Definitive Guide, O'Reilly Media, USA, 2010.

[33] Fay Chang, J. Dean, S. Ghemawat, W.C. Hsieh, D.A. Wallach, M. Burrows, T. Chandra, A. Fikes, R.E. Gruber, BigTable: a distributed storage system for structured data, in: Proceedings of the 7th USENIX Symposium on Operating Systems Design annd Implementation (OSDI), 2006.

[34] D. Borthakur, N. Jan, J. Sharma, R. Murthy, H. Liu, Data warehousing and analytics infrastructure at facebook, in: Proceedings of ACM International Conference on Management of Data (SIGMOD), 2010.

[35] Michael Isard, Mihai Budiu, Yuan Yu, Adrew Birrell, and Dennis Fetterly, Dyrad: distributed data-parallel programs from sequential building blocks, in: Proceeding of the 2nd ACM SIGOPS/EuroSys European Conference on Computer Systems (EuroSys'07), 2007.

[36] Prasan Roy, Mukesh Mohania, Bhuvan Bamba, Shree Raman, Towards automatic association of relevant unstructured content with structured query results, in: ACM Conference on Information and Knowledge Management (CIKM), 2005.

[37] A. Okcan, M. Riedewald, Processing theta joins using Map-Reduce, in: Proceedings of ACM International Conference on Management of Data (SIGMOD), 2011.

[38] S. Blanas, J.M. Patel, V. Ercegovac, J. Rao, A comparison of join algorithms for log processing in MapReduce, in: Proceedings of ACM International Conference on Management of Data (SIGMOD), 2010.

[39] C. Zhang, F. Li, J. Jestes, Efficient parallel kNN joins for large data in MapReduce, in: Proceedings of Extending Database Technologies (EDBT), 2012.

[40] A. Metwally, C. Faloustous, V-SMART-JOIN: a scalable MapReduce framework for all pair similarity joins of multisets and vectors, in: Proceedings of Very Large Databases (VLDB), 2012.

[41] J. Jestes, K. Yi, F. Li., Building wavelet histograms on large data in MapReduce, in: Proceedings of Very Large Databases (VLDB), 2012.

[42] K. Wang, J. Han, B. Tu., J. Dai, W. Jhou, X. Song, Accelerating spatial data processing with MapReduce, in: International Conference on Parallel and Distributed Systems (ICPADS), 2010.

[43] B. Bahmani, R. Kumar, S. Vassilvitski, Densest subgraph in streaming and MapReduce, in: Proceedings of Very Large Databases (VLDB), 2012.

[44] C. Wang, J. Wang, X. Lin, W. Wang, H. Wang, H. Li, W. Tian, J. Xu, R. Li, MapDupReducer: detecting near duplicates over massive datasets, in: Proceedings of ACM International Conference on Management of Data (SIGMOD), 2010.

[45] W. Lu, Y. Shen, S. Chen, B.C. Ooi, Efficient processing of k nearest neighbor joins using MapReduce, in: Proceedings of Very Large Databases (VLDB), 2012.

[46] IBM InfoSphere DataStage. <www.ibm.com/software/data/infosphere/datastage/>.

[47] Informatica-The Data Integration Company. <www.informatica.com/>.

[48] C. Chambers, A. Raniwala, F. Perrry, St. Adams, R.R. Henry, R. Bradshaw, N. Weizenbaum, FlumeJava: easy, efficient data-parallel pipelines, in: Proceedings of the 2010 ACM Conference on Programming Language Design and Implementation (PLDI), 2010.

[49] Alexander Alexandrov, Stephan Ewen, Max Heimel, Fabian Hueske, Odej Kao, Volker Markl, Erik Nijkamp, Daniel Warneke, MapReduce and PACT comparing data parallel programming models, in: Proceedings of the 14th Conference on Database Systems for Business, Technology, and Web (BTW), 2011.

[50] Cascading: Application Platform for Enterprise Big Data. <www.cascading.org>.

[51] Compliance Regulatory Overview: Sarbanes-Oxley. <http://www.techrepublic.com/article/compliance-regulatory-overview-sarbanes-oxley/5843010>.

[52] Health Insurance Portability and Accountability Act (HIPAA). <http://www.gpo.gov/fdsys/pkg/PLAW-104publ191/content-detail.html>.

[53] UK Data Retention Requirements: Information Data Retention and Disposal. <https://www.watsonhall.com/resources/downloads/paper-uk-data-retention-requirements.pdf>.

[54] S. Papadimitriou, DisCo: distributed co-clustering with Map-Reduce: a case study towards petabyte-scale end-to-end mining, in: Proceedings of Eighth IEEE International Conference on Data Mining (ICDM), 2008.

ABOUT THE AUTHORS

Rajeev Gupta received Bachelors of Technology (B.Tech) in Electronic and Communications Engineering, from Indian Institute of Technology (IIT) Kharagpur and a Ph.D. in Computer Science and Engineering, from IIT Mumbai. He has been with IBM Research for last 13 years. His research interest include data integration, distributed data processing, streams processing, distributed computing, and networking. He has published more than 20 papers in reputed conferences and journals such as VLDB, WWW, TKDE, ICDE, SIGMETRICS, INFOCOM, etc.

Himanshu Gupta is working as a Technical Staf Member at IBM India Research Lab, New Delhi. He received BTech degree in Computer Science in 2004 from Indian Institute of Technology, Kanpur and MS degree in Computer Science in 2010 from Indian Institute of Technology, New Delhi. His research interests include data management, data mining, mapreduce processing. machine learning and related areas. He has published more than 15 papers in international scientific journals, books and proceedings of international conferences and he holds multiple US patents.

Mukesh Mohania received his Ph.D. in Computer Science & Engineering from Indian Institute of Technology, Bombay, India in 1995. He was a faculty member in University of South Australia from 1996-2001. Currently, he is a Distinguished Engineer and IBM Master Inventor in IBM Research Lab, India. He has worked extensively in the areas of distributed databases, data warehousing, data integration, and autonomic computing. He has published more than 100 papers and also filed more than 30 patents in these or related areas. He is an IEEE and ACM Distinguished Speaker.

AUTHOR INDEX

SUBJECT INDEX

A

Abstract Data Type (ADT), 107
ACID (Atomicity, consistency, integrity, and durability) properties, 374
Acquisition board (MDA320CA), 69–70
Active data archival, 393
Activities of Daily Living (ADLs), 51
Adaptive and Robust Topology control (ART), 34–35
ad hoc wireless network, 30
Agent-based systems
    IRIS NET, 152
    SWAP, 154–155
Aggregation with Increasing Scopes (AIS), 325, 330
Algorithms
    cascading movement, 211
    DFP-SVM training, 231
    energy efficient, 207
    Equal Cost Multipath (ECMP), 300
    event coverage enhancement, 209
    K-means, 245
    limited mobility, 208
    maximum weighted flow, 202
    minimax, 194
    NLP, 225
    Weighted DFP-SVM training, 231
    optimal sensor mobility, 206
    randomized movement, 197
    scan-based movement, 195–196
    VECtor-based, 193
    virtual force movement, 192–193
    Voronoi-based movement, 194, 209
    See also DM algorithms, classification of
A Nearly-New Information Extraction (ANNIE) System, 261
Application Data Unit (ADU), 8
Application-oriented architectures
    Agent-based systems
        IRIS NET, 152
        SWAP, 154–155
    overview of, 159
    rule-based data transformation

Content-based Publish/Subscribe, 146–147
    mapping rules, 148–149
    SWASN, 149
service-composition
    Hourglass, 139, 141
    IBM, 143–144
    SONGS, 141, 143
service-oriented-architecture
    OGC SWE, 131, 137
    SemSOS, 137–138
    TinyREST, 130, 132
Application Programming Interface (API), 297
A Practical Transit Mapping Service (APT), 327
Architecture
    AAA architecture, 121
    CTP, 16–17
    database centered, 106
    data-oriented, 106, 158
    DONA, 334
    FARA, 318
    FlashDB, 56
    for energy management, 38
    HAIR, 340
    HIDRA, 341
    HRA, 337
    IvIP, 327
    kernel, 61
    Lance, 8–9
    layer, 22
    LIMA, 338
    link layer security, 48
    LNA, 318
    MILSA, 339
    MLA, 22
    multihoming, 296
    new and routing-centric, 348
    NIIA, 341
    node software, 71
    OASIS node software, 71
    object storage, 54

415

CONTENTS OF VOLUMES IN THIS SERIES